Virtual, Distributed and Flexible Organisations

Virtual, Distributed and Flexible Organisations

Studies in Organisational Semiotics

edited by

Kecheng Liu

The University of Reading,
Reading, Berkshire, United Kingdom

KLUWER ACADEMIC PUBLISHERS

DORDRECHT / BOSTON / LONDON

Library of Congress Cataloging-in-Publication Data

ISBN 978-90-481-6603-9 (PB)
ISBN 978-1-4020-2162-6 (e-book)

Published by Kluwer Academic Publishers,
P.O. Box 17, 3300 AA Dordrecht, The Netherlands.

Sold and distributed in North, Central and South America
by Kluwer Academic Publishers,
101 Philip Drive, Norwell, MA 02061, U.S.A.

In all other countries, sold and distributed
by Kluwer Academic Publishers,
P.O. Box 322, 3300 AH Dordrecht, The Netherlands.

Printed on acid-free paper

Printed in the Netherlands.

Contents

Contributors

ABRAHAM K. LOMI
Atma Jaya University-Indonesia, Software Competence Center, Hagenberg (SCCH) - Austria, Institute of Technology National (ITN) -Indonesia

ANDERSEN, PETER BØGH
Center for Human Computer Interaction, Department of Computer Science, Aalborg University, Denmark, pba@cs.auc.dk

BORIS SHISHKOV
Faculty of Information Technology and Systems, Delft University of Technology, Delft, 2600 AJ, The Netherlands,
b.b. Shishkov, j.l.g.dietz@ewi.tudelft.nl

CARLOS ALBERTO COCOZZA SIMONI
Institute of Computing - State University of Campinas, Brazil, cacs@ic.unicamp.br

DANIEL GALARRETA
Centre National d'Etudes Spatiales, France, Daniel.Galarreta@cnes.fr

DARREN WHOBREY
School of Public Administration, University of Victoria, B.C., Canada and School of Information Systems, Technology and Management, University of New South Wales, Australia, d.whobrey@unsw.edu.au

DUNCAN STRANG
Sheffield Hallam University, United Kingdom, lyallex@yahoo.co.uk

ELENA REVILLA
Instituto de Empresa & Fundación EOI, Spain.

GÖRAN GOLDKUHL
CMTO, Linköping University, SE-581 82 Linköping, Sweden and Jönköping International Business School, P.O. 1026, SE-551 11 Jönköping, Sweden, ggo@ida.liu.se

HART WILL
School of Public Administration, University of Victoria, B.C., Canada and School of Information Systems, Technology and Management, University of New South Wales, Australia, hart_will@acl.com

HENK W. M. GAZENDAM
University of Groningen, The Netherlands, h.w.m.gazendam@bdk.rug.nl

HONGWEI XU
University of Paisley, United Kingdom, xu---ci0@wpmail.paisley.ac.uk

IAIN W. PHILLIPS
Modelling and Reasoning Research Group, Department of Computer Science, Loughborough University, United Kingdom, I.W.Phillips@lboro.ac.uk

JAMES NOBLE
Department of Mathematical and Computing Sciences, Victoria University of Wellington, New Zealand

JAN L.G. DIETZ
Faculty of Information Technology and Systems, Delft University of Technology, Delft, 2600 AJ, The Netherlands, j.l.g.dietz@its.tudelft.nl

JOAQUIM FILIPE
Escola Superior de Tecnologia do Instituto Politecnico de Setubal, Rua Vale de Chaves, Estafanilha, 2910 Setubal, Protugal, jfilipe@iceis.org

JOHN CONNOLLY
Department of Computer Science, Loughborough University, Loughborough, LE11 3TU, UK, J.H.Connolly@lboro.ac.uk

JONAS SJOSTROM
Jönköping International Business School and Linköping University, Sweden, jonas.sjostrom@ihh.hj.se

JOSE SANCHEZ-ALARCOS
Instituto de Empresa & Fundación EOI, Spain, SANCHEZALARCOS@telefonica.net

JOSEPH A. GOGUEN
Department of Computer Science & Engineering University of California, San Diego. United States., goguen@cs.ucsd.edu

JUNKANG FENG
School of ICT, University of Paisley, United Kingdom.

KECHENG LIU
Department of Computer Science, University of Reading, Reading, RG6 6AY, UK, k.liu@reading.ac.uk

KEN COSH
Lancaster University, United Kingdom, k.cosh@lancaster.ac.uk

MARTIN HELMHOUT
University of Groningen, The Netherlands, j.m.helmhout@bdk.rug.nl

M. CECILIA C. BARANAUSKAS
Institute of Computing, State University of Campinas, Caixa Postal 6176 - 13083 970 Campinas, SP - Brazil, cecilia@ic.unicamp.br

OSCAR MANGISENGI
Atma Jaya University-Indonesia, Software Competence Center Hagenberg (SCCH)- Austria, Institute of Technology National (ITN) -Indonesia

PETE SAWYER
Lancaster University, United Kingdom.

PIERRE-JEAN CHARREL
Universite Toulouse 2 Grimm & Institut de Recherche en Informatique De Toulouse. France. charrel@univ-tlse2.fr.

PIPPIN BARR
Department of Mathematical and Computing Sciences, Victoria University of Wellington, New Zealand, chikken@ihug.co.nz

RENA J JORNA
Castor-Project, Faculty of Management and Organisation, University of Groningen, P.O.-Box 800, NL-9700 AV Groningen, The Netherlands, r.j.j.m.jorna@bdk.rug.nl

RICARDO R. GUDWIN
Department of Computer Engineering and Industrial Automation - DCA - Faculty of Electrical and ComputerEngineering - FEEC - State University of Campinas - UNICAMP – Brazil, gudwin@dca.fee.unicamp.br

ROBERT BIDDLE
Department of Mathematical and Computing Sciences, Victoria University of Wellington, New Zealand,

RODRIGO BONACIN
Institute of Computing, State University of Campinas, Caixa Postal 6176 - 13083 970 Campinas, SP - Brazil, rbonacin@yahoo.com.br

RUSDY HARTUNGI
Atma Jaya University-Indonesia, Software Competence Center Hagenberg (SCCH)- Austria, Institute of Technology National (ITN) –Indonesia, hartungi@yahoo.com

SIMON POLOVINA
Sheffield Hallam University, United Kingdom, S.Polovina@shu.ac.uk

WEI HU
School of ICT, University of Paisley, United Kingdom, hu-ci0@wpmail.paisley.ac.uk

WILLIAM FONE
Staffordshire University, United Kingdom, W.Fone@staffs.ac.uk

ZHIWU XIE
Department of Computer Science, University of Reading, Reading, RG6 6AY, UK, zxie@unm.edu

Foreword

Organisational Semiotics has a vital role to play in the post-industrial age, which has information as its key resource. At present we have well-developed disciplines concerned with the 'hard' and 'soft' extremes of the information field[1]. The practitioners of computer science and software engineering stand on the one side of an intellectual chasm facing others dealing with the social impacts of IT and they view each other with suspicion across the void. Organisational Semiotics can provide a bridge between them because it builds on the fundamental concepts of a *sign* that lends itself to empirical investigation.

Organisational Semiotics can meet the needs of the 'hard' sciences for formality and precision without which IT systems cannot be designed. At the same time, it accommodates the concepts and categories essential for solving 'soft' problems in the organisational domain. Thus our new discipline can link the mechanical to the social, combining as far as possible the strengths of both.

Organisational Semiotics links two fields of study where empirical methods can be difficult to apply. Computer scientists deal with formal sign structures and operations upon them; software engineers implement them on computers; neither group has to bother with the rather philosophical issues of what the data (signs) mean, what intentions they express or what social consequences they produce. Social scientists either face unique or complex problems that do not lend themselves readily to empirical investigation in the manner of the natural sciences (e.g. Zuboff) or they work with gross categories about which statistical data may be gathered (e.g. Castells, Strassmann). Semiotics, the doctrine of signs, leads us directly into

[1] See the work of our keynote speaker, Joseph Goguen, who is expert at both poles.

empirical investigations via ranges of derived concepts (physical, empiric and syntactic sign properties) appropriate to investigating 'hard' issues and others (semantic, pragmatic and social) for the 'soft' problems. Can we build on this foundation to create a body of scientific knowledge in the style of the natural sciences?

Modern science's remarkable success derives from the way it handles information. Pre-scientific scholarship produced many interesting, speculative papers about the natural world written by great thinkers; these were held in libraries and copied in their scriptoriums for other libraries; grateful readers awed by the reputations of the authors, believed in their speculations. This did not result in any scientific discipline, as we now know them today.

In those earlier times, three factors inhibited the development of a reliable body of empirically based knowledge: the manuscript technology; the sparse connectivity of the scholarly community; and their lack of critical apparatus and attitudes. Let us examine each of them and enquire how well our nascent discipline measures up.

Modern science certainly could not have begun in the era of manuscript or even in the earliest days of printing. Error-prone copying injected noise into the small stream of information, making it difficult to bring an idea to a critical mass of scholars. There was only an attenuated broadcasting system with limited and slow feedback. But by the 17th Century the quality and efficiency of printing made possible the dissemination of multiple, accurate copies. Then, complex figures, details of processes, extended mathematical arguments and so on could reach a sizeable scholarly community.

Technological advances in printing accurately and cheaply were not enough. The intense constructive criticism of ideas depends upon having a richly connected network of scholars. The Royal Society and *Philosophical Transactions,* its journal, provided the institutional harness for the new technology. Many similar bodies set up throughout Europe brought scholars into a closer collaboration. The enhanced accuracy of communication among larger well-connected groups made the critical examination of ideas more cogent than before. Not only could each person work on the internal arguments of exactly the same texts but the accurately described observations and experiments allowed them to be replicated so that theoretical or speculative ideas were brought face-to-face with nature, which then became their judge. Gradually this overcame the traditional reliance, of Classical and Medieval times, upon the empirically untested opinions of accepted thinkers circulated in manuscript. By subjecting theories to open, rigorous, critical assessment modern science was born.

Technically accurate information circulated through well-connected networks could not alone have led to science. A new way of thinking was required. Throughout the Middle Ages it was dangerous to question the truths established by powerful hierarchies. The Reformation no doubt contributed to the growing confidence of scholars in their own judgment. But the notion of empirical testing through experiment and observation only grew rapidly when the infant sciences fed on the interaction between theory and observation within the new scholarly communities. Chicken and egg! We now have the evolved epistemological instrument that enables us to produce knowledge that we can justify using as a practical tool; it has three interlinked functions: creating ideas, ensuring their internal consistency and testing them against reality.

Does Organisational Semiotics have the right technologies, the strong community and the right mixture of creative, logical and critical faculties to follow the established model? No well-developed empirical science will result from merely writing our own papers, no matter how internally sound they are, unless they are adequately digested by our colleagues and paid the supreme compliment of careful critical analysis and empirical testing. So let us check what advantages we have and identify any shortcomings.

Today we have the most wonderful technology. But do we make the best use of it? No longer are we bound by the slow cycle for print journals. Indeed, at this present time (Autumn 2003) Peter Andersen and Göran Goldkuhl are creating the on-line journal that received the unanimous endorsement of the OS Workshop reported in this volume. We shall know the name of the journal in 2004 but it will serve those interested in "action, communication, representation, and interpretation mediated by information technology in work organisations". This journal will be a distinct advantage.

On-line publication should help us to replicate in cyberspace the geographical closeness of the early scientific societies in European cities. In our workshops we have already formed a community that welcomes new ideas and lively, open discussion. Perhaps we need to take more time for detailed, constructive critical analysis.

We must not loose our receptiveness to new ideas. So let me defend imaginative speculation more explicitly. It has an essential role to play along side more rigorous work, especially in the formative years of a new discipline. In my own experience, sometimes only wild speculation leads us out of sterile, established ways of thinking towards new kinds of questions that were not being asked before. Sometimes these lead on to new rigorous theories. A truly worthy advocate of this position, Clerk Maxwell, wrote a verse expressing this rather well:

What combination of ideas,
Nonsense alone can wisely form?
What sage has half the power that she has,
To take the towers of truth by storm?

This defence of wild speculation in science comes from the father of Maxwell's demon, inspiration for information theory, originator of statistical thermodynamics and electro-magnetic theory (from which he predicted radio waves), and maker of the first colour photograph.

But science needs to balance conjecture with critical analysis, which must be of two kinds: to establish internal consistency and to establish a reliable connection to external reality. Our colleagues in computing and software engineering look for consistency within their formal systems. Their work lies on the syntactic level of semiotics but an empirical science must get the semantic level right.

Established disciplines have less difficulty in this respect than we do. They work with a settled core of theory, making anomalies easier to spot, especially under the watchful eyes of much larger communities. A nascent discipline like ours faces more risks. For example, the field of educational psychology in the UK failed badly when in its early years it let Cyril Burt use made-up data from his own imaginary population of identical twins to support his eugenically-tainted theories (Beloff, Halla,1980, and Eysenck, H.J. & L. Kamin,1981). Burt (mis)guided government policy and thereby, some would say, damaged the education of a whole generation but won himself a knighthood. Sir Cyril Burt was only exposed posthumously.

What justifies accepting the work of a scientific community as valid knowledge? To some extent, as the educational psychology example illustrates, it depends upon the community functioning effectively. That effectiveness depends on their honesty, openness to new ideas and readiness courteously to criticize them – conditions that I believe have already developed within our community.

What can we do to ensure a healthy balance between the generation of new ideas and their critical scrutiny? Of course those who review papers submitted to workshops, conferences and journals play a key role but critical analysis must form a significant part of our overall output. Exchanges through writing, though very important, assume that the writers and readers have established a clearly understood body of shared concepts. In the early years of a discipline, that probably presumes far too much. The slow feedback loop through text does not allow the subtle misunderstandings of meanings to be picked up and resolved. That calls for face-to-face encounters. One can imagine the 17th-19th Century scientists, in their less frenetic age, gathering to discuss and minutely dissect each interesting paper. Perhaps our on-line technology will help but I believe that we should do all we can to visit one another to work together for several days at a time, preferably on concrete problems that will put our ideas to the test.

In addition to testing ideas against concrete problems, we must also think about the scientific methods we adopt. In their face-to-face encounters the early natural scientists developed an understanding of the categories of issues that they should investigate. They also arrived at their methodology of enquiry with its clear criterion of empirical testing to gauge their progress. We too must arrive at a clear understanding about what constitutes well-founded knowledge in our field.

We must tackle two problems. First we must develop a clear understanding of the categories that constitute the subject matter of our studies before we can even begin to formulate theories or make statements relevant to our discipline. Then we can decide how to test those hypotheses and statements. A new discipline has to make do with traditional categories, some of which may turn out to be fuzzy and confusing on closer examination. Early natural scientists took long established concepts, gradually discarding many of them as a result of experiment and observation: for example, caloric gave way to the kinetic theory of heat, phlogiston to the chemistry of combustion; the clarity of mathematics revealed that the medieval notion of a vital force to explain the dynamic properties of objects was just a confusion of many precise concepts such as kinetic and potential energy, linear and angular momentum and so on. They had first to discard the old mysterious categories.

Organisational Semiotics has similar difficulties to overcome, not least in the form of traditional categories of 'information', 'data', 'meanings' and so on. Natural science deals with observations of and experiments with tangible things but then builds theories about the invisible forces and particles but in a precise language that links the tangible and invisible together by chains of logical and mathematical argument. Signs, our primary subject matter, seem rather intangible at first, especially when asked to account for such properties as their meanings. The physical materials of natural science are interesting in their own right but signs are of limited interest unless they tell us about something else. That extra step causes problems, as I shall illustrate below.

We semioticians, no less than natural scientists, have to talk about objects and their properties with operational precision. In other words, when we refer to x (some thing or property or category), we invite the challenge:

"You talk about x, so take me by the hand and show it to me." . . (1)

We must reply by means of a reliably reproducible set of operations. It is no good substituting some words for x unless their operational meanings have already been established. Although no one can take us by the hand to see an atom, theoretical models link that concept to experiments on tangible objects.

In our field, in place of the category of physical objects, we have the notion of a 'sign' that we can confidently account for operationally by taking the questioner by the hand to see innumerable examples of signs in operation until they get the idea and we can test them on it. This simple step takes us far beyond the people talking about 'information'. Ask that awkward question with x = information and you will receive, even from experts in the field, a host of incompatible responses. I am sure you have heard them philosophising about the spectrum

data – information – knowledge – wisdom ...... (2)

and how we distil each from its cruder raw material. These remind me of the mediaeval elements

earth – air – fire – water ...... (3)

Our treatment of (2) ranks along with (3) as pre-scientific. Can we put the notions in (2) onto a firm operational footing?

The IFIP 8.1 Task Group charged with arriving at a Framework of Information Systems Concepts (Falkenberg *et al*, 1996) tackled this question. Our work exposed a deep philosophical difference between my own and the mainstream of information systems thinking. My colleagues – broadminded, technically oriented, socially aware computer scientists and software engineers – became good friends and I have the greatest respect for their position. Nevertheless I was forced to recognize that our positions are incompatible. But I must thank them for their clear, precise statement of the theoretical position of the FRISCO majority without which I could not have so readily formulated my own. I believe that the difference between our views helps to define the distinct character of Organisational Semiotics.

FRISCO adopted a strategy (why not emulate them?) of building a hierarchy of concepts, each one defined in terms of other concepts until they reached a few fundamental notions that one must take on trust. From an OS perspective, it seemed to me only natural to escape from the network of verbal definitions by supplying *operational definitions* in the sense of (1) above. For example, they defined information in terms of increments of knowledge and defined knowledge in terms of conceptions possessed by an actor (FRISCO Report, p.92). At this point, I filled out formula (1) with x = conceptions. Clearly no one can take you by the hand to see some conceptions without entering the mind of a person in some way to make the conceptions manifest. In physics this would be like defining 'apple' by relying on an understanding of 'atom'. Ultimately the meaning of 'conception', a fundamental notion, was left to the enquirer's imagination. That is a perfectly acceptable solution provided that one works within the limited domain of signs manipulated in either a formal system or in a computer: that is, in computer science or software engineering.

The elegant mathematical reformulation of the network of definitions in FRISCO does not remove assumptions about the chosen primitive concept but it underlines my observation that the mainstream of information systems thinking, mainly derived from computer science, is content with the consistency of a theory as it affects the internal structure of machines, program and data structures. Organisational Semiotics must always examine how a sign-system connects externally to the substantive world.

Our own domain of study stretches far beyond the world of computers, actual and virtual. We have to deal with people using information (signs!) to handle steel bars (physical world) and insurance contracts (social world). Just as FRISCO does we sometimes define one term using others terms, but we have a duty to provide an operational bridge from any undefined term and reality. Moreover, we have to make clear what we understand by 'reality'. Software engineers have enough to do solving the problems of representing and manipulating complex sign-tokens in electronic devices. They can justify leaving aside some philosophical issues that Organisational Semiotics cannot shrug off! Why not start by criticizing the arguments I have introduced above?

REFERENCES

Beloff, Halla, (1980), *A Balance Sheet on Burt,* Leicester, The British Psychological Society

Castells, Manuel, (1996/97/98), *The Information Age: Economy, Society and Culture,* Oxford, Blackwell,
Vol I – *The Rise of the Network Society,* Vol II – *The Power of Identity,*
Vol III – *End of the Millennium,*

Eysenck, HJ & L Kamin, (1981), *Intelligence, The Battle for the Mind,* Pan Books, London.

Falkenberg, E (ed), W Hesse, P Lindgreen, BE Nilsson, JLH Oei, C Rolland, RK Stamper, FJM van Assche, AA Verrijn-Stuart and K Voss, (1996), *A Framework of Information Systems Concepts,* IFIP Geneva, on line edition at ftp://ftp.leidenuniv.nl/fri-full.zip

Lakoff, G, (1986), *Women, Fire and Dangerous Things,* Chicago, University of Chicago Press

Strassmann, Paul A, (1990) *The Business Value of Computers,* Strassmann Inc, New Canaan, Conn.

Zuboff, S, (1988), *In the Age of the Smart Machine: the Future of Work and Power,* Heinemann, Oxford.

Ronald Stamper
December 2003

Preface

As usual, this book contains selected papers from a recent International Workshop of Organisational Semiotics. The last workshop took place on 11-12 July 2003 in Reading (UK). Attended by 40 delegates from 13 countries, the research community continued its effort in the development of a new discipline of organisational semiotics (OS). It focused not only on theory-building, but also on practical benefits gained so far through application of methods and techniques derived from various OS approaches.

Building on some principles of the long established discipline of Semiotics, the theory of signs, OS has developed a new perspective to study the functions of information and communication in organised activities. The fundamental notion of a sign - anything that stands for something else within a certain community – offers a handle for the in-depth understanding of human and technical aspects of information and information systems. Signs in a simple or complex form (e.g. icon, index, symbol, mark, token, gesture and language) are constantly created and consumed within a social and organisational context. To study the nature, properties, roles and functions of these signs is the primary goal of OS.

The emergent information and communication technology (or ICT) has certainly increased the velocity of change in organisational behaviour; and has also introduced new opportunities, challenges and complexity. Distribution of responsibility and operations within a company and collaborative work across different organisations, time zones and geographic locations become readily adoptable practice rather than fiction. Hence, there arises the need for a sound theoretical underpinning and rigorous methods for understanding and describing the organisational behaviour and the interrelationship between organisational components and technological devices. To this end, the workshop set the following scope of investigation:

- Semiotic analysis of the nature of virtuality and virtual organisations
- Co-design of business and IT systems for distributed and flexible organisations
- Organisational behaviour and changes: modelling and simulation in organisational understanding, organisational re-design, process re-engineering and change analysis
- Interaction between semiotic and material processes in organisations
- Actability and transparency in information systems: under which conditions will system behaviour be interpretable to users and support proper actions?
- Interface design and the division of labour in organisations: who needs access to what information?
- Pervasive computing: designing an environment of computer based signs. Physical space as the new interface to information systems.

This book is divided into three parts. Part one, Organisational Behaviour, deals with modelling and design of organisations. Papers in this part range from analysis of organisational values, culture and governance to examination of activities and processes. The papers in the second part, Systems Interface, mainly focus on the relationship between the business and IT systems. An adequate understanding of the relationship and the interface for the user is crucial for the effectiveness of any well-designed system. The last part, Communication and Action, emphasises the effect of proper use of information and communication in business contexts. From these papers, one can see that information and communication can result in social and pragmatic impact on business operations and our social life. The papers in this book represent the current state of the work as well as new search in the theory, methods and techniques rooted in Organisational Semiotics to date.

The workshop received support from The Engineering and Physical Sciences Research Council (EPSRC) of the United Kingdom (Grant No. GR/S17710/01), in conjunction with an EPSRC funded project "Semiotic Enterprise Design for IT Applications" (Grant No. GR/S04840/01).

Colleagues and research students in the Applied Informatics with Semiotic Laboratory (or the AIS Lab, http://www.ais.rdg.ac.uk) at the University of Reading have offered their support to the workshop unreservedly. Simon Tan of the University of Reading has done tremendous work in assembling the materials and converting them into the manuscript.

Kecheng Liu
December 2003

Programme Committee

Kecheng Liu (chair), The University of Reading, United Kingdom
Peter Andersen, Aalborg University, Denmark
Cecilia Baranauskas, UNICAMP, Brazil
Rodney Clarke, Staffordshire University, United Kingdom
Joaquim Filipe, Escola Superior de Tecnologia de Setubal, Portugal
Henk Gazendam, Groningen University and Twente University, The Netherlands
Göran Goldkuhl, Linköping University, Sweden
René Jorna, University of Groningen, The Netherlands
Ronald Stamper, University of Twente, The Netherlands
Workshop Secretary: Steven Xie

Additional Reviewers

Jim Underwood, University of Technology, Sydney, Australia
John Krogstie, SINTEF Telecom and Informatics, and Norwegian University of Science and Technology, Norway
Junkang Feng, University of Paisley, United Kingdom
Lily Sun, The University of Reading, United Kingdom
Renchu Gan, Beijing Institute of Technology, China
Steve Peters, Free University, Amsterdam, The Netherlands

I

ORGANISATIONAL BEHAVIOUR

Chapter 1

SEMIOTICS, COMPASSION AND VALUE-CENTERED DESIGN

Joseph A Goguen

Department of Computer Science & Engineering University of California, San Diego. United States.

Abstract: It is difficult to design systems that satisfy users; failure is common, and even successful designs often overrun time and cost. This motivates user-centered design methods. But users often don't know what they need or else cannot articulate it (due to tacit knowledge), and also are often not aware of key impacts of organisational context on how they work. This motivates using ethnographic methods. However these can be slower and more expensive, and can still fail. We argue that values are keys to the promise of socially sensitive design. Algebraic semiotics provides a rigorous notation and calculus for representation that is explicitly value sensitive, while compassion supports both better analysis and better ethics in design. Together with discourse-based value discovery methods and iterative design, these enable a method that we call value-centered design; some case studies are discussed.

Key words: Semiotics, Ethnomethodology, Value-Centred Design, Requirement Engineering

1. INTRODUCTION

The history of computing hardware can be summarized as a progression from a focus on low level components towards integration on larger and larger scales, from vacuum tubes and transistors to LSI, VLSI, chipsets, personal computers, LANs, WANs, and now the global internet. But this machine oriented view is far too narrow, because progression on the human side has been at least as dramatic and important, from isolated single users, to time sharing, to groupware and support for community activities, to the frontier where ubiquitous, wireless, context-aware multimodal mobile

K. Liu (ed.),
Virtual, Distributed and Flexible Organisations: Studies in Organisational Semiotics, 3–14.

computing enables currently unknown social possibilities, conjured in the startling visions for education, art, politics, medicine, and business that regularly appear in the media. There has also been a parallel evolution of organisations, as the increasing integration of communication and computation (known as ``convergence") has enabled ever closer coordination of quasi-independent units. On the other hand, the landscape is littered with failed schemes, e.g., from the ambitions of early logic-based AI to the more recent dot.com meltdown.

Few would deny that design today lacks mature principles and methods, is more an art than a science, and often fails to deliver satisfying results. The following are among the challenges that a mature design discipline would have to overcome:

1. develop systematic reliable ways to discover appropriate requirements that take account not only of the cooperative, distributed and dynamic social aspects of use, but also the values of user communities;

2. formulate mathematically precise definitions for basic notions such as structure, action, event, representation, and metaphor;

3. develop an abstract specification notation, including both dynamic and static (display) aspects, building on 2. above;

4. find and use general measures for the quality of designs, especially as expressed in 3. above;

5. find general principles for the use of media and their combinations, especially new media;

6. find ways to automatically generate a realization from abstract descriptions (as in 3. above), e.g., for information visualizations; and

7. integrate all this with other disciplines, e.g., software engineering.

Note that this article interprets ``design" in a broad sense, ranging from traditional crafts like user interface design, industrial design, book and magazine layout, up to organisational aspects of management, such as re-engineering, flexible organisation, and synergy of organisation with IT support.

Much of the literature in design and management seeks theory-based, replicable methods for solving problems, in the style of mathematics, physics, or (at least) engineering. However, the rapid evolution of fads and buzzwords, and the ubiquity of spectacular failures (e.g., Enron and Windows1, to take just one example from each area) attest to the lack of significant progress. Two often cited obstacles are: giving precise formulations of realistic problems; and giving realistic metrics for the adequacy of solutions. I suggest that in general, these obstacles cannot be overcome, and in fact, that they are not even genuine problems, but rather are artifacts of a misguided reductionist program that attempts to apply successful methods from the hard sciences to domains having completely different characteristics.

Instead of longing for the stable, grounded world that seems promised by reductionist science, and seeking reductionist solutions, managers and designers should learn to live in the groundless semiotic world of social reality. Although certain specific problems can be reduced to predictable routine methods, management and design operate in open social environments, which implies that their most important problems are not reducible. Philosophers including Heidegger and Nishitani have developed deep insights into the groundlessness of the human condition, and how to live with it, as discussed here later. I believe that extreme reductionist tendencies are harmful, because they raise expectations that cannot be fulfilled, thus leading to disappointment, and fueling further cycles of hope and fear. For example, (Heidegger 1977) gives a powerful and very influential discussion of the dark side of technology, and (Burstall 1991) describes some of the ways in which our involvement with computing may bias our overall point of view, leading to additional confusion and pain in our lives, both our working and our personal lives.

This article suggests that, although extreme reductionism remains sterile, semi-formal approaches that take account of social processes can be valuable. It argues that values are the key to unlocking the mysteries surrounding the enormous opportunities and enormous dangers of contemporary technologies. Claims are often made that better engineering will solve the problems, or better management, or further progress in basic technical areas such as distributed algorithms, user interface design and ontologies, and no doubt all this can help, but until we understand not only what users want (as in requirements analysis, defined in (Goguen 1994) as the reconciliation of what is desirable with what is possible, so that a useful system can actually be built), but much more fundamentally, why they want, i.e., their fundamental underlying motivations, progress will be heavily interleaved with failure, and will continue be very expensive when it does occur, since users are notoriously unreliable at saying what they want, and traditional requirements engineering is very error-prone, as shown by the shockingly common failures of large software systems. A design method called algebraic semiotics is sketched, combining ideas from sociology and computer science.

We also reject extreme relativism, which claims that all social phenomena and human values are equally valid. However, it is not claimed that merely denying both absolutism and relativism solves any hard problems in design or management. Instead, our view that there are no definite foundations for such disciplines leads us to explore groundlessness, the lack of any definite foundation, and to discover that groundlessness can spark compassion, ethics, and perhaps even better design.

The research described in this paper draws on insights and methods from ethnomethodology, activity theory, discourse analysis, symbolic interactionism, etc., but it is focused on practical results, rather than ideological purity. CSCW (Ackerman 2000, Dourish 2001, Robinson and Bannon 1991) and related work in sociology of technology (Agre 1995, Bowker 1994, Bowker and Star 1999, Star 1989, Star 1989a) suggest relating activity to "institutions of practice" within particular communities, while ethnomethodology suggests viewing context as situated interaction, rather than attempting to reify it with precise (allegedly context independent) descriptions (Sacks 1992). Such insights naturally motivate the idea that values are inherent in all situations, and indeed, are what give them the coherence that allows us (whether as participants or as observers) to see them as situations. The formal side of the research also uses algebraic abstract data type theory as a basis for semiotic theories. However, this is not the place for a detailed exposition of the mathematics involved; for this, readers may wish to consult (Goguen 1999).

2. ALGEBRAIC SEMIOTICS

Communication is always mediated by signs, which always occur in structured systems of related signs (Saussure 1976). This insight is formalized in algebraic semiotics, an emerging theory of design, which has mainly been applied to user interface design (Goguen 1999, Goguen 1999a). Semiotic systems are a central notion of algebraic semiotics; these are axiomatic theories for systems of signs, including hierarchical "constructors" for signs, and (socially determined) measures of their relative importance; an example is the space of potential displays for some application running on a PDA. Context, including the setting of a given sign, can be at least as important for meaning as the sign itself. In an extreme example, the word "Yes" can mean almost anything, given an appropriate context. This corresponds to an important insight of Peirce (1965), that meaning is relational, not just denotational (i.e., functional); this is part of the point of his famous semiotic triangle. In algebraic semiotics, certain aspects of context dependence can be handled by constructors that place signs within larger signs, so that the original signs become contextualized subsigns. However, human interpretation is still needed for signs to have meaning in any human sense. Moreover, human interpretation is needed in deploying the formalism of algebraic semiotics, since it is intended to be used flexibly, in much the same manner as musical notation is used in musical performance.

In design, it is often important to view some signs as representing other signs. This motivates the systematic study of representation, including what makes some representations better than others. Although transformations are fundamental in many areas of mathematics and its applications (e.g., linear transformations, i.e., matrices), transformations of signs seem not to have been previously studied in semiotics; in algebraic semiotics, semiotic morphisms are mappings between such spaces which preserve various significant properties (Goguen 1999). Just as semiotic systems are theories rather than models, so their morphisms translate from the language of one semiotic system to the language of another, instead of just translating the concrete signs. This may seem indirect, but it has important advantages over more common approaches based on set theoretic models, in that it is open, in allowing multiple models, as well as in permitting new structure to be added at a later stage.

Algebraic semiotics also provides precise ways to compare the quality of representations, and to combine representations, such that conceptual blending (in the sense of cognitive linguistics (Turner 1997, Fauconnier and Turner 1998, 2000)) is a special case. A number of algebraic laws have been proved about operations for combining representations, constituting the beginnings of a calculus of representations. Case studies for this theory include web-based displays for mathematical proofs that integrate motivation, background and explanation with formal details (Goguen 1999a, Goguen and Lin 2001), and information visualization (Goguen and Harrell 2003).

In many real world examples, not everything can or should be preserved, so that semiotic morphisms must be partial. For example, the table of contents of a book preserves structure and the names of major parts, but completely fails to preserve content (which is what makes it useful). The extent of preservation gives a way to compare the quality of semiotic morphisms (Goguen 1999). It is notable that semiotic spaces and semiotic morphisms are qualitative rather than quantitative, in that they concern structure, and their quality measures are partial orderings, rather than linear numerical scales. Design is the problem of massaging a source space, a target space, and a morphism, to achieve suitable quality, subject to constraints. This formulation applies just as well to managing an organisation as it does to designing a website. In addition, various design principles can be stated and justified, including the following:

1. The most important subsigns should be mapped to correspondingly important subsigns in the representation of a sign;

2. The most important axioms about signs should also be satisfied by their representations; and

3. It is better to preserve form (i.e., structure) than content, if something must be sacrificed.

These can be given much more precise formulations using the mathematical definitions in (Goguen 1999); for example, the first rule can be broken into two principles, one concerning sort preservation according to level, and the other concerning constructor preservation according to priority. The third principle is called Principle F/C in (Goguen 1999); many instances of it are familiar to designers in special cases.

The situated abstract data type (SADT) notion arose from noticing many situations in which users recognize quite different complex signs as "representing the same thing" (Goguen 1994). For example, sports events often involve elaborate data, presented in different ways in different contexts, e.g., on TV screens, in newspapers, and on real-time scoreboards at the event. Moreover, specific events, e.g., the legality of a particular play, may be negotiated by various combinations of players, referees, coaches, rule bodies, etc. Thus, both producing and interpreting these displays are social achievements. Three other examples discussed in (Goguen 1994) are the value hierarchy of a small corporate recuirtment firm (see Figure 3), a taxonomy of requirements engineering methods (Figure 2), and the so called ``waterfall model" (Figure 1), a normative process model of how software engineering should be done.

3. GROUNDLESSNESS AND COEMERGENCE

There appears to be a conflict between grounding design in a mathematical formalism like algebraic semiotics, and in claiming that design is groundless. This appearance arises from an implicitly assumed Platonism for mathematical modelling in general, and semiotics in particular, instead of positioning them in social reality, which is groundless due to its being continually reconstructed through the work of its members. This ongoing reconstruction is an instance of the Buddhist notion of pratityasamutpada, which is literally ``dependent arising," often translated as codependence or coemergence. Found in the earliest teachings of the Buddha, and developed further by Nagarjuna, Vasubandhu and others, coemergence is the notion that nothing exists by itself, but instead, everything is interdependent, or more precisely, everything arises together with other things. It is similar to the Western notion of ``hermeneutic circle," which has origins in ancient Greece, but has been especially developed in more recent times, e.g., by Schleiermacher, Heidegger, and (under a different terminology) Derrida.

The lack of any definite ground for phenomena follows from coemergence. The groundlessness of the human condition is discussed in depth by (Nishitani 1982), who points out (following his teacher Heidegger) that much of the recent history of Western thought can be seen as a progressively refined questioning of absolutes. Among the responses to this questioning, two extremes are identified: nihilism, which is absolute relativity, the denial of any meaning; and absolutism, which is the denial of the questioning. Such absolutism may take the form of dogmatism, fundamentalism, or extreme reductionism. Moreover, there tends to be an unstable oscillation between these two extremes Thus groundlessness is not a stable, fixed state; indeed, it makes even less sense to reify groundlessness than other things. Nor is it passive. All living systems are dynamic, constantly rebalancing their state in order to achieve equilibrium within their environment.

Nishitani says there is a "middle way"' which avoids the extremes of both nihilism and absolutism, as well as the unstable oscillation between them, by accepting groundlessness as a basis for being. The experience of groundlessness, and a path based upon it, have been described in many traditions with phrases such as "dark night of the soul" and "cloud of unknowing". Results of practicing this middle way are said to include openness, compassion, and harmony with nature; joy, strength, and peace are also said to result. This is advocated in (Varela, Thompson and Rosch 1991) as a fruitful approach to cognitive science. Here, I suggest it also makes sense as an approach to design, dwelling in neither relativism nor reductionism, and drawing energy and inspiration from silence.

4. COMPASSION, ETHICS AND VALUES

A book by the Dalai Lama (which reached number one on the New York Times best selling business list) discussed some inner possibilities of groundlessness from the viewpoint of Tibetan Buddhism (Dalai Lama 1999), though its approach is not so different from that of Meister Eckhardt, Maimonides, Rumi, Lao Tzu, and many others. A major argument of this book is that everyone wants to be happy and content, and that an important way to achieve this is to live ethically, for example, to avoid harming others. Fortunately, everyone has an innate capacity for compassion, for feeling the condition of others, and this makes it possible to act in a humane way. This capacity may have a basis in mirror neurons (Rizozolatti et al 1996), which for primates are known to respond to specific gestures in others, and which might well be further developed in humans. In any case, it is clear that empathy and compassion are inhibited by preconceptions and prejudices.

Arguments against rule based approaches to ethics are well known, e.g. (Johnson 1993); they are similar to arguments against reductionist approaches to other areas, e.g., management and design. Fixed rules can never anticipate the complexities of the human condition, and in any case require interpretation, while second order rules (such as Kant's categorical imperative) require even more interpretation than first order rules (like "Thou shalt not kill'"). Although rules can certainly be very valuable as guidelines, as argued above with respect to design, the usual philosophical problems of reductionism arise when they are elevated to universal principles. A perhaps surprising result is that human nature is sufficient for ethical behaviour, once it has been sufficiently refined. Groundlessness then becomes a ground for authentic behaviour, including genuine ethics, as well as effective and creative design; indeed, from this perspective, effective behaviour cannot be separated from genuine ethical behaviour. Compassion is the central value here, and other values include an appreciation for groundlessness, and the avoidance of both nihilism and absolutism. Clearly, other, more specific, values arise in the many specific situations of life.

According to ethnomethodology, when events occur in a social context, members apply their concepts and methods to account for what happened: the technical term accountability refers to this process, which simultaneously produces new assertions, and expresses what the group values by highlighting some aspects while ignoring or downplaying others. Thus information and values do not exist as abstract ideal entities, but rather emerge interactively through accountability in actual situations; everything in social life attains meaning through the relations of accountability in which it participates, and therefore always has an inherent ethical component. Moreover, information always arises through the particular relations of accountability that tie it to a particular social group and the work done in a particular context to produce particular interpretations. A foundational approach to values based on these ideas is developed in (Goguen 1997), where the following definition is given:

An item of information is an interpretation of a configuration of signs for which members of some social group are accountable.

To summarize, groups, values, and information are ``coemergent" in the sense that each produces and sustains the others: groups exist because members share values and information with one another; values exist because they are shared and communicated within groups; and information arises as groups with shared values cope with a dynamic world. None of these three should be considered more basic than the others. Values are also a necessary presupposition of analysis, because it is members' accounting, based on their shared values, that renders their concepts and methods visible to analysts. Jayyusi (1991) puts this point as follows:

What emerges from both Garfinkel's and Sacks' work is the understanding that all communicative praxis presupposes, and is founded in, a `natural' ethic - an ethic, that is, which is constitutive of, and reflexively constituted by, the natural attitude of everyday life. The sense of reflexivity here is the same as that of coemergence above.

But all this theory leaves open the question of how a working designer (or manager, or systems analyst) can actually discover values. For this, we can draw on practical ethnography (participant observation, field notes, audio and video recordings, etc.), the work of Labov (1972) on the embedding of evaluation in stories, and of Sacks (1974) on interactions of speakers and audience during the telling of jokes. Case studies (Goguen 1996) with small groups show that value systems can be obtained by using Labov (1972) and Sacks (1974) plus discourse analysis, to extract value-laden discourse fragments, and the KJ method (Kawakita 1975) to classify them. For example, part of a "`value tree"' expressing the value system of a small corporate recruitment firm is given in section 3.6 of Goguen (1996). Later case studies have probed the values implicit in database interfaces (Goguen 2003) and in mathematical proofs (Goguen 2004).

It is interesting to look at the four examples in Goguen (1994) in light of the definition of information above, because each is socially situated in a different way. Sports scores are constructed by players, referees, etc., while the value hierarchy consists of discourse fragments from firm members, as chosen and arranged by the analysts, the taxonomy of methods is purely an analysts' construction, and the waterfall model is a traditional diagram found (in varying forms) in many texts.

Actor network theory (Latour 1987, 1988) can contribute to system design through its emphasis on the whole network of relations that constitute, support, and use a system. For example, not only end users and their local environments should be included, but also equipment manufacturers, supplies of communications infrastructure, system maintainers, etc. Also the notion of "immutable mobile" can shed light on how different SADTs (and even different parts of the same SADT) can be socially situated to different degrees, in different ways (Goguen 1994). Finally, the negotiations that occur along edges between actants crucially involve value translations.

5. VALUE-CENTERED DESIGN

Since values are the essence of what holds communities together, if we can design systems that embody the values of a community, we will have gone a long way towards being able to reliably design systems that will be embraced by that community. But understanding how values relate to current and future computer based systems is no simple task; values must be considered as situated, embodied, and enacted, rather than as abstract, disembodied, and eternal, and must be related to the use of material artifacts (Vygotsky 1962). This requires a design method that is not just user-centered, and certainly not technology-centered, but is community-centered, and more than that, is value-centered; i.e., we need a value-centered design method.

In brief, our proposed method calls for first extracting values, and using this information to determine key SADTs; these should be expressed as semiotic systems, which are then implemented; for user interfaces, defining semiotic morphisms is a useful intermediate step, and here it is also important to examine natural situations, rather than what users say they might do in imagined situations (Goguen and Linde 1993), though the latter can be useful for discovering values. Appropriate actors should be involved in all processes as much as feasible, and iterative development should be employed throughout. For example components could be procured in partnership with manufacturers, and interested end users could be supported in customizing applications, or even programming their own. It is hoped that exploring such ideas will lead not only to systems that better satisfy users and/or their managers, but that also better satisfy all the actors involved, are ethically produced and used, and enhance society as a whole.

REFERENCES

Ackerman, M. 2000, The Intellectual Challenge of CSCW: The Gap between Social Requirements and Technical Feasibility. Human-Computer Interaction, 15:pp. 179-203.

Agre, P. 1995, Institutional Circuitry: Thinking about the Forms and Uses of Information. Information Technologies and Libraries: pp. 225-230.

Bowker, G. 1994, Information Mythology and Infrastructure. In Lisa Bud, Editor, Information Acumen: The Understanding and Use of Knowledge in Modern Business, pp. 231-247. Routledge.

Bowker, G and Star, S, L. 1999, Sorting Things Out. MIT.

Burstall, R. 1991, Computing: Yet Another Reality Construction. In Software Development and Reality Construction. Springer.

Dalai Lama. 1999, Ethics for the New Millenium. Riverhead.

Dourish, P. 2001, The Foundations of Embodied Interaction. MIT.

Fauconnier, G. Turner, M. 1998, Conceptual Integration Networks. Cognitive Science, 22, pp. 133-187.

Fauconnier, G. Turner, M. 2002, The Way We Think. Basic.

Garfinkel, H. 1967, Studies in Ethnomethodology. Prentice-Hall.

Goguen, J. 1994, Requirements Engineering as the Reconciliation of Social and Technical Issues. In Marina Jirotka and Joseph Goguen, editors, Requirements Engineering: Social and Technical Issues, pp. 165-200.

Goguen, J. 1996, Formality and Informality in Requirements Engineering. Proceedings, International Conference on Requirements Engineering, pp. 102-108. IEEE Computer Society.

Goguen, J. 1997, Towards A Social, Ethical Theory of Information. In Geoffrey Bowker, Les Gasser, Leigh Star, and William Turner, editors, Social Science Research, Technical Systems and Cooperative Work, pp. 27-56. Erlbaum

Goguen, J. 1999, An Introduction to Algebraic Semiotics, with Applications to User Interface Design. In Chrystopher Nehaniv, editor, Computation for Metaphors, Analogy and Agents. Lecture Notes in Artificial Intelligence, Volume 1562, pp. 242-291. Springer.

Goguen, J. 1999, Social and Semiotic Analyses for Theorem Prover User Interface Design. Formal Aspects of Computing, 11:pp. 272-301. Special Issue on User Interfaces for Theorem Provers.

Goguen, J. 2003, The Ethics of Databases. In Tara McPherson and Nina Wakeford, editors, Confronting Convergence. Erlbaum, to appear.

Goguen, J. 2004, The Reality of Mathematical Objects, In Preparation.

Goguen, J and Harrell, D. 2003, Information Visualization and Semiotic Morphisms. To appear in Multidisciplinary Approaches to Visual Representations and Interpretations, ed. Grant Malcolm. Elsevier. Papers from the Second International Conference on Visual Representations and Interpretations, Liverpool UK, 9-12.

Goguen, J and Lin, K. 2001, Web-Based Support for Cooperative Software Engineering. Annals of Software Engineering, 12:pp. 25-32.

Goguen, J and Linde, C. 1993, Techniques for Requirements Elicitation. In Stephen Fickas and Anthony Finkelstein, editors, Requirements Engineering '93, pp. 152-164. IEEE. Reprinted in Software Requirements Engineering (Second Edition), ed. Richard Thayer and Merlin Dorfman, IEEE Computer Society.

Heidegger, M. 1962, Being and Time. Blackwell. Translation by John Macquarrie and Edward Robinson of Sein und Zeit, Niemeyer, 1927.

Heidegger, M. 1977, The Question Concerning Technology and other Essays. Harper and Row. Translated by William Lovitt.

Jayyusi, L. 1991, Values and Moral Judgement: Communicative Praxis as a Moral Order. In Graham Button, editor, Ethnomethodology and the Human Sciences, pp. 227-251. Cambridge.

Johnson, M. 1993, Moral Imagination: Implications of Cognitive Science for Ethics. Chicago.

Kawakita, J. 1975, KJ Method: a Scientific Approach to Problem Solving. Kawakita Research Institute.

Labov, W. 1972, The Transformation of Experience in Narrative Syntax. Language in the Inner City, pp. 354-396. University of Pennsylvania.

Lakoff, G and Johnson, M. 1980, Metaphors we Live by. Chicago.

Latour, B. 1987, Science in Action. Open.

Latour, B. 1988, The Pasteurization of France. Harvard.

Nishitani, K. 1982, Religion and Nothingness. University of California. Translated by Jan Van Bragt.

Peirce, C. 1965, Collected Papers of Charles Saunders Peirce. Harvard. In 6 volumes; see especially Volume 2: Elements of Logic.

Rizzolatti, G, Fadiga, L, Gallese, V and Fogassi, L. 1996, Premotor Cortex and The Recognition of Motor Actions. Cognitive Brain Research, 3, pp. 131-141.

Robinson, M and Bannon, L. 1991, Questioning Representations. In Mike Robinson, Liam Bannon, and Kells Schmidt, editors, Proceedings, Second European Conference on Computer-Supported Cooperative Work. Kluwer.

Sacks, H. 1972, An Analysis of the Course of A Joke's Telling in Conversation. In Richard Baumann and Joel Scherzer, editors, Explorations in the Ethnography of Speaking, pp. 337-353. Cambridge.

Sacks, H. 1992, Lectures on Conversation. Blackwell. Edited by Gail Jefferson.

Saussure, F, 1976, Course in General Linguistics. Duckworth. Translated by Roy Harris.

Star, S. 1989, Layered Space, Formal Representations and Long-Distance Control: The Politics of Information. Fundamenta Scientiae, 10:pp. 125-155.

Star, S. 1989a The Structure of Ill-structured Solutions: Boundary Objects and Heterogeneous Problem-Solving. In Les Gasser and Michael Huhns, editors, Distributed Artificial Intelligence, volume 2, pp. 37-54. Pitman.

Turner, M. 1997, The Literary Mind. Oxford.

Varela, F, Thompson, E, and Rosch, E. 1991, The Embodied Mind. MIT.

Vygotsky, L. 1962, Thought and Language. MIT.

Chapter 2

SEMIONICS: A PROPOSAL FOR THE SEMIOTIC MODELLING OF ORGANISATIONS

Ricardo R. Gudwin
DCA-FEEC-UNICAMP gudwin@dca.fee.unicamp.br Brazil.

Abstract: In this paper, we present Semionics, a contribution to the field of Computational Semiotics, and propose its use in order to build and simulate models of organisations. Computational Semiotics refers to a research area where semiotic techniques are used in order to synthesize semiotic processes in computers and computer-based applications. Semionics is the main technology developed by our research group, based on Peircean semiotics, with the aim of providing both modelling and simulation artifacts for the design of such semiotic systems. Here we present the main backgrounds of semionics - the semionic network - what it is and how it works. Further, we show an application example of a semionic network for the modelling and simulation of a small business organisation.

Key words: Semionics, Computational Semiotics, Organisations

1. INTRODUCTION

The notion of "organisation" is a fairly abstract concept that can be applied to many kinds of physical systems. This notion comes from the greek word "organon", which means "tool". Tools are artifacts or systems which have a purpose, or functionality associated with them. In this sense, we may think of organisations as special kinds of systems, where there is a purpose for their existence, and these systems continuously work doing their best in order to achieve this purpose. Many different things can be classified as organisations: biological systems as cells, organs, organisms, societies, etc., or economical systems as business organisations, markets and even national and international economies. But from these examples we may guess that it is not so easy to define what an organisation really is. Let's take

K. Liu (ed.),
Virtual, Distributed and Flexible Organisations: Studies in Organisational Semiotics, 15–33.

the example of a business organisation (even though the following conclusions are valid also for other kinds of organisations). This organisation is not simply the sum of its employees, installations and resources. It is much more. It is its brand, its name, its connection to its market, its customers and its suppliers. And this is not all! If we change all the employees, move to a different installation and renew all its resources, it will keep on being the same organisation. So, this is not an easy task defining what an organisation is.

Many different models of organisations were attempted (Sterman 2000). One particular approach that proved to be of special interest is to model them in terms of the signs being processed during its behaviour. In this sense, the semiotic modelling of organisations (Van Heusden & Jorna 2002) led the way to the creation of a new area of research that was called organisational semiotics (Alderson *et al.* 1999; Liu et.al 2000). But how can we pragmatically do such semiotic modelling of organisations? What are the artifacts that allow us to consider organisations as flows of signs in semiotic systems? The main purpose of this work is to present Semionics, a pragmatical proposal for a both formal and computational model of sign systems, and to apply it on the semiotic modelling of organisations.

2. SEMIOTICS - THE STUDY OF SIGNS

Semiotics is the science which studies the phenomena of signification, meaning and communication in natural and artificial systems (Noth 1995). Its main artifact is the notion of *signs,* and its main approach is to explain different kinds of phenomena as being *sign processes.* The study of sign processes is documented in literature since the works of Plato and Aristotle (Noth 1998), but Semiotics, as an independent area of research was organized and structured only with the work of Charles S. Peirce, an American philosopher, during the middle of the 20th century (Peirce 1960). Even though we consider Peirce as the great exponent on developing semiotics, there are many different approaches developed in order to account for the notion of signs, and many others have contributed to the development of semiotics, like Saussure, Hjelmslev, Jakobson, Greimas and Morris - more recently Eco, Sebeok, Merrell and others (Noth 1996; Morris 1947; Morris 1964; Morris 1971; Sebeok 1997).

Both natural and artificial systems can be modelled semiotically. There are some constraints, though. When we are considering natural systems, i.e., systems that are already working in nature, the only way of semiotic modelling is due to semiotic analysis. Now, considering artificial systems, we can apply both semiotic analysis and semiotic synthesis. We use semiotic synthesis in order to artificially create semiotic processes. In this case, we are not mere expectants of the miracles of nature, but actants in order to fully synthesize devices where semiotic processes do occur. Of course, after making the synthesis, we are also able to employ semiotic analysis on the synthesized systems, but we will see that the synthesis problem is sometimes harder than its analysis counterpart.

Many different strategies may be employed for semiotic synthesis. In the next section, we will present Semionics, our proposal for semiotic synthesis.

3. SEMIONICS

We may understand Semionics as a particular way of implementing the notion of a sign in a formal and computational way. So, before describing the details of semionics, it is important to analyse the different models of signs available within semiotics, in order to characterize the power and constraints of each available option.

Let's start with the dyadic sign as proposed within structuralist semiotics, presented in figure 1.

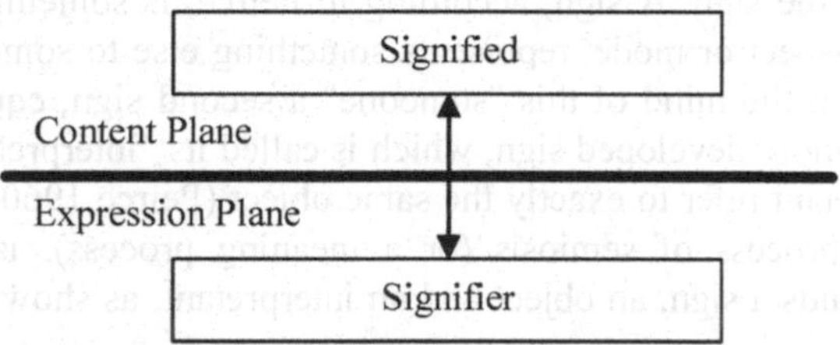

Figure 1 - The Structuralist Model of the Sign (dyadic)

In this model, there are two planes, bi-univocally connected - the so-called expression plane and the content plane. Within the expression plane, we find discriminable unities which we call "signifiers". On the content plane, we find discriminable unities we call "signifieds". Unities on the expression plane and on the content plane are related to each other, forming cartesian pairs of the type (signifier, signified). A sign (according to the structuralist view) is then defined as being such a pair (signifier, signified). So, in this model, a sign is viewed as a dyadic relation that connects a signifier to a signified. This model has its origins in the work of Saussure (Nöth 1996), being further enhanced by Hjelmslev and others. In its original inceptions, both signifier and signified were supposed to be mental units. So, an example of a signifier would be the sound of the word "car", defined on an expression plane of sound waves, encoded accordingly to become a mental term, and its signified will be the idea we have of a car, also encoded in a mental way. Some variations on this model may associate the expression plane to an inner world, and the content plane to the external world. Then, to each signifier in the inner world (mental world), there should be a natural correlate on the external world (content plane). The problem with this view is that such correlation is totally arbitrary. This is the vision proclaimed by cognitivism within cognitive sciences, which says that if in a computer memory a given set of signals represent the proposition "Socrates is mortal", the connection between these signals with the historic Socrates (the individual), and the fact that this man has a property of "being mortal" would be "automatic". This totally arbitrary connection between signifier and signified is apparently the fragility of this model, being the origin of the symbol grounding problem in artificial intelligence (Harnad 1990). With this model, it is also impossible to model the said natural signs - the icons and the indexes, but only symbols.

As a contraposition to the dyadic model of the sign, Peirce developed a more elaborate, triadic (Noth 1995) model, which splits the notion of "signified" into two different parts, one of them connected to an element of real world - the so called "object" of the sign, and the other connected to the effect of the sign on the mind of a potential interpreter, called the "interpretant" of the sign. A sign, according to Peirce, is something which, under a certain aspect or mode, represents something else to someone. This sign will create in the mind of this "someone" a second sign, equivalent to itself - that is, a more developed sign, which is called its "interpretant". Both sign and interpretant refer to exactly the same object (Peirce 1960; Santaella 2000). So, the process of semiosis (or a meaning process), is a triadic relation that bounds a sign, an object and an interpretant, as shown in figure 2:

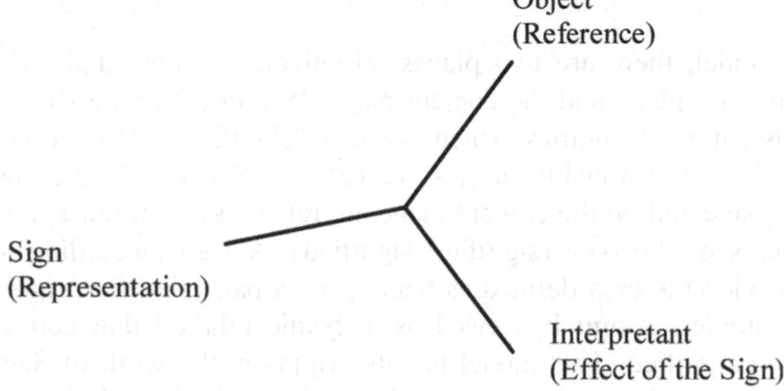

Figure 2 - The Peircean Model of the Sign (triadic)

In this process, the object, by means of its relation to the sign, confers to the sign the power to represent it. This power is consolidated during the generation of the interpretant, within the mind of a potential interpreter (even though the notion of interpreter is not necessary, according to Peirce). Note that in this case, there is no "automatic" connection between a signifier and a signified, as in the dyadic model, but a process in which a sign only becomes a sign, when it possess this capacity of generating an interpretant, and it will only have this capacity, in virtue of the relation that it has with its object. This allows the definition of natural signs, i.e., the icons and indexes, which were not allowed in the dyadic model.

The Peircean model (Peirce 1960; Santaella 2000) is elaborated and full of details (which we omit in this article, as they are beyond its scope here). But let us better appreciate the relation between a sign and its object, which is what gives the sign its character of being interpretable. So, according to the nature of the relation between a sign and its object, signs can be divided into icons, indexes and symbols.

Icons are signs which have in their structures some relation of similarity to their designated object. In other words, they have in themselves the same qualities (or a subset of them) that the object itself has. This is the main reason they are entitled to represent their object. Icons can be divided into three different sub-categories - images, diagrams and metaphors. Images have in themselves, the same qualities as their objects. This happens, for example, when we use a picture to represent something that was photographed. So, by viewing the picture of a house, and appreciating its qualities, we know which house it is. This meaning is so split into two parts. From one side, we have the real house, the one which was photographed, and which is referred to by the picture. On the other side, there is the idea that we have of such a house, idea that is triggered in our mind, due to the presence of the sign. Diagrams, as opposed to images, do not possess in themselves directly the same qualities as their object. But they present a relation between their parts which are equivalent to the relations that hold for the object's parts. So, the relation among the parts of a diagram is equivalent to the relations among the parts of the object in the real world. This is a different kind of icon. The metaphors, which are another kind of icon, are connected to their objects by means of abstractions that we are able to make from both the sign and the object. So, even though sign and object do not share the same qualities, the abstractions we make for both sign and object do share these qualities. So this constitutes a more sophisticated kind of icon. In a general way, we say that icons do not depend on their objects (that is, they do not depend on the simultaneous presence of their objects for the interpretation), because they hold in themselves the object's qualities, which allows them to be interpreted as signs of it. On the contrary, we will see that indexes and symbols will depend on their objects and interpretants, respectively, in order to be interpreted (Peirce 1960).

The symbol, in the same way as the icon, carries in itself an absolute meaning. But, on the other hand, it has no need to have in itself the same qualities present as in the object. Its power to represent an object is instead related to an arbitrary convention, or law, that binds the sign to the object. The interpretation of a symbol comes in two steps. In a first step, something presented to the system is recognized due to its attributes as an icon, corresponding to the identification of the sign in itself (as something known). In a second step, a convention linking this already known icon to something else is invoked and used to connect the preliminary sign to the final object. We see that an important element on the interpretation of a symbol is the arbitrary convention that binds the sign to the object. This convention occurs due to a personal decision of the interpreter (e.g. ... "from now on I will call this xyzt" ...), or due to a pact with other interpreters, to whom this interpreter wants to communicate. The celebration of this pact involves a sophisticated protocol, still not known in its entirety, involving icons and indexes.

The third kind of sign, the index, does not have an absolute meaning, as the icon and the index. Its meaning is otherwise relative to some existing connection to the object. A good way of understanding what is an index is to think of it as a "key" to a procedure which will in turn point to the object. An example will be referential indexes, like "this" or "that". The meaning of "this", or "that" is not absolute, but will depend on the context where these words appear.

Now, in order to understand "Semionics", let us relate these concepts, well known within semiotics, to a computational procedure that is proposed in order to materialize semiotics within computers. We will start with the Peircean model of the sign, as presented in figure 3. In figure 3(a), we have the Peircean model of the sign, as a triadic relation mediating amongst sign, object and interpretant. The idea is that we have three distinct entities that are related to each other in the sense that there is a relationship between the sign and the object, which confers to the sign its power to be turned into an interpretant. At the same time, this interpretant needs to be related to the same object, allowing the possibility of a potentially infinite chain of similar successive transformations, in the course of which each new interpretant keeps a relationship with the same original object.

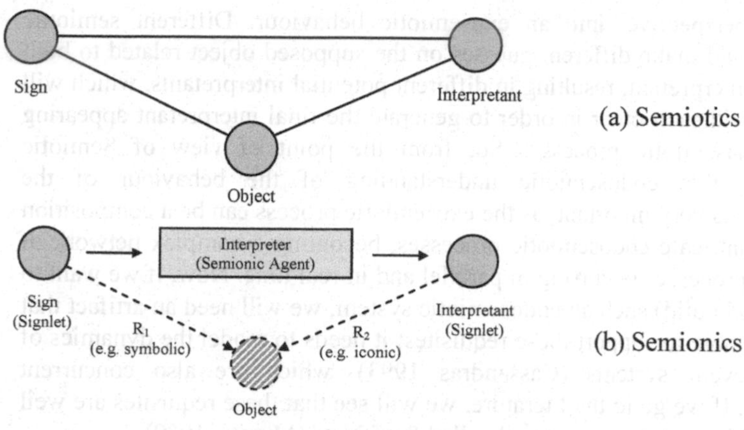

Figure 3 - Linking Semiotics to Semionics

In figure 3(b), we show our proposal for an equivalent relationship between three distinct entities, in a computational version of the same triadic relation found in figure 3(a). In this case, each entity in figure 3a is turned into a computational entity that we call a "signlet". We also propose the notion of a "semionic agent", which performs the role of an interpreter, translating a given signlet, performing the role of a sign, into another signlet, performing the role of an interpretant. In order to generate the signlet performing the role of an interpretant, the semionic agent supposes that the other signlet (the one which performs the role of a sign) should have a link to a third element, their object (which is also supposed to be a signlet). Based on this supposed relationship, it tries to propose a signlet that should maintain some kind of link with this same object. In the example on figure 3b, an input signlet has a symbolic relation to a presumed object, and after the interpretation, the semionic agent generates a signlet which has an iconic relation to this same object.

This process, of generating an interpretant from a sign, based on a supposed relation of both of them to a same object can be a very complicated procedure. Although it appears to be a sequential process, we need to decompose this external, or exosemiotic view, into an internal, or endosemiotic view, in order to better understand it, (figure 4).

From an internal, endosemiotic view, the same process of interpretation, where a given semionic agent takes a signlet and transforms it into another signlet can be performed by a great number of other (internal) semionic agents, creating a whole network of interpretations, that will result, from an external perspective, into an exosemiotic behaviour. Different semionic agents would make different guesses on the supposed object related to both sign and interpretant, resulting in different potential interpretants, which will compete witheach other in order to generate the final interpretant appearing at the exosemiotic process. So, from the point of view of Semiotic Synthesis, this endosemiotic understanding of the behaviour of the interpreter is very mportant, as the exosemiotic process can be a composition of many intricate endosemiotic processes, becoming a complex network of semiosic processes occurring in parallel and in real time. Now, if we want to model (and build) such an endosemiotic system, we will need an artifact that should be able to support these requisites: it needs to model the dynamics of discrete event systems (Cassandras 1993), which are also concurrent processes. If we go to the literature, we will see that these requisites are well supported in a mathematical tool called Petri Nets (Murata, 1989).

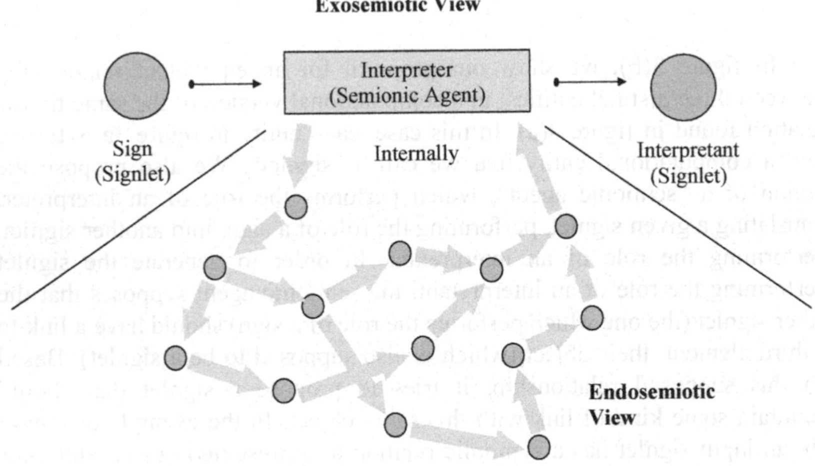

Figure 4 - Exosemiotic and Endosemiotic View of an Interpretation

But standard Petri Nets are not enough for our purposes, because their tokens are unstructured and their transitions have no processing capabilities. We may thus consider extensions and variations of Petri Nets, such as Higher Level Petri Nets (Genrich & Lautenbach 1981), Coloured Petri Nets (Jensen 1990) or Object-based Petri Nets (Lakos 2001), where the tokens are structured, and the transitions have (at least some) processing capabilities. But, again, Coloured Petri Nets and Object-based Petri Nets are inadequate for our requirements, because we have two different kinds of entities in our system, signs and interpreters, both of them structured, something that is not supported within these Petri Net extensions. So, we have deviseda new extension of a Petri Net, taking into consideration the requirements we envisioned for semionics, culminating in a model we have called "Semionic Networks". Semionic networks (Gudwin 2002) are a development that came after many other previous developments, such as Object Networks (Gudwin 1996; Gudwin & Gomide 1997a,b,c, 1998) and Agent Networks (Guerrero et. al. 1999).

4. SEMIONIC NETWORKS

An example of a semionic network can be viewed in figure 5. Signlets and semionic agents are distributed within a network of locations, where each location may have different ports. These locations are connected by means of arcs linking two ports in different locations. Semionic agents perform their role by taking a signlet and generating a newer signlet. This is shown in figure 5a. The semionic agent in the location with the double line takes a signlet from the place on its left, and generates a newer signlet that is put into the location on its right. This could be a very simple procedure, if we consider that there is only one signlet and one semionic agent. But in fact, if we are going to use this to model the endosemiosic processing we suggested in figure 4, we need to cope with the existence of many signlets and eventually many semionic agents competing with each other. This is the situation presented in figure 5b. In the first case, we show the situation in which a semionic agent in the middle place has many options of signlets to process. Which one will it process? The second situation shows that this can be either more complex, if we consider that we need to compose many signlets in order to perform the interpretation. So, we need to better elaborate the behaviour of our semionic agents.

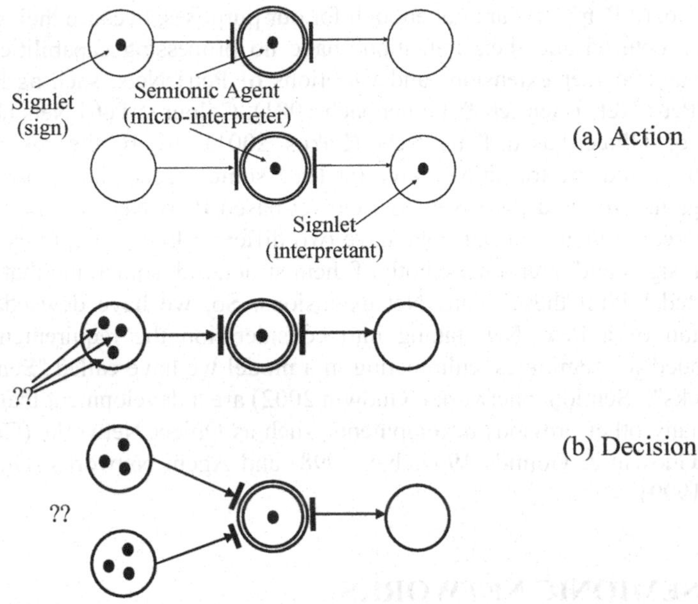

Figure 5 - Action and Decision in a Semionic Network

As suggested by the examples in figure 5, a semionic agent needs to perform two main tasks: decision and action. In the decision task, it needs to choose which sign (or which signs, in the case of a composition) it is going to interpret, and also what is going to happen to this sign, if it is going to be preserved or not. In the action task, the semionic agent needs to materialize the interpretation, generating the interpretant, based on the chosen sign.

The *decision task* is performed by means of two distinct phases, the evaluation phase and the assignment phase. The *action task* is also performed by means of two other phases, the assimilation phase and the generation phase. In order to understand how those phases work together, we need first to dig into the structure of signlets.

A signlet is a computational entity that is basically a tuple of compartments, just like in figure 6 below:

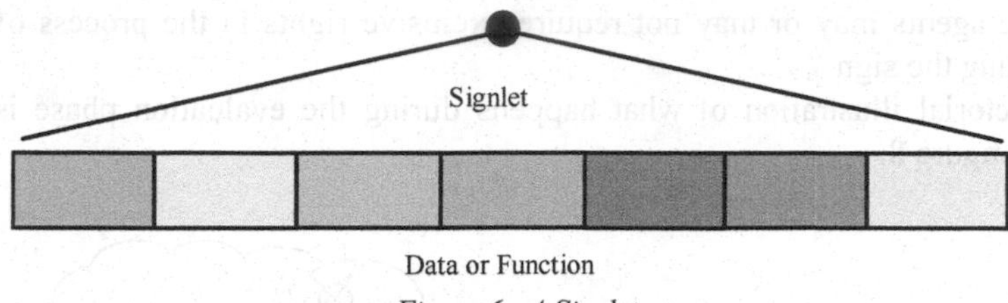

Figure 6 - A Signlet

Signlets can be organized into classes, according to the types of its compartments, which can be either data or functions. In this sense, we will see that semionic agents can be defined also as signlets, but with a special arrangement of compartments, as shown in figure 7 below:

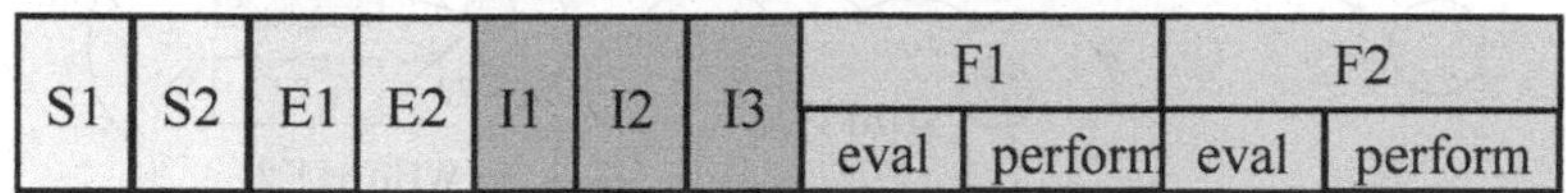

Figure 7 - Semionic Agents are Signlets

In the case of a semionic agent, the compartments are divided into four sections. They can be sensors, effectors, internal states or mediated transformation functions. Each mediated transformation function is described by two different functions, the eval function and the perform function. They are called mediated transformation functions, because the perform functions are executed only mediated by the result of the eval functions, according to the phases described in the sequence.

4.1 The Decision Task

In the decision task, the semionic agent needs to decide which signlet (or signlets) it is going to interpret, and what is going to happen to this signlet. This is not an easy task, because there may be many different signlets available for the semionic agent, and also many possible semionic agents interested in the same signlet. So, the decision task must be implemented in a coordinated way, in order to allow multiple chains of semiosis to happen in parallel and concurrently. The decision task is split into two different phases, the evaluation phase and the assignment phase.

The evaluation phase starts when a given semionic agent is faced with the many available signlets, and considers the different transformations it is able to apply to them, it must evaluate each available signlet, and at the same time decide what is going to happen to it after the interpretation. This last step is necessary because signs may or may not be persistent and also semionic agents may or may not require exclusive rights in the process of interpreting the sign.

A pictorial illustration of what happens during the evaluation phase is given in figure 8.

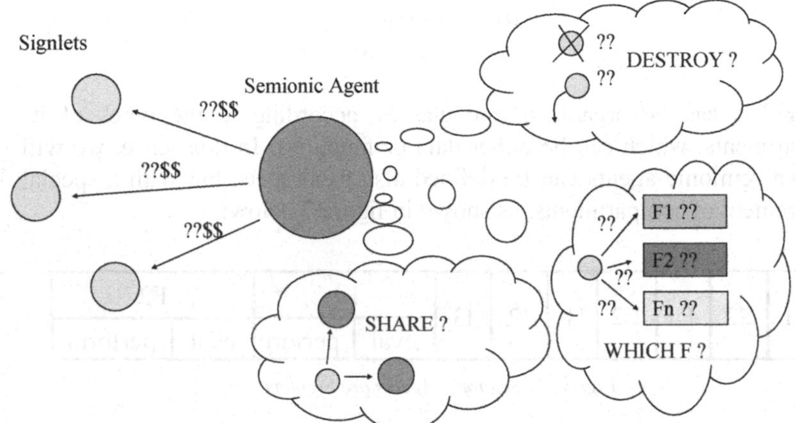

Figure 8 - The Evaluation Phase

Basically, for each transformation function available within the semionic agent, a set of signlets required to perform it is determined from among the available signlets. All possible combinations of available signlets that match the function requirement must be evaluated. Each possible combination, in the form of a list of potential signlets, is called an enabling scope. Each possible enabling scope must be evaluated by means of an evaluation function, which should provide a score for the enabling scope, and also a destiny for it. The possible destinies are:

- a signlet could be modified and sent to a different place
- a signlet could be dropped back to its original place
- a signlet could be destroyed after the interaction

The evaluation phase ends when the semionic agent evaluates all available enabling scopes and attributes to each one an interest value and a pretended access mode.

The pretended access mode describes the semionic agent's planned actions to each input signlet. It should report whether or not the semionic agent plans to share the signlet with other semionic agents and if it plans to destroy the signlet after its use.

After all the enabling scopes are evaluated and rated, a second phase starts, the assignment phase. The assignment phase is responsible for solving possible conflicts with the plans of each semionic agent in the network. In order to overcome this, a central supervisory algorithm computes the plans of each semionic agent and selects an enabling scope for each of them. This selection should avoid any kind of conflict with the plans of the other semionic agents. Many different algorithms can be used in this phase to solve this scheduling problem. For test purposes, our group (Guerrero et al, 1999) developed an algorithm, which we called BMSA (Best Matching Search Algorithm), which attributes a signlet to the semionic agent that best rated it, respecting the pretended access modes of each semionic agent.

4.2 The Action Task

In the action task, the semionic agent simply follows the plan assigned in the assignment phase, generating a new signlet, destroying signlets or modifying them. The action task is also divided into two sub-phases, the assimilation phase and the generation phase. In the *assimilation phase,* the semionic agent decides on a course of action, depending on the access mode given by the decision task. Depending on this access mode, the semionic agent will *read* or *get* the signlets on its inputs. In the case of a *read*, the semionic agent only retains a link to the signlet, so it can have access to its internal contents, but it is not supposed to change the internal content of the signlet. In the case of a *get*, the semionic agent fully assimilates the input signlet, becoming its owner, and in this case, it is able to modify the signlet contents and change it for further reuse. After assimilating the necessary information, the semionic agent then, depending on the given plans, may leave the signlet in its original place, destroy it permanently or take it from its original place, in order to process it. This is the end of the assimilation phase. After managing the future of input signlets, the semionic agent turns to the generation phase, where it will generate new signlets, if it is the case. In the generation phase, after getting the available information from input signlets, this information is used to generate new signlets, or to modify an assimilated signlet. This information is then processed, applying a transformation function that will generate new signlets, which are then sent to the proper places in the network.

4.3 Special Cases

There are two special kinds of semionic agents, which it is useful to point out. These are the *sources* and the *sinks.* Sources are special kinds of semionic agents that don't have inputs, only outputs. The result is that signlets are constantly being generated and being inserted into other places, in a semionic network. Sinks, in contrast, are semionic agents that have no outputs, but just inputs. These semionic agents are used to take signlets from places on the network and destroying them. Sources and sinks can be used in a semionic network to link the network to external systems.

4.4 The SNToolkit

In order to create computational models of semionic networks, and use them to simulate organisational processes, our group built the SNToolkit (Guerrero 1999), the Semionic Network Toolkit, a software tool for editing and simulating semionic networks. A view of this tool is presented in figure 9 below:

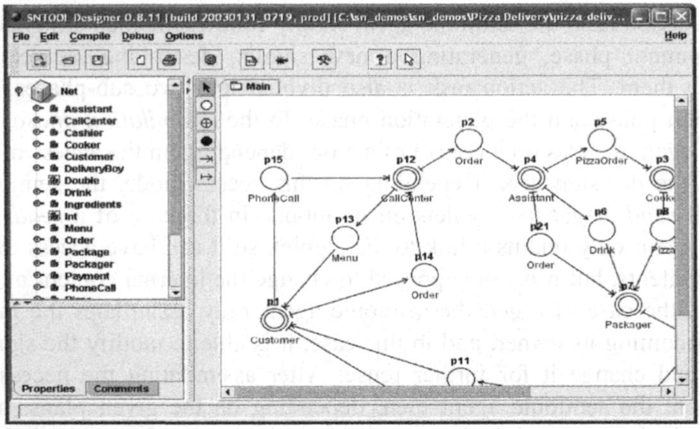

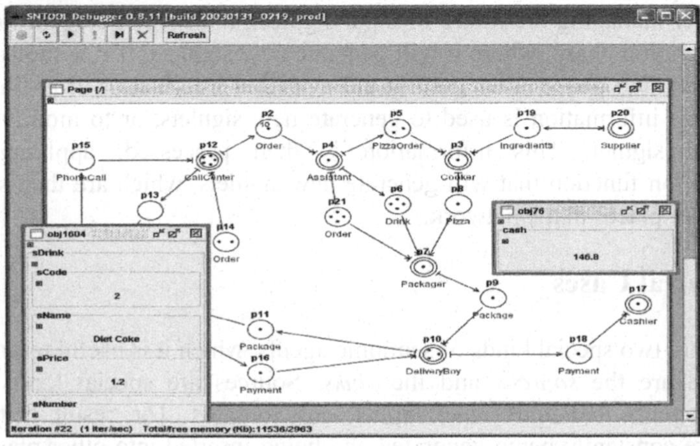

Figure 9 - Screenshots of the SNToolkit

5. MODELLING ORGANISATIONAL PROCESSES

Now, in order to understand how to semiotically model organisational processes, using semionics, we need to introduce some fundamental concepts. The first concept we will start with is our own notion of what characterises an organisation. We will define an organisation as a network of resource processing devices performing a purposeful role. In this sense, we may understand a resource as a very abstract concept that can be applied to many different domains of knowledge. These resources may have an associated "value" or "cost", which can be used on the models being developed. A resource can be almost anything: something substantive, some information, a machine, a person, whatever plays a meaningful role in an organisation. We differentiate between two major kinds of resources: passive resources and active resources. Passive resources are resources that are passively managed or manipulated during the organisational activities. They can be material resources such as objects, parts, products, raw-materials, money, etc... , or informational resources, like texts, documents, diagrams, data, sheets, tables, etc... Active resources are processual resources, or in other words, resources that execute activities of resource processing. Active resources can be mechanical resources (or processors without decision-making) or intelligent resources (or processors where there is some kind of decision-making). Examples of active resources are machines, human resources (workers), etc...

The main idea now, here, is that organisational processes can be described in terms of sign processes, which is the main idea behind organisational semiotics. Resources within an organisation can be modeled in terms of signlets and semionic agents. Passive resources are modeled as signlets and active resources as semionic agents. So, a network of resource processing (an organisation), can be modeled in terms of a semionic network. It is important to notice that both intelligent and mechanical active resources can be modeled in terms of a semionic agent. But the most interesting case, of course, is the case of intelligent active resources, as mechanical processes can be easily modeled by standard Petri Nets. From Peircean semiotics, we borrow the notions of abduction, deduction and induction as the elementary operators being applied to signs. Abduction refers to the generation of newer knowledge structures (signlets). Deduction is related to the extraction of explicit knowledge structures from implicit knowledge structures. And induction is the evaluation of a given knowledge structure in terms of the system purpose. We propose that semionic agents are able to perform decision-based actions, and that the coordination between evaluation and transformation functions in semionic agents allows a semionic agent to perform the three main semiosic steps: abduction, deduction and induction. So, the coordinated work of a network of semionic agents may allow the representation of full semiotic processes (the endosemiosic view) and in this sense, we say that actions performed by semionic agents are mediated actions, where the transformation function is mediated by the evaluation function. An example of a model of a business organisation using a semionic agent is given in figure 10.

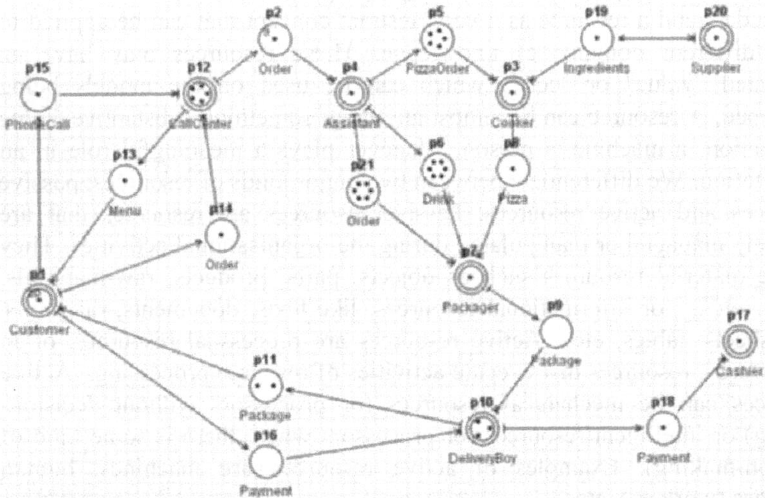

Figure 10 - An Example: A Pizza Delivery Organisation

In this example, there are many active resources on the organisation, performing the roles of customers, call center attendees, assistants, cookers, suppliers, packagers, delivery boys and cashiers. Each active resource is represented by means of a semionic agent and is placed into a location on the network. Passive resources are phone calls, menus, orders, ingredients, pizzas, drinks, packages, payments, and others, which are represented by means of signlets and put on different places around the network, according to its role in the organisation. A semionic network like the one in figure 10 can be simulated on SNToolkit, and many different kinds of results can be collected. We may change the number of employees performing the different roles, give them different organisational procedures, and with that re-engineer the whole organisation and simulate the results of the changes

So, many different things can be done with this framework. We can use it to model and simulate multiple levels of abstraction of an organisation, focusing on the resources processed and on the deliverables created and used. We may test and simulate multiple configurations, making a simulated reengineering of an organisation. They can also be used as a both formal and computational model of the organisation, which can be used to better understand the dynamics of such an organisation. And we can also build information systems better suited to the organisational structure, and which better represent the control demands of the organisation.

6. CONCLUSIONS

We have presented a new approach for semiotic modelling and analysis of organisations, which we have called semionics. The main artifact in semionics is the semionic network, which is a potentially interesting tool for the semiotic modelling of organisations, as simulated in the example given. Although the main guidelines for this approach are already delineated in this work, we are conscious that there is still a lot of work that remains to be done. For example, a comparison between our approach and other approaches used in the study of organisations and workflows, is a must. In order to do that, there are many standards and proposals that need to be checked, like those from the Workflow Management Coalition Standards (Hollingsworth 1995), the Enterprise Distributed Object Computing (OMG 2002) and other models of business processes found in the literature. We also need a more complex study case of a real organisation, as, so far only demonstrations and proof-of-concept implementations were generated. A real study case may suggest new features to be included in the approach, or even changes to the current features. We also need a better understanding of the semiotic contributions to this kind of modelling, which is an issue to be analysed by the organisational semiotics community. This is just a preliminary presentation of a promising tool for the modelling and simulation of organisations, which still needs a lot of work.

REFERENCES

Alderson, A. Yap, J, Liu, K. and Shah, H.U. 1999, Relating Organisational Semiotics, Process Modelling and Stakeholder Viewpoints to Elucidate and Record Requirements, Proceedings of Systems Modelling For Business Process Improvement March 1999, pp. 168- 220

Cassandras, C.G. 1993, Discrete Event Systems: Modelling and Performance Analysis, Aksen Associates Incorporate Publishers.

Genrich, H.J. and Lautenbach, K. 1981, System Modelling with High Level Petri Nets - Theoretical Computer Science 13, pp. 109-136.

Gudwin, R.R. 1996, Contributions to the Mathematical Study of Intelligent Systems - Ph.D. Thesis - DCA-FEEC-UNICAMP - (in portuguese) available on-line at http://www.dca.fee.unicamp.br/~gudwin/Publications/thesis.html

Gudwin, R. R. 2002, Semiotic Synthesis and Semionic Networks S.E.E.D. Journal (Semiotics, Evolution, Energy, and Development), Volume 2, No. 2, p. 55-83.

Gudwin, R.R. and Gomide, F.A.C. 1997, Computational Semiotics: An Approach for the Study of Intelligent Systems, Part I: Foundations Technical Report RT-DCA09-DCA-FEEC-UNICAMP, http://www.dca.fee.unicamp.br/~gudwin/ftp/publications/rep1_97.pdf

Gudwin R.R. and Gomide, F.A.C. 1997, Computational Semiotics: An Approach for the Study of Intelligent Systems, Part II: Theory and Applications Technical Report RT-DCA09-DCA-FEEC-UNICAMP, http://www.dca.fee.unicamp.br/~gudwin/ftp/publications/rep2_97.pdf

Gudwin, R.R.and.Gomide, F.A.C. 1997, An Approach to Computational Semiotics- Proceedings of the ISAS Conference, Gaithersburg, pp.467-470.

Gudwin, R. and Gomide, F. 1998, "Object Networks – A Modelling Tool" – Proceedings of FUZZ-IEEE98, WCCI'98 - IEEE World Congress on Computational Intelligence, 4-9, Anchorage, Alaska, USA, pp. 77-82

Guerrero, J.A.S Gomes, A.S.R. Gudwin, R.R. 1999, A Computational Tool to Model Intelligent Systems - Anais do 4o SBAI - Simpósio Brasileiro de Automação Inteligente, 8-10 September, São Paulo, Brasil , pp. 227-232

Harnad, S. 1990, The Symbol Grounding Problem, Physica D, 42:335-346.

Hollingsworth, D. 1995, Workflow Management Coalition - The Workflow Reference Model, Document Number TC00-1003, Issue 1.1, Workflow Management Coalition - http://www.wfmc.org.

Jensen, K. 1990, Coloured Petri Nets : A High Level Language for System Design and Analysis - Lecture Notes in Computer Science 483 - Advances in Petri Nets, pp. 342-416.

Lakos, C. 2001, Object Oriented Modelling with Object Petri Nets - In G. Agha et al. (Eds.): Concurrent OOP and PN, Lecture Notes in Computer Science, pp. 1-37.

Liu, K. Clarke, R.J. Andersen, P. B. Stamper, R.K. 2000, Information, Organisation and Technology - Studies in Organisational Semiotics (Information and Organisation Design Series, Volume 1), Kluwer Academic Publishers, Boston.

Morris, C.W. 1947, Signs, Language and Behavior - New York : Prentice Hall.

Morris, C.W. 1964, Significant and Significance – New York – Prentice Hall.

Morris, C.W. 1971, Foundation for a Theory of Signs - in Writings on the General Theory of Signs - The Hague : Mouton.

Murata, T. 1989, Petri Nets : Properties, Analysis and Applications - Proceedings of the IEEE, vol. 77, n. 4.

Noth, W. 1995, "Handbook of Semiotics" - Indiana University Press - Bloomington & Indianapolis.

Noth, W. 1996, A Semiótica no Século XX - (Semiotics in the 20th Century - in portuguese), Annablume Editora, São Paulo, Brasil.

Noth, W. 1998, Panorama da Semiótica: De Platão a Peirce - (A Semiotic Panorama : From Plato to Peirce - in portuguese) Annablume Editora - São Paulo, Brasil, 1998 2d edition.

Object Management Group, 2002, UML Profile for Enterprise Distributed Object Computing Specification- OMG Adopted Specification ptc/02-02-05, http://www.omg.org/docs/ptc/02-02-05.pdf

Peirce, C.S. 1960, "Collected Papers of Charles Sanders Peirce" - vol I - Principles of Philosophy; vol II - Elements of Logic; vol III - Exact Logic; vol IV - The Simplest Mathematics; vol V - Pragmatism and Pragmaticism; vol. VI - Scientific Metaphysics - edited by Charles Hartshorne and Paul Weiss - Belknap Press of Harvard University Press - Cambridge, Massachussets.

Santaella, L. 2000, A Teoria Geral dos Signos, Editora Thomson Pioneira.

Sebeok, T.A. 1997, The Evolution of Semiosis, Tutorials 1 – Semiotics - ISAS Conference, Gaithersburg.

Sterman, J.D. 2000, Business Dynamics: Systems Thinking and Modelling for a Complex World - McGraw-Hill Companies.

Van Heusden, B. Jorna, R.J. 2002, "Reconsidering the Standard: A Semiotic Model of Organisations" In: Kecheng Liu, R.J. Clarke, P.B. Andersen & R.K. Stamper (Eds.) Coordination and Communication Using Signs: Studies in Organisational Semiotics 2. Dordrecht: Kluwer Academic Publishers, p. 153-67.

Chapter 3

ANTICIPATED ACTIVITIES

In Maritime Work, Process Control, and Business Processes.

Peter Bøgh Andersen
Department of Computer Science, Aalborg University, Denmark

Abstract: Most activities are anticipated before they are executed. The paper presents methods for describing this anticipated state and the processes that may lead to a new state where the activities are executed. The method builds on linguistic case-theory.

Key words: Maritime work, Process control, Business processes, Case theory.

1. INTRODUCTION

Many activities live much of their life in a half-baked shape, as anticipated activities. It means that although some of their parts are in place, other parts are too vague to be executable, or consist of a set of undecided options, while still other parts are completely missing. In addition, half-baked activities are continually revised, some options are removed, others are added, and vague information becomes more definite. This paper presents a conceptual framework for describing such unfinished plans and the transformations they undergo. It analyses an authentic anticipated activity (that took 9 h 30 min to accomplish) from the maritime domain and extracts relevant concepts from it; it tests the robustness of the concepts by applying them to two other domains, namely maritime automation, and business processes.

K. Liu (ed.),
Virtual, Distributed and Flexible Organisations: Studies in Organisational Semiotics, 35–59.

2. MARITIME PLANS

We will start with an authentic example from a field study of communication and work onboard Sally Maersk, a large container ship (Andersen 2000, 2001).

Maritime work is planned to a large degree, but although there is a *passage plan* and a schedule for departures and arrivals, factors outside the control of the crew may change the plan. We depart at three o'clock in the morning from Felixstowe in England heading for Rotterdam in Holland. Gudrun, which occupies our berth in Rotterdam, is delayed and Sally has been notified before leaving Felixstowe. From now on, the detailed plan for entering Rotterdam harbour is continuously discussed and modified.

2.1 Overview

Gudrun cannot estimate the exact delay, and the ETD (Expected Time of Departure) varies from 13.00 to 14.30. (She sails in fact at 14.10). Therefore the crew has to plan under uncertainty.

There are three possibilities for Sally. The best one is to *kill time* by going slow, since this saves fuel. Number 2 is to *anchor in the parking area* outside Rotterdam harbour, and this is the one actually adopted; only she does not anchor but sails in a circle. Number 3 is the worst, namely getting to Rotterdam before the berth is free and *parking in the basin*. This is unadvisable because of possible current, wind, and traffic.

The main communication takes place between Sally, VTS (Vessel Traffic service) and Gudrun. This communication spreads in ripples: the changing times for Gudrun's departure must be routed to the sailors and to the engine, and it must be mentioned during reliefs of the watch. It has consequences as to when the sailors are scheduled for duty, and when they are called.

The crew tries to make Gudrun announce her departure via VHF radio, but she fails to do so. When Gudrun becomes visible, they try to follow the process by observing the number of active cranes. This pattern can be seen in other places: first information is gathered by communication, later it is verified through observation.

The whole sequence takes 9 ½ hours and consists of 24 episodes:

- 03.18: Chief Officer comments on possible problem: Gudrun occupies our berth.
- 05.01: Captain informs (engine?) of problem. ETD: 13.00.
- 05.46: Captain and Chief Officer discuss alternative ways of entering the harbour.
- 06.55: Chief Officer informs replacement of problem. ETD: 14.00.

- 08.34: 2nd Officer tells VTS about the decision to head for an anchoring place.
- 09.28: Captain starts to kill speed and informs engine.
- 10.46: Captain, 1st officer, and sailor discuss whether to inform the other sailors. ETD: 13.30.
- 10.56: Pilot, captain, and 1st officer discuss the size of the delay and communicate with Gudrun. Pilot embarks.
- 11.03: Commenting the waiting time and observing the booms on the ship.
- 11.27: Observing the booms on the ship.
- 11.29: Discussing manoeuvres when Gudrun has sailed.
- 11.29: Discussing future traffic situations and observing the booms.
- 11.38: Communicating with Gudrun, discussing consequences of delay, and communicating delay to engine. ETD: 14.30.
- 11.41. Comments on the frequency of delays.
- 11.43. Reasons for waiting outside harbour.
- 11.54. Comments on waiting.
- 12.04 Comments on waiting.
- 12.10 Complaining.
- 12.12: Pilot Maas informs that Gudrun is sailing. Departure: 14.10. Sails without giving notice.
- 12.27. Observation of cranes.
- 12.33: Complaining of lack of communication. Routing information and replanning.
- 12.44 Complaining.
- 12.49: Observing Gudrun.
- 12.52: Observing Gudrun.

The problem in this situation is that the captain cannot fix on one course of action, but must work with more than one scenario. If Gudrun sails earlier, he can kill time, but if she sails later, he must stay in the parking lot outside the harbour. He must keep more than one option open all the time. He has to plan under uncertainty and delay decisions and communication until better information is available. This means that plans are seldom developed in all details, but will contain undecided options or vague elements. The crew handles the uncertain situation in various ways:

- Revising and discussing plans and forecasting future scenarios when new information is available in order to maintain consensus.
- Legimitising and explaining plans to one another.
- Informing crew of the current situation.
- Commenting on the waiting situation and complaining.
- Seeking new external information by communication and observation.

In addition, planning and execution are intermingled, since the final planning of the last part of the plan may only be possible after the first part has been executed.

How does one go about handling a plan that contains undetermined parts? An undetermined part can verbalized in various ways:

– it is spoken about as a set of alternatives one of which has not yet been selected ("either this or that"),
– it is spoken of in a vague and non-operational way ("somehow"),
– it is modalized ("maybe, probably"),
– the lack of knowledge is directly focused ("we don't know"),
– the uncertainty is viewed as something a third party can reduce, either Gudrun or the pilot ("he will tell us"),
– the uncertainty is viewed as something that direct observation can reduce ("we shall see").

2.2 Examples

In the following I give a few examples from our tapes (C = captain, P = Pilot, A, B = officers, K = helmsman). Tables 1-3 illustrate uncertainty as alternatives, modal expressions, lack of knowledge and vagueness.

Table 1. Uncertainty as alternatives

Officer	If only this there Gudrun is not further delayed, then we can *kill time by idling*, but if it begins to drag on, then we will have to *anchor*, right, we'll have to see

Table 2. Uncertainty as modal expressions and expressions of lack of knowledge

C	It is the skipper... yes, we will be there by noon....but, um, there is another one that has to sail first, Gudrun must sail before we can get in, so we really *don't know*, it will *probably* be... he *was to* sail at one o'clock, but we will be there at bit before noon, so now we must see what happens if he is delayed...OK.

Table 3. Uncertainty as vagueness.

B	And must exchange quay with Gudrun...
A	Yes, that was twelve o'clock, right?
B	Well, she now says that it is to sail at two o'clock, so...
A	Yes.
B	It will be *something like that.*
A	Okay.

At 09.28 the decision to start to killing speed is communicated to the engine room, which is requested to be on standby from twelve o'clock.

Table 4. Communicating choice

C	Yes, it is the skipper, it will probably be OK that M, that we begin to *reduce* at bit, and then we can just say that we are standby from twelve o'clock...because then we can just as well *kill time* now and then...surely, nothing happens before one o'clock, since he will not sail until two o'clock...

The uncertainty is not only a problem for the officers; it also affects the crew, since it does not know when to stand by. The dilemma is whether to keep the crew posted on the current situation or to wait for more precise information until informing. The former solution can create confusion if too many different messages are sent out. The captain decides to wait for the pilot that may reduce uncertainty (*We will just hear what the pilot says, then hopefully we will get better information*).

A theme for the whole planning sequence is of course the departure time of Gudrun, and it is very pronounced in Table 5 (*when, one thirty, one*).

Table 5. Time as a set of options

D	*When* do you want the crew ready?
C	I just wanna hear what the pilot ways, but if he does not sail until now, what was it it said in the telex, was it *one thirty* now?
D	*One...*
C	...this is the last one here...
D	*... one thirty, yes.*
C	*One thirty...one thirty,* we will hear what the pilot says, when he wants us in...
K	(...)
D	What do you say, we just wait until the pilot comes up, *then we hopefully get better information*

At 11.03 it is suggested that direct observation may reduce uncertainty by using the position of the booms as an index of Gudrun's work progress *(all booms, only one, foredeck is finished).*

Table 6. Direct observation

P	Maybe we can *see* the Gudrun from here.
	(P)
P	Yes I *see* her.
C	*All booms down?*
P	*No only one.*
C	*Only one?*
P	Yeah.
P	On the aft part of the ship, the *foredeck is finished.*
C	Yeah.

During the waiting time, they keep forecasting future scenarios in order to be prepared for action when the waiting is finished *(The outgoing ship will pass us. When Gudrun has gone we can back in. Maybe we are not alone).*

Table 7. Forecasting in order to be prepared

P *And the outgoing ship will pass us* on the stern .. so *when Gudrun is gone* we back in.
C We can back in.
P That's better than passing .. closer to corner ().
C Yeah.
P and *maybe we are not alone there,* maybe barge and other ships around so...

Table 8. Forecasting and watching the booms

D It looks like we *will start a fight* with the small one there, when we are going in...
P I think the crane is going up now.
C Which one are you talking about?
D On the starboard beam there, it...
C Oh, this one, yeah.
P No, no (...).
C But *he will probably eventually overtake us*, and then, we are still lying here waiting, and...
D Yeah.
P (...) *not a crane.*
C *And then we speed up.*

At 11.43 the captain repeats the reason for the anchoring choice: if we had gone straight into the harbour, we would have been in real trouble as the situation has turned out. His decision turned out to be a good one!

Table 9. Legitimising decisions

C Because *if* he sails two thirty, right, then we won't go in, and then be caught in there, *if* he is further delayed, then we cannot keep it up, *then it is better to wait out here* so...so for the time being it is an hour, right?

3. WHAT IS AN ANTICIPATED ACTIVITY?

We will normally conceive of anticipated activities as a psychological category: they are something inside our heads. The methodological problem is of course that we have no access to other people's minds except by observing what they do and listening to what they say. In addition, it is not true that anticipated activities only exist in our minds; as the example shows, the plan for going from Felixstowe to Rotterdam also exists as written text, as the passage plan, and as spoken language, in the lengthy discussions on the bridge.

What is the relation between the activity as anticipated and as executed? A simple answer is that the plan controls the execution, like a computer program controls the computer. The example shows that this is only a small part of the whole picture. Although it is true that the waypoints of the voyage plan have been designed with the purpose of arriving in Rotterdam harbour in a safe and efficient way, one could just as well say that the plan is controlled by its execution. The reason for saying this is that the environment is only partially known, and new information causes the plan to be specified and rescheduled as a part of its execution.

One may also say that the plan constitutes a basis for interpreting the actions of the crew and the significance of incoming information. In the following we shall explore the idea of viewing anticipated actions as *interpretations* (Peirce's interpretant) of activities, relating a *representation* of the action, e.g. a control or display used in the action, to its *object*, the changed state which the action intends to accomplish.

Peirce's interpretant concept is complex but very fruitful.

> A sign addresses somebody, that is, creates in the mind of that person an equivalent sign, or perhaps a more developed sign. The sign which it creates I call the interpretant of the first sign. *Collected Papers, §2.228. Quoted from Nöth 1995: 43*

We shall use the concept in two of Peirce's three senses: the first one is the *dynamic* interpretant which is "the direct effect actually produced by the sign upon an Interpreter of it" (Quoted from Nöth 1995: 43).

The second one is the *final* interpretant: in Peirce's philosophy, the category of the final interpretant is "thirdness", habit or law (in opposition to the category of the representamen which is "firstness", quality, and that of the object which is "secondness", quantity, brute cause). In my reading of Peirce, the final interpretant occurs when we see an action as an instance of a more general regularity or habit; as something that is performed according to some rule. The idea is that plans are such regularities and that plans are a type of final interpretants.

This is unproblematic with semiotic activities, like conversations and interpretation of instruments and observations. For example, the booms are interpreted as signs of Gudrun's imminent departure which is again a sign that our berth will be free in a short time. This dynamic interpretation is only warranted because we can guess Gudrun's voyage plan (she will be leaving soon) and our own plan (we are scheduled to take Gudrun's berth). If these rule-oriented interpretations were not available we would have no reason for seeing the booms as a sign of a free berth. The same information is used in Table 10, where Gudrun is calling Sally to inform her of an hour's delay (Representation = VHF radio, Object = Gudrun's delay): if we did not know that, according to plan, we would take over Gudrun's berth, then we would not understand the reason for the captain's remark *Yeah, Yeah, then we are in a bad position.*

Table 10. VHF conversation and the captain's reaction.

Q This is Gudrun Mærsk calling, over (VHF).
D Sally Mærsk (VHF).
Q This is Sally Mærsk, time of departure has been delayed for about one hour, so we will (...) (VHF).
D Okay thank you very much ... we will standby on sixteen (VHF)
C One hour.
P Suppose he (...).
C *Yeah, Yeah, then we are in a bad position.*
P That's right.
D Will you inform your colleagues?

But the crew does not spend its entire working time with interpretation and communication (Goldkuhl 2001). They also sail the ship. They manipulate controls that make the huge ship move physically, and this instrumental activity is influenced by the voyage plan, among other things. In order to account for this non-semiotic part of the work, I shall tentatively combine the basic pattern of activity theory (Raeithel 1992) with the Peircean sign concept as shown in Figure 1 (cf. Andersen 2003. On material and semiotic processes, see Rossi-Landi 1975, 92).

The basic abstraction of activity theory is very simple: A *Subject* influences an *Object* by means of a *Mediator*. Semiotics also rests on a simple abstraction: A *Representation* stands for an *Object* under some rule of *Interpretation.* Although almost anything can be used as a representation to stand for something else, instrument usage can often be analysed as an activity where the Mediator is also a Representation, and the work Object of the activity coincides with the semiotic Object, as shown in Figure 1.

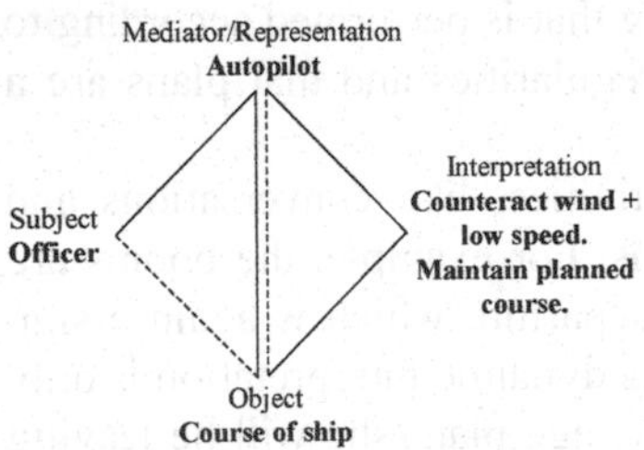

Figure 1. Combining instrumental and semiotic activities. Analysis of Table 11.

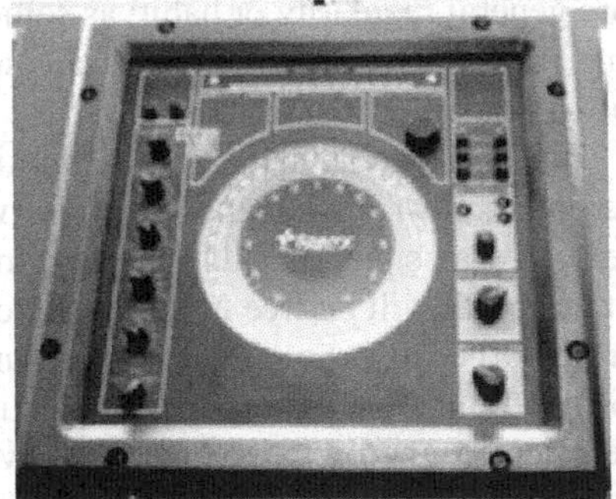

Figure 2. The autopilot

Consider the manoeuvring situation illustrated in Table 11 below, where the 2nd officer and captain discuss a problem with manoeuvring at low speed.

Table 11. Battling wind and low speed

C	Now look here, now you have to take care, now we are reducing speed, right, then the wind gets more power over the ship and...
A	Yes
C	...and start to...There may be current too, so try and give it five degrees leeway to port.
A	We are already high up, we are steering seventy so...
C	Yes
A	...and the course in the map says seventy eight...but it did take hold when I came over Noordhinder.
C	Yes, but it changes all the time here, right, but particularly when you reduce speed, then of course you become more sensitive to ...
A	Yes
C	...both wind and current.

We are still on our way to Rotterdam and have decided to kill time so that we will not arrive until the berth is free. The problem is that when we reduce speed, the water flow along the rudder decreases, and this in turn decreases the effect of the rudder. We are having heavy side-wind, and therefore use the supporting rudder, so when speed decreases, we need to increase the rudder angle to achieve the same effect. The goal of the 2nd officer is to maintain a course of 78 degrees, as indicated in the voyage plan. In this case, the Subject is the 2nd officer, the Mediator is the autopilot, and the object of his work is to maintain the course of the ship. A glance at the autopilot in Figure 2 shows that this Mediator is also a Representation of the course: it displays *the steered course* (the digits to the right) *and the course made good* (the digits to the left). The steered course signifies the intention of the officer, and the course made good the actual result of his activity.

However, the officer's remark, *and the course in the map says seventy eight...but it did take hold when I came over Noordhinder*, is only understandable with respect to the voyage plan in the map, which thus forms the Interpretation according to which we should view the course displayed by autopilot. It involves both the particular manoeuvring situation with strong wind and low speed, and a reference to the general plan.

Figure 1 asserts that any (social) activity is interpreted and socially reflected upon, and the example shows that this is indeed true: the captain is able to reconstruct what the 2nd officer is trying to do by looking at the autopilot and recalling the voyage plan and the manoeuvring circumstances. Although the autopilot in itself only represents the steered course and the course made good, the captain can add a lot of extra information to these pieces of evidence because he knows the voyage plan and the type of manoeuvring situation we are in.

Thus, it seems to make sense to see plans as a kind of final Interpretation that views the concrete action instance as an example of a more general regularity – in our case, the voyage plan and the type of manoeuvring situation. We shall return to Figure 1 in Section 7.

4. CASES, INTERPRETATIONS, AND GLUE

What is the structure of interpretations and how can we describe them? If we stick to the idea that plans may be interpretations, these are questions about the nature of half-baked plans.

The plan for sailing from Felixstowe to Rotterdam must surely contain the following information:

We berth Sally at Gudrun's berth in Rotterdam harbour by means of tugs (?) at one o'clock (?).

Although we can recognize the Subject (*we*), the Mediator (*the tugs*) and the Object (*Sally*) from the activity theory abstraction, there are some elements left, namely place and time: *in Rotterdam harbour at one o'clock*. This is a problem since it was precisely the time-element which was discussed 24 times during the voyage, cf. Table 5! Thus, in order to make sense of this conversation, we must enrich the structure of activities with more elements. The two question marks show two undecided parts of the plan: use of tugs, and the time of arrival.

4.1 Cases

One theory of the morphology of actions is *case-theory*. Case theory is about the verbal categories we use to describe actions; specifically, it is about the roles sentence parts can play in a sentence, and it is an old invention, since it goes back to the case-inflexion of classical Latin grammar. It was revived by the American linguist Charles Fillmore (Fillmore 1968, 1977) who re-defined cases as pure semantic units, and allowed prepositions and word order to mark cases as well. In this paper we use the cases to describe the roles which participants of activities are assigned to in verbal descriptions of the activities, and we shall define activities by means of the case-roles their verbalization involve, in a manner similar to Halliday 1994. Cases predict the linguistic forms the utterances will take, and have a relation to corresponding action categories, but probably not in any straightforward fashion. The reason for possible discrepancies is that cases are used to express a variety of perspectives on actions (Fillmore 1977) and therefore allow variation in the way activities are viewed. For example, do the different grammatical roles of the medium of communication in *We communicate by walkie-talkie* (instrument) and *We listen in on walkie-talkie* (location, literal translation from the Danish original) indicate that the action structure is different, or is the same action structure just staged in two different ways?

Table 12 presents a standard version of the principal cases:

Table 12. Case roles. Adapted from Jurafsky & Martin 2000:609

Role	*Definition*
Agent	The volitional cause of an event
Experiencer	The experiencer of an event
Force	The non-volitional cause of an event
Theme	The participant most directly affected by an event
Result	The end product of an event
Content	The proposition or content of a propositional event
Instrument	An instrument used in an event
Beneficiary	The beneficiary of an event
Source	The origin of the Theme of a transfer event
Goal /Destination	The destination of an Theme of a transfer event
Purpose	The purpose of the event
Time	The time of the event
Place	The place of the event

If we assume that activities can not only contain Agent (= Subject), Instrument (= Mediator) and Theme (= Object), but also Time and Place, then we have a method for understanding the relation between the voyage plan and the bridge communications. Figure 3 shows the half-baked plan for berthing Sally[2].

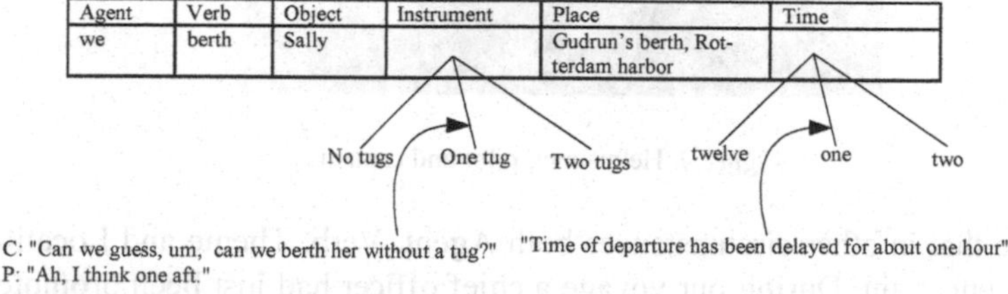

Figure 3. Half-baked plan for entering Rotterdam harbour

The categories of Agent, Verb, Theme and Place are filled and do not change: there is no doubt that our captain is the Agent responsible for berthing Sally, or that it is Sally that must be berthed, or that our destination is Rotterdam harbour; but the Time role has at least three possible fillers, *twelve, one* and *two,* and the Instrument role also contains a choice between zero, one or two tugs. The Time slot becomes filled with certain information by the VTS informing us of Gudrun's departure, and the contents of the Instrument are is decided by the Pilot recommending one tug aft. This effect

[2] The formalism used in the following resembles the ORM notation described by Halpin 1996, 1998, and no year, with one exception: Halpin formalizes actions as predicates whereas in our notation, actions are objects, although of a fast-changing and short-lived sort; the only predicates are the thematic roles. This solves a number of irritating problems identified in Jurafsky & Martin 2000: 523 ff.

of the conversation is illustrated by arrows pointing from the utterance to the line connecting a filler to a slot. This line represents the propensity of the filler to fill the slot, and in both cases, the utterance strengthens this propensity. We shall develop this "propensity" further in Section 4.2.

Thus, the function of communication is to modify the propensity of fillers to occupy slots in the Interpretation; some of these slots are empty, others are filled with too vague material, or with incompatible alternatives (e.g. *moving straight ahead and anchor,* versus *killing time*, cf. above), while still others are filled with material that turns out to be wrong (not one o'clock but later).

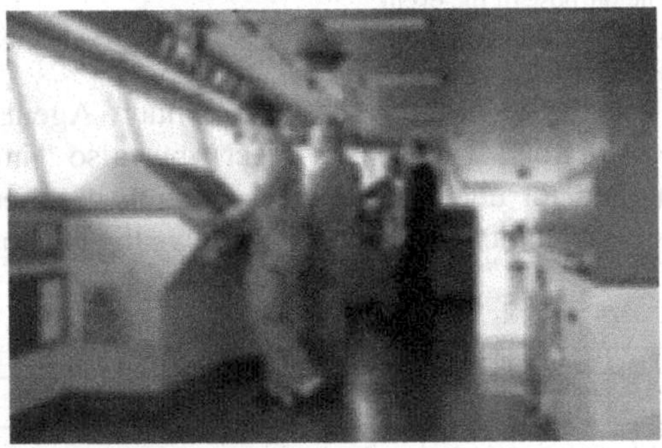

Figure 4. Helmsman, pilot and captain

Note that in other circumstances both Agent, Verb, Theme and Location may be uncertain. During our voyage a chief officer had just been promoted to captain, and it might have been a possibility for him to take over the berthing activity; similarly, if we were an oil tanker, we might be redirected to another Location if the oil had been sold during our voyage.

The example above was a long-term plan, but the analysis also works in very short term ones. Consider a situation where pilot and captain stand amidships on the bridge, with the helmsman placed at the helm. The pilot issues rudder commands, as in Table 13, to the helmsman (Figure 4).

Table 13. Rudder commands

Pilot:	Starboard twenty
Helmsman:	Starboard twenty
Helmsman:	(turning rudder and watching the rudder angle display)
Helmsman:	Starboard twenty

Notice that the full command is not given: the pilot neither bothers with the Agent (the helmsman does it), the Time (it is now), the Verb (turn), or the Theme (the wheel).

Table 14. All roles except the Manner slot are filled out beforehand.

Agent	Modality	Verb	Theme	Manner	Time, place
Helmsman	should	turn	wheel	starboard or port, 1-30?	Now, at the helm stand

The choices are reduced to the Manner slot with a few degrees of freedom (the wheel can be moved about 30 degrees to each side) as shown in Table 14. It describes the Interpretation of the activity shared by all parties; the Interpretation so to speak lives a life of its own, and the only input it needs to become complete is a verbal command to fill the missing slot.

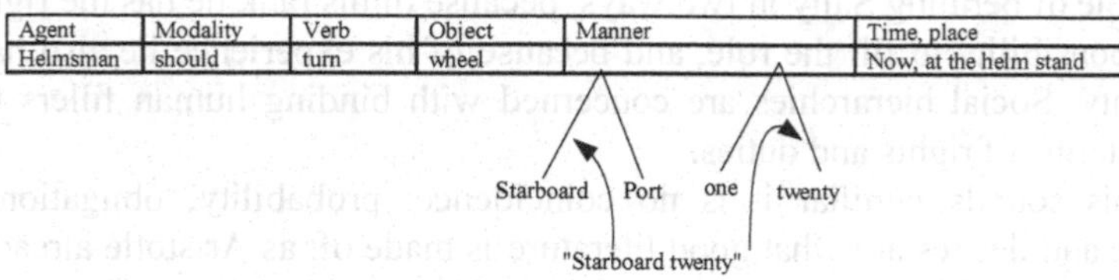

Figure 5. Rudder commands

Andersen, Carstensen & Nielsen (2002) presents a classification of communicative functions based on the distinction between *backgrounded* slots that are already filled out and *focus* slots open for discussion. In this classification, rudder commands are *instructions* since the manner slot is focused. Figure 5 illustrates how the command "starboard twenty" selects one of the 60 degrees of freedom in the manner slot.

4.2 Glue

How can communication influence fillers of an anticipated activity? The conversation about Gudrun's departure time is clear enough. It concerns the certainty of the time, and the information from VTS changes uncertainty into certainty. But what about the rudder command? This does not seem a case of probability, but rather one of obligation. The command requires the Manner slot of this activity to be filled with "twenty". To see the difference, consider what happens if the activity was not performed as indicated. In the case of Gudrun, no reprimand would follow, since Gudrun has the right to stay in her berth until she is loaded. But if the helmsman turns the rudder ten degrees where the command was "twenty", he will be reprimanded since "twenty" is obligatory. In this case we seem to be concerned not with *epistemic* logic (true, probable, false), but with *deontic* logic (is required, allowed, or forbidden to) dealing with duties and rights. The tug-example is a third case: on the face of it, we are concerned with *ability*: how many tugs are necessary to pull Sally safely to her berth? But in reality it may contain politics, since Rotterdam harbour may want to keep its tugs employed. It could be a duty imposed by the harbour upon Sally.

It turns out that semiotic and instrumental activities influence one another by manipulating at least four forces that bind fillers to roles: *truth, obligations, abilities, and desires* (cf. Ryan 1991). The backgrounded fixed fillers of the activities have in fact been bound previously by these means: the helmsman has been bound to the Agent role by the watch schedule that requires him to be on duty on the bridge, and the captain is bound to the Agent role of berthing Sally in two ways: because of his rank he has the right and responsibility to fill the role, and because of his experience he also has the ability. Social hierarchies are concerned with binding human fillers to roles in terms of rights and duties.

If this sounds familiar it is no coincidence: probability, obligations, abilities, and desires are what good literature is made of, as Aristotle already knew. Oedipus killed his father and married his mother but did not *know* the identity of the Theme of his actions. He *desired* a woman whom he *ought not* to desire. Or to take a modern saga, the Lord of the Rings. Frodo's duty is to *destroy* the ring, but he is lacking *ability*. He is torn between the *desire* to claim it for himself and his *duty* to destroy it.

This indicates that the concepts developed here have a broader range of application than landing a container ship safely in Rotterdam harbour. In fact, the first systematic description of narrative structure, Propp 1975, used a slot and filler formalism. Elsewhere I have used the formalism for literary analysis, and it does seem to be able to capture the main conflicts in my material.

I have talked about "binding" fillers to slots, and it has turned out that this binding can be manipulated. This means that it ought to become an object in its own right. I shall term the object "glue". A glue object is associated to exactly one slot in one activity, and to exactly one filler.

Table 15. Dimensions of glue-objects.

	Negative	Neutral	Positive
Obligations	Forbidden	Allowed	Mandatory
Desires	Abhorred	Tolerated	Desired
Capabilities	Incapable		Capable
Truth	False	Probable	True

It consists of the four dimensions mentioned above – truth, obligation, ability, and desire – and describes the probability, obligation, ability and desire of a filler to fill the role in question (Table 15). The individual dimensions require specific fillers to make sense; for example, only humans can be bound by obligations or desires, only physical bodies can be capable, and only representations can be true or false. We shall discuss this further in Section 6.

As an example, consider the task of mowing the lawn: *I (Agent) mow the lawn (Theme) by means of my lawn mower (Instrument).* All three fillers can be wanting: if I lack the ability or moral stamina to do it, my morals can be heightened by sweet remarks like "the lawn is like a jungle", whereas overcoming the lack of ability requires exercise. The lawn may be unmowable, too uneven and bumpy, which requires leveling it with a roller in order to increase the ability of the lawn to be mowed. Finally, the lawn mower may refuse to start when the cord is pulled. This lack of ability to fulfill the role of an instrument can be remedied by repair activities. In Figure 6 the glue is represented by lines between fillers and roles and arrows show the way utterances and actions influence the glue. The arrows are annotated by the glue-dimension they influence, and by the direction of influence (+/-). In the situation depicted my ability may be positive, but my moral obligations are negative. I do not feel obliged to mow the lawn and the utterance is intended to change this: we ought to be ashamed of the mess. The two material actions influence the ability of the garden to be mowed, and ability of the mower to mow.

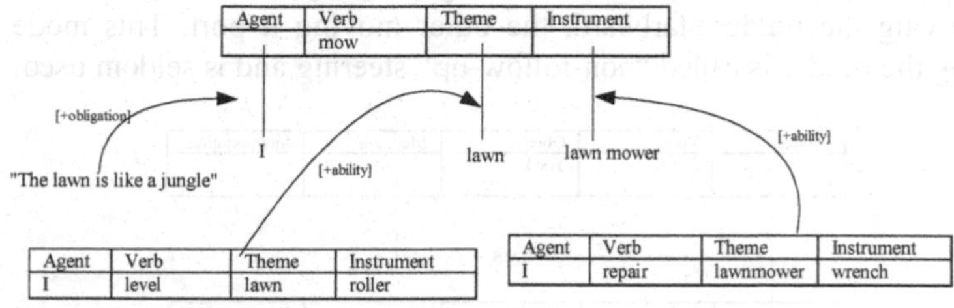

Figure 6. Mowing the lawn

5. AUTOMATED SYSTEMS AS ANTICIPATED ACTIVITIES

After having shown how to use the formalism for describing work and communication, I shall discuss its application to automated systems. Viewing automated systems as anticipated activities is not a new idea, but a very natural thought, especially when one designs interfaces. The designer tries to anticipate the actions the user may want to do. Let us see whether our notation can capture characteristic features of maritime automation.

Maritime automatic systems are designed to function in a high-risk environment, and this motivates the following principle:

> First and foremost it must be required that every process that is crucial for the safe operation of the ship must be executable, even if the integrated system does not work. Therefore, it is always possible to control the most important engine and navigation elements manually – "in the old-fashioned way" – independently of the state of the integrated system. *Lem & Nordseth 1996: 26.*

Thus, for the important processes, the automatic system can be switched off and manual operations used.

In the terms developed in the preceding we can say that the Subject role can be filled with a crew member *or* with automatic machinery. As illustrated in Figure 7 with respect to the steering gear, a whole hierarchy is designed in this way. If we start at the bottom, there is an activity we can term "setting the rudder angle". The Object of this activity is the rudder angle and the Mediator is the hydraulic rudder machine. The rudder machine can be controlled manually from the bridge, e.g. by means of two buttons, one moving the rudder starboard, the other moving it port. This mode of working the rudder is called "non-follow-up" steering and is seldom used.

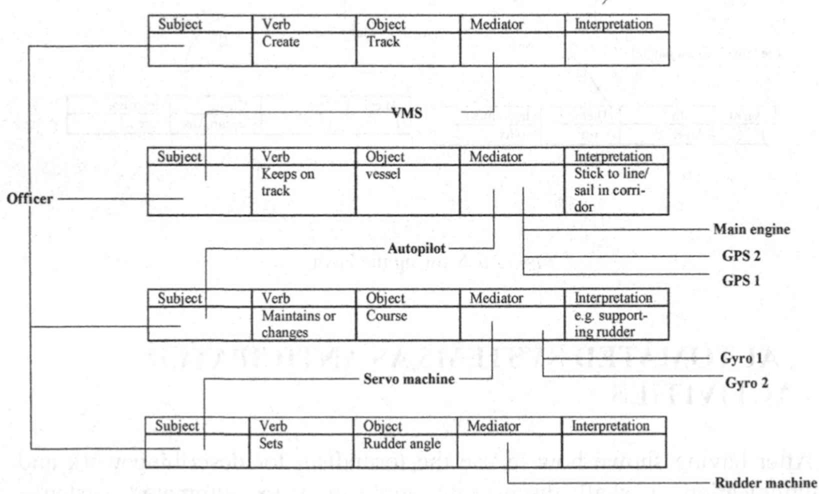

Figure 7. The Control hierarchy of steering

Instead, a servo system is allowed to control the rudder machine. The servo system is given a certain desired rudder angle and influences the rudder machine until the actual rudder angle is equal to the desired one. This is normal hand-steering that is used in the activity of maintaining or changing the course of the ship.

The Subject of the activity of maintaining the course can be a crew member, but it can also be the autopilot. In both cases, the servo system acts as the Mediator between Subject and rudder machine (in the following I shall use the term "Subject" for automatic systems as well. This is a questionable step, but lack of space prevents a thorough discussion).

Maintaining or changing course is a part of the higher-level activity of keeping the vessel on the track of the voyage plan, and the story repeats itself: the officer can be the subject and control the autopilot manually by entering course commands (turning the knob in the right upper part of Figure 2), but the Voyage Management System (VMS) can also act in this capacity and send course commands to the autopilot. In both cases, the autopilot acts as Mediator, and the result of automatic or manual operation is shown in the same way, namely as course commands in the upper right display of Figure 2.

The top level activity in Figure 7 consists of creating the voyage plan and the track to be followed, and here only human Subjects are possible. The VMS system is used for this purpose and e.g. allows the officer to "draw" the track directly on the electronic map.

One can say the hierarchy is a means-end hierarchy in the sense that the component in charge of lower level activities functions as a mediator of the higher level activity.

The Subject role is not the only role whose fillers can be exchanged. This is also true of Mediators: for example, there is normally more than one GPS-receiver and gyro, and both can be switched while the ship sails. The same is true of the radar and the echo sounder. Finally, it is possible, although ill-advised, to sail without any sensor at all, since dead-reckoning can be used.

From this description it seems to make sense to view automatic machinery as anticipated activities. It is possible to define activities, most of which can be executed by humans or machines, and which are related as means to ends. The automatic machinery and the crew functions can act as fillers of the roles of the activity, and, as was the case in the planning example from Section 2, the filling of some roles is undetermined in the beginning and can be changed during execution.

The description given above has three advantages:

1. It takes its departure in work activities and specifies technology according to the role it plays in these activities. It thus clearly shows the function of technology in relation to work.

2. It can describe dynamic features, such as one filler replacing another, and it can deal with incomplete work processes.
3. By means of the glue-concept, it can describe suboptimal states of equipment, which makes it more realistic. For example, the 4 cm radar may be better suited than the 10 centimeter radar in some situations.

We have only exemplified actions that maintain or create a certain state (attractors), but we also find repellers that hinder the functioning of a filler in a certain role. For example, there are delimiters that limit the size of the rudder angle or the rate of turn, so if the ROT delimiter is set to 5, the ship will only be able to turn at a rate of 5 degrees. The purpose of this is to save fuel when sailing in open water. In terms of the preceding statement we can say that the delimiters weaken the ability of the rudder servo system to fulfill the role of mediator in the activity of changing course (Figure 8). Much safety equipment can be analysed in this way: it lowers our ability to perform some dangerous action. For example, the crash stop button on a ship can be protected by a small plastic housing in order to prevent it from being unintentionally pushed, and road humps are a very physical way of inhibiting our ability to drive fast in cities.

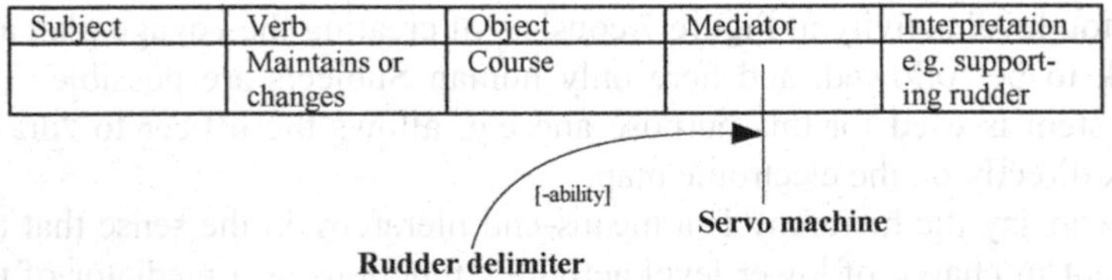

Subject
Verb
Object
Mediator
Interpretation
Maintains or changes
Course
e.g. supporting rudder
[-ability]
Servo machine
Rudder delimiter

Figure 8. Delimiters

We need to make one modification to Figure 7, since the crew obviously does not directly influence the autopilot, servo machine or rudder machine. Instead they act through the displays and controls. This can be described by saying that humans accomplish two things (Cf. Petersen 2002): (1) they *do* something to the displays and controls, and thereby (2) *bring about* a change in the ship.

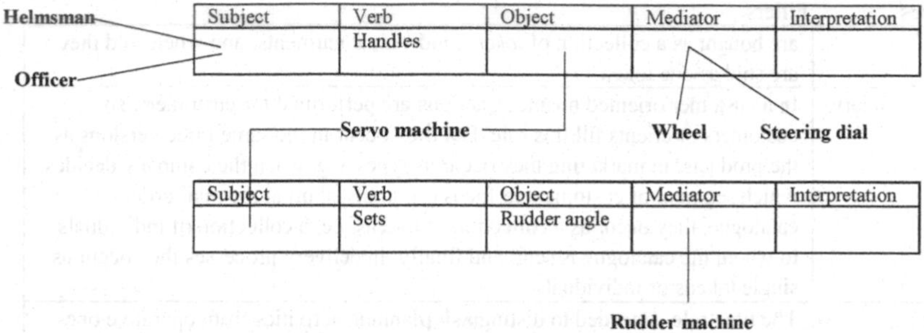

Figure 9. Doing and bringing about

In the first activity the Object is the automatic component and the Mediator represents the controls and displays. In the second activity, the Subject is the automatic component and the Object is the part of the ship they want to influence (see Andersen 2003 for examples of how this is interpreted by the crew).

Figure 9 shows the two processes: (1) helmsman or officer use the wheel or the steering dial to influence the servo machine; and (2) the servo system influences the rudder angle by controlling the rudder machine.

6. BUSINESS PROCESSES

The preceding examples are well-founded in the sense that we have carried out empirical work in the domain and know a reasonable amount of the relevant literature. This last example, however, arises from a previous paper but only limited domain knowledge in that the author has carried out some field work in the relevant administrative domain, cf. Andersen 1997). The purpose is to investigate how well an existing analysis of business processes can be translated into the framework presented, but the following should be taken with a grain of salt.

We use a mail order firm selling fashion clothes as an example and build on the classification of business processes proposed in Lind 2003.

The following cases are used:

Table 16. Four cases and their function in business processes

Cases	Fillers
Agent	The company is the Agent for most actions; the customer is the Agent of *ordering*.
Theme	The products fill the Theme role, but in three different ways: when the assortment is planned, the products appear as *types*, e.g. as models; when they

Cases	Fillers
	are bought as a collection of *tokens*, individual garments; and when sold they are sold as one token.
Beneficiary	In a customer oriented business, actions are performed *for* customers, so customers or clients fill this role. But they occur in the same three versions as the products: in marketing they occur as types, e.g. when the company decides which segment of customers to focus on; in distributing the mail order catalogue, they occur as a collection of tokens, i.e. a collection of individuals to whom the catalogue is sent; and finally, in delivery processes they occur as single tokens or individuals.
Time	The time role is needed to distinguish planning activities from operative ones. The former has a time horizon of a year, whereas that of the operative actions is counted in days.

Apart from these cases, we also need Instruments (tools used in the business), Sources (the physical location from where products are procured. In our case, products are bought overseas in countries with cheap labour costs, so the transportation distance is large), and Destinations (the physical location to which products are delivered, e.g. the home address of the customers).

Lind (2003) distinguishes between three main types of business processes: in *delivery* processes the Beneficiary is filled by customer *individuals*, whereas this role is a *type* (or a collection of tokens) in the *providing* and *condition creating* processes. Examples of *delivery* processes are the selection, packing and mailing of a piece of garment to a particular customer, whereas the purchase of a collection of garments from suppliers is a *providing* process, since the Beneficiary for whom it is bought is a customer *type*, not an individual.

The difference between *providing* and *condition creating* processes consists in the fact that the former are *operative*, the latter *development oriented.* Lind does not give an explicit definition of these concepts, so I have to make a guess from his examples of condition creation: *assortment design and planning*, *catalogue production and distribution*, and *marketing and campaign planning.*

In the following I characterise business processes by describing the change they cause to the fillers of the basic operative process of delivering products to customers, where the firm is the Agent, the products the Theme, and the customers the Beneficiary.

The *condition creating processes* determine the following fillers: the Time case is filled by "next season", the Theme slot by a *type* of garment, and the Beneficiary by a *type* of customer. The main function of these actions is thus to provide a *type* or *collection* filler of the Theme and Beneficiary cases.

In the subtypes *campaign planning* and *assortment planning,* the Theme (the garment models or types) and Beneficiary (the customers) are types, as we expect from the definition: we decide which models to choose and which costumer types to target. In the difference between the two lies the result they are intended to have, i.e. which roles are focused and liable to change and which ones are backgrounded and temporarily stable, cf. Section 4.1. *Campaign planning* addresses the Beneficiary and backgrounds the Theme: we discuss which customer types to concentrate on. *Assortment planning* does not focus on the customers but selects suitable garments based on the background of the customer types.

The Theme of *procurement of products* is a collection of tokens, whereas its Beneficiary is a type of customer: a collection of individual garments is transported to Sweden, but at this time one cannot know which individuals are to benefit from them. The focus is clearly on the Theme, the garments. *Distributing the catalogue to customers* is the opposite: in the catalogue the garments occur as types, whereas the customers appear as a collection of individuals with individual addresses. The Theme is backgrounded since the models have already been decided; the focus is on the collection of customers, since the aim is to increase the probability of a customer to become the Beneficiary of a *delivery* action, i.e. turn potential into actual customers.

However, there is another difference between *procurement* and *catalogue distribution*: the theme in the former consists of a collection of real objects, not representations of objects, whereas in the *catalogue distribution* the theme is representations, such as pictures and texts.

This means that we need to add a final distinction: does an action provide *the real Object* to fill the role or just a *Representation* of it? The same distinction was in fact implicit in the previous Sections: in the maritime planning example, we knew all the time which berth in Rotterdam harbour we were to have, i.e. the Representation was in place; what we needed was the material availability of its Object, the real berth that Gudrun occupied. Normally, communicative actions are used to provide a representation of the filler, whereas material actions are necessary for inserting the real filler. The name of our berth was communicated to us before we left Felixstowe, but Gudrun had to remove herself before the real berth was capable of being used by us. Types always seem to be representations, whereas tokens and collection of tokens can be either representations or real objects. Even if a model exists as a physical object – as a prototype – it is still a representation, since it is not identical to the garment the customer receives.

We also need the Representation-Object distinction to describe the difference between *order reception, packing,* and *distribution*. *Reception* furnishes Representations of individual products and customers, since the mail order only contains numbers and letters identifying the two. This is changed by the *packing* activity that replaces the product representation in the Theme slot by the real product. The *distribution* activity starts with a representation of the customer (name and address) plus the real object, the garment, and aims at exchanging the representation of the customer with the real customer. It does this by transporting the product to him.

Thus, some activities like berthing a ship or delivering goods to a customer require their roles to be filled with real objects. The costumer has every right to complain if she received a parcel with a picture instead of the real dress. But other activities accept representations in some of their roles. This is true of communication. A maritime example is *reporting communication*, as in: I (Agent) said to him (Beneficiary) *that as soon as you were finished steering, you would come down so that we could get it in* (Content). The Content slot contains a *representation* of an activity, not the activity itself.

Table 17 summarizes this analysis. The difference between a Representation and its Object is marked by black versus grey colour, and the focus slot is underlined.

Table 17. Seven business processes. Underline: focus roles. Gray: representations.

	Theme: garments	Beneficiary: customers
Campaign planning	Type	Type
Assortment planning	Type	Type
Procurement	Collection	Type
Catalogue distribution	Type	Collection
Reception	Token	Token
Packing	Token	Token
Distribution	Token	Token

The diagram in Figure 10 shows the same classification, only this time the connection to the central "delivering" process is shown explicitly

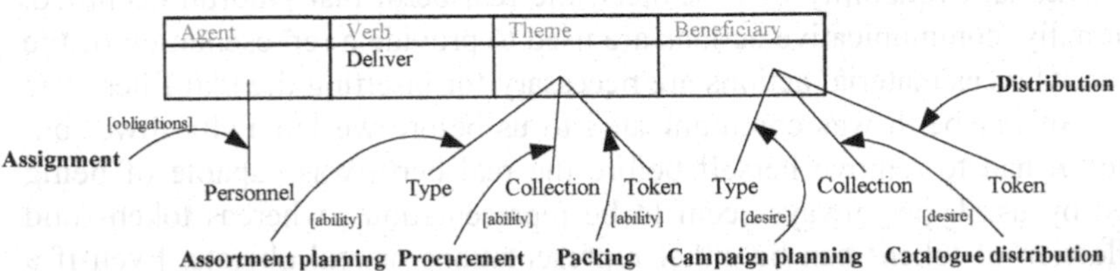

Figure 10. Seven business processes defined in relation to the process of delivering products to customers

In fact, all the other business processes are analysed as steps in creating an operational version of the delivery process which exists as an anticipated half-baked action for about a year. The figure also shows the place for organisational processes, such as assigning staff to jobs. They form the glue of the Agent slot.

Lind (2003) does not deal with the payment processes in the mail-order firm. However, in a naïve analysis at least, the concepts seem applicable here too. Modern payments are done by a financial institution on behalf of a client: *an Agent (bank) transfers Theme (amount) for a Beneficiary (the client) from a Source (account) to a Destination (account).* Like all other actions, payment actions must be constructed: the bank must be authorized by the client to fill the Agent role; the purchase of the clothes creates a bond of obligation between the amount and the Theme, the buyer and the Beneficiary, and the mail-order firm's account and the Destination role of the transfer action. Finally, the buyer's ownership of the Source account strengthens its right to participate in the transfer. If any of these pieces of glue are not in order, the payment process cannot execute.

7. SUMMARY AND PERSPECTIVES

Figure 1 can be used as a road-map that summarizes the processes described in the preceding example. Maritime work is rulebased; planning and execution are intermingled; execution consists in using controls and machinery to manipulate the ship. This means that we have a repeated trajectory of the form *Representation → Interpretation → Representation → Object → Representation*...One example is the rudder commands in Table 14, where a command fills out the Manner slot of the helmsman's current Interpretation, which causes him to turn the wheel (Representation) in order to change the course of the ship (Object), which again is represented on the course display (Representation), which again... Another example is Table 11 where the captain interprets the 2nd officer's instrument settings (Representation), reminds him of the manoeuvring type of the situation (Interpretation), which again may cause the officer to give more supporting rudder (Representation → Object).

The mail-order firm exhibits a different trajectory: there is a long preparatory period that only deals with Representations and Interpretations, *Representation → Interpretation → Representation →*..., Lind's *condition creating processes*. In the subsequent operative activities there is continual conversion of Representations to Objects, *Representation → Object*: when an order is received, the catalogue number must be exchanged with the real garment it denotes, and the transport firm must exchange the name and address of the customer with the real customer.

Although both domains contain the trajectory *Representation → Object*, the trajectory is realized in different ways. On the ship, it is part of a continuous feed-back loop, *Representation$_1$ → Object → Representation$_2$*, where Representation$_1$ (e.g. the machine telegraph) physically changes the object (e.g. the revolutions of the propeller and the speed of the ship) and Representation$_2$ (e.g. the Doppler log) measures the change of the object. In the mail-order firm, the garments are not changed by the representation, but simply replace it in the delivering activity.

This paper has benefited from discussions in the Elastic Systems group under the Danish Centre for Human Machine Interaction, and from a joint paper with Susanne Bødker.

REFERENCES

Andersen, P. B., 1997, A Theory of Computer Semiotics. Semiotic Approaches to Construction and Assessment of Computer Systems. Cambridge: Cambridge University Press.

Andersen, P. B. 2003, Communication and Work on Maritime Bridges. Center for Human-Machine Interaction. Report CHMI-1-2000, 2000. Retrieved May 2003 from http://www.cs.auc.dk /~pba/ElasticSystems.

Andersen, P. B., 2001, Maritime Work and Communication. Australian Journal of Information Systems (AJIS) 8 (2): pp. 83-102.

Andersen, P. B., 2002, Dynamic Semiotics. Semiotica; 139(1/4): 161-210.

Andersen, P. B., 2003, Saying and Doing at Sea. In ALOIS 2003, Action in Language, Organisations and Information Systems, G. Goldkuhl et al. (Eds.). Linköping: The research network VITS. Will be available at http://www.vits.org/alois/.

Andersen, P. B., P. 2002, Carstensen & M. Nielsen, Means of Coordination. In Coordination and Communication Using Signs. Studies in Organisational Semiotics, K. Liu, R. J. Clarke, P. Bøgh Andersen & R. K. Stamper, eds. Boston: Kluwer, pp. 32-58.

Fillmore, Ch. J., 1968, The Case for Case. In Universals in Linguistic Theory, E. Bach & R.T. Harms, eds., 1-90. London, New York, Sydney, Toronto: Holt, Rinehart and Winston.

Fillmore, Ch. J., 1977, The Case for Case Reopened. In Syntax and Semantics: 8. Grammatical Relations, 59-81, P. Cole and G. M. Sadock, eds. New York: Academic Press.

Goldkuhl, G., 2001, Communicative vs. Material Actions: Instrumentality, Sociality and Comprehensability. CMTO Research Papers no. 2001: 06. Centre for Studies of Humans, Technology and Organisation. Lindköping: Lindköping University.

Halliday, M.A.K., 1994, An Introduction to Functional Grammar. London: Edward Arnold.

Halpin, T., 1996, Business Rules and Object Role Modelling. Database Programming & Design, 9(10): pp. 66-72. Retrieved May 2003 from http://www.orm.net/overview.html

Halpin, T., 1998, Object Role Modelling (ORM/NIAM). In Handbook on Architectures of Information Systems, Bernus, P., Mertins, K. & Schmidt, G., eds. Berlin: Springer. Retrieved May 2003 from http://www.orm.net/overview.html

Halpin, T., 2003, Object Role Modelling: An Overview. Retrieved May 2003 from http://www.orm.net/overview.html

Jurafsky, D. & J. H. Martin, 2000, Speech and Language Processing. New Jersey: Prentice-Hall.

Lee, J. D. & T. F. 1996, Sanquist, Maritime Automation. In Automation and Human Performance: Theory and Applications, 365-384, R. Parasuraman & M. Mouloua, eds. Mahwah, New Jersey: Erlbaum.

Lem, S. E. & A. 1996, Nordseth, Integreret Skibskontrol (Integrated Ship Control). Copenhagen: I. C. Weilbach.

Lind, M., 2003, The Diversity of Work Practices – Challenging the Existing Notion of Business Process Types. In ALOIS 2003, Action in Language, Organisations and Information Systems, G. Goldkuhl et al., eds. Linköping: The research network VITS: pp. 123-138.

Nöth, W., 1995, Handbook of Semiotics. Bloomington: Indiana University Press.

Petersen, J., 2002, Modelling Control Situations for the Design of Context Sensitive Human-Machine Systems. In Proc. of the 21st Conference on Human Decision Making and Control. 15-16 July. Glasgow, Scotland.

Propp, V., 1975, Morphology of the Folktale. Austin: Univ. of Texas Press.

Raeithel, A. 1992, Activity Theory as a Foundation for Design. In Software Development and Reality Construction, C. Floyd et al. (Eds.). Berlin: Springer, pp. 389-413.

Rossi-Landi, F. 1992, Between Signs and Non-signs. Amsterdam/ Philadelphia.

Rossi-Landi, F. 1975, Linguistics and Economics. The Hague: Mouton.

Ryan, M-L. 1991, Possible Worlds, Artificial Intelligence and Narrative Theory. Bloomington & Indianapolis: Indiana University Press.

Chapter 4

LAUNCHING ORGANISATIONAL SEMIOTICS IN THE REAL WORLD: HOW TO PREPARE FOR IT?

Carlos Alberto Cocozza Simoni and Maria Cecília Calani Baranaukas
Institute of Computing - State University of Campinas, Brazil

Abstract: Organisational Semiotics has been presented in the academic literature as a promise for system analysts to construct a better understanding of organisational issues, promoting better adherence between the software to be designed and the organisational needs. In this work we focus on how to carry a semiotic-based approach from the academy to the "real world" of systems development. The paper aims at discussing a training approach and investigating the meaning people in the role of developers make for the semiotic-based methods. The work is illustrated with a case study in which three teams of academics with previous experience in software development were exposed to a training situation in which they had to model a problem using methods and techniques from Organisational Semiotics. Findings of the case study inform the design of instructional material for training information system analysts and developers. The results achieved also point out difficulties experienced by the teams that could promote further discussion by the OS community of theorists and practitioners.

Key words: Information Systems Training, Organisational Semiotics, Information System Development.

1. INTRODUCTION

As discussed in Ehn and Lowgren (1997), the early approaches to Information System (IS) development can be characterized by a strong belief in methods for systematic design grounded in mathematical theories. Research interests in accuracy and technical control have guided these approaches. The main assumptions behind them seem to be that the users

K. Liu (ed.),
Virtual, Distributed and Flexible Organisations: Studies in Organisational Semiotics, 61–82.

(end-user, client, customer, stakeholder or problem owner) are supposed to give complete and explicit descriptions of their demands in terms of the system to be developed. This tradition was inherited by some widely spread methods of Software Engineering (SE) and had a profound influence on the curricula of courses in Computing and Information Systems Engineering. Non-mainstream movements in IS development have tackled this problem with software process models such as evolutionary development, incremental development, etc. Sommerville (2001) offering a basis for a solution to the problem of requirements. Nevertheless, even these efforts lack good methods for investigating social constructs that influence the signification of these systems to their users in the real world.

One of the major sources of inspiration for changes in orientation is the theoretical discussion about the phenomenon of designing computer artefacts. A reframing of the objectivist understanding of computer systems has given place to a subjectivist view. Within this new paradigm, reality is understood as being created subjectively and socially with subtle differences between groups of agents. As a consequence, we can understand an Information System as a semiotic system and the role of the analyst as being to assist users to articulate their problems, discover their information requirements and evolve a systemic solution. In other words, the role of the analyst resembles a designer and "design" is understood in Winograd and Flores (1986) and Adler and Winograd (1992): as the interaction between understanding and creation.

Users, as mentioned before, do not have a clear and closed specification about their needs and they have expectations in the analyst role in helping them to elaborate a picture of the situation. We have had difficulties in using methods from the objectivist tradition to deal with this problem. The alternative usually adopted is to adapt the conventional models of system development to include concepts from quality approaches, ISO series, reengineering etc, which deal with process, behaviour and organisational issues. We envisage in Semiotics and Organisational Semiotics, a way of smoothly bringing together aspects of development process and organisational issues. Our concern in this work is with how to carry an approach grounded in OS from the academy to the "real world" of systems developers working in companies. During this investigation, some questions were raised, such as: How to prepare information system development teams to apply Organisational Semiotics in a real business environment? What kind of syllabus and text references should be used in this preparation? What previous knowledge background would be necessary? Would the time spent with theoretical foundations adequate for them?

In this paper we briefly show the project we have conducted in our University, trying to answer the above questions and anticipating questions that could be raised in real situations of system development. We also had as goals, both to adapt and to document a method to be applied in training situations outside the University. It was our intention to test the approach with the participation of people with a theoretical and practical background in systems development to help us in evaluating it and adapting it for external training. Research and practice of Organisational Semiotics is recent, specially in our country, and we do not have as much didactical literature and documentation to be used in training situations as we have for traditional approaches such as the Unified Process with UML or Structured Analysis.

The main reference for the project was the book "Semiotics in Information Systems Engineering" (Liu 2000) where we got the basis for using MEASUR – Methods for Eliciting, Analysing and Specifying Users' Requirements, with three of its basic methods: PAM – Problem Articulation Methods, SAM – Semantic Analysis Method e NAM – Norm Analysis Method. We also took inspiration from the book "Employing MEASUR Methods for Business Process Reengineering in China" by Liu (2001) in order to understand the techniques in practical situations and generate didactical examples of usage.

Those and other theoretical references were compiled, translated to a course format and introduced into a postgraduate course in Semiotic Perspectives in Information Systems, referred in this paper as "internal training". Through presentations of the subject, readings from literature and discussions carried out in classes, we led the participants in studying Semiotics, Organisational Semiotics and Semiotics in System Development as a requirement for starting practical work. The same process was employed to introduce semiotic approaches in user interface design. In this paper we present and discuss the process of sensemaking as it occurred during the activities, illustrating it with some of the results presented by the teams on the proposed work. Discussions raised, questions presented and solutions found by the teams are also set out as examples.

The work resulted in a dynamic process for training software development teams in a process based on Organisational Semiotics, which will be applied to situations of system development in organisations (external training). Also, we have worked some theoretical issues related to user interface considerations, discussed in other papers.

The paper is organized as follows: Section 2 briefly presents the theoretical and methodological basis for our work, with emphasis in the MEASUR methods. Section 3 briefly describes the context of the case study and present preliminary results of using MEASUR. Section 4 discusses results of a brainstorming session about the experience and Section 5 gives the conclusion.

2. THEORETICAL AND METHODOLOGICAL BASIS

Organisational Semiotics (OS), as a branch of Semiotics, seems to offer an adequate basis to fill the lack we found in traditional system development methodologies concerning the study of organisations in their values and behaviour. We are mainly considering the MEASUR methods, from Ronald Stamper (1973 and 2000) and Kecheng Liu (2000) School of OS. Within their framework, an organisation can be seen as an information system in which interdependent links between the organisation, the business processes and the IT system occur Liu (2000). At an *Informal Level* there is a sub-culture where meanings are established, intentions are understood, beliefs are formed and commitments are made, altered and discharged. At a *Formal Level,* form and rule replace meaning and intention. At a *Technical Level* part of the formal system is automated by a computer-based system.

The conventional information system development models propose several ways of grouping the activities of system development, which in general involve: establishing the scope of the system, requirement analysis, system design, implementation, validation, management and evolution. MEASUR, as an acronym for Methods (Means, Models) for Eliciting (Exploring, Evaluating), Analysing (Articulating, Assessing) and Specifying (Structuring) User's Requirements, deal with the aspects of information system development related to the three upper layers of the Semiotic Framework, which are concerned with the use of signs, their function in communicating meanings and intentions, and their social consequences.

The MEASUR methods related to elicitation and analysis of requirements, our focus in this study, are briefly described below, according to Liu (2000) and Liu (2001):

- Problem Articulation Methods (PAM): consist of a set of methods to be applied in the initial phase of a project, when the problem is still vague and complex. The analyst is supported during definition of units that will be validated by stakeholders using the Semiotic Diagnosis.
- Semantic Analysis Method (SAM): assists the users or problem owners in eliciting and representing their requirements in a formal and precise model. With the analyst in the role of a facilitator, the required functions of an envisaged system are specified in the Ontology Model, which describes a view of responsible agents in the focal business domain and their behaviour or action patterns called *affordances*. The meaning of words used in the semantic model to represent the business world is treated as a relationship between the signs and appropriate actions.
- Norm Analysis Method (NAM): focuses on social, cultural and organisational norms that govern the actions of agents in the business domain. A norm, in a formal or informal sense, defines a responsibility of

an agent engaged in a task or condition by which certain actions should (should not, must, etc) be performed by the agent. Each specified norm is associated with an action pattern described in the computer system. Norm Analysis is used to identify norms and to link them to parts of the semantic model.

Using this theoretical and methodological basis, complemented by other references from the literature on OS, Semiotics and Semiotics in Interface design, we have organized a theoretical and practical course to introduce graduate students with a Computer Science background to the Organisational Semiotic approach. Results of the proposed activities have contributed to evaluation and improvement of the approach towards training project leaders and professional system analysts to use it in their companies.

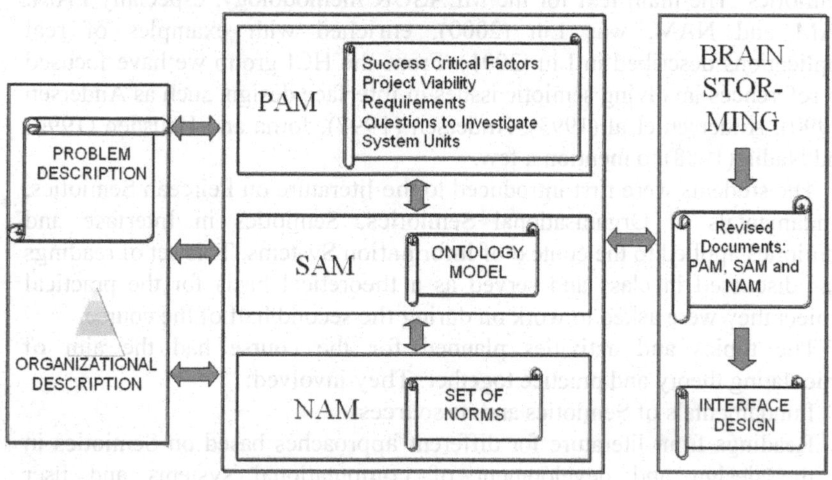

Figure 1. Training Scheme Proposed.

Figure 1 shows the way we have worked with MEASUR in the process of our internal training. As an input to this process we have presented a brief problem definition and organisational structure of the company. Afterwards the main MEASUR concepts and PAM methods were presented. The students applied PAM in a case study, and presented and discussed their results. Before working with SAM, they reviewed the work done in PAM. The same process was employed for SAM and NAM. After the review in results of NAM we conducted a brainstorming session to discuss the whole process aiming at both to capture misunderstandings and to get elements to improve this process towards its application in external trainings. After the brainstorming, the PAM, SAM and NAM documents were revised, worked in the system interface prototype and a final project presentation concluded the process.

2.1 The Proposed Syllabus and Scenario of the Course

The course outline was motivated by a discipline offered to graduate students in their programmes of master and PhD studies in Computer Science using a Semiotic perspective. In this course we aimed at presenting and discussing the basic principles and the main theories, models and methods for designing computational systems based on semiotic approaches.

Initially we planned the contents of the course, having literature references from both Human-Computer Interaction and Organisational Semiotics. The main text for the MEASUR methodology, especially PAM, SAM and NAM, was Liu (2000), enriched with examples of real applications described in Liu (2001). From the HCI group we have focused on references involving semiotic issues in interface design, such as Andersen (1990), Andersen et al (1993), Andersen (1997), Jorna and Heusden (1996) and Nadin (1988) to mention a few.

The students were first introduced to the literature on Peircean Semiotics, fundamentals of Organisational Semiotics, Semiotics in Interface and Semiotics applied to the context of Information Systems. This set of readings was discussed in class and served as a theoretical basis for the practical project they were asked to work on during the second half of the course.

The topics and activities planned for the course had the aim of articulating theory and practice together. They involved:

- Fundamentals of Semiotics and its sources.
- Readings from literature for different approaches based on Semiotics in the design and development of computational systems and user interfaces.
- Presentation and discussion of methods from the Organisational Semiotics to deal with different aspects of information system development: Problem Articulation Methods (PAM), Semantic Analysis Method (SAM), and Norm Analysis Method (NAM).

The contents were worked in lessons, seminaries and tasks carried out individually and/or in groups, according to the agenda of the discipline. Complementary bibliographical references, tasks, acknowledgments, etc. were announced gradually in the agenda. Activities in group involved the development of parts of a project and individual activities involved presentations and participation in class discussions.

The course was carried out during 16 weeks, according to the distribution summarised in Table 1.

Table 1. Main covered subjects.

Subject	*Hours*
Discipline Presentation and Administration	2
Semiotics, HCI and Organisational Semiotics Theoretical Foundations	36
MEASUR Methods	6
Case Study – Practical Work	16

3. DESIGNING THE CALL CENTER SYSTEM OF AN ORGANISATION: THE HANDS ON EXPERIENCE

In this section we present and discuss the learning process as it occurred during the internal training activities, illustrating it with examples of results presented by the teams as well as discussions raised, questions presented and solutions found.

For the hands on experience the students organized themselves into 3 groups of 3 persons each. The problem to be worked on was the design of a Call Center System for a particular organisation. Each participant had a different level of knowledge and experience with Call Center Systems. The concept of the system was familiar to all of them as they had been already reached by some phone call from this kind of business and coincidentally two students had previously had jobs as attendants in the Call Center section of the organisations. Nevertheless no one had worked on the design or development of this type of system.

The work was developed in four phases: the first three related to the application of MEASUR methods and the fourth one related to the construction of interface prototypes for the proposed system. The groups were engaged in activities involving: analysis and modelling with the use of the methods previously discussed, followed by presentation and discussion of results in each phase of the project. At the end of the process, a brainstorming session was conducted and recorded aiming at evaluating and discussing the approach and their role in it. The fourth phase of the training and the relationship made between the Ontology and Norm Models and the User Interface Design is discussed elsewhere in Baranauskas e Simoni (2003) and Simoni e Baranauskas (2003).

The problem proposed involved the Call Center department of an organisation. Our aim was to investigate the use of the methods and their contribution to the interface design of the system. As in any problem the students were presented with a vague definition of the problem and a short description of the structure of the organisation, its main functions (attendance to calls, active marketing and support to selling) and the roles of people working in it. The main requirements and requests from managers and main users were also presented. A brief summary of the requirements included the following:

> "*The system should support the answering to calls, to facilitate and make the process agile, as it was noticed that the clients desire a more dynamic and error proof answering system. The system should be rich in graphical resources to facilitate the access and minimize the use of the keyboard. It was expected to diminish the time needed to access the information related to clients´ records and contacts. The system should enable the worker in charge of answering the call, to initiate new contacts and to record and control them in the same way done for the contacts automatically generated*".

Using this brief description for the problem, we have observed that the methods drove the teams to get the main concepts, terms, roles, etc in the problem domain. In the next sections we present the first results of using MEASUR in this problem. As instructors in charge of the course we had the opportunity to verify the acceptance of the methods and to observe the misunderstandings that could denote conceptual difficulties and drawbacks of our training.

3.1 PAM – Problem Articulation Methods

The teams were intentionally presented with a vague and short description of the problem, allowing them to investigate the domain, the main questions and feasible solutions, stakeholders directly or indirectly involved in the process, conditions, effects for each area in the organisation, the system units etc.

3.1.1 Semiotic Diagnosis

Traditional system development methods emphasize technical issues and the analyst misses the opportunity of analysing other levels of relationship (semantic, pragmatic and social), which direct or indirectly affect aspects of the system. Semiotic Diagnosis allows us to analyse strategic factors and to examine the organisation as a social system that is constructed through the use of information. Table 2, a result of Team 1 work, shows at social level that the team understands that the "commitment to the improvement in quality of services offered to the customer" is a feasible solution for "increasing trust from the customer". This comment suggests that IT is not the only solution to improve the perception of quality of services. The involvement of the whole organisation would be important and it would be necessary to explore how each area of the organisation could contribute to this improvement. In subsequent levels, the team explores this issue to achieve the commitment with the customer.

Table 2. Semiotic Diagnosis for the problem by Team 1.

Level	*Description*	*Questions*	*Feasible Solutions*
Social World	Legal structure/ Consolidate customer relationship	How to increase trust from customer?	Commitment with improvement of quality in services offered to customer.
Pragmatics	Trust / Customer satisfaction	How to give evidence of the importance of customer satisfaction?	Register customer suggestions for improvement.
Semantics	Non ambiguous meanings	How to assure that the customer understands the company?	Use customer language when contacting people.
Syntactic	Structural Language	How to simplify meanings?	Use standard reports. Company / Customer communication guideline. Questionnaire to collect opinions.
Empirics	Interaction between company areas and the customer	How to assure that information flows from customer to company areas?	Reports of Customer Contacts (sales, support, marketing etc).
Physical World	Structures to physical communication	How to settle contact with the customer with agility and feasible resources?	Using phone lines, fax and internet (e-mail and attendance site).

We have observed that each team focused on a different aspect of the problem. Team 1 worked with quality of services; Team 2 discussed about customer profiles and how to communicate with them in a personalized way; and Team 3 paid attention to information and message flow. Using Semiotic Diagnosis the analysts went beyond the technical issues of IT, considering other possible solutions to the questions.

3.1.2 Stakeholder Analysis

This kind of analysis allows the analyst to investigate interesting areas which are not so evident in a first observation, but could interfere with some organisational or technical issues. For example, the "government" could define regulations related to the workplace or work time, which should be obeyed using internal norms and the system would be affected by them. Would it be necessary to consider the Call Center physical environment, e.g. furniture layout, designation of staff common room aea etc? Must the computer system control the employee work time e.g. dictating the timing and duration of breaks? These are some examples of issues that could directly affect the project costs and schedule.

Figure 2 presents the Stakeholder Analysis resulted from Team 2 work. The solutions of the other two teams are very similar. The only difference is that Team 2 included the Support groups as stakeholders in this process.

The team have explained the analysis resulting in the representation in the following way:

"In the most internal level we have the operation, which directly involves the attendants, who operate the system. In the second level we have the group in charge of supporting operation (attendance support); i.e., they support the attendants towards a better system operation, providing information about products, problem solutions, promotions etc. On this level we have also a group to maintain the software (infra structure group), providing an adequate operation, and groups interested in information about attendance (supervisor, manager and owner), to control or to use the information to improve sales. On the third level we have groups interacting with the Call Center (customer, marketing and sales). Finally, in the fourth level we have any people that could contact the Call Center or access published advertisement; the press, which publishes the marketing advertisements and also judges the company products and services and the government, which makes rules and laws which must be respected on all levels".

This analysis, used in association with the two following tools, resulted in a strong approach to the analyst to explore the pragmatic and social levels of the Semiotic Framework.

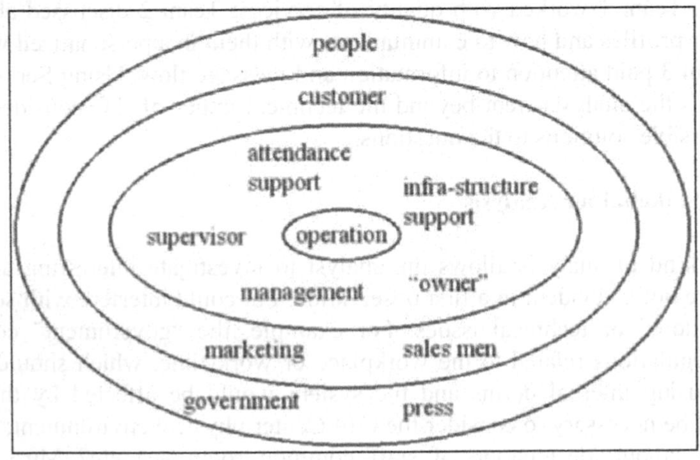

Figure 2. Stakeholder Analysis by Team 2.

3.1.3 Conditions, Consequences and Questions

This method aims at verifying problems in the process and the important conditions and questions to be addressed for each interested person (stakeholder), area or sector. Table 3 presents the analysis produced by one of the teams. They have focused on the interaction between the Call Center and other areas, directly or indirectly involved with the attendance. They pointed out the main conditions necessary to provide consistent information to the whole team. For each area they also pointed out one question considered relevant to the context.

Table 3. Dealing with Conditions and Questions by Team 2.

Area	*Conditions / Consequences*	*Questions*
Marketing	Sales promotion transmitted to attendants and salesmen.	Has the area good ways to transmit and organise the existent promotions?
Infrastructure technical support	Technical support problems existing in the Call Center.	Has the area the tools to contact, attend and quickly solve the problems?
Attendance technical support	Solve attendant questions (promotions, products, computational system).	Has the area tools for a quick contact?
Supervisor / Sales manager	Attendance quality evaluation and the number of appointments.	Has the area tools for quality evaluation and for dealing with the appointments?
Salesman	Plan for visits according to appointments.	Has the area ways to visualise, access and maintain the agenda?
Attendant	Solve customer questions, make products advertising and make salesmen appointments. Verify customer satisfaction level. Maintain customer register.	Has the area tools to get information about products, promotions, sales contacts, customer contacts, order situation and list of activities to do?

This approach allowed the analyst to focus in points related to the problem, to establish priorities and conduct further investigation.

3.1.4 Anthropologic Framework

This method is suggested for each stakeholder and interested person to analyse his/her requirements using an evaluation framework based on the anthropological classification of cultural norms. This framework drives the analyst to consider many aspects of the culture of groups such as: interaction, association, subsistence, taxonomy, time, space, learning, creativity, defence and exploitation. The analyst should observe the problem using a different lens or perspectives.

We have observed that the teams used this method in two different ways. One of the teams explored the cultural aspects for each group of people involved with the problem, e.g. attendants (shown in Table 4), salesmen and customers. This method has allowed the team to get important requirements for each area, conditions, constrains, controls etc. This information is also important for setting goals and quality measures, not only for the software application but also for the system and its expected behaviour. Another team has used the method, in the format of a questionnaire to verify the actual status of the information system, for each stakeholder. This approach helped to identify critical points, priorities issues, constrains, expectancies etc, for all aspects of the information system.

Table 4. Anthropologic framework created by Team 1.

Aspect	*Description*	*Attendant*
Interaction	Communication	Easy access to products information, promotions, support group, salesmen and customer agenda.
Association	Involved groups	Cooperation with other attendants, supervisor, manager, support and customer.
Subsistence	Economics	Quick and satisfactory attendance.
Taxonomy	Record data	Personalized attendance according to customer profile, customer / business / product specific attendant.
Time	When? How long?	Deadline to give feedback to the customer.
Space	System availability	Quick attendance and short breaks.
Learning	Knowledge / experiences	Products knowledge and experience in customer and prospect attendance.
Creativity	Attractive	Ability in showing clues to avoid other similar problems.
Defence	Classified information	Maintain information security.
Exploitation	Information	Stimulate customer to seek information on the company site.

With the Anthropologic Framework we could observe that the teams had made a wide exploration of the problem, observing the organisation, issues, groups, etc under several perspectives, allowing them a comprehensive understanding of the problem context.

3.1.5 Morphologic Analysis

This analysis is proposed to allow investigation of the norms that govern people's behaviour within the unitary systems. Three main components of the analysis are the substantive, which focuses on aspects that contribute directly to the organisation's objectives, the communicational and the control aspects. We have observed that the teams did not explore this method sufficiently. They have partially represented the main norms for each component (substantive, communication and control). This seems to be related to the "toy" character of the problem. Table 5 presents the result of one of the teams work.

Table 5. Morphologic Analysis created by Team 1.

Substantive	*Message*	*Control*
To answer customer calls.	To acknowledge customer suggestions.	Reports about customer contacts to: Sales, Support and Marketing
To make calls to customers and prospects.	Customer / Company communication guidelines.	Report about calls to prospects.
To measure customers' satisfaction levels.	Customer opinion questionnaires.	Report about received calls.
To manage salesmen agendas.	To acknowledge salesman agenda modifications.	
To provide information about new products, and promotion to the customer.	To acknowledge contact interest with specific salesman.	
To record complaints.	Promotion product and new product lists.	
To record orders.		
To maintain customer files.		

3.1.6 Collateral Analysis

This method allows the analyst to investigate many components of the entire project, which could impact costs, schedule and the success of the project if not treated in time. We have observed that only Team 2 had made an in depth analysis of the systems that would interact with the focal system. They had considered the system in use as the predecessor system; the focal system was considered the first version of the computational system (shown in Figure 3) with the successors considered as the new releases of the application. This team also explored the Predecessor as a Focal System, discovering its own system units. The other two teams did not present concrete simulations using this method.

The analysis made by Team 2 shows aspects of system construction, the resources involved and evaluation of the human resources necessary to the new situation. Would the new system reduce the number of some professionals and increase others? The impact of this type of discussion could be crucial in preparing the areas to receive the system.

Another analysed situation that could impact the computer system is related to the operation of backup; the necessity of having a secure copy of the database was pointed out. The analyst should verify technical alternatives in the market, ways to get access to this copy, etc. Each one of these questions impact the system operation, resources and costs depending on the solution adopted.

```
A. Focal System:  The new system:
   Life Cycle:
      Predecessor: previous system based on paper-based records.
      Successor: future new versions of the system considering the
   use of the computer.
   Operation:
      Fall: system fall (energy, user error, telephonic system
      etc.).
      Backup: security copy of the system data.
      Recovery: recovery of stored information and tables.
   Construction:
      Available: time interval where the system will be operating,
      from its implementation until a new version.
      Ending: finishing of first version of the system.
      Decommissioning: initial data base for a new version
      generation.
      Resources: verification of available resources to support the
      system functions. There are human resources as attendants,
      supervisors and technician for maintenance and other resources
      as the telephonic system and the computers.
      Construction: construction of first version based on the
      resources and initial files.
      Launching: implantation of first version of the system and
      training for employees.
      Description: the proposal of this system is the automation of
      the previous process of attendance.
   Execution:
      Inputs: telephonic linking that will feed the system.
      Environment: graphical resources for the communication between
   users.
      Outputs: updating tables with information received from the
   operator.
```

Figure 3. Collateral Analysis by Team 2.

This method seemed to be very important when used as a checklist to investigate many different aspects related to the future system.

3.1.7 Some Considerations about the Use of PAM

After using PAM methods the teams reviewed and rewrote the problem description, not only amplifying it, but also confirming or changing the original requirements. With this analysis the project owners could realistically decide whether the project was feasible or not, concerning costs, resources and schedule, establish critic factors of success, weak points to be improved and strong points to be sustained. They also got a complete list of stakeholders, their main requirements and interests. This analysis favours an improvement in commitment among the technical team, owners, stakeholders and users.

Having finished this step the teams discussed their solutions in class and reviewed their steps, changing the products of each phase when necessary. Despite the valuable results of PAM, they had difficulties in transposing from PAM to the next methods (Semantic an Norm Analysis).

3.2 SAM – Semantic Analysis Method

Semantic Analysis allows the analyst to model the problem context, the agents involved and their patterns of behaviour - affordances, in the ontology chart. In this section we illustrate some findings using part of the Ontology Model constructed by one of the teams (Figure 4). Demarked areas are commented below.

Starting from the problem definition, the teams underlined semantic units, separating candidates from agents and affordances, then classifying and grouping the affordances and constructing the ontology chart.

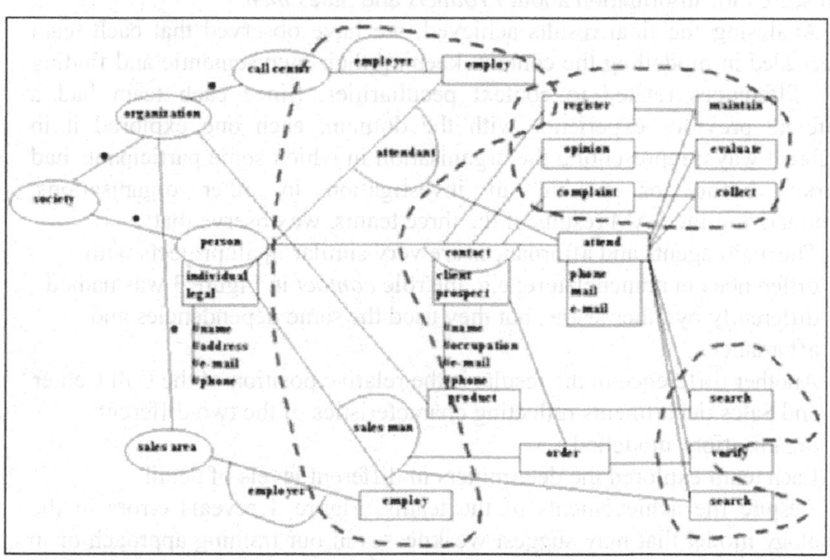

Figure 4. Part of Ontology Model constructed.

In the model shown in Figure 4, *Society* is the root agent, and it has two affordances: *Organisation* and *Person*. Both of them are agents, part of *Society* and ontologically dependent on it. *Person* is a generic agent and the designers captured *Individual* and *Legal* as its specifics. The *Individual Person* is related to *Call Center* and *Sales* Departments, both are agents and part of *Organisation*. Both *employ Person* adopting the *employer* role.

Employ is an affordance of both. The person employed by the Sales Department adopts the *sales man* role and the person employed by the Call Center department adopts the *attendant* role. *Person* has determiners such as *name*, *address*, *e-mail* and *phone*; in other contexts other determiners could have been specified for an *individual* or *legal person*. When someone makes a phone call to the *Call Center*, he or she is in the role of a *contact* person, which is a generic role having *Client* and *Prospect* as specifics. The *contact* role has the determiners *name*, *occupation*, *e-mail* and *phone*. The action *Attend* is ontologically dependent on *Contact* (the role) and *Attendant*. This means that the attendance is only possible within the existence of an *Attendant* and a *Contact*. The affordance *Attend* has *phone*, *mail* and *e-mail* as specifics and this means the ways by which the *Attendant* can answer to the *Contact*. Information in *Register*, *Opinions*, *Complaints* and *Order* are affordances of *Contact* and can be respectively *Maintained*, *Evaluated*, *Collected* and *Verified* during an attendance. In the same way, the *Attendant* can search for information about *Products* and *Sales men*.

Analysing the final results achieved, we have observed that each team succeeded in modelling the context, keeping their own semantic and finding out differences related to context peculiarities. Since each team had a different previous experience with the domain, each one explored it in different ways: representing the organisation in which some participants had worked before or making an investigation in other organisations. Summarizing the SAM results of the three teams, we observe that:

- The main agents and affordances are very similar in all projects with differences in nomenclature; e.g. the role *contact* in Figure 3 was named differently by other teams, but they used the same dependencies and affordances.
- Another difference in the results is the relative position of the Call Center and Sales departments reflecting characteristics of the two different organisations modelled.
- Each team explored the determiners in different levels of detail.

Despite the achievements of the teams, Figure 4 reveals errors in the ontology model that may suggest weaknesses in our training approach or in the SAM itself, that deserves some considerations. The double occurrence of "employer", for example, could have been avoided if they had realised that "organisation", not departments, should have the "employ" affordance and the role name "employer". The same type of conceptual misunderstanding is revealed by the two occurrences of the affordance "search". Another error refers to issues of reification. Some affordances found in Figure 4 such as "register", "opinion", "complaint", etc. might be specifics of the behaviour of the Person asking for attendance.

The chart produced revealed the difficulties that the teams had in deciding on an appropriate level of abstraction. The general feeling was that if a very high level of abstraction had been achieved, the chart would be correct but could be useless to their specification problem. The balance between abstraction and reification is difficult to reach in the models and some best practice should be provided to help the prospective practitioners with this issue.

The concept of ontological dependency is another issue with which the teams presented difficulties in elaborating. Part of this difficulty we believe is related to the brief period of training. Nevertheless, the difficulty was explained by the teams, as being a result of the influence of traditional methodologies, which emphasise causal dependencies. Another difficulty observed was the classification of agents representing groups such as: Company, Organisation, Department, etc. In spite of the difficulties, the discussions occurring during their presentations were very important in order to clarify some misunderstandings and misuses.

Having finished this analysis the teams worked in the norms that govern agents, actions, behaviours and relationships, which we present in the next section.

3.3 NAM – Norm Analysis Method

The teams worked on the norms which related not only to the computer-based system, but mainly to the general behaviour of the organisation. Table 6 shows a summary of some norms pointed out and associated to the Ontology Model in Figure 4.

Table 6. Some norms detected by Team 1.

N°	*Character*	*Content*	*Condition*	*Subject*
1	Obliged	To attend the customer	A call occurs	Attendant
17	Permitted	To work in attendance activities	Call Center area exists	Attendant
18	Obliged	To maintain customer data	Call Center area exists	Attendant
22	Permitted	To make a break	To be in attendance work during 2 hours	Attendant
23	Obliged	To record customer complaint	Customer makes a complaint	Attendant
25	Must not	To make public data about customer	To be an attendant	Attendant

In order to show the relations established by the teams between the Ontology Model and the Norms raised, we highlight some observations:

- Based on the model shown in Figure 4 and the combination of norms 1 and 17, we observe that the access to the system must be allowed only to the attendants. In the model, the affordance *attend* is ontologically dependent on *attendant* and *person*, in the *contact* role. Norms 1 and 17 define that the Call Center has responsibility for the customer attendance and the attendant is the responsible agent.

- Norm 18 is related to the attendant obligations in maintaining customer data. In terms of the computer-based system the attendant should be supported in getting relevant information during the attendance.
- Norm 22, based on social labour rules, allows the *attendant* to take a break after 2 hours working on the *attendance*. This norm impacts in organisational issues, such as the definition of a special place to rest. The computer-based system is affected by controlling the work time.
- Norm 23, similar to norm 18, shows the organisation concerns with improving quality of attendance. They could explore the necessity of creating a procedure to deal with the complaints, which impact in both the organisational operations and the computer-based system.
- Norm 25, related to information protection, affects the relationship among the organisation, attendants and customers, also impacting the computer-based system.

These examples show us that this approach guided the teams in exploring many aspects of organisational relations, which impact and enrich the analysis. We also observed that using Semantic and Norm Analysis the teams did not need to be working with processes, workflows, activity nets etc, as is common in traditional methodologies. One interesting point observed by the teams was the strong existing link between Semantic and Norm Analysis. Changes in one of them imply the need to review the other and the teams have not presented difficulties in doing this.

After concluding this phase, we conducted a brainstorming session to evaluate the whole process. Afterwards, the teams reviewed the models and made a system interface prototype considering the modelled needs, constrains, roles, etc. In the next section we present some results of this brainstorming and illustrate the interface prototypes constructed.

4. DISCUSSION - BRAINSTORMING ABOUT THE EXPERIENCE

In the brainstorming session that we conducted to discuss the use of MEASUR methods in the case study, one of us played the mediator role and the other recorded the discussion. The brainstorming session lasted around 2 hours and we recorded the session using a camera, to complement the written record and to allow us to review the session and capture more details. We present some results achieved, describing the students feelings, points of view, restrictions etc, and illustrating these with fragments of some comments.

The initial concerns about the proposed methodology reflected an *"initial fear in making errors"* or *"of being below the class expectations"*, *"The new brings the feeling of fear and we are accustomed with other methodologies"*. They mentioned that a second project would be easier and the time spent in the process would decrease.

The first impression caused by the PAM method was *"... confusion, because it is a very open set of artefacts, different from other approaches, which have a lot of rules to guide you..."*. In fact, we have observed that the students felt more comfortable in using SAM and NAM because they believed that these methods *"are more systematic"*. They said that other methodological approaches have much more rules and guidelines than observed in PAM methods. Another point raised was that they felt they did not use much information from PAM methods to work in SAM and NAM. Another problem pointed out was *"we had some problems because of lack of technical understanding"*. We have been considering using this feedback to improve our training strategies with more examples of usage, output expected from each step, best practices, etc. In PAM, for example, we could have as output a list of Success Critical Factors, Project Feasibility, Requirements, Questions to Investigate, System Units, etc.

Despite the critics they considered PAM "*a tool set much wider than the majority of approaches used before*". "*There is a gap in other methodologies in dealing with Requirement Analysis*". They agree that there are many things to do, analyse and observe before designing the system. "*These tools seem to be better at capturing what the customer wants*". "*If we hadn't used PAM, the Semantic and Norm analysis would have been different from what we got*".

Another issue pointed out was the shift from function or process orientation to information system analysis. "*We used to be oriented to functions. Seek functions ... and think in the software earlier*". "*We need to forget the software and try to understand the context situation*". "*We did not need to think about the software, but about the organisation, instead*".

Despite the errors committed, the work with the Ontology Model was considered *"... very simple and gave us a different view of the problem"*. *"We could easily modify the model many times as our problem understanding increased"*. They considered SAM and NAM better defined. *"The Ontology Model is more explicit. There is less ambiguity"*. Another issue pointed out was *"the possibility of going back to review previous results"*.

Regarding Norm Analysis, the teams succeeded in dealing and capturing many kinds of norms. "*There are norms related not only to the software, or impacting in it, but also related to the organisational functions and work*".

Another interesting result of this case study, was related to the system interface design, the final product of this internal training. The mapping from SAM and NAM to the user interface design is discussed in Baranauskas and Simoni (2003) and Simoni and Baranaukas (2003). On a general level, it was possible to perceive the way Semiotics can lay a foundation for the analysis of a problem and the creation of an interface. All the three considered methods (PAM, SAM and NAM) contributed to the elaboration of the interface, informing its conception. The methods provided support for identification of the relevant categories of users to be involved with the interface (such as Attendant, Customer, etc), the crucial operations for the adequate functioning of the Attendance and the norms that drive the relations between Attendance and Customers.

Specifically from the Semantic Model, they took the main characteristics that guided the interface design: the domain relations and classes of users, the different arrangements for composing menu options, the privileges and adequate filters of operations relatives to each type of user, the available operations that would define buttons and labels of folder identification, the fields for data entry and information exhibition/delivery, the processes of navigation among screens and windows of the interface.

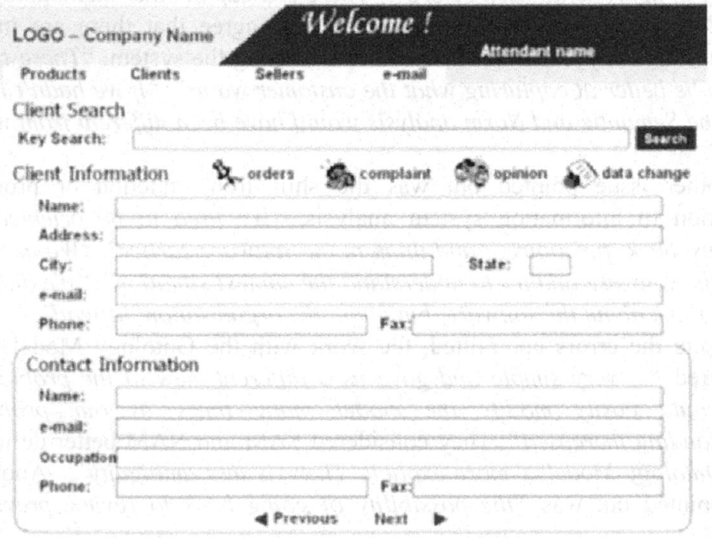

Figure 5. Example of system interface prototype.

To illustrate these results, Figure 5 shows one example of system interface prototype created by one of the teams. In this Figure we see the proposed screens to support the attendant, when s/he is in contact with the customer, to maintain her/his data file. The interface prototype was directly modelled from the Ontology Model shown in Figure 4.

The interface created from this analysis reflects the dialectics between system design and organisational issues. This observation comes from the fact that Organisational Semiotics allows us to analyse organisations as live structures, in constant mutation, as an agent who makes semiosis on the basis of the signs he/she/it perceives in the organisation.

5. CONCLUSION

Summarizing, the proposed work resulted in feedback for training software development teams in a development approach based on Organisational Semiotics. Also, we intended to extend the models to include user interface considerations.

We have verified that the participants perceived the values of the semiotic-based approach. To illustrate with some participants comments: "*there is an improvement in eliciting requirements*"; "*the problem substance was understood even with a brief problem description*"; "*the focus is on the Organisation Information System and not only in Software Development, as is usual in other methodologies*"; "*the methodology is cyclic and revisions are easily made*". Furthermore, the results achieved by the different teams in the final project demonstrated the consistency of the approach.

Another point that deserves consideration is the relationship the teams made between the Ontology and Norm Models and the User Interface Design, as a way of building an interface that considers the users language and reflects the dynamics and spaces modelled. Requirement studies share with HCI many fundamental issues. They both need to address how people understand the world and how to represent their understanding. Meaning of symbols and languages used in modelling is a fundamental issue for both. Results achieved with the case study suggest that the students that participated as designers had a good understanding of the approach, which enabled them to practice the Semantic Analysis, mapping concepts from the Ontology Model to elements in the interface design. Layout delimitations, sequences of screens, structuring of menus, etc. are some examples of elements mapped from the OM.

The discussion with the teams that participate in the case study and the final results achieved encourage future work on a systematic basis towards formalizing the approach. Although we acknowledge the importance of analysing the achievements in comparison with other methods, it was out of the scope of this paper. Our next move, which we have already started, involves training people working outside the academy, in organisations that develop information systems.

REFERENCES

Adler, P.S., Winograd, T. 1992, The Usability Challenge. In P.S. Adler and T.A. Winograd (eds.), Usability: Turning Technologies into Tools, Oxford University Press, USA.

Andersen, P.B. 1990, A Theory of Computer Semiotics: Semiotic Approaches to Construction and Assessment of Computer Systems. Cambridge University Press, Cambridge.

Andersen, P.B., Holmqvist,B., Jensen, J.F. 1993, The Computer as Medium, Cambridge University Press, USA.

Andersen, P.B. 1997, A Theory of Computer Semiotics, Cambridge University Press, USA.

Baranauskas, M. C. C., Simoni, C. A. C. 2003, From Requirements Analysis to Interface Design: Understanding a Subjective Approach to Information Systems, work in progress.

Ehn, P., Lowgren, J. 1997, Design for Quality-in-use: Human-Computer Interaction Meets Information Systems Development. In M. Helander, T.K. Landauer, P. Prabhu (eds.), Handbook of Human-Computer Interaction, Second completely revised edition, Elsevier Science. The Netherlands.

Jorna, R., Heusden, B. 1996, Semiotics of the User Interface. In Semiotica 109-3/4, 237-250.

Liu, K. 2000, Semiotics in Information Systems Engineering, Cambridge University Press, Cambridge.

Liu, X. 2001, Employing MEASUR Methods for Business Process Reengineering in China, Ph.D. Thesis University of Twente, Enschede, the Netherlands.

Nadin, M. 1988, Interface Design: A Semiotic Paradigm. Semiotica 69:269-302.

Simoni, C. A. C., Baranauskas, M. C. C., (2003), Da Análise de Requisitos ao Projeto de Interface: uma Abordagem Subjetivista para Sistemas de Informação, CLIHC2003, Rio de Janeiro, Brazil.

Sommerville, I., 2001, Software Engineering. International Computer Science Series. Addison-Wesley Publishers Limited - USA, 6th edition.

Winograd, T., Flores, F. 1986, Understanding Computers and Cognition – A New Foundation for Design. Norwood, NJ: Able.

Stamper, R, K. 1973, "Information in Business and Administrative Systems". John Wiley and Sons, New York apud Liu, K. (2000), "Semiotics in Information Systems Engineering", Cambridge University Press, Cambridge.

Stamper, R. et al, 2000, "Understanding the Roles of Signs and Norms in Organisations – a Semiotic Approach to Information System Design", Behaviour & Information Technology, v.19/1, pp. 15-27.

Chapter 5

WHAT IS IN A COMMITMENT?

A Glimpse of The Social Level of the Semiological Ladder Using Eda Glasses

Joaquim Filipe
School of Technology of Setúbal, Portugal

Abstract: This paper discusses the notion of commitment, a central element of the social level of the semiological ladder, in the scope of the EDA (Epistemic-Deontic-Axiological) agent model. We introduce how the EDA model can accommodate the notion of Information Field and suggest how information fields can be used to manage commitments, based on information field servers. Both the psychological notion and the social notion of commitments are analysed and compared. We also describe how commitments are represented and used in the EDA model, including the structural and functional properties of commitments as well as the main operations on them.

Key words: Organisational Semiotics, Commitment, Agents

1. INTRODUCTION

The semiological ladder (fig. 1) was proposed by Stamper (1973) as an extension to Morris semiotics framework, which divided semiotics in three levels only: syntax, semantics and pragmatics. Stamper added three more levels, creating a fuller framework that spans from the Physical World to the Social World. Here we will focus our attention on the *Social World.*

K. Liu (ed.),
Virtual, Distributed and Flexible Organisations: Studies in Organisational Semiotics, 83–102.

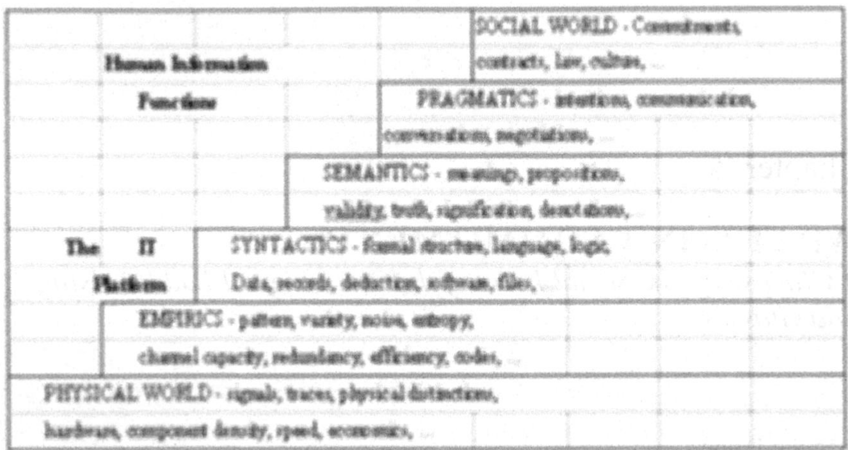

Figure 1. Semiological ladder between the Physical and the Social World (Stamper 1973)

We believe commitments are one of the key elements for the coordination of social systems. Therefore, we are particularly interested in studying them – their nature and their usefulness – in human information systems and in artificial distributed systems. Given the normative nature of social information systems, and inspired in the social-psychology classification of norms, we have proposed the Epistemic-Deontic-Axiologic (EDA) model (Filipe, 2000) as a normative agent model for supporting the coordination of intelligent multi-agent systems.

In this paper we briefly present the normative EDA agent model and then we discuss different aspects of the notion of commitment relating it to the EDA model and to the social world – the top level of the semiological ladder.

2. THE EDA MODEL

Social psychology provides a well-known classification of norms, partitioning them into perceptual, evaluative, cognitive and behavioural norms. These four types of norms are associated with four distinct attitudes, respectively (Stamper, 1996):

- Ontological – to acknowledge the existence of something;
- Axiological – to be disposed in favour of or against something in value terms;
- Epistemic – to adopt a degree of belief or disbelief;
- Deontic – to be disposed to act in some way.

Our agent model is based on these attitudes and the associated norms, which we characterize in more detail below:

- Perceptual norms, guided by evaluative norms, determine what signs the agent chooses to perceive. Then, when a sign is perceived, a pragmatic function will update the agent EDA model components accordingly.
- Cognitive norms define entity structures, semantic values and cause-effect relationships, including both beliefs about the present state and expectations for the future. Conditional beliefs are typically represented by rules, which being normative allow for the existence of exceptions.
- Behavioural norms define what an agent is expected to do. These norms prescribe ideal behaviours as abstract plans to bring about ideal states of affairs, thus determining what an agent ought to do. Deontic logic is a modal logic that studies the formal properties of normative behaviours and states.
- Evaluative norms are required for an agent to choose its actions based on both epistemic and deontic attitudes. If we consider a rational agent, then the choice should be such that the agent will maximize some utility function, implicitly defined as the integral of the agent's axiological attitudes.

Using this taxonomy of norms, and based on the assumption that an organisational agent behavior is determined by the evaluation of deontic norms given the agent epistemic state, we propose an intentional agent model, which is decomposed into three components: the epistemic, the deontic and the axiological.

Together, these components incorporate all the agent informational contents, according to the semiotics ladder depicted in figure 2, where it is shown that information is a complex concept, and requires different viewpoints to be completely analysed.

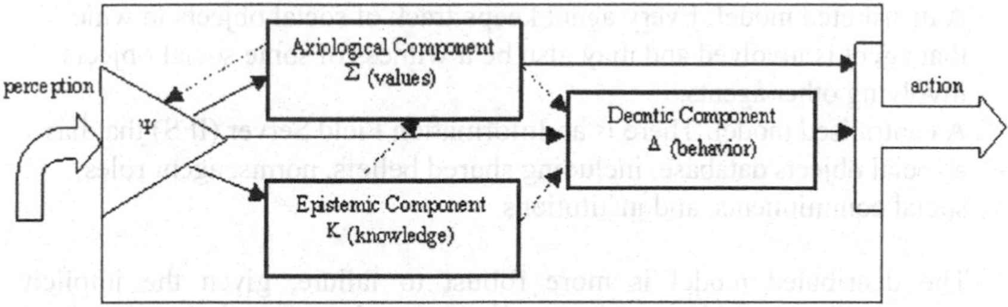

Figure 2. The EDA agent model.

Ψ is a pragmatic function that filters perceptions, according to the agent perceptual and axiological norms, and updates one or more model components.

Σ is an axiological function, that is used in two circumstances: to decide which signs to perceive and to decide which actions to execute.

K is a knowledge based component, where the agent stores his beliefs both explicitly and implicitly, in the form of potential deductions based on logical reasoning.

Δ is a set of available plans, either explicit or implicit, that the agent may choose to execute.

3. INFORMATION FIELDS

Following Stamper (1973) and Habermas (1984) we postulate the existence of a shared ontology or inter-subjective reality that defines the social context (information field) where agents are situated. This kind of social shared knowledge is not reducible to individual mental objects (Conte and Castelfranchi, 1995). For example, in the case of a commitment violation, sanction enforcement is explicitly or tacitly supported by the social group to which the agents belong, otherwise the stronger agent would have no reason to accept the sanction. This demonstrates the inadequacy of the reductionist view.

Once again, we look at human organisational models for designing multi-agent systems; for example, contracts in human societies are often written and publicly registered in order to ensure the existence of socially accepted, and trusted, witnesses that would enable the control of possible violations at a social level. Non-registered contracts and commitments are often dealt with at a bilateral level only and each concerned agent has its internal contract copy. This observation suggests two representational models:

- A distributed model: Every agent keeps track of social objects in which that agent is involved and may also be a witness of some social objects involving other agents.
- A centralised model: There is an Information Field Server (IFS) that has a social objects database, including shared beliefs, norms, agent roles, social commitments, and institutions.

The distributed model is more robust to failure, given the implicit redundancy. For example, a contract where a number of parties are involved is kept in all concerned agents' knowledge bases, therefore if an agent collapses the others can still provide copies of the contract. It is also more efficient assuming that all agents are honest and sincere; for example, commitment creation and termination involved in business transactions would not need to be officially recorded – a simple representation of a social commitment at the concerned agents EDA model would suffice.

However, since these assumptions are often unrealistic, the distributed model cannot completely replace the role of certified agents, trusted by society to keep a record of shared beliefs and social commitments. We assume here that these social notions are part of the ontology that is shared by all members of an information field; that is why we call these trusted repositories of the shared ontology "Information Field Servers". These servers have the following characteristics:

- Different information fields must have different IFS because the shared ontology may differ among specific information fields.
- Each information field may have several non-redundant IFS, each representing a small part of the shared ontology.
- The robustness problems of IFS are minimized by reliable backup (redundant) agents.

Considering the empirical semiotics level, communication bandwidth is another relevant factor to consider: if all social objects were placed in central IFS agents these might become system bottlenecks.

A conceptual problem that exists but is not in the scope of this paper is related to the representation of social objects resulting from the interaction of agents belonging to different information fields. Possible solutions range from the unification of the different conceptual frameworks to the creation of new information fields where the ontology is constructed from a continuous meaning negotiation process via the interaction of the concerned agents.

In figure 3 the architecture of the inter-subjective level is depicted with respect to the localisation of social objects in addition to an example showing how social objects are used at the subjective level.

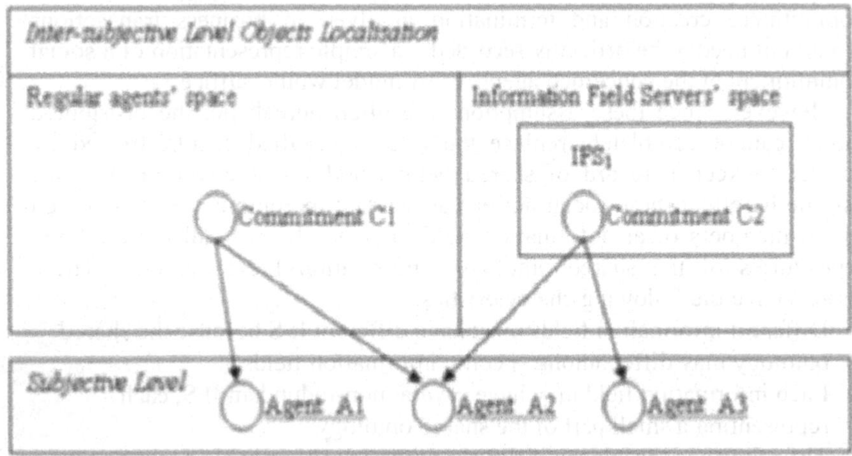

Figure 3. Social objects representation and usage

Commitments are first class objects, which can be represented either in the agents' EDA models (which we designate as the agents' space) or in the IFS' EDA model (which we designate as the Information Field Server's space). In the example above, agents A1 and A2 have only an internal representation (in each EDA model) of a shared commitment C1, whereas Agents A2 and A3 do not have an internal representation of commitment C2 because this commitment is represented in IFS1. All agents A2 and A3 need is a reference (i.e. a pointer) to that shared commitment, although for implementation reasons related to communication bandwidth and efficiency copies may be kept internally.

One problem that we need to analyse is the fact that the word commitment is overloaded: it can be used to signify different things. In the next sections we discuss the differences and similarities between psychological and social commitments.

3.1 Psychological Commitments

An agent who has an intention is in some way *committed to act* – it intends to achieve a certain goal. This attitude does not occur only at a particular point in time but it lasts for a substantial period of time, even if circumstances change.

The agent is also said to be *committed to its beliefs* if it resists reconsideration even in the face of new data.

This suggests the unifying role of psychological commitments for agent intentions and beliefs. Both constrain the deliberation of an agent about its cognitive state, thus entailing a certain amount of irrationality.

Theoretically, perfectly rational agents should be able to derive all possible logical conclusions from their belief set and only after having total knowledge of all possible logical consequences of every possible action at a certain point in time (logical omniscience) should they take a decision and choose the action with highest expected utility. However, the assumption of logical omniscience is almost always inappropriate. One of the most obvious examples occurs when we consider human reasoning. People are simply not logically omniscient: a person can know a set of facts without knowing all the logical consequences of this set of facts. Organisations and even artificial agents too are resource bounded, thus they also are not logically omniscient.

Therefore, commitments should be reconciled with rationality for rationally bounded agents (Simon, 1996), who lack the resources to reason at every moment from *first principles*. Well-designed agents have the relevant commitments so that they can succeed despite ignoring a number of aspects that they might otherwise reason about. Furthermore, by adopting psychological commitments the agent reduces its choices (voluntarily – therefore without loss of autonomy), thus becoming more predictable which can enhance multi-agent co-ordination.

3.2 Social Commitments

Commitments are conditional obligations. They have been studied in the scope of Deontic Logic, the logic of obligations. This modal logic is based on the obligation operator *O*. Hintikka (1970) which presents the advantages and disadvantages of each of the two typical deontic representations of commitment:

a) $O(p \supset q)$, the so-called prima facie duty (obligation)

b) $p \supset O(q)$, the so-called absolute duty (obligation)

In the first case the implication is represented in the context of a deontically perfect world, therefore in such a world it is not possible to realise *p* and not bring about *q*. However, if a conflict of duty occurs, and we are no longer in a deontically perfect world, then the obligation to do q may be overruled by other obligations.

In the second case, whether or not we are in a deontically perfect world, if *p* is the case then an obligation *q* is created and cannot be overruled.

Using the EDA model we presume, by default, that we are always in a sub-ideal world, and we hide, in the axiologic component, the decision concerning which obligations to fulfil and which to violate, therefore we prefer to adopt a notion of commitment based on absolute duties (option b above). If an obligation is violated, even if justified by the existence of a higher priority obligation, we prefer to let the right to enforce the corresponding sanction be created. Then, the actual sanction enforcement may be prevented if the controller agent accepts the responsible agent justification.

Social commitments may be implicit. For example, consider the following rule and commitment: $r \supset p; p \supset O(q)$. In this case, although r is not directly related to q and is not part of any commitment, r existence brings about an obligation to do q.

Commitments may not be explicitly represented in the agent knowledge base, but could also instead exist only at the social level, being derived from social architectures or situation dynamics, where agents may adopt successive different social roles. This also applies to the particular case of commitments inherent to organisational roles.

An important observation is that behavioural norms, which are essentially social commitments implicitly accepted by an agent α in favour of the contextual social group (information field where the norm is valid), may not be to the immediate benefit of the agent, but since they bring a benefit for the social group to which the agent belongs there is an indirect benefit for the agent that must be accounted for in rational terms, *e.g.* by evaluation norms represented in the axiologic component of the EDA model.

Furthermore, the maximization of social utility is translated into the costs of sanctions attached to the violation of social norms, which constitutes an additional factor relevant to the local utility evaluation of a rational agent. This mechanism is a way to circumvent the bounded rationality of social agents, which is unavoidable in any kind of social system not totally deterministic.

3.3 Social Commitments vs Psychological Commitments

According to our model, whilst social commitments are related to and justified in terms of social obligations, psychological commitments are related to and justified in terms of individual goals.

A social commitment is a notion that represents the obligation of one agent to act in a certain way and the corresponding right of a second agent to sanction its eventual violation; a psychological commitment is a notion that involves only one agent and that represents an epistemic entrenchment (Gardenförs, 1988): a meta-level notion involving the agent's beliefs or intentions that do not involve any liability in the case of commitment violation.

Social commitments have a natural connection with individual rationality: they assist in negotiation processes. Agents never bargain about their psychological commitments. However, they may bargain about their social commitments, guided in the negotiation by the rational principle of utility maximization. For example, if agent α agrees to do something for agent β then necessarily α will receive compensation (although it may not come from β, it may not be quantifiable, and it may even not be external to α). Whether or not compensation is enough is determined by the axiologic component of the EDA model.

Ideally, an agent who has a social commitment also is psychologically committed to achieve it. However, given agent autonomy in goal selection, this need not be the case. Then again, the violation of a social commitment implies a sanction whose expected negative value must be considered in the decision. Psychological commitments do not generate social commitments even if they are a reason why a rational selfish agent accepts a social commitment.

The social relationship between the concerned agents is essential for enabling social commitments even if they enter into the commitment consciously and deliberately. Consequently, social commitments are fundamentally more complex than psychological commitments, suggesting that it is not trivial to map social commitments on to psychological commitments. Some researchers, however, have proposed formal definitions that assume that social commitments can be reduced to statements involving mutual beliefs among the participating agents (Cohen and Levesque, 1990; Grosz and Sidner, 1990). Mutual beliefs arise when each of a set of agents believes something, and believes that each of the other does so, and so on *ad infinitum*. This has a number of shortcomings (Singh, 1996):

- Given the assumption that agents know of each other and keep each other perfectly informed, mutual beliefs fail for systems whose membership is large and changing.
- It assumes that the all agents contribute the same in terms of what they know of the joint action, *i.e.* that the system is homogeneous and symmetric.
- Joint action becomes impossible when the mutual beliefs break down, which easily can happen in the context of unreliable communication channels.

We adopt a quite different direction, motivated by the work of Shoham (1993), defining an individual goal as a conditional obligation of α to do Q in favour of α the same way as we defined a social commitment as a conditional obligation of α to do Q in favour of β. Singh (1996) warns that this reduction can only succeed if an additional primitive of *self* is added, referring to the argument of the *essential indexical* where an agent's actions depend on whether it knows that the "other" party is itself. Both conceptually and in terms of implementation, this has not presented any problems in the EDA framework since this additional primitive of *self* is a natural and useful reflective notion to ensure that the EDA agent has an identity and is able to refer to the self.

An essential aspect of the EDA model is that the Deontic component is based on the notion of a *generalised goal* as a kind of obligation, that encompasses both social goals (social obligations) and individual goals (self obligations). This idea is inspired by Shoham's work (1993). Following a traditional designation in DAI, we designate those individual *generalised goals* that are inserted in the agenda as *achievement goals,* as in (Cohen and Levesque, 1990). Figure 3 describes the parallelism between mental and social constructs that lead to setting a goal in the agenda, and which justifies the adoption of the aforementioned generalised obligation. Here, p represents a proposition (world state). $B_\alpha(p)$ represents p as one of agent α 's beliefs. $O_\alpha^\beta(p)$ represents the obligation that α must see to it that p is true for β . $O_\alpha^\alpha(p)$ represents the interest that α has on seeing to it that p is true for itself – a kind of self-imposed obligation. In this diagram $p \in \mathrm{E}_\alpha(W, D)$ means, intuitively, that proposition p is one of the goals on α 's agenda.

Interest is one of the key notions that are represented in the EDA model, based on the combination of the deontic operator 'ought-to-be' (von Wright, 1951) and the agentive 'see-to-it-that' *stit* operator (Belnap, 1991). *Interests* and *Desires* are manifestations of *Individual Goals*. The differences between them are the following:

- *Interests* are individual goals of which the agent is not necessarily aware, typically at a high abstraction level, which would contribute to improve its overall utility. Interests may be originated externally, by other agents' suggestions, or internally, by inference: deductively (means-end analysis), inductively or abductively. One of the most difficult tasks for an agent is to become aware of its interest areas because there are too many potentially advantageous world states, making the full utility evaluation of each potential interest impossible, given the limited reasoning capacity of any agent.
- *Desires* are interests that the agent is aware of. However, they may not be achievable and may even conflict with other agent goals; the logical translation indicated in the figure, $O_\alpha^\alpha(p) \wedge B_\alpha(O_\alpha^\alpha(p))$, means that desires are goals that agent α ought to pursue for itself and that it is aware of. However, the agent has not yet decided to commit to it, in a global perspective, *i.e.* considering all other possibilities. In other words, desires become intentions only if they are part of the preferred extension of the normative agent EDA model (Filipe, 2000).

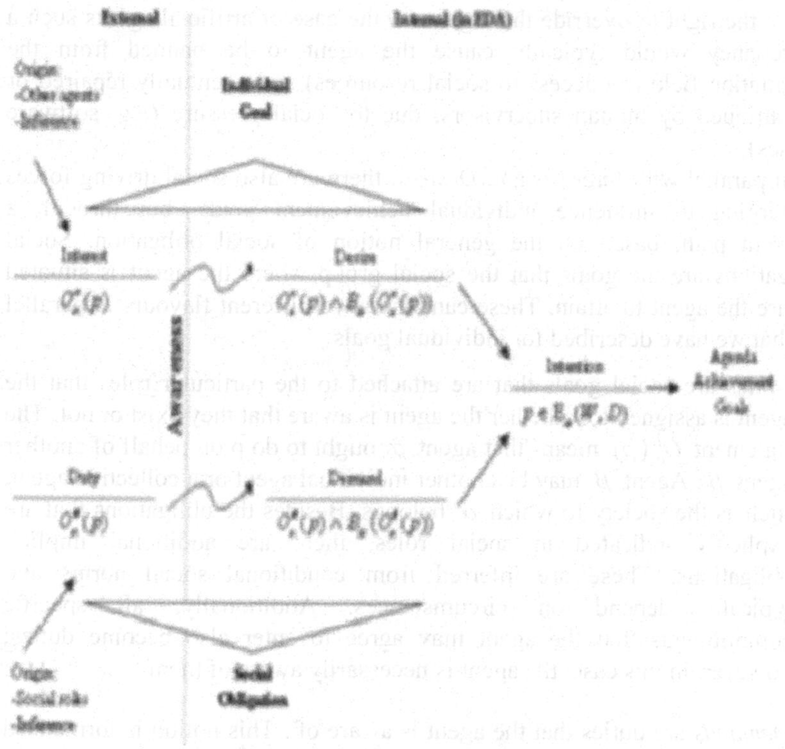

Figure 4. Social and Individual goals parallelism in the EDA model.

It is important to point out the strong connection between these deontic concepts and the axiologic component. All notions indicated in the figure should be interpreted from the agent perspective, *i.e.* values assigned to *interests* are determined by the agent. Eventually, external agents may consider a particular goal (*interest*) as having a positive value for the agent and yet the agent himself may decide otherwise. That is why *interests* are considered here to be the set of all goals to which the agent would assign a positive utility, but which it may not be aware of. In that case the responsibility for the *interest* remains with the external agent.

Not all interests become desires but all desires are agent interests. This may seem contradictory with a situation commonly seen in human societies of agents acting in *others' best interests,* sometimes even against their desires: that is what parents do for their children. However, this does not mean that the agent's desires are not seen as positive by the agent; it only shows that the agent may have a deficient axiologic system (by way of its information field standards) and in that case the social group may give other agents the right to override that agent. In the case of artificial agents such a discrepancy would typically cause the agent to be banned from the information field (no access to social resources) and eventually repaired or discontinued by human supervisors, due to social pressure (*e.g.* software viruses).

In parallel with *Interests* and *Desires*, there are also social driving forces converging to influence individual achievement goals, but through a different path, based on the general notion of social obligation. Social obligations are the goals that the social group where the agent is situated require the agent to attain. These can also have different flavours in parallel to what we have described for individual goals.

- *Duties* are social goals that are attached to the particular roles that the agent is assigned to, whether the agent is aware that they exist or not. The statement $O_\alpha^\beta(p)$ means that agent α ought to do p on behalf of another agent β. Agent β may be another individual agent or a collective agent, such as the society to which α belongs. Besides the obligations that are explicitly indicated in social roles, there are additional implicit obligations. These are inferred from conditional social norms and typically depend on circumstances. Additionally, all specific commitments that the agent may agree to enter also become duties; however, in this case, the agent is necessarily aware of them.

- *Demands* are duties that the agent is aware of[3]. This notion is formalised by the following logical statement: $O_\alpha^\beta(p) \wedge B_\alpha(O_\alpha^\beta(p))$. Social demands motivate the agent to act but they may not be achievable and may even conflict with other agent duties; being autonomous, the agent may also decide that, according to circumstances, it is better not to fulfil a social demand, and rather, accept the corresponding sanction. Demands become intentions only if they are part of the preferred extension of the normative agent EDA model – see (Filipe, 2000 section 5.7) for details.

- *Intentions*: Whatever their origin (individual or social) intentions constitute a non-conflicting set of goals that are believed to offer the highest possible value for the concerned agent. Intentions are designated by some authors (Singh, 1990) as psychological commitments (to act). However, intentions may eventually (despite the agent sincerity) not actually be placed in the agenda, for several reasons:
    - They may be too abstract to be directly executable

[3] According to the Concise Oxford Dictionary, *demand* is "*an insistent and peremptory request, made as of right*". We believe this is the English word with the closest semantics to what we need.

- They may need to wait for their appropriate time of execution.
- They may be overridden by higher priority intentions.
- Required resources may not be ready.

4. COMMITMENT REPRESENTATION

4.1 Structure and Functional Properties

In the EDA model, the notion of commitment is the common, essential entity that underlies all the notions required to describe the goal-governed behaviour in the EDA model.

We need to consider commitments as first-class named entities, instead of just aliases of other deontic notions, because of their importance for modelling the social interaction of EDA agents. A commitment ξ_i is formally represented as a named generalised goal:

$\xi_i = O^{\beta/\chi}_{\alpha/\rho}(Q,\tau,\sigma) \supset O\,([\alpha\ stit: Q]$ in-time-window τ subject-to-sanction $\sigma)$

This can be read as: α (under the responsibility of ρ) has the goal of ensuring Q, in reply to a request of β (under the control of χ); α is the performing agent, β is the client that requested the service, χ is a controller agent – which Castelfranchi (1993) calls a witness, Singh (1996) calls a context, and we associate to the information field. ρ is the responsibility chain for α [4]; O is the standard deontic operator 'ought-to-be'; $[\alpha\ stit: Q]$ is an agency statement, saying that agent α sees-to-it-that proposition Q becomes true. This means that α will perform a plan to bring about Q in time window □, where □ is a time expression specifying the time window during which proposition Q is intended to be satisfied; □ may be specified in absolute time or relative to some event; □ indicates the sanction cost of violation.

If agent α is different from agent β then we have a social commitment; otherwise we have a psychological commitment. In the latter case there is no controller agent χ and the sanction σ is typically null (represented by $\varnothing$) with expected value zero. However it has been pointed out by Albert Alderson (2000, personal communication) that the case where the sanction is

[4] The responsibility chain is a list constituted by one (only if α is human) or more agents: if the performing agent is artificial then an human agent must ultimately be responsible for the commitment to service performance and may be brought to the scene if there is a breakdown during the service performance that the artificial agent is not able to handle satisfactorily.

not null may be interesting in discussing psychological situations (e.g. “the centre forward was angry with himself for not scoring the penalty”).

Using BNF, the syntactic structure of *commitment* is defined by the following 7-tuple:

```
<commitment> ::= Obligation <responsible>/< responsibility chain>
                 stit: <goal state>
                 <beneficiary>/<controller>
                 <time-window>
                 <sanction>
<responsible> ::= <agent>
<responsibility chain> ::= <human agent> | <agent>/<human agent>
<beneficiary> ::= <agent>
<controller> ::= <agent>
<agent> ::= <human agent> | <artificial agent> | <abstract agent>
<abstract agent> ::= <role>
<time window> ::= [<time>, <time>]
<sanction> ::= <action> | ∅
```

Besides its structural properties, commitments have the following functional properties:

- *Type*: there are two basic commitment types, according to sources:
    - *Individual* commitments: if it corresponds to an individual goal.
    - *Social* commitment: if <in favour of> is another agent.
- *Epistemic state*: a commitment may be *known* of the agent or not. If a commitment is not in the EDA agent model then it necessarily is an Interest or a Duty. Since we use an auto-epistemic logic, $O^{\beta/\chi}_{\alpha/\rho}(Q,\tau,\sigma) \Box B(O^{\beta/\chi}_{\alpha/\rho}(Q,\tau,\sigma))$ *i.e.*, an agent knows about its commitments.
- *Deontic state*: a known commitment may be *preferred* or not, according to the agent axiologic component. If a commitment is preferred it becomes an intention.
- *Validity*: a commitment is *valid* if its terms are considered acceptable by the controller agent, who is normally the social group to which belong both the <responsible> and the <in favour of> agents.

- *Activation state*: a commitment may be *active* or inactive, according to the semantic value of its pre-conditions. A commitment is active if $(p \supset O(q)) \wedge p$.

4.2 Operations on Commitments

We define the following elementary operations on commitments, extending a list of operations proposed in (Singh, 1996):

- Create
- Release
- Modify
- Inspect

Each of these four operations yields a social action. Below we analyse the social impact of each operation.

4.2.1 Create

This operation produces an explicit commitment, which is stored in the agents' knowledge bases or at an IFS in the inter-subjective zone (typically as part of a contract). This operation may be invoked by agents or by norms. As will be shown below there are also commitments that are implicit in social norms; when such a commitment is instantiated it becomes explicit and acquires an identity (is created).

However, the most frequent situation is to establish a commitment as a result of a request. Agent β (the initiator) makes a request/proposal to agent α (the responder), who can then take one of three decisions:

1. Accept the request,
2. Counter-propose to accept the request with modifications,
3. Reject the request.

Figure 5 shows some typical scenarios for establishing a commitment, using simplified role-activity diagrams. The initiator is the beneficiary agent and the responder is the responsible agent.

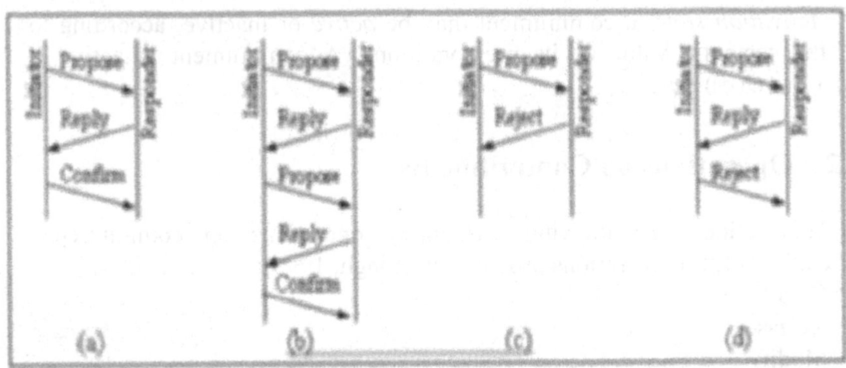

Figure 5. Scenarios for establishing a commitment (Hagg, 1998)

When commitments are created by agents, there are two possibilities: either the commitment is shared between the two concerned agents or it is kept centrally at an official *information field server*.

- If the commitment is shared then it requires that both the responsible agent and the beneficiary agent know of the commitment and have accepted it[5]. The commitment is kept simultaneously in both agents' EDA models, authenticated in such a way that no agent can modify its copy without the other's agreement.
- If the commitment is kept centrally then it exists only in one place (the IFS). None of the concerned agents can modify it without the other's agreement.

In the discussion above, both agents concerned (the responsible agent and the beneficiary) were aware of the commitment. However, it is possible that commitments exist without the knowledge of either concerned agent. The following example illustrates this situation:

- In a certain society S all workers are entitled to the services provided by a national health agency (NHA). Formally: $\forall_{\beta \in S, \alpha \in NHA} : Auth_{\beta}^{\alpha}(Q)$, where $Auth_{\beta}^{\alpha}(Q)$ means that β is authorised to obtain service Q from α, who in turn has an obligation to stit Q in favour of β, i.e. $\forall_{\beta \in S, \alpha \in NHA} : O_{\alpha}^{\beta}(Q)$.
- β_1 is a worker in S. Formally: $\beta_1 \in S$
- α_1 is an agent of NHA. Formally: $\alpha_1 \in NHA$.

From the statements above it is possible to infer that $O_{\alpha_1}^{\beta_1}(Q) \wedge Auth_{\beta_1}^{\alpha_1}(Q)$. However, unless agents α_1 and β_1 believe all three statements above, they

[5] This condition is considered trivial if both are the same agent, although the previous discussion about interest conflicts (section 6.3.1) becomes relevant in some cases.

do not recognise the existence of the inferred commitment. The question is: if an agent ignores norms or facts that support commitments where it is a concerned agent, is the commitment valid or not? We adopt the affirmative answer, which is coherent with the answer provided, for example, by most human legal systems, although this entails the acceptance of the omniscient agent concept, which we have declared to be an unrealistic assumption. We are facing a case of a commitment that is implicit but that can be inferred by an omniscient social agent who is aware of all shared norms and facts, therefore can instantiate that commitment at the social level.

4.2.2 Release

A commitment may be released in one of three ways (Hägg, 1998):

- The commitment is successfully fulfilled.
- The responsible agent cancels the commitment.
- The beneficiary agent cancels the commitment.

In the normal situation the commitment is released when the desired state Q is obtained. This corresponds to case 1, which includes as a special case a situation where the duration time for the commitment elapses, freeing the responsible agent from its responsibility.

However, it is possible that due to lack of resources or agent capability a commitment becomes impossible to be discharged (satisfactorily); furthermore, since agents are autonomous, it is possible that the responsible agent may not wish to discharge the commitment. Therefore, another way to terminate a commitment is by cancellation.

In real life, almost any kind of commitment can be cancelled. However, cancellations usually affect the responsible agent, in some way, who has cancelled the commitment, at least through the important social concepts of *trust* and *reputation.*

The responsible agent may cancel a commitment explicitly by sending an informing message to the beneficiary agent. When the beneficiary agent detects a violation the commitment is also automatically cancelled.

Although the beneficiary agent can conceptually get support from the controller agent of the violated commitment (typically the context group or society to which the agents belong) this controller agent may not be explicitly involved when sanction policies are explicitly defined in advance.

4.2.3 Modify

This operation could be thought of as a commitment cancellation followed by another commitment creation. However, the new commitment would have a different identity and, in the case of social commitments shared by several agents, this could lead to a cumbersome sequence of complex operations. An alternative is to just modify some aspect of the commitment keeping the commitment identification.

This operation requires mutual agreement of all agents involved. For example, if a set of agents had scheduled a meeting and later on one of them discovered that it could not attend then it must either cancel the commitment, or suggest a modification (*e.g.* change the starting time) but in the latter case it must obtain the agreement of all the other concerned agents – a two-phase commit, like in the distributed databases algorithm.

When modified, the commitment looses its validity certification, thus requiring the controller agent to re-evaluate it.

4.2.4 Inspect

This is an operation that is meaningful only when an agreement is stored in an information field server, and thus is not available locally, and an interested agent needs to access the details about the commitment object. This is not a social operation because it does not require more than one agent to perform it and its performance does not impact any agent other than the performer. However, it requires access rights (that are automatically granted to all agents involved in the commitment).

5. CONCLUSIONS

Commitments are a key element of the social world – the top level of the semiotics ladder. In this paper we have analysed the nature of commitments, showing that commitments can be interpreted in several different ways, including a psychological perspective and a social perspective. Yet, the two perspectives are not completely separable and we have shown how they can be related in agents that exhibit goal-governed behaviour.

This unification is captured by the EDA model – a normative model for designing goal-governed agents that is based on the social-psychology classification of norms. This model, meant for understanding and developing coordination mechanisms for intelligent multi-agent systems, incorporates many of the basic concepts of organisational semiotics and, in particular, the notion that commitments are the key to coordination. Using this model we discussed the representation of commitments, especially in the scope of information fields, and the kind of operations on commitments that are required for coordination.

One of the conclusions of our research is that it makes sense to use central repositories of shared knowledge for at least some semiotic levels, including the social world, which we designate as information field servers. These shared structures seem to provide an adequate way to centralise shared commitments, which need to be certified by a mutually trusted agent and thus cannot be kept in individual agents' knowledge bases only. This would lead to the study of the notion of trust, which is an important notion closely related to that of commitment, but which lies outside the scope of this paper.

We suggest that the theoretical framework presented in this paper provides a well-founded and promising method for developing coordination mechanisms for intelligent multi-agent systems. Some small experiments have been done, with the implementation of intelligent agents using this framework. Lastly more work needs to be done in this promising line of research.

REFERENCES

Belnap, N. 1991, Backwards and Forwards in the Modal Logic of Agency. Philosophy and Phenomenological Research, vol. 51.

Castelfranchi, C. 1993, Commitments: from Individual Intentions to Groups and Organisations. In Working Notes of AAAI'93 Workshop on AI and Theory of Groups and Organisations: Conceptual and Empirical Research, pp.35-41.

Cohen, P. and H. Levesque. 1990, Intention is Choice with Commitment. Artificial Intelligence, 42:213-261.

Conte, R., and C. Castelfranchi. 1995, Cognitive and Social Action, UCL Press, London.

Filipe, J. 2000, Normative Organisational Modelling Using Intelligent Multi-Agent Systems. Ph.D. thesis, University of Staffordshire, UK.

Gärdenfors, P. 1988, Knowledge in Flux. MIT Press, Cambridge, MA.

Grosz B. and C. Sidner. 1990, Plans for Discourse. In P. Cohen, J. Morgan and M. Pollack (Eds.), Intentions in Communication, pp.417-444, MIT Press.

Habermas, J. 1984, The Theory of Communicative Action: Reason and Rationalization of Society. Polity Press. Cambridge.

Hägg, S. 1998, Commitment in Agent Cooperation, Applied to Agent-Based Simulation. In Proceedings of the 5th International Conference on Intelligent Autonomous Systems, IAS-5, Sapporo, Japan.

Hintikka, J. 1970, Deontic Logic and its Philosophical Morals. In Models for Modalities, Selected Essays, pp. 184-214, D. Reidel Publishing Co., Dordrecht.

Shoham, Y. 1993, Agent-Oriented Programming. Artificial Intelligence, 60, pp.51-92, Elsevier Science Publishers.

Simon, H. 1996, The Sciences of the Artificial (3rd Edition). MIT Press. Cambridge, Massachussets, USA.

Singh, M. 1990, Towards a Theory of Situated Know-How. 9th European Conference on Artificial Intelligence.

Singh, M. 1996, Multiagent Systems as Spheres of Commitment. Proceedings of the International Conference on Multiagent Systems (ICMAS) - Workshop on Norms, Obligations and Conventions. Kyoto, Japan.

Stamper, R. 1973, Information in Business and Administrative Systems. John Wiley & Sons.

Stamper, R. 1996, Signs, Information, Norms and Systems. In Holmqvist et al. (Eds.), Signs of Work, Semiosis and Information Processing in Organisations, Walter de Gruyter, Berlin, New York.

Stamper, R. 1996, Signs, Information, Norms and Systems. In Holmqvist et al. (Eds.), Signs of Work, Semiosis and Information Processing in Organisations, Walter de Gruyter, Berlin, New York.

Wright, G. von. 1951, Deontic Logic. Mind, 60, pp.1-15.

Chapter 6

INFORMATION SYSTEM DESIGN AS A PERSISTENT MULTI-VIEWPOINTS REQUIREMENTS ELICITATION PROCESS

Pierre-Jean Charrel
Université Toulouse 2 GRIMM & Institut de Recherche en Informatique de Toulouse, 21 Allée Antonio Machado, F-31958 Toulouse Cedex 9, France. Tel: (33) 561 50 39 84. Fax: (33) 561 12 41 73. Email: charrel@univ-tlse2.fr. France.

Abstract: Requirements Engineering, as the first stage of any system design project, often implies that respecting diversity during the upstream stages is an unavoidable feature of the design process. In the field of Information Systems, the ability to evolve is currently a pivotal quality of its computerised components. In order to introduce the necessary flexibility of any current organisation in its Information System, a framework is presented to view an Information System in a persistently evolving design state space where requirements are continuously elicited. The framework considers the Information System in terms of a system of signs. Viewed from this semiotic angle, each actor is a stakeholder of a particular viewpoint on the Information System and gives it some sense. We also introduce a new actor, the Requirements Semiotic Engineer, whose task is to organize the elicitation of the other actors' requirements. A six-stage method is then sketched to organize the information system so that it is similar to a persistent multi-viewpoint requirements elicitation process.

Key words: Information System Design, Viewpoint, Semiotics Engineer, Requirement Elicitation Process

1. INTRODUCTION

System Engineering defines the early phase of a system designing project as the Requirements Engineering activity which elaborates what the future system must do. Its goal is to obtain a complete and consistent set of the

K. Liu (ed.),
Virtual, Distributed and Flexible Organisations: Studies in Organisational Semiotics, 103–118.

system's features (Pohl, 1993). We share the opinion of other researchers in the Requirements Engineering field that respecting diversity is an unavoidable feature of the designing process (Easterbrook, Finkelstein, Kramer & Nuseibeh, 1994, Finkelstein & Fuks, 1989, Kontonya & Sommerville, 1992, Leite & Freeman, 1991, Leite, 1988, Mullery, 1979, Nuseibeh, Kramer & Finkelstein, 1994, Zave, 1997).

A typical Requirements Engineering process is constituted by the following tasks (cf. Figure 1) which are organized in a loop:

- requirements elicitation: discovery, collection, analysis of users' and other actors' needs;
- requirements analysis: translation into elementary requirements techniques, technical requirements analysis, requirements categorisation, synthesis;
- requirements verification and validation: individual analysis of the requirements quality, checking of consistency and completeness (client, other actors, technical);
- modification: correction, evolution of requirements due to other system engineering activities;
- allocation: decomposition and allocation of requirements to system components (in parallel with system design);
- project management (preparation, control).

In Requirements Engineering, eliciting requirements is one of the basic issues studied. It involves the collection of all information available concerning what users know about exactly what they want the system to be and to do. In the field of the Information Systems, users' needs evolve between the first interview and the time when they use the system: users change, the environment of the organisation and the organisation itself change. "There are very good reasons why clients often do not, or cannot, know exactly what they need; they may want to see models, explore alternatives, and envision new possibilities" (Goguen, Linde, 1994).

We have already considered that the requirements elicitation process of a System *"to be"*, according to the Viewpoint Paradigm, is the multi viewpoint integration process which produces the sense of this System viewed as a particular Object (Charrel, 2002a). In this paper, the Viewpoint Paradigm aims at considering an Information System as though it were a persistent requirements elicitation process, where each relevant Actor has "to find or give sense" to it, despite the evolution of his / her intentions. This forms part of the dynamic – living – feature of an Information System.

Section 2 presents the Viewpoint Paradigm and its semiotic source. Section 3 depicts the close links between signs and the notions of Viewpoint and <X>-Correlation between Viewpoints. Section 4 deals with the Graph of Viewpoints which traces all the Viewpoints and all their pertinent relations that occur during the requirements elicitation process of an Information System. At last, section 5 put forward the interest of a new Actor, member of the Information System who will warrant the evolution of the Graph of Viewpoints: the Requirements Semiotic Engineer.

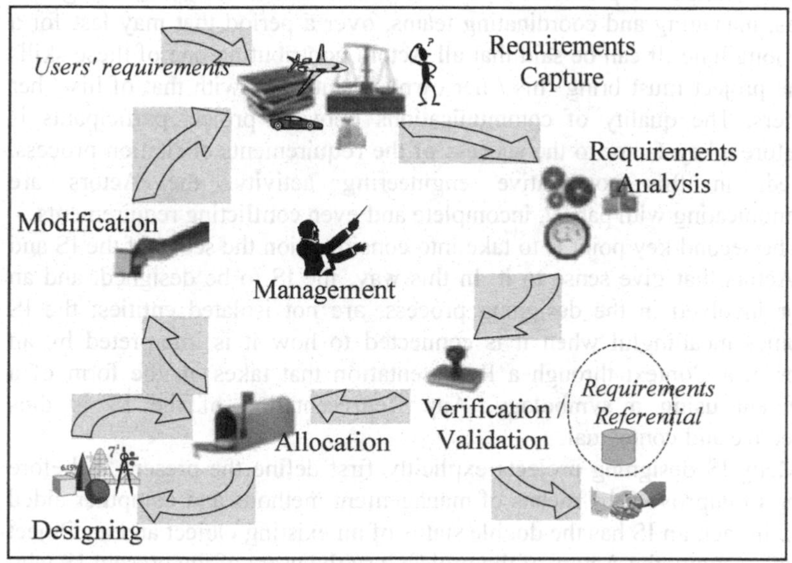

Figure 1. *Requirements engineering loop process (adapted from GTIE, 2001)*

2. THE VIEWPOINT PARADIGM

The sense of an object to be created is the integration of the viewpoints exerted on it.

This statement founds what we have already called the Viewpoint Paradigm, which reconciles semiotics and the designing process of any object that is an artefact. The Viewpoint concept is central to two processes, the process whereby Actors in the requirements elicitation process communicate with each other and the process whereby the Object "to be" achieves sense.

In the context of designing an Information System (IS), the integration of the future users into the system is necessary to warrant the success of the project. In general, a new IS replaces an old one, with the same users but with a new organisation which changes their daily schedule. Users must accept the new organisation before accepting the new IS. In other words, the new IS is a success if all actors can “give sense” to it. One key point arises out of the following observation: the activity of eliciting requirements brings into play a great many technical, organisational and financial skills in order to find solutions to problems such as technical constraints, controlling cost prices, managing and coordinating teams, over a period that may last for a very long time. It can be said that all Actors contributing one of these skills to the project must bring "his / her own" IS into line with that of his / her partners. The quality of communications between project participants is therefore a key factor to the success of the requirements elicitation process. Indeed, in this cooperative engineering activity, the Actors are communicating with partial, incomplete and even conflicting requirements.

The second key point is to take into consideration the sense of the IS and the Actors that give sense to it. In this way, the IS to be designed, and an Actor involved in the designing process, are not isolated entities: the IS becomes meaningful when it is connected to how it is interpreted by an Actor in a Context through a Representation that takes on the form of a statement using a symbology. Any Representation of the IS is thus subjective and contextual.

Many IS designing projects explicitly first define the present IS before trying to improve it by means of management methods and computer aided tools. In fact, an IS has the double status of an existing Object and an Object "to be". Among the Actors of the project, are the users of the present IS who produce requirements which are often expressed as improvements of the existing system: they express *differences* that should be implemented in the system "to be".

These statements suggest that the requirements elicitation of an IS could be organized as endless controls loop which:

- controls the two previous communication and meaning processes;
- does not end when design begins, but persists as long as the system is alive;
- emphasizes requirements expression in natural language by all the relevant Actors, especially users and designers.

This position is conducive to a global – systemic – view of the IS, the Actors, the Representations and the requirements elicitation process: it identifies the sense of an IS and the result of the process by which it is designed.

3. VIEWPOINTS AND SIGNS IN THE REQUIREMENTS ELICITATION PROCESS

Reconciling the Viewpoint notion with semiotics leads us first of all to a representation of the basic concept of Viewpoint and the relationships between Viewpoints.

3.1 A Viewpoint as a situated sign

Let us explicitly extend Peirce's sign triad figure < Object, Expression, Content > (Peirce, 1932), to the Actor, who uses or produces the sign, i.e. who uses or produces the Expression – the signifier – with Content – the Signified – to give sense to the Object and to the Context – the conditions in which the sign is used or produced (cf. Figure 2).

A Viewpoint implements the conditions for an Actor A in order to interpret a sign, i.e. to give sense to an Object O, in a Context C: it is defined by the Object about which the interpretation is made, the Actor making it, the Expression E and Content CO of the interpretation of the Object by the Actor, and the Context C in which this interpretation is made.

A Viewpoint thus comprises five poles: the Actor, as a "member" of the Information System, holds at least one Viewpoint, in the Context of which he/she uses or produces a sign, i.e. an interpretation of the Object to be; the Object is interpreted by an Actor exerting a Viewpoint on it; the Context defines the condition governing the way the Actor exerts his/her Viewpoint, e.g. the place from which the Viewpoint is exerted, the moment in time it is exerted, the tool used by the Actor to exert his/her Viewpoint. The Expression is a statement, formalised in a symbolic system, that is attached to the Object by the Actor within the Context of the Viewpoint to express his/her interpretation of the Object; the Content is the sense given within the Context by the Actor to the Object by means of the Expression.

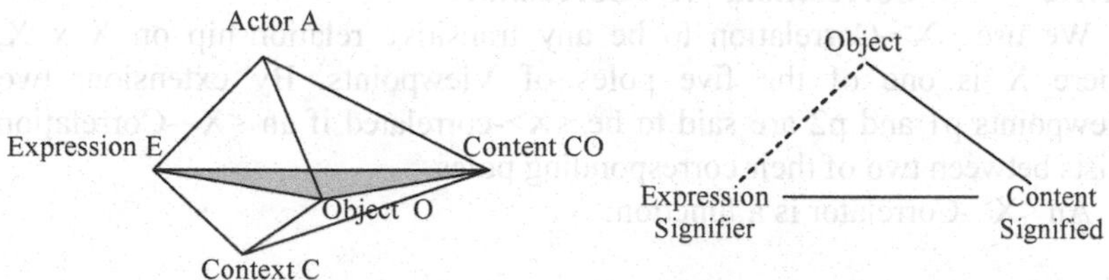

Figure 2. *Viewpoint and Peirce's triadic sign*

When the symbolic system used in the Expression is a formal one, i.e. when semantics are associated with each statement, the two poles Expression and Content merge as a Representation R. Since the early 80s, studies about IS have invited users and designers to share such Representations expressed by the use of graphic notations (Entity-relationship diagrams, data flow diagrams, use cases...).

Thus a Viewpoint comprises Peirce's sign triad and namely the Actor and the Context: who and in what conditions a sign is produced. There is a strong analogy with what W. Clancey defines as "situated" (Clancey, 1993): "...not rejecting the value of planning and representations in everyday life, rather seeking to explain how they are created and used in already coordinated activity; not claiming that representing does not occur internally, in the individual brain (e.g., imagining a scene or speaking silently to ourselves), rather seeking to explain how perceiving and comprehending are co-organized...".

Thanks to this analogy, a Viewpoint appears as a *situated sign* in the requirements elicitation phase of the Requirements Engineering activity: the Expression is created by an Actor who has an Object in mind. This Expression is related to a given Context and is reified by a Content which can be another expression.

3.1.1.1 Universe of Viewpoints

The Universe P of Viewpoints is the Cartesian product:

P = A x O x C x E x CO

in which A, O, C, E, CO are respectively the aggregate of Actors, Objects, Contexts, Expressions, and Contents, each one being referred to as a pole of the Universe. We use dotted notation to designate one component of a Viewpoint. For example, p.a is Actor a of Viewpoint p in the Universe P.

For the following definitions, the Universe is implicit. In fact, it is the reference from which all the Viewpoints can be defined.

3.1.1.2 <X>-Correlation, <X>-Correlator

We use <X>-Correlation to be any transitive relationship on X x X, where X is one of the five poles of Viewpoints. By extension, two Viewpoints p1 and p2 are said to be <X>-correlated if an <X>-Correlation exists between two of their corresponding poles.

An <X>-Correlator is a function:

cr: X → X

where X is one of the poles.

The transitive closure of each <X>-Correlator cr defines an <X>-Correlation:

$$\{(x, cr(x)), x \in X\}$$

This notion is extended to Viewpoints in the same way as an <X>-Correlation.

3.1.1.3 Examples

The relationship "is the department chief" is an <A>-Correlator; "the work organisation" is an <A>-Correlation over all Viewpoints; if the Expressions of Viewpoints p1 and p2 are two knowledge bases made of logical formulae, an <E>-Correlator can define the formulae of p2 deducible from the formulae of p1.

3.1.1.4 System of Viewpoints

A System of Viewpoints is defined as the couple:

$$S = < P, CR >$$

where P is a Universe of Viewpoints and CR is a set of <X>-Correlators defined on P.

The next section explores an analogical representation of the System of Viewpoints as a Graph.

4. THE REQUIREMENTS ELICITATION PROCESS AS A PARTIALLY ORDERED GRAPH OF VIEWPOINTS

According to the Viewpoint Paradigm, the process whereby requirements are collectively elicited gives rise over time to a partially ordered subset of <X>-Correlated Viewpoints which constitute the nodes of a partially ordered graph, the edges of which are the different <X>-Correlations between the Viewpoints.

Reasoning both about Viewpoints and the requirements elicitation process facilitates the discovery and management of all significant differences which are the sources of sense. Here, the pole Context C of all Viewpoints is a two-dimensioned entity <C.T, C.RE>: C.T represents Time and C.RE the Remainder elements of the interpretation context. The first and last nodes of the Graph of Viewpoints respectively relate to two Viewpoints whose Actor is the project's customer, and the intermediate nodes are the various Viewpoints exerted throughout the process (cf. Figure 3).

For the initial Viewpoint i of the graph, the Object is the assignment on the Actor-customer's purchase order, the Context is the instant when the project is launched, the Expression is the entire set of written documents produced by the Actor-customer for the project team and the Content is the formal acknowledgement of the Expression.

For the final Viewpoint of the graph, the Object is the collection of requirements produced – and all knowledge acquired on its maintenance and operation –, the Expression is the integration of all the Expressions of the Viewpoints in the final Context, and the Content then represents the formal acceptance by the customer of the Object. The process is complete when the final Viewpoint of the customer Actor is able to prevail: at last, the Object acquires its sense for all the Actors involved in the requirements elicitation process, who exerted a Viewpoint on it.

When the process is complete, the Graph of Viewpoints traces both the communications and the meaning process that constitute the final collection of requirements. The Graph of Viewpoints constitutes a kind of referential repository for analysing and understanding the requirements elicitation process. No particular formalisation is required for the poles of the Viewpoints: either for Expressions, or for Objects. They may refer to texts or diagrams or any other media. The key point is the collection of relationships between the elements which either take place inside one Viewpoint or are mediated via an <X>-Correlation. In particular:

- the sub-graph defined by the projection of the Graph of Viewpoints on the triad Object-Expression-Content <O,E,CO> poles deploys all the signs produced during the process;
- the sub-graph defined by the projection of the Graph of Viewpoints on each triple of poles Actor-Expression-Context.Time <A, E, C.T> is a rough trace of the activity of Actor Ai during the process.

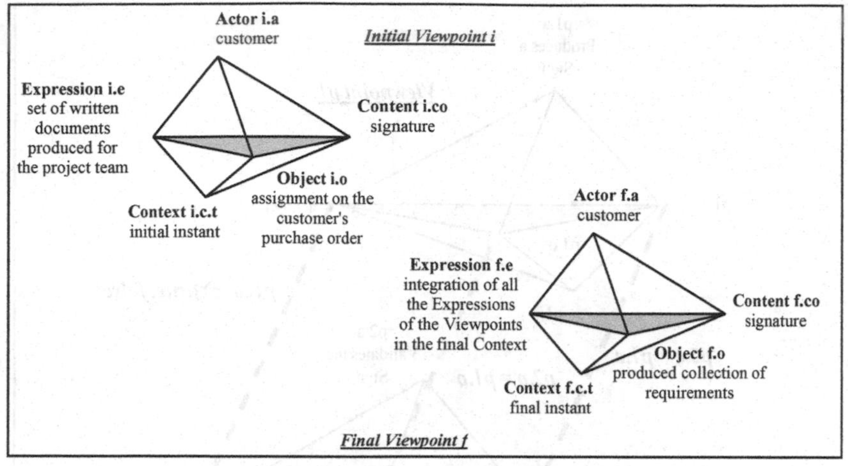

Figure 3. *Initial and final nodes of the Graph of Viewpoints of a requirements elicitation process*

In the Graph of Viewpoints, the level of observation may be zoomed towards simple <X>-Correlations to identify the tiniest events that occur during the process. The following subsections show some examples.

4.1.1 Integration of elements in a whole

"Integrate components in a whole" is an <O,E>-Correlation which matches a source tuple of Viewpoints vi = <ai, c, o, ei, co> and a targeted Viewpoint w = <a, c, o, e, co> where the Actor a is responsible for the integration, o is the Object composed, e is the integration of all the partial Expressions ei, c defines the context of the integration (time, tools used...) and co is a truth value which either validates or invalidates the integration.

4.1.2 Sign Validation

"Validate an Expression" is an <O, E, CO>-Correlator which links the Viewpoint p1 of the Actor who produces the Expression to be validated and the Viewpoint p2 of an Actor who validates it. The <CO>-component is the Boolean function: p1.co → {true, false}, and the <O> and <E> components are identities (cf. Figure 4).

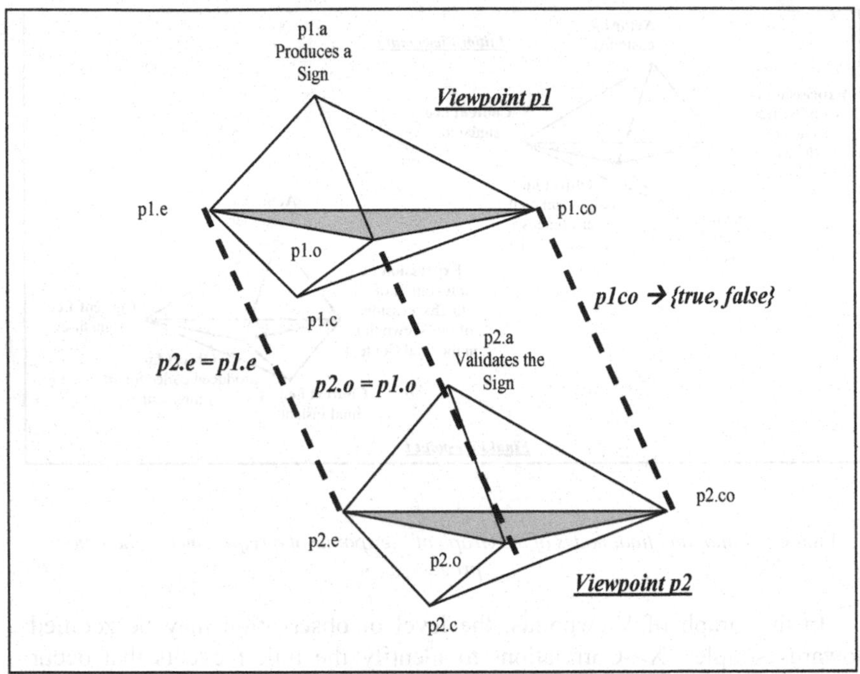

Figure *4.* An < E >-Correlator "Validate a Sign

4.1.3 Versioning

Partial Objects (versions, schemata, mock-ups...) are created throughout the requirement elicitation process. They are assembled and modified in order to constitute the final body of requirements. Let us consider the history of the different versions of such an Object produced by the same Actor during the process. Each version is related to one Viewpoint, and all these Viewpoints are linked to each other by <A,O,C>-Correlators, where the <A> and <O> components are the identity relationship, and the <C.T> component is the sequence t → t + 1 (cf. Figure 5).

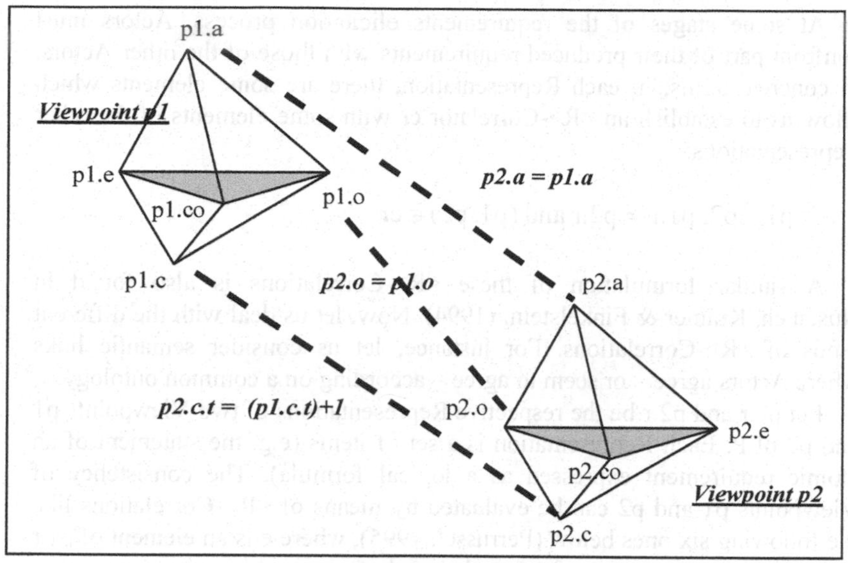

Figure 5. An Information System Designing as a Persistent Multi-Viewpoints Requirements Elicitation Process

4.1.4 Management of Consistency between Requirements

The Viewpoint Paradigm generates specific Viewpoint meta models and Correlation meta models (Charrel, 2002a, Charrel, 2002b, Charrel, Perrussel, Sibertin-Blanc, 2003). The following meta model uses a logical framework to address the management of consistency between requirements by avoiding conflicts.

The Viewpoint Paradigm rids us of the constraint of having a permanent and total consistency between the different Representations. The tolerance of inconsistencies allows us not to prematurely limit the requirements elicitation process, and, for example, can allow a better investigation of alternatives. In contrast with a centralized process whose goal is to prevent any inconsistency in the requirements, the goal in this process is to manage the inconsistencies. These characteristics are also found in the ideas put forward in Easterbrook, Finkelstein, Kramer & Nuseibeh, (1994), Nuseibeh, Kramer & Finkelstein, (1994). Thus the Requirements expression are the relationships between different Representations, i.e. the <R>-Correlations of the Viewpoint Paradigm. Here, we focus on the Expression of particular <R>-Correlations.

At some stages of the requirements elicitation process, Actors must confront part of their produced requirements with those of the other Actors. In concrete terms, in each Representation, there are some elements which allow us to establish an <R>-Correlator cr with some elements of the other Representations:

$$\forall p1, \exists p2, p1.r \neq p2.r \text{ and } (p1, p2) \in cr$$

A similar formulation of these <R>-Correlations is also found in Nuseibeh, Kramer & Finkelstein, (1994). Now, let us deal with the different kinds of <R>-Correlations. For instance, let us consider semantic links where Actors agree – or seem to agree – according on a common ontology.

Let p1.r and p2.r be the respective Representations of two Viewpoints p1 and p2 of P. Each Representation is a set of items (e.g. the statement of an atomic requirement expressed as a logical formula). The consistency of Viewpoints pl and p2 can be evaluated by means of <R>-Correlations like the following six ones below (Perrussel, 1995), where e is an element of p1.r and e' is an element of p2.r deduced from e by means of some transformations:

$$(p1, p2) \in R1 \text{ iff } p1.r \neq \phi \Rightarrow p2.r \neq \phi;$$

if the Representation p1.r exists then the Representation p2.r must also exist;

$$(p1, p2) \in R2 \text{ iff } e \in p1.r \Rightarrow p2.r \neq \phi;$$

if an element e is present in p1.r then p2.r is not empty;

$$(p1, p2) \in R3 \text{ iff } e \in p1.r \Rightarrow e' \in p2.r;$$

if an element e is present in p1.r then another element e' must be present in p2.r;

$$(p1, p2) \in R4 \text{ iff } e \in p1.r \Rightarrow e \in p2.r;$$

if an element e is present in p1.r then e must also be present in p2.r.

$$(p1, p2) \in R5 \text{ iff } e \in p1.r \Rightarrow e' \notin p2.r;$$

if an element e is present in p1.r then another element e' must not be present in p2.r;

$$(p1, p2) \in R6 \text{ iff } e \in p1.r \Rightarrow e \notin p2.r;$$

if an element e is present in p1.r then e must not be present in p2.r.

These general rules allow us to detect inconsistencies. These rules represent templates which can be instantiated according to the formalism of any CASE tool.

5. THE REQUIREMENTS SEMIOTICS ENGINEER

According to the Viewpoint Paradigm, the Graph of Viewpoints is the trace of the signification of the IS: all the Actors of the IS are present in the Graph of Viewpoints because they express a Viewpoint on the System or a part of it, at least once.

When the collection of requirements of the future IS is complete, the IS is implemented using CASE tools which generate forms, databases schemas, etc. But the Graph still exists as a referential and can contribute the revision process of the IS. This skill corresponds to a pivotal Actor who will feed the Graph of Viewpoints. This Actor belongs to the set of Actors involved in the process and has a semiotic skill.

The next time a revision of the IS is planned, the implementation can be automated from the revised Graph. Moreover, such revisions can be implemented immediately if the consequences on all the IS are slight, i.e. if the <X>-Correlation surrounding the concerned signs is not embedded in an over dense sub-graph. The Viewpoint Paradigm and its related Viewpoint Graph render all the Actors responsible for their *intentions* towards the System. It raises up the issue of distribution and flexibility because it renders the IS reactive to the Actors' and to the organisation's needs.

The requirements elicitation process can no longer be a first stage in a design process, but rather an endless loop activity. Figure 6 sketches the six steps of a design process. It includes a special requirements discovery step from written documents that we discussed earlier (Charrel, 2002a):

Step 1: Viewpoint elicitation: ontology capture and translation with text classification tools.

Step 2: Infometrical analysis: Implementation of the Infometrical Correlation.

Step 3: Completeness control of the requirements elicitation process.

Step 4: Implementation of the Consistency Management <R>-Correlation: organisation of the requirements.
Step 5: Code Generation.
Step 6: Evolution Control.

One direction for future work is to identify the properties of the Graph of Viewpoints in order to facilitate its administration. This graph seems very similar to Goguen's sign systems the definition of which is the following (Goguen, 2001):

(1) A set S of sorts for signs, not necessarily disjoint;
(2) A partial ordering of S, called the subsort relation and denoted as <=;
(3) A set V of data sorts, for information about signs, such as colours, locations, and truth values;
(4) a partial ordering of sorts by level, so that data sorts are lower than sign sorts, and such that there is a unique sort at the maximal level – called the top sort;
(5) a set Cn of level n constructors used to build level n signs from signs at levels n or less, and written r: s1…skd1…dl → s, indicating that its "ith" argument must have sort si, its "jth" parameter data sort dj, and its result sort is s; constants c → s are also allowed;
(6) a priority (partial) ordering on each Cn;
(7) some relations and functions on signs;
(8) a set A of sentences, in the sense of logic – called axioms – that constrain the possible signs.

An interesting challenge is simulation: finding a form to present the Graph of Viewpoints to all the Actors so that they themselves can evaluate the consequences of a new requirement. Socio-psychological skills must then be added to the Requirements Semiotics Engineer. It will also be necessary to organize experiments on such simulations to improve the requirements elicitation process in a concrete way. The expected result is an Information System which is organised as an autonomous system with a persistently evolutionary component.

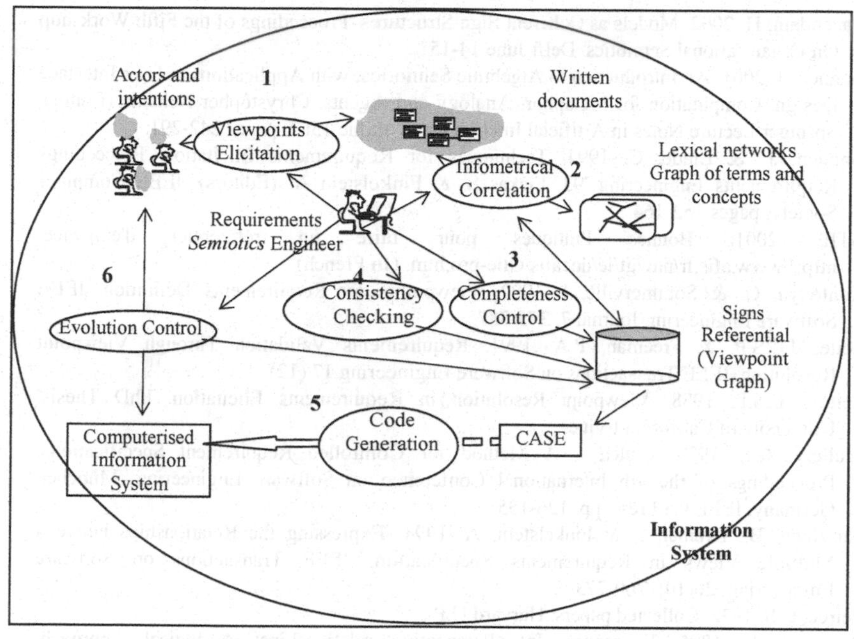

Figure 6. An Information System Designing as a Persistent Multi-Viewpoints Requirements Elicitation Process

REFERENCES

Charrel, P.J. 2002a. Viewpoints for Knowledge Management in System Design. Proceedings of the Fifth Workshop On Organisational Semiotics. Delft June 14-15.

Charrel, P.J. 2002b. The Viewpoint Paradigm: A Semiotic Based Approach for the Intelligibility of a Cooperative Designing Process. Australian Journal of Information Systems. Vol. 10, n° 1.. pp. 3-19.

Charrel, P.J., Perrussel, L., Sibertin-Blanc C. 2003. "Multi-Viewpoint Requirement Engineering for Lyee Methodology. Proceedings of The 13thEuropean Japanese Conference On Information Modelling and Knowledge Bases. Kitakyush, Japan, June 3-6, (to appear).

Clancey, J. 1993. Situated Action: A Neuropsychological Interpretation; Response to Vera and Simon. Cognitive Science. 17:87-107. 1993.

Easterbrook, S.M., Finkelstein, A., Kramer, J. & Nuseibeh, B. 1994. Co–ordinating Distributed Viewpoints: The Anatomy of Consistency Check. Proceedings of Concurrent Engineering Research and Applications. West Bloofield USA.

Finkelstein, A. & Fuks, H. 1989. Multi–party Specification. Proceedings of the 5th Workshop on Software Specification and Design, Pittsburgh. IEEE C.S. Press.

Gazendam, H. 2002. Models as Coherent Sign Structures. Proceedings of the Fifth Workshop On Organisational Semiotics. Delft June 14-15.

Goguen, J. 2001. An Introduction to Algebraic Semiotics, with Applications to User Interface Design. Computation for Metaphor, Analogy and Agents. Chrystopher Nehaniv (Editor). Springer Lecture Notes in Artificial Intelligence. volume 1562. pages 242-291.

Goguen, J., & Linde, C. 1994. Techniques for Requirements Elicitation. Proceedings Requirements Engineering '93. Fickas S. & Finkelstein A. (Editors). IEEE Computer Society. pages 152-164.

GTIE 2001. Bonnes Pratiques pour faire un référentiel d'exigence. http://www.afis.fr/nav/gt/ie/docafis/Gtie-pro.htm. (In French)

Kontonya, G. & Sommerville, I. 1992. Viewpoints for Requirements Definition. IEEE Software Engineering Journal 7, 375-387.

Leite, J.C.S.P. & Freeman, P.A. 1991. Requirements Validation Through Viewpoint Resolution. IEEE Transactions on Software Engineering 17 (12).

Leite, J.C.S.P. 1988. Viewpoint Resolution in Requirements Elicitation. PhD Thesis. University of California Irvine.

Mullery, G.P. 1979. CORE – A Method for Controlled Requirement Specifications. Proceedings of the 4th International Conference on Software Engineering. München Germany. IEEE CS Press, pp. 126-135.

Nuseibeh, B., Kramer, J. & Finkelstein, A. 1994. Expressing the Relationships between Multiple Views in Requirements Specification. IEEE Transactions on Software Engineering, 20(10), 760-773.

Peirce, C.S. 1932. Collected papers. Harvard U.P

Perrussel, L. 1995. Expressing Inter-Perspective relationships: A logical Approach. Proceedings of APSEC '95, Brisbane, Australia, IEEE CS Press, December 1995.

Pohl, K. 1993. The Three Dimensions of Requirement Engineering, Proceedings of Software Engineering - ESEC '93, 4th European Engineering Conference. Garmish-Partenkirchen. Germany.

Zave, P. 1997. Classification of Research efforts in Requirement Engineering. Computing Surveys 29(4), 315-321.

Chapter 7

ORGANISATIONAL LEARNING IN COMPLEX ENVIRONMENTS

Aviation Safety as the Case Study

Elena Revilla & José Sánchez-Alarcos
Instituto de Empresa & Fundación EOI, Spain

Abstract: In this paper we will be analysing the effort made by many organisations concerning the design of technical and structural mechanisms with which to improve performance of work processes. However, improvement in rules and procedures seems to *backfire* leading to obstacles to the solution when unforeseen problems arise. Each new rule or device can prove to be a good way to handle a planned event (Reason, 1997) and, at the same time, it can prevent the reaction to an unplanned one. As a result of this process, the pace of improvement of many organisations has come to a halt or decreased. Technology-based development generates new events through unexpected interactions among parts of the system. Consequently, this kind of development reduces the capacity of the system to handle these new events. In order to explain this issue, we will use semiotics-related concepts and we will proceed as follows: In the first epigraph, we will analyse briefly the development of information technologies and the effects produced on organisations, especially on human-operator capacity. Then, we will study this situation in a specific industry -air transport- focusing our interest on safety-related issues. Finally, some conclusions can be drawn from this analysis for future organisational development.

Key words: Organisational evolution, semiotics, sense, complex environments, air safety

1. THEORETICAL BACKGROUND

Information and communication technologies together with detailed procedures have become an essential element for organisational development in recent years. From this point of view, an evolving system

K. Liu (ed.),
Virtual, Distributed and Flexible Organisations: Studies in Organisational Semiotics, 119–127.

acts as a machine. This machine needs to gather and process information and, supposedly, reflects an external reality as closely as possible. Information technologies have been very useful in obtaining these representations. In this respect, the definition of Varela (1988) of a computer as a device that manages symbols but only handles their physical shape and not their sense is relevant. This feature of information technologies leads to a lack of systems-capacity in the handling of unforeseen events. Therefore, these events should require human operators. However, information systems design is complex enough to become opaque for those operators who, in many situations, do not understand how these systems work.

Winograd and Flores (1987) show that "opacity of implementation is one of the key intellectual contributions of computer science" since every level of design can become independent from the one below, maintaining its own logic. This issue does not appear in mechanical systems. Mechanical systems are more complicated since every level of design has to be justified by the one below. This means that, if the required knowledge is present, a contingency can be traced to its origin in these kinds of systems. This does not happen in an information system. The opacity of implementation of information systems breaks up the logical chain into different levels of design. The hardware designer, the software designer and the operator live apart and they can become experts in their respective fields having no idea about the others' fields since they have become functionally independent.

When everything runs as planned, this blind-to-meaning model works fine. However, in situations where unplanned contingencies appear, the feasibility of dealing with them decreases if compared with the old mechanical systems. Reason (1997) explains this fact under his "SRK" model where "S" stands for Skill, "R" for Rules and "K" for Knowledge. Each character represents a specific level. Skill is the basic level and Knowledge is the top level in this model. An opaque system only allows its operators to reach the Rules Level since the opacity of its design makes it impossible for the operators to reach the Knowledge Level.

The model of five stages (Novice, Advanced Beginner, Competence, Proficiency and Expertise) by Dreyfus (1986) draws similar conclusions. For Dreyfus, the important thing to learn is the overall perspective we can build from recent events. If these events are hidden by the system, operators do not have the opportunity to reach the following learning stage.

Therefore, both models can prove to be useful in understanding a single concrete fact: Actions coming from the operators are channelled through systems that add their own inputs and select the information outputs. Since operators do not know how the system works internally, they lack the information required to know the real meaning of their actions. In the field of Knowledge Management, Choo and Bontis (2002) introduced the concepts of meaning and sense-making as important issues for the improvement and learning in organisations. In the field of Organisational Semiotics, Gazendam (2001) explains the importance of active exploration as a key for the operator to build a world model that allows its author to manage it. If the design of the system prevents active exploration and, therefore, access to the meaning of the activity, the introduction of new features to a system could transfer capacities from the operators to the technical part of the system instead of adding new capacities.

The loss of meaning makes the human operator act at the Skill and Rules Levels instead of using the Knowledge Level (Reason, 1997). Every new added feature could reinforce this process. Therefore, real improvement – viewing the system as a whole- is lower than expected since increases in technical capacity go together with decreases in human capacity: The technical model of development adds capacity to the system by extracting capacity from one of its components and transferring it to the other one. As a consequence, the capacities of the system that can be performed by technology are increased and the capacities that cannot be performed by technology but by its human operators are decreased.

Since information technologies do not have access to the meaning but to symbols (Varela, 1988), those activities requiring access to meaning –i.e., those events representing exceptions to the general rule and not included in the system design- could impose serious limitations on the operator. On the other hand, actions included in the system design can be performed efficiently, thus decreasing the number of errors.

The risk involved in some industries, such as air transport, proves to be too high to accept this development model. The improvement of many activities actually leads to a decrease in performance in a few of them. If these few activities lead to situations -important in terms of human or material losses- the basis of this model of development should be re-examined.

In the next epigraph, air safety will be analysed in order to show how these effects happen even in industries that can demonstrate a high improvement rate.

2. THE CASE OF AIR SAFETY

Results in air safety show a successful example of the feasibility of real improvement in very complex organisations. The figure (Boeing, 2002) illustrates the development of safety until the present moment:

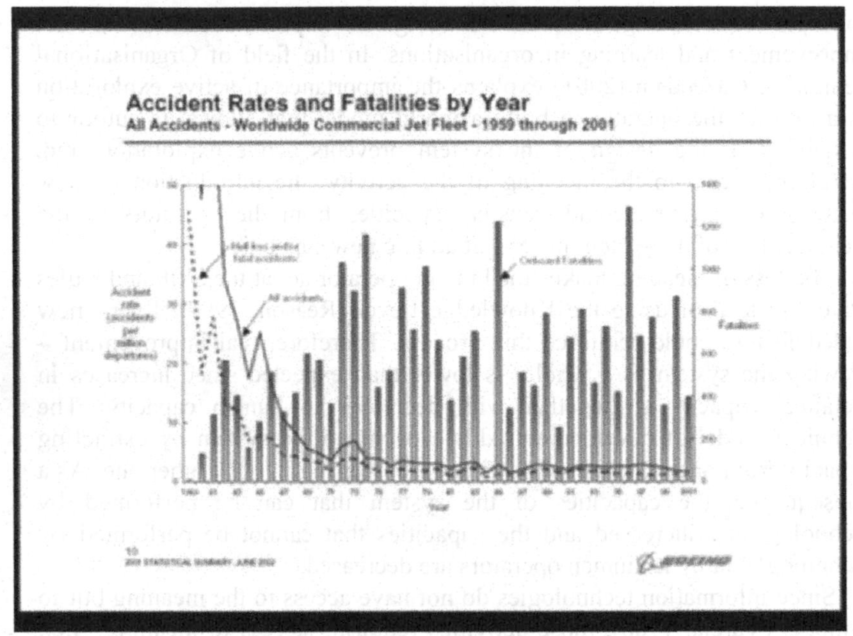

Figure 1. Boeing Statistical Summary (2002)

It is especially interesting to observe that since 1975 the improvement rate, in terms of accidents per million departures, has decreased. A high-level analysis of the graph could dismiss the problem as an ordinary diminishing returns phenomenon. However, Boeing forecasts a weekly major accident in 2015 if both present accident rate and traffic increase expectations are maintained. Therefore, there is a real necessity to go beyond the diminishing returns level. Furthermore, this decrease in improvement occurred alongside significant technological developments in the air-field. Since technology has been one of the key drivers for improvement in this field, another different factor or a secondary effect of this technology must be responsible for the decreasing improvement rate.

Reason (1990) identifies this factor by explaining that we can produce a new accident trying to avoid the last one. In other words, limiting the freedom of human operators can avoid mistakes but, at the same time, can prevent actions that, in any unforeseen event, would be required. In complex environments, there are unforeseen contingencies where required actions could be unforeseen too. Therefore, these actions would be unforeseeable and unmanageable due to the design of the organisation.

If human operators are allowed to act but are part of a system that they do not fully understand, the feasibility of acting is more theoretical than real since operators may not know how to act. The development of information technologies in aviation shows how this can happen: An old aircraft provided the human operator with many data sources allowing the experienced operator to obtain an overall picture of the situation. A new aircraft is very different, having few multifunctional screens and giving information that the system itself has integrated beforehand. The new Boeing 747 generation has about one third of the indicators that the old Boeing 747 generation had and even the flight engineer is not required anymore on the new flightdeck.

Information technology has led to major improvements in the air industry: Automated flightdecks can be handled by fewer people and, at the same time, common flightdeck designs installed in different planes allow some of the crews to fly them with a very short period of adaptation (Airbus, 2002). Furthermore, since automation can prevent human mistakes in previously defined situations, some actions are performed close to the operating limits without any danger of surpassing them. Aircraft manufacturers can design fuel-efficient planes even when this design can make a plane unstable since automatic systems would prevent dangerous situations from arising.

Therefore, information technology in aviation is an efficiency-booster. The efficiency comes from design improvement, payroll reductions and training cost reductions due to simpler interfaces. However, this efficient environment has given human operators a new role limiting their accessibility to the real meaning of their actions.

Some accidents in new planes have demonstrated this effect very clearly. Once the operator has adopted a passive attitude and his/her job is "serving the system", s/he becomes useless in situations that exceed the system capabilities –precisely those that could justify his/her presence on the flightdeck.

Accidents such as AeroPeru 603 or American Airlines 965 (Walters & Sumwalt, 2000), both involving technologically advanced planes, can only be explained due to an established passive role on the part of the responsible air crew in relation to the aircraft information systems. Once the information systems started to give confusing indications, the operators were then unable to take the right actions by themselves.

Both situations could have happened in old planes. The accident of AeroPeru occurred because of a piece of tape that someone left on the outside part of the plane, giving false speed and height indications. The accident of American Airlines was due to confusion with radio-frequencies.

However, if we think about procedures in an old plane, probably, neither of these accidents would have happened:

- AeroPeru 603: The wrong indications issue is analysed even for lower licenses such as glider and private pilot licenses. Why did these experienced pilots not do take appropriate action? They never thought of their plane as a normal plane and merely focussed on looking for an explanation in the information system part.
- American Airlines 965: The confusion between two radio-stations with the same frequency disoriented the pilots in a high-mountain area. If, instead of a multi-functional screen with a keyboard, they had had a paper-made chart, they would probably not have got confused and, if so, they could have quickly corrected the mistake.

Information technology designers have traded meaning for legibility and paid special attention to designing inputs and outputs with visual representations familiar to operators coming from older systems. In this way, operators can obtain friendly interfaces and tend to think that a new plane is quite similar to the old one. Likewise, the independence among design levels in information systems (Winograd & Flores, 1987) makes the transition from one plane to another easy. Different kinds of planes can share identical flightdecks (Campos, 2001) leading to a situation similar to a PC-user who can handle computers from different manufacturers as long as they share the same software.

This solution increases the complexity of the system, since it gives the operators an image of how the system supposedly works but such an image is an added construct implied by the output of the system and does not necessarily correspond with the internal functional logic of the aircraft sub-systems. The disparity between the two modes –the real (logical mode) and the output received by the operator (operational mode) – can cause operator confusion: If an operator has been using the operational model "as if" it were coincident with the logical model, thenin crisis situations, the operator has to learn, very rapidly indeed, that such taken for granted assumptions are incorrect. .

Consequently, the expert operator becomes aware of this fallacy through various episodic "microevents" whereby the output of the information system does not work as expected. Baberg (2001) explains this fact through a very common joke among pilots: Supposedly, the most common sentence spoken on a modern flightdeck is: "What is this bastard doing now?" referring to the plane. Therefore, the operator learns to mistrust a system designed to provide him/her with the information supposedly required and nothing else. In this way once something happens that makes evident the contradiction between the operational and the logical mode, the operator get confused and feel powerless to resolve the situation.

Dennett (1996) uses two metaphors to illustrate the contradiction between these modes. Dennett contrasts the model of an information agency with the model of a commando group. In the first model, the operator knows only the information required to perform the specific task. In the second model, operators are provided with all the information about a situation where unforeseen events are expected and they are asked to resolve them.

The increasing complexity of organisations has led to situations in which operators are managed under the "information agency" model. Consequently, they only receive the operational model since the logical model would be very complex for them to understand. The key issue should be as follows: Under what conditions would some opacity of the meaning for the operator be a sound design option for the system designer?

3. CONCLUSIONS: NEW CHALLENGES.

The case shown in this paper is not an exception. Many organisations use advanced information systems and operators are given an operational model but not a logical one. In situations where serious contingencies are not expected, limiting the knowledge required of operators can be an efficient way to act. However, this model has a serious flaw when contingencies are frequent and/or significant. The kind of development that can make the organisation more efficient can, at the same time, prevent human operators from becoming an alternative resource in unforeseen events.

Operators do not learn how the system works through their activity because of the incomplete knowledge they have received with which to perform their tasks. Learning other design levels of the system could be very far from their training and experience. Consequently, the development drives the system far beyond the understanding capacity of the operator.

Therefore, operators provided with incomplete knowledge are not a good solution, especially in those fields where contingencies can be serious. At the same time, training and experience of these operators do not allow them to acquire a deeper understanding of increasingly complex systems. That poses a dilemma which is hard to escape from.

The next challenge to be faced by engineers concerns this dilemma: Since full understanding of the systems by operators is difficult, time-consuming and expensive, the requirements for simpler systems are hard to meet. This happens especially in those systems that deal with high-risk activities. The reasonable limit for technological design should not come from technological potential but from the level of complexity where human operators begin to be unable to perform their role as an alternative to the system.

This solution goes far beyond ergonomic issues and the idea of making interfaces as easy as possible. The real issue is in the organisational semiotics field and the transparency requirement, especially in high-risk activities. New programming languages and new logical models are required to make systems meaningful to operators.

Rassmussen (1986) pointed out a requirement for information system designs: They had to be *cognitively run* by their human operators. In this way, these operators are able to know the real state of the system at any given moment. So far, this requirement has not been met by new developments in technology.

The independence among design levels (Winograd & Flores, 1986) has some advantages and the temptation to get the most out of the information system is constant. However, the existence of different modes –both logical and operating- has to be avoided. The "as-if" way, giving far more importance to operational knowledge rather than to conceptual knowledge, is not enough in high-risk environments. This means working with the logical model of the systems and keeping it easy to understand for its operators. The next step in organisational development would be to make this logical model easier instead of hiding it.

REFERENCES

Airbus Industries 2002. Cross Crew Qualification. http://www.airbus.com.

Baberg T. W. 2001, Man-Machine-Interface In Modern Transport System from an Aviation Safety Perspective. Aerosp. Sci. Technol; 5: 495-504.

Boeing 2002. Statistical Summary of Commercial Jet Airplane Accidents Worldwide Operations 1959-2001. http://www.boeing.com

Campos L. 2001, On the Competition between Airbus and Boeing. Air & Space Europe.

Choo, C.W. and Bontis, N, 2002, The Strategic Management of Intellectual Capital and Organisational Knowledge. Oxford: Oxford University Press.

Daft, R.L. and Huber, G.P. 1987, How Organisations Learn: a Communication Framework. Research in the Sociology of Organisations 5: pp. 1-36.

Daft, R.L. and Lengel, R.H. 1986, Organisational Information Requirements, Media Richness and Structural Design. Management Science 32: pp. 554-571.

Dennett, D.C. 1996, Kinds of Minds. New York. Basic Books.

Gazendam. 2001, Semiotics, Virtual Organisations and Information Systems. In Information, Organisation and Technology, Liu, Clarke, Andersen & Stamper, Boston: Kluwer Academic Publishers.

Dreyfus, H.L. and Dreyfus, S.E., 1986, Mind Over Machine. New York: The Free Press.

Liu, K., Clarke, R.J., Andersen, P.B., and Stamper, R.K, 2001, Information, Organisation and Technology: Studies in Organisational Semiotics. Norwell: Kluwer Academic Publisher.

Maturana H. and Varela F., 1998, The Tree of Knowledge. Boston: Shambala.

Nevis, E.C., DiBella, A.J. y Gould, J.M. 1995, Understanding Organisations as Learning Systems. Sloan Management Review, 36: pp. 73-85.

Rasmussen, J., 1986, Information Processing and Human-Machine Interaction: An Approach to Cognitive Engineering. New York: North Holland.

Reason, J.,1990, Human Error. Cambridge: Cambridge University Press.

Reason, J., 1997, Managing the Risk of Organisational Accidents. Cambridge: Cambridge University Press.

Varela, F., 1988, Conocer. Barcelona: Gedisa.

Walters, J.M. and Sumwalt III, R.L., 2000, Aircraft Accident Analysis. New York City: McGraw Hill.

Winograd, T. and Flores, F. 1986, Understanding Computers and Cognition. Indianápolis. Addison Wesley.

Chapter 8

THE ASSURANCE PARADIGM

Organisational Semiotics Applied to Governance Issues

Hart Will and Darren Whobrey
School of Public Administration, University of Victoria, B.C., Canada and School of Information Systems, Technology and Management, University of New South Wales, Australia

Abstract: Major organisational scandals, such as the Enron accounting fiasco and the demise of Arthur Andersen, have driven the financial world to seek more rigorous methods for explaining and possibly regulating financial reporting and auditing. As the principal guarantor of information quality, the public accounting sector is presently confronted with a credibility gap that it tries to bridge with an assurance paradigm. In this paper the growing demand for, and reliance on assurance techniques, is discussed from the semiotic point of view. Using this as an increasingly more important applications domain, the organisational semiotic modelling requirements of a methodologically tenable assurance approach are set out. Based on a review of current modelling techniques, extensions are suggested that would be needed to support the objectives of the public accounting sector in its adoption of organisational semiotics to governance issues.

Key words: accountability, assurance, audit, risk, risk management, integration, modelling, organisational semiotics, technologies.

1. INTRODUCTION

The recent scandals in commerce, such as the demise of Enron and WorldCom as auditees and Arthur Andersen as auditors and the necessary adjustments to the financial statements of over 250 of the largest American corporations for the fiscal year 2001 have raised serious questions about corporate governance and (public) accountability and auditability. The public accounting profession has responded with an "assurance" paradigm in order to bridge the acknowledged (IFAC 2003) credibility gap created by

K. Liu (ed.),
Virtual, Distributed and Flexible Organisations: Studies in Organisational Semiotics, 129–152.

pursuing financial accounting and auditing in traditional ways. "Assurance" is a term used to distinguish traditional auditing from responses to new governance demands for the integrity, protection, and security of modern information systems and information generated by them. However, it is presently only loosely circumscribed, conceptualised and defined, as the following definition quoted from the American Institute of Public Accountants (AICPA) illustrates:

> [Assurance services are] independent services that *improve the quality of information and its context for decision-makers*. This information can be financial or non-financial, historical or prospective. (AICPA-SCAS 2002, italics added)

Note that this description as well as the recent discussions of assurance in the contemporary accounting and audit literature leave both its conceptualization and its definition wide open with the surprising expectation that "the market" will define it in terms of services to be demanded from and subsequently supplied by the audit profession (Boritz 2002, Alles, Kogan and Vasarhelyi, 2002, Elliott, 2002, Vasarhelyi 2002). Instead, the use of artificial intelligence (AI) and "intelligent agents" (IA) has been advocated by the AICPA as follows:

> Electronic *sensors and software agents* (some of which may be owned or controlled by the CPA) will be introduced at key checkpoints throughout the [financial statement] preparer's set of business activities. The CPA may provide general parameters to the software agent, such as industrial, macro-economic, and technical factors, but *give the software agent discretion* to add other factors or information appropriate in the circumstances. Agents may have *adaptive, quasi-learning algorithms* embedded *to adjust to a constantly changing model*. (AICPA *Special Committee on Assurance Services*, 1998, italics added)

The initial enthusiasm about AI and IA has been slightly dampened in the recent literature as follows:

> *[Artificially] intelligent agents* used in electronic commerce applications have the potential to dramatically affect the supply value chain. Some significant hurdles, however, must be overcome before *multi-agent societies* can truly thrive and reach their full potential (e.g., agent interfacing mechanisms, data security, and *trust of agents*). (Greenstein and Vasarhelyi 2002: 430, italics added)

These references are broad claims rather than proper definitions. To address the new demands of governance, auditability needs to be considered as a cognitive problem faced by everyone requiring "assurance" in the electronic world, rather than just that of external or internal auditors.

2. THE ASSURANCE PARADIGM

To overcome the methodological vacuum with respect to assurance it is suggested that we attempt to link accountability, assurance, auditability, confidence, governance, information, and knowledge cognitively, epistemologically, ontologically, and technologically in an elegant, proper, and methodologically consistent and tenable way.

> Assurance is necessary and sufficient evidence that information (or information systems) meet their recipients' (or their users') knowledge (or belief, trust or confidence) requirements in support of rational action in one or more contexts.

The need for assurance arises as a semiotic phenomenon at and across various ontological and representational levels of contextual-sentience[6] as illustrated in Figure 1: Assurance Contexts and Requirements. There would be no requirement for observations in the "real" world and data representing relevant aspects of the real world without a problem (Popper 1994: 19). The collected data must fit an appropriate model context describing the problem; however, the generated information may not represent knowledge understood as "warranted belief" (Fetzer 1981, 1990, 2000, 2003). Moreover, what is considered knowledge may even be false in the user's (current, next or previous) action context (Will 2002).

Semiotics as the theory and use of signs originated with Charles S. Peirce (1839-1914) (Hartshorne et al. 1958) and was initially and repeatedly applied to intelligence, knowledge, and mentality by Fetzer (1988, 1990, 2000, 2001, 2003). Its application to: (1) accounting, auditing, and modern information systems (MIS) by Will (1990, 2001), Fetzer (2000) and Stamper (1987); (2) minds and machines by Fetzer (1990, 2000, 2001, 2003) and Whobrey (1999, 2000, 2001); (3) the assurance paradigm (Will, 2002, Will and Whobrey 2003); (4) information systems design (Liu 1993, 2000); (5) organisations (van Heusden and Jorna 2000, 2001; de Moor 2002; de Moor and Whitworth 2003); (6) IT governance (Jamieson and Will 2003) and (now in this paper) (7) relevant modelling technology, illustrates that semiotics provides an elegant conceptual framework that overcomes the

6 Contextual sentience is defined in the semiotic sense as the ability to use signs and being able to exercise that ability – see Fetzer (1998, p384).

limitations of behaviourism, extensionality, and reductionism (Fetzer 1990: 21-27) in various fields and contexts.

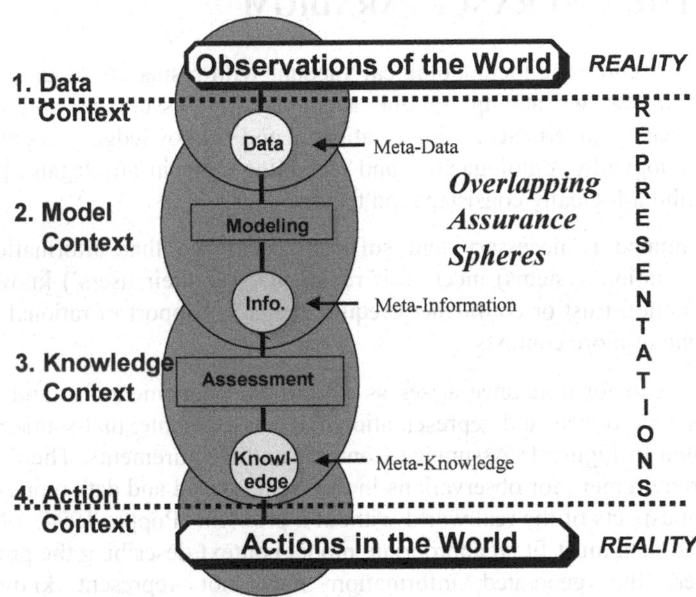

Figure 1. Assurance Contexts and Requirements.

For example, the semiotic trichotomy between a sign and its user, the sign's meaning, and the user's interpretation helps to surmount the conceptual limitations of the conventional but simplistic "input to process to output" dichotomy used traditionally to "explain" data, models, information, and information systems. This is illustrated in Figure 2: Assurance of Accountability Information in Double Semiotic Perspective. This diagram shows the semiotic relationships between accountability information (or accountability information systems) understood as signs; the (relevant) events, objects or subjects and their respective internal states that the (protected) information represents; and the interpretation the respective situation receives by both the informing agents (e.g., in terms of rationally respecting the principals and their belief systems) and by the informed principals (e.g., as rational confidence in the agents) in a governance context (understood as their common knowledge context). Both the agents and the principles are facing their own "problems with the rest of the world" in their personal efforts to succeed and to survive; however, the agent is more embedded in the common knowledge context and is therefore less free to act outside it than the principal.

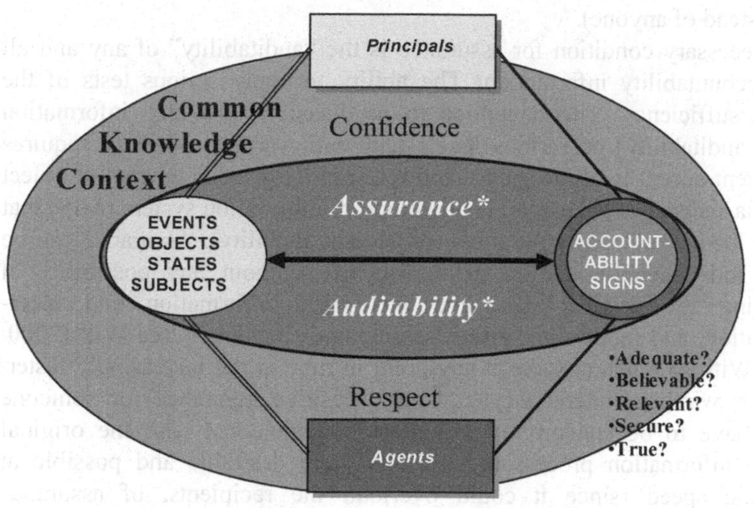

Figure 2. Assurance of Accountability Information in Double Semiotic Perspective.

To qualify as "knowledge" (Fetzer 1981, 1990, 2000, 2003), electronically generated or communicated accountability information (signs) has to be adequate, believable, relevant, secure, and true to the extent rationally justifiable or warranted in any (type of) user's knowledge or action context. Applying these attributes to accountability information establishes merely sufficiency criteria for assurance to be gained or had - not as "surety," but as "relatively or sufficiently sure" warrants for knowledge, understood as warranted belief (Fetzer 1981, 1990).

For example, without some kind of explicit evidence *that* and *why* the agents' accountability information is adequate, believable, not false, necessary, protected, and sufficient in a specific context, a principal can hardly have any confidence in an agent and rely on the agent's actions as proper stewardship. Confidence is therefore rationally related to accountability provided auditability facilitates tests of any and possibly all accountability information for adequacy, credibility, integrity, protection, relevance, and for appropriate conceptions of truth. For example, assurance as "a positive declaration intended to give confidence" (Random House Dictionary, 1982) can refer to specific types and instances of accountability at specific points in time (*ex nunc* and *ex post*) and to accountability for specific kinds of performance over periods of time (*ex nunc* and *ex post*), but it is always time-dependent and must be contextual to be meaningful to some one (instead of anyone).

A necessary condition for assurance is the "auditability" of any and all such accountability information: The ability to apply serious tests of the various sufficiency criteria applied to produced or provided information (active auditability) at various levels and with varying intensity requires convenient access to all necessary and relevant knowledge tokens (in object and meta-language statements) in any modern information system (MIS) that is used for accountability purposes (passive auditability). Assurance can be gained independently and meta-linguistically without any possibility of modifying the original data and meta-data, information and meta-information, and models and risk assessments – for details see Will (2000, 2002). With so much at stake at any point in time in the increasingly faster, wired or wireless, interconnected world, positive assurance for someone would have to be concurrent (or almost simultaneous) with the original (object) information processing – if this were desirable and possible at electronic speed (since it could overload the recipients, of assurance messages, with even more information than the large volumes they are already constantly bombarded with).

Even if various types of assurance warrants (i.e., serious audit, test procedures and the evaluation of their results) could be automated as part of process control methods, models, and procedures, assurance statements would be perfect and could serve as guarantees only if *all causally relevant* changes in, or states of, the recipients' e-world (as it represents their real world) could be and were constantly monitored at several levels in specific knowledge and action contexts. However, then a positive assurance statement would be unnecessary, because only an indication of negative assurance would make sense. It would be an ethical requirement to notify someone immediately of the lack of warrants for belief in the "proper" (or expected) functioning of the world if the audit and (internal) control procedures indicated errors, disinformation (Fetzer 2002), failures, fraud, misinformation or omissions. Therefore, an undefined (or improperly defined) "automated audit capability" (Razaee *et al.* 2002) without a consistent and reliable methodology and reference to a specific knowledge context (and a related action context) can never result in assurance.

Assurance at the cognitive level requires information users with a critical mentality and matching cognitive and meta-linguistic support, who can either question and assess the quality of their own information or do it on behalf of other users. Assurance may result in negative rather than positive declarations (meta-reports) by assurors to the recipients of the original object information (assurees). This is illustrated in Figure 3: Auditability as Meta-Accounting and Assurance as Meta-Reporting, for accountable agents (auditees); for principals as the legitimate recipients of the original accountability information to be assured (assurees); and for auditors as the assurors who must be able to audit the accountability information (understood as meta-accounting by means of a meta-language). In the semiotic sense auditing would be defined as follows:

> Auditability is meta-accounting understood as rational criticism, rather than re-accounting, within the legal constraints of the respective profession, such as the International Accounting Standards (IAS), or the Generally Accepted Accounting Principles (GAAP).

Auditees and assurors can each be considered as complex (human, person-machine, and possibly even machine-machine) agents according to agency theory (Jensen and Meckling 1976) or as minds (according to semiotic theory) with various abilities, capabilities, ethics, motivations and perceived opportunities (Fetzer 1990). Whether such minds are limited to persons or extend to machines remains an open, but very relevant question, because if "mindful" machines (Whobrey 2000, 2001, 2002) can be designed then they may as well be used for assurance purposes.

There would be no requirements for assurance, auditability or protection if principals could trust their agents. Trusting principals would simply believe the accountability information provided by the agents, because the agents' loyalty or respect would prohibit deliberate abuse, disinformation, and fraud, although (innocent) error and misinformation would still be possible without proper controllership. Any and all knowledge extracted from the information by the agents by means of critical thinking and logical reasoning would be sharable (and actually shared) with the principals. However, how can information or information systems be "trusted" (Will 1992) or believed in the e-world if they may be insufficiently monitored and protected against various threats and vulnerabilities and if one cannot be "assured" about the effectiveness and efficiency of such protection without a proper risk assessment? One of the most important questions in the e-world is therefore: How well monitored and protected are (or can be) the uses of various knowledge objects *and* their users?

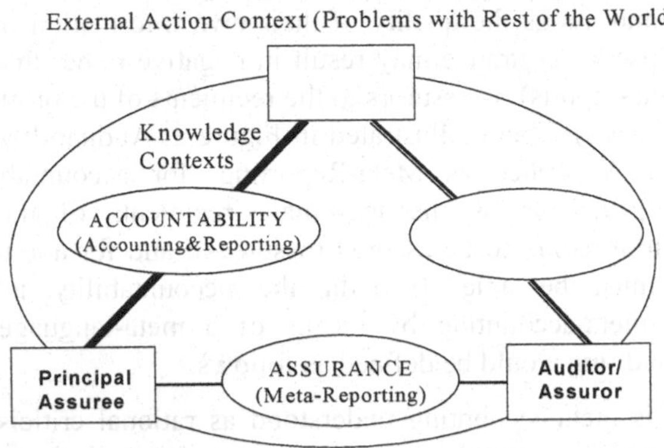

Figure 3. Auditability as Meta-Accounting and Assurance as Meta-Reporting.

It is therefore important to distinguish two categories of accountability: the first concerned with the meaning or content of the data, information or knowledge, and the second, concerned with the protection and integrity of the meaning of the data, information, or knowledge. Both types of accountability may be abused, but lack of knowledge (data or information) protection may facilitate abuse, disinformation, fraud, loss of integrity, and misinformation, especially in the e-world. Users of accountability information need to be assured against violations of both types of accountability (Will 2000b, 2002a, 2002b). In fact, awareness of these problems allows one to establish criteria for the proper design and use of MIS and for the proper design and use of audit and assurance support methodologies, processes, and software (see, e.g., Will 1974, 1975a, 1975b, 1983, 1990a, 1995b, 1995c, 2000a, 2002).

While the initial conception for a pragmatic assurance paradigm arose from issues with present practices in the accounting and auditing industry when viewed in an information systems perspective (Will 1974), the organisational semiotics community has finally encountered the problem on its own by recognizing the need for similar assurance methodologies, processes, techniques and tools. For example, de Moor and Whitworth (2003) raise the issue of legitimacy (of effecting actions) as a growing system design problem.

With the uptake of semiotic oriented business process redesign (BPR) practices and their filtration into the system design process itself (see

Katzenstein and Lerch, 2000), an organisation's IS systems will become more amicable to a semiotic based assurance paradigm in IT governance (Jamieson and Will 2003) and specific knowledge and action contexts.

3. ASSURANCE MODELLING REQUIREMENTS

Models are concepts and constructs: "Concepts have the properties of habits of mind (in processing informational stimuli) in relation to habits of action (in producing appropriate responses)." (Fetzer 2000: 473). As constructs models are created either *l'art pour l'art* or with a special purpose in mind, but in both cases with a variety of means in a variety of ways. Either as concepts or as constructs, models represent some aspect of the imagination of the creator or some aspect of the world that is of interest to the creator and to any of the model users. In other words, models are signs in the semiotic sense as illustrated in Figure 4: Models and Model Results as Signs. Especially in the e-world, users of models require assurances that they are adequate, believable, protected, relevant and true according to the user's knowledge and action contexts - either as games or as useful tools in support of manual or mental tasks. Regardless, it is important to distinguish between the three semiotic dimensions of models when they are considered as signs for their users:

(M1) *Syntactic.* Do the models make the users syntactically aware of something or do they represent merely "noise"?

(M2) *Semantic.* Do the models represent something "real" for the users such as specific (types of) events, objects or states of the world?

(M3) *Pragmatic.* Do the users interpret the models (as syntactic signs corresponding semantically to something else that they represent) as being pragmatically appropriate in their respective knowledge and action contexts?

All three semiotic aspects represent corresponding assurance problems for the users:

(A1) *Relevance.* How can the users be sure or assured that a particular model result (sign) that they become aware of at any specific point in time and at any specific location is *relevant* for them and not merely noise in their respective knowledge and action context?

(A2) *Faithfulness.* How can the users be sure or assured that the model results (signs) *truly* represent something "real" (objective, observable and inferable) rather than "unreal" (highly subjective or purely theoretical) in their respective knowledge and action contexts?

(A3) *Utility*. How can the users be sure or assured that the model results (signs) serve their purposes in their respective knowledge and action contexts?

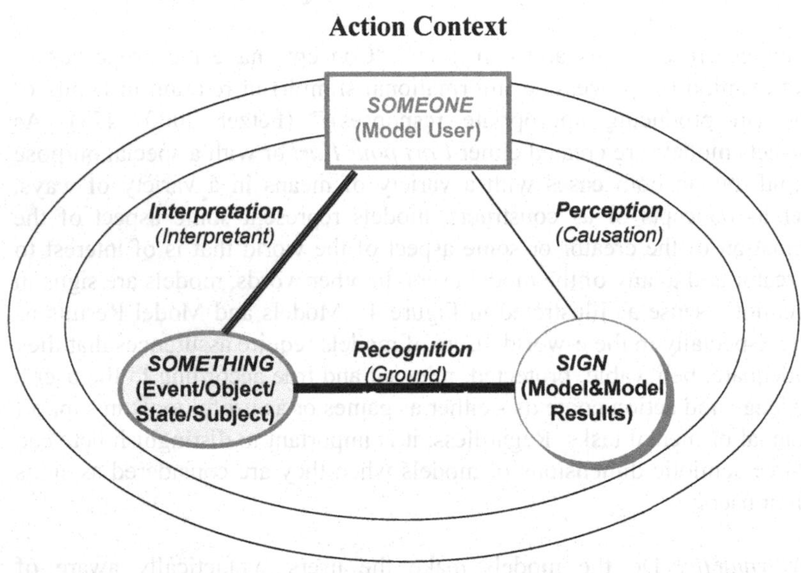

Figure 4. Models and Model Results as Signs.

While the model dimensions M1, M2, and M3 require mental assessments, those described in A1, A2, and A3 require critical re-assessments.

3.1 Semiotic Modelling Dimensions

The three semiotic dimensions (M1, M2, M3) for modelling, models, and model results (understood as signs) apply independently both of the technological implementation of the models; how they fit into the technological user context; and how they relate to the knowledge and action context. However, they do refer to object models, whereas A1, A2, and A3 refer to meta-models. Notice that treating models as signs, implies that, firstly, the model or the model results have to be perceivable and perceived by users who are sentient (in the semiotic sense defined earlier) and able to use all or any of their senses. For example, a blind person cannot perceive the model and its result visually, but may do so acoustically or tactilely. Secondly, they must be recognized as representing something else in a semantic sense; however, this does not mean that what they represent is observable by means of the same senses as the model. For example, a blind person who cannot see an object may be able to *feel* a model of it to recognize its meaning. Finally, the user's interpretation of the model in a pragmatic context completes the cognitive process, but that does not guarantee that the one and the same model will also be adequate, believable, relevant or true in a different context.

3.1.1 Syntactic Modelling Criteria: Sentience of Models or Model Results

In Figure 4, the syntactic relation between the sign (model & model results) and someone (observer/user) corresponds to the representational structure of the conceptual manner in which the sign is perceived. From this it follows that unless the structure of a model itself (or its behavioural or computational results) can be perceived and comprehended with the senses, it will merely represent syntactic noise. This means that at least acoustic, tactile, and visual presentations of models and modelling results in various forms are important dimensions to make users aware. For example, modulated acoustic and tactile signs such as vibrations of various frequencies as well as static and dynamic graphical, numeric, or textual formats in various colours, are important dimensions of modelling from a syntactic point of view.

3.1.2 Semantic Modelling Criteria: Correspondence

The semantic correspondence dimension of models can be viewed differently depending on the type of sign produced: Iconic, Indexical, and Symbolic (Peirce and Fetzer).

Models can resemble something if they depict what they represent as *icons* such as photographs of objects or persons, films of events, images or scans of internal system states. Model results can indicate causes and effects if they represent causes, effects, or both in some way as *indices.* Descriptive models represent important structural components and their behaviourally relevant couplings of interest to users by means of *symbols* in the Peircean sense. They rely on mental associations such as denotations, diagrams, metaphors or synonyms and the (various) linguistic conventions of such different natural languages as Arabic, Chinese, English, French, German or

Thai or artificial languages such as *accountese*, *riskese*, and *auditese* (Will 2003), formal logic(s) and mathematics.

Descriptive models can be used for explanatory or predictive purposes. *Explanations* consist of an *explanans* and an *explanandum* formulated within a language framework according to the *requirement of maximal specificity* if they are to be adequate, and the *requirement of strict maximal specificity* if they are to be true, as defined by Fetzer (1990: 152-162). *Predictions* are likewise based on descriptive models; however:

> When either (a) the laws of [modelled] systems …are not known or (b) the description available for that system is not closed [i.e., has not been described maximally specifically]…then precisely how that system would behave over a corresponding interval of time…cannot be predicted with – invariable or probabilistic - confidence, because essential information remains unknown. Even when the laws of systems of that kind are known, moreover, that knowledge could be incomplete when there is no end to the number of factors whose presence or absence makes a difference to the occurrence of the outcome of interest. (Fetzer 1990: 160)

Can individual human behaviour, social human behaviour, and organisational behaviour (ever) be sufficiently well described in complex semiotic models to facilitate "assured" predictions? Can predictions about complex systems' behaviour that is described by means of (integrated) syntactic, semantic and pragmatic models be made without simulations, replications or emulations of expected or likely behaviour at a higher level (see below)?

3.1.3 Pragmatic Modelling Criteria: Monitoring and Regulation

Pragmatic criteria for modelling and the proper use of model results are dependent on whether one wants to use the model for monitoring the system under observation or for regulating it. While "black box monitoring" of input-output relationships may invite tinkering with inputs (e.g. by "fixing" data syntactically or semantically, or pragmatically by "throwing money at problems"), *proper monitoring* requires understanding the context (e.g., culture, environment and systems), determining the expected behaviour, and having the means for discovering misbehaviour (e.g., as dangerous exception conditions).

To *regulate* a system means to change it structurally such that it cannot misbehave and stays the course. How can there be assurances about appropriate system behaviour without adequate, believable, relevant and true information about its (possible or potential) misbehaviour over (past) time and about its disposition(s) at any point in time?

Consider the following assertion about assurance understood as "continuous auditing:"

> Continuous auditing is … a comprehensive electronic audit process that enables auditors to provide some degree of assurance on continuous information simultaneously with, or shortly after, the disclosure of the information. (Razaee, Sharbatoghlie, Elam and McMickle, 2002: 147)

How assuring can "continuous audits" be, when the models applicable for "continuous monitoring" may be very difficult to define (as alluded to above) and when they should be designed to identify exceptions to the expected behaviour rather than to look for confirmations of it? Note also that they may not be taking full cognisance of the risks in a structured, consistent and reliable manner (Bergman 2003).

As illustrated in Figure 1, semiotic models are contextually relevant for assurance purposes at different levels and with different effects. Note that syntactic correctness or integrity and protection does not imply semantic correctness or integrity and protection and that semantic correctness does not guarantee pragmatic correctness or integrity and protection. The applicability and usefulness of the models may also depend on the respective governance context and their technological implementation.

3.2 Contextual modelling: Knowledge Content and Knowledge Protection

Semiotic modelling is contextual and refers, in the context of governance and accountability, *by* agents, to them providing adequate, believable, protected, relevant and true knowledge content *to* their principals. It requires appropriate specification and execution of the information systems along with the means for their protection in general, similarly for the various relevant knowledge elements and processes and their protection in particular. "Assurance of accountability" depends on the proper specification and implementation of information systems as semiotic knowledge management and administration systems (SKMAS) as illustrated in Figure 5: Semiotic Knowledge Management and Administration in Governance Context. Note that a SKMAS is qualitatively different to a knowledge management system (KMS) based on the symbol system hypothesis, which was most recently assumed as the basis for a KMS by O'Leary (2002, p. 273).

Proper MIS design implies accessibility to explicit descriptions of states, events and objects of a SKMAS (typically via log files) both for knowledge content and for knowledge protection. This transparency to auditability has been dubbed "passive auditability." On the other hand, "active auditability" implies *rational criticism* (Fetzer 2003) and requires meta-linguistic support for serious tests of adequate, believable, relevant and true knowledge content, and for the adequacy, credibility, relevance and truth of knowledge protection of SKMAS in their users' respective knowledge and action contexts (Will 2000, 2002).

3.2.1 Sufficient Knowledge Content: Criteria

For agents to deserve the confidence of their principals means to provide the principals with information that is adequate, believable, protected, relevant and true in the principals' knowledge context. For agents to be able to act on behalf of principals in organisations created to achieve the principals' objectives requires semiotic knowledge management and administration systems. They need to be able to access, assess, collect, maintain, and produce adequate, believable, protected, relevant and true data, information and models within the observations-actions spectrum illustrated in Figure 1 both to support themselves in their respective cognitive tasks and to share (at least some of) their relevant knowledge with their principals.

To model such governance and accountability systems organisationally requires awareness of the respective users' knowledge and action contexts in order to provide appropriate information to them as an accountability obligation. To model them for assurance purposes in support of a positive declaration intended to give confidence to an assuree requires not only awareness of the respective user's knowledge and action contexts but also an ability to develop appropriate meta-models of the accountability model(s) that were designed to represent the respective "accountability reality" truthfully in a governance context.

3.2.2 Sufficient Knowledge Protection: Risk and Threat Assessments

Especially in the e-world where information is not visible at its source and vulnerable to manipulations by hackers and fraudsters, any information needs to be of high integrity and sufficiently protected before it can be believed by any of its users as relevant and sufficiently true to (dare to) act on it. This means also that the information systems that produce information need to be likewise of high integrity and similarly protected as more aggregate, complex and compound signs as illustrated in Figure 4 with respect to models.

To assess knowledge protection requires contextual modelling of the controls, threats and vulnerabilities in an appropriate and methodologically defensible manner. Risk assessment has been (typically) defined as "the process by which a firm determines what resources need to be protected…and classifies resources into sensitivity levels…" (Greenstein and Vasarhelyi 2002: 241). How can one classify vulnerable resources into sensitivity levels when one cannot assess the causality and specificity of the sensitivities without reference to specific assurance conditions and risk criteria and actually existing vulnerabilities? How can one assess the (potential) threats of a (likely) hostile environment without considering ones own protective and regulatory actions and their (actual or hypothetical) effects on the world, including the possible or likely reaction of the rest of the world?

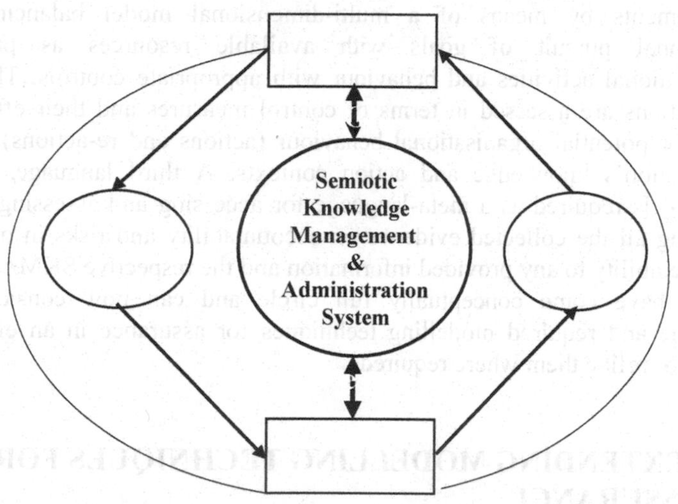

Figure 5. Semiotic Knowledge Management and Administration in Governance Context.

Can risk assessment be simply an inductivistic,[7] linear, sequential, and easily programmable "observational discovery process" without some hypothetical constraints or contextual specifications - even in "simple" and relatively closed traditional bookkeeping and financial accounting contexts? Regardless of the misrepresentation potential contained in traditional

[7] Hume's Inductivism (commonly referred to as *the scientific method*) is characterized by four phases of scientific effort: (1) *Observations*; (2) *Classification*; (3) *Generalization*; and (4) *Prediction.* For a critical distinction between four different kinds of *scientific methods* see (Fetzer 1990, 1993, 2003) and below.

financial accounting information, any one user of a computer-based accounting system may pose a rather complex threat. Can that be (simply) analysed by, (1) *observing* unspecific events, objects, and states of any system; (2) *classifying* the various (types of) information resources relatively arbitrarily into "sensitivity levels"; (3) *generalizing* the (types of) risks somehow; and then (4) attempting to *predict* the vulnerability of the system to specific (types of) attacks?

Proper risk assessment (analysis and evaluation) is clearly not two-dimensional, but essentially semiotic and requires a language, *riskese,* above the language of accountability, call this *accountese*. Then *riskese* serves as a meta-language for statements in the object language *accountese* to gather evidence and to describe the complexity and riskiness of the organisational arrangements by means of a multi-dimensional model balancing the operational pursuit of goals with available resources as part of organisational activities and behaviour with appropriate controls. The risk implications are assessed in terms of control measures and their effect on actual or potential organisational behaviour (actions and re-actions) in the organisation's knowledge and action contexts. A third language, call it *auditese*, is required as a meta-language for accessing and assessing or re-assessing all the collected evidence on accountability and risks in order to lend credibility to any provided information and the respective SKMAS.

We have come conceptually full circle and can now consider the available and required modelling techniques for assurance in an effort to extend or refine them where required.

4. EXTENDING MODELLING TECHNIQUES FOR ASSURANCE

The above suggests that in providing assurance it is necessary to confront how an organisation manages its data, information, and knowledge, how this is accessed, continuously meta-modelled, and most importantly, cognitively assessed in a "virtuous circle" (cf. the cycle of data analysis, see Ovum Evaluates: Data Mining), and consequently how it is monitored and regulated in a governance context. Corresponding to Figure 1, the terms object language, meta-language, and meta-modelling were used to categorise and label these requirements.

4.1 Requirements Arising From Trends in Information Systems

Mickhail (1996) analyses the application of a semiotic interpretation to audit judgement when viewed as an information system. The conclusion reached can be treated as general requirements for assurance oriented systems: "(i) to develop behavioural auditing research beyond its current limitations and, in particular to facilitate the emergence of new methodologies to tackle problem-situations in auditing judgement; (ii) to reflect upon the relationship between different organisational and societal interests and the dominance of particular behavioural (Psychological) methods and techniques; (iii) to provide practically useful, theoretically sound approaches to problematic 'audit judgement' situations, which will assist in the larger process of progressive social change."

Bacon and Fitzgerald (2001), in discussing a systemic framework for the field of information systems, highlight that various models are used depending on the objective: "All of these contributions describe a particular *part* of the subject and field. They describe (a) an information system, (b) strategic systems planning approaches, (c) types of development, (d) types of system/application, and (e) research themes." They conclude that it is no longer solely about developing IS systems, but "It is proposed that the central theme of the field of information systems is *Information for Knowledge Work, Customer Satisfaction & Business Performance.*"

Katzenstein and Lerch (2000), review business process redesign tools and process models with the aim of deriving a set of criteria that good process models should satisfy – their Goal-Exception-Dependency framework was devised to meet these criteria, i.e. process content criteria: the need to capture social and psychological context; process status criteria: 1) the need to capture process emergence, 2) the need to capture multiple operational routines, 3) the need to show missing resource and information flows; and presentation and use criteria: 1) the need for visual utility, 2) the need to facilitate qualitative reasoning, 3) the need for process redesign heuristics.

4.2 Addressing these Requirements

In some of the above respects the organisational semiotics (OS) and knowledge management fields have been making inroads – see van Heusden and René Jorna (2000, 2001) and their work under the CASTOR-Project for establishing a theoretical and methodological framework to these fields.

To this end, analysts modelling organisations, with one goal being to simulate its behaviours, face recurring representational issues: modelling knowledge, rules and actions. There are now many notations for accomplishing this, e.g., within the field of OS, descriptive languages such as MEASUR (see Stamper et al., 1988), NORMA (Liu, 1993) and LEGOL (Stamper, 1996). In discussing the RENISYS method for specification (which "combines the conversational Transaction Process Model from the language / action perspective (LAP)-based DEMO [see Dietz (1999)], with the normative basis provided by OS-representative MEASUR."), de Moor et al. (2002), present a brief comparative review of descriptive techniques from the fields of the language / action perspective (LAP – see Denning and Medina-Mora, 1995) and organisational semiotics, e.g. the ToP (theory of practice) modelling approach. In this approach, Braf et al. (2001) suggest the need for generic models encompassing knowledge, artefacts, signs and business processes of an organisation, which includes actions, products, technology and other organisational assets. Accommodating change is starting to be addressed, e.g., a change in regulations or procedures with respect to a particular temporal period. In simple cases of object existence, this has been conventionally handled by adding existence clauses to the entities / data concerned, e.g. as in MEASUR and via (Start-time, Finish-time) fields in database tables – see Liu and Sun (2000).

Postulating norms as the basic building blocks for producing (and, therefore, modelling) organised behaviour, Filipe (2002) claims, "Although organised activity is possible either with or without communication, it is not possible without a shared set of norms." Conformance to norms turns out to be a central concern in providing assurance. Filipe, drawing upon the work of Stamper (1996) reviews the social psychological classification of norms, into perceptual, evaluative, cognitive and behavioural norms and how they are associated with four distinct attitudes, respectively: "Ontological – to acknowledge the existence of something; Axiologic – to be disposed in favour or against something in value terms; Epistemic – to adopt a degree of belief or disbelief; Deontic – to be disposed to act in some way." Behaviours are formally modelled; using deontic logic, as partial plans, where a goal is an abstract plan and an instance of behaviour is a particular sequence of actions. However, these are all effectively, what this paper has been calling, descriptive object languages rather than meta-languages that permit meta-modelling and rational criticism.

The OS community is now actively researching into more comprehensive organisational modelling tools, such as tools that can accommodate continuous change to regulations. For example, de Cesare et al. (2002) review business-modelling techniques with the goal of determining whether an extension of the Unified Modelling Language (UML) would be a suitable technique. In summarising the domain of discourse, they refer to the work of Homans (1950), who "identifies the elements related to the behaviour of social groups and then applies them within a business context. These elements are: concepts, activities, interactions and sentiments," and Ould (1995), who "identifies the following basic concepts in business process modelling: roles, actors, activities, interactions, process goals and entities." Other business concepts mentioned include services, rules and events. In conclusion, they suggest the current mechanism for extending UML, via profiles (which "are containers for the three extension mechanisms that are currently legal within the UML: stereotypes, tagged values and constraints."), is still not semantically (e.g. diagrammatic activity diagrams are of little programmatic use especially as a means of modelling agent roles) or ontologically rich enough to conceptually facilitate business modelling in a natural and transparent manner.

Advances in organisational semiotics that may help meet the assurance paradigms requirements may spring from related fields. It is evident that there is a growing, mutually beneficial, interaction between the fields of OS and intelligent agents, e.g., see Joslyn and Rocha (2000), and Rocha (1999). The interest in the latter, from the information systems and computer science communities, has led to the development of powerful simulation engines, e.g. Swarm – see www.swarm.org. The flow of ideas has been in both directions, for example, Gudwin and Gonçalves (1998) address "issues concerning the development of a semiotic oriented software engineering methodology, aimed at the analysis and design of autonomous intelligent systems." Filipe et al. (1999) have used concepts from the field of artificial agents to model an organisation based on normative knowledge and role-modelling using the JAVA based JESS rule engine. The agent technology is interesting to the assurance paradigm since agents that learn could be used to model ongoing regulatory changes.

The information technology world in general, with the drive toward open standards and interoperability is becoming more assurance "friendly." For example, the global popularity of the Simple Object Access Protocol (SOAP) standard – see "http://www.w3.org/TR/SOAP/", as an XML based integration protocol providing semantic tagging of information, can be seen as an enabling technology that will act as a technological infrastructure coupling mechanism facilitating the incorporation of semiotic techniques in information systems. Similarly, the development of the extensible Business Reporting Language (XBRL) as an XML-based, royalty-free, and open standard is intended to provide a common platform for critical business reporting processes and improves the reliability and ease of communicating financial data among users internal and external to the reporting enterprise – see "http://www.xbrl.org".

4.3 The Nature of Future Assurance Tools

Nevertheless, whatever technological solution is arrived at for the assurance paradigm, it will have to be user-friendly enough to be accepted by the business community. This suggests that any tool will be a mixture of diagrammatic and textual representations. A strong contender would have to be some variation on a visual tool supporting UML class and object like diagrams used in an ERD fashion for the gross logical description of the IS systems. This would need to be underpinned by a set of formal textual - operational - modelling languages for describing behaviours, laws and assets (such as data) etc. Specifying regulations and norms that govern behaviours through equations is expedient, such as permitted in BOBJ (see Goguen et al., 2002), since it allows reasoning about behaviours by means of (extensional) equational logic as a possible mechanism in testing statements of assurance. This, when combined with the kind of analytical functionality offered in statistical applications, such as Excel, Matlab and SAS, could act as basis for addressing the assurance paradigm requirement for meta-modelling and rational criticism.

Of the current tools available for assurance, Will (1974...2003) developed ACL as an intensional (contextual) meta-language for critical thinkers (such as assurors, auditors, controllers, and forensic accountants) in accountability and auditability contexts. ACL changes the traditionally implicit *instrumental* techniques-orientation of accountants and auditors into a semiotic and explicit process of critical thinking and logical reasoning in data, information, knowledge, and action contexts.

5. SUMMARY AND CONCLUSION

It was suggested that in providing assurance it is necessary to confront how an organisation manages its data, models, information, and knowledge; how they are accessed, collected, communicated, maintained, protected, and cognitively assessed in a virtuous semiotic circle; and consequently how they are finally monitored, reviewed, and regulated in governance contexts. The advantages of semiotic modelling, as illustrated in Figure 4, are that one can clearly distinguish three dimensions characterized by specific criteria: 1) syntactically, the sentience of models or model results; 2) semantically, the correspondence of the model to events, objects, subjects and internal states of real world systems; and 3) pragmatically, the ultimate purposes of modelling such as monitoring and regulation – all within overlapping assurance spheres as illustrated in Figure 1; according to a double semiotic governance model as illustrated in Figure 2; in terms of meta-accounting and meta-reporting as illustrated in Figure 3; and within a semiotic knowledge management and administration framework as illustrated in Figure 5.

Models are needed to simulate, replicate or emulate our understanding of the world in order to assess or re-assess the adequacy, believability, protection, relevance, and truth of data, information, and knowledge in the users' respective contexts within their observations-actions spectrum. The acceptance of a methodologically tenable assurance paradigm will stimulate research and development in organisational semiotics, and vice versa, given the direction of current advances and expectations in both fields.

Semiotics and semiotic modelling seem to provide the proper conceptual framework for addressing the governance, accountability, and auditability issues in organisations and societies because they overcome the limitations of behaviourism, "culture", extensionality, and reductionism. Business modelling tools need to be (or resemble) intensional languages in order to facilitate subjunctive descriptions of individual and organisational behaviour in knowledge and action contexts. Whether assurances are sufficient warrants depends on specific criteria for their adequacy, credibility, protection, relevance and truth in specific knowledge and action contexts and on the technology available to test and assess them.

The conceptual and practical deficits in and the failures of traditional accounting and auditing suggest that the influential and large public accounting community will rally around the "assurance paradigm" – understood as the beliefs, concepts and technologies of a scientific (or professional) community (Kuhn 1970). To be a member of the community of assurors will require the ability to think critically and to reason logically in a semiotic perspective and with appropriate tools already in existence or under development. To provide adequate assurance consistently, convincingly, ethically, and truthfully is to know rather than to pretend to know (especially after the application of mythical language, dazzling techniques, and expensive technology). Nevertheless, since knowledge is never "really" certain and may depend on different conceptions of adequacy, relevance, risk, security and truth, an assuror can only have "relative assurance" rather than "surety" when providing warrants for beliefs to an assuree in a governance and specific knowledge or action contexts.

In the e-world, critical thinking, appropriate logical reasoning, and rational criticism (Fetzer 2003) are more important than ever before in order to be able to assess both the knowledge content and the knowledge protection of MIS and the information they contain, purvey and share among various (types of) users. Assurance requires intensional object and meta-languages that facilitate semiotic modelling and meta-modelling of organisational behaviour and information processing. This way, critical assessments and re-assessments of knowledge content and knowledge protection are feasible in any governance context both in the private and public sectors of accountable, democratic, just, and transparent societies.

REFERENCES

AICPA – SCAS. Assurance. 2002, "http://www.aicpa.org/assurance".

Alles, M.G., Kogan, A., Vasarhelyi, M. 2002, Feasibility and Economics of Continuous Assurance. Auditing: A Journal of Practice and Theory. 21 (1):pp. 125-138.

Arbib, M. Brains, 1964, Machines and Mathematics. New York: McGraw-Hill.

Bacon, J., Fitzgerald, B. 2001, A Systemic Framework for the Field of Information Systems. Data Base, Vol. 32, No. 2.

Bergman, J. 2003, Audit Risk Language™ (ARL™) - A Conceptual Framework. University of New South Wales IS Audit and Accounting Information Systems (AIS) Course Material, AIS Unit 1, 7-8. Version 2.

Boritz, E. 2002, Information Systems Assurance. In, Researching Accounting as an Information Systems Discipline. Eds. V. Arnold, S. G. Sutton. Sarasota, Fl.: American Accounting Association, pp. 231-255.

Braf, E., Goldkuhl, G., Röstlinger, A. 2001, Organisations as Practice Systems - Integrating Knowledge, Signs, Artefacts and Action. IFIP 8.1 Working Conference on Organisational Semiotics: Evolving a Science of Information Systems, July 23-25.

de Cesare, S., Lycett, M., Patel, D. 2002, Business Modelling with UML: Distilling Directions for Future Research. 4th International Conference on Enterprise Information Systems, 3-6 April, Ciudad Real, Spain.

Denning, P.J., Medina-Mora, R. 1995, Completing the Loops. Interfaces, 25 (3).

Dietz, J.L.G. 1999, Understanding and Modelling Business Processes with DEMO. Proc. 18th International Conference on Conceptual Modelling (ER'99), Paris.

Elliott, R.K. 2002, Twenty-first Century Assurance. Auditing: A Journal of Practice and Theory 21 (1):pp. 139-146.

Fetzer, J. H. 1981, Scientific Knowledge. Dordrecht; Reidel.

Fetzer, J. H. 1988, Aspects of Artificial Intelligence. Ed. Dordrecht: Kluver.

Fetzer, J.H. 1990, Artificial Intelligence: Its Scope and Limits. Kluwer Academic Publishers,.

Fetzer, J.H. 1998, People Are Not Computers. J. Experimental & Theoretical AI. Vol.10, pp. 371-391.

Fetzer, J. H. 2000, Information and Representation. Proceedings SCI'2000, Volume X: Concepts and Applications of Systemics, Cybernetics, and Informatics, 472-477. Orlando: International Institute of Informatics and Systemics.

Fetzer, J. H. 2001, Computers and Cognition: Why Minds are not Machines. Dordrecht: Kluver.

Fetzer, J.H. 2003, The Evolution of Intelligence. Chicago, Il.: Open Court, forthcoming.

Filipe, J., Liu, K., Sharp, B. 1999, Organisation Simulation Based on Normative Knowledge and Role Modelling. American Association for Artificial Intelligence.

Filipe, J. 2002, A Normative and Intentional Agent Model for Organisation Modelling. ESAW02, Third International Workshop, Engineering Societies in the Agents World.

Goguen, J., Lin, K., Rosu, G. 2002, Conditional Circular Conductive Rewriting with Case Analysis. 16th Workshop on Algebraic Development Techniques. Frauenchiemsee, Germany, pp. 24-27.

Goncalves, R., Gudwin, R. R. 1998, Semiotic Oriented Autonomous Intelligent Systems Engineering. Proceedings of ISAS'98, Intelligent Systems and Semiotics, International Conference. 14-18 September, Gaithersburg, USA. pp. 700-705.

Greenstein, M. and M. Vasarhelyi, 2002, Electronic Commerce - Security, Risk Management and Control, McGraw-Hill Irwin.

Hartshorne, C., P. Weiss and A. Burks (eds.). 1958, Collected Papers of Charles Sanders Peirce. Boston: Harvard University Press.

van Heusden, B.P., Jorna, R.J. 1999, Toward A Semiotic Theory of Cognitive Dynamics in Organisations. Second Workshop on Organisational Semiotics in Almelo (NL). In, Organisational Semiotics. Ed. Kecheng Liu. (In press).

van Heusden, B.P., Jorna, R.J. 2001, Reconsidering the Standard: A Semiotic Model of Organisation(s). 3rd International Workshop on Organisational Semiotics. Stafford, UK. In, Semiotics in Organisational Theory. Ed. Kecheng Liu. Amsterdam: Kluwer.

Homans, G. C. 1950, The Human Group. New York, Harcourt, Brace.

IFAC: 2003, International Federation of Accountants. Study on Rebuilding Public Confidence in Financial Reporting. http://www.ifac.org/.

Jamieson, R., Will, H.J. 2003, What Can and Does IT Governance Mean? Oceania CACS 2003 Handbook: Crooks, Lies and IT Governance. ISACA: Sydney: pp. 102-107.

Jensen, M.C. and Meckling, W. 1976, Theory of the Firm: Managerial Behavior, Agency Costs and Capital Structure. Journal of Financial Economics, 3:pp. 305-360.

Joslyn, C., Rocha, L. 2000, Towards Semiotic Agent-based Models of Socio-Technical Organisations. In, Proc. AI, Simulation and Planning in High Autonomy Systems. Ed. H.S. Sarjoughian et al. pp. 70-79.

Katzenstein, G., Lerch, F.J. 2000, Beneath the Surface of Organisational Processes: A Social Representation Framework for Business Process Redesign. ACM Transactions on Information Systems, Vol. 18, No. 4, pp. 383-422.

Kuhn, T.S. 1970, The Structure of Scientific Revolutions. 2nd. Edition. Chicago: University of Chicago Press.

Liu, K. 1993, Semiotics Applied to Information Systems Development. PhD Thesis, Twente University, Holland.

Liu, K., Sun, L. 2000, Capturing Temporality and Intentionality in Information Systems. In: Proceedings of the Fifth International Workshop on the Language-Action Perspective on Communication Modelling (LAP 2000). Eds. M. Schoop, C. Quix.

Mickhail, G. 1996, Meaning: A Niche or A Necessity for Audit Judgement. CPA96. The 4th Critical Perspectives on Accounting Symposium. Harcourt Brace Inc.

de Moor, A. 2002, Language / Action Meets Organisational Semiotics: Situating Conversations with Norms. Information Systems Frontiers. 4:3, pp. 257-272. Kluwer.

de Moor, A., Whitworth, B. 2003, Legitimate by Design: Towards Trusted Virtual Community Environments. Behaviour & Information Technology. 22:1, pp. 31-51.

O'Leary, D.E. 2002, Knowledge Management in Accounting and Professional Services. In, Researching Accounting As An Information Systems Discipline. Eds. V. Arnold, S.G. Sutton. Sarasota, Fl.: American Accounting Association. pp. 273-283.

Ould, M. 1995, Business Process: Modelling and Analysis for Re-engineering and Improving. Wiley.

Popper, K. R. 1994, Alles Leben ist Problemlösen: Űber Erkenntnis, Geschichte und Politik. Műnchen Zűrich: Piper.

Razaee, Z., Sharbatoghlie, A., Elam, R., McMickle, P.L. 2002, Continuous Auditing: Building Automated Auditing Capability. Auditing: A Journal of Practice and Theory. 21 (1):pp. 147-163.

Rocha, L. 1999, Review of Agent Models: Encounters, Strategies, Learning, and Evolution. Los Alamos National Laboratory Internal Report. (LAUR 99-5475).

Stamper, R., 1987, Semantics. In, Critical Issues in Information Systems Research. Eds. R.J. Boland, R.A. Hirschheim, pp. 43-78. Wiley.

Stamper, R., 1996, Signs, Information, Norms and Systems. In, Signs of Work, Semiosis and Information Processing in Organisations. Eds. Holmqvist et al. Walter de Gruyter, Berlin, New York.

Vasarhelyi, M. 2002, Concepts in Continuous Assurance. In, Researching Accounting as an Information Systems Discipline. Eds. V. Arnold, S. G. Sutton. pp. 257-271. Sarasota, Fl.: American Accounting Association.

Whobrey, D.J.R. 1999, Aspects of Qualitative Consciousness: A Computer Science Perspective. Ph.D. Thesis. Dept. of Computer Science. City University, London.

Whobrey, D.J.R. 2000, Developing Mindful Machines Requires More than Information. In, Proceedings SCI'2000, Volume X: Concepts and Applications of Systemics, Cybernetics, and Informatics, pp. 489-494. Orlando: International Institute of Informatics and Systemics.

Whobrey, D.J.R. 2001, Machine Mentality and The Nature of The Ground Relation. Minds and Machines. 11(3):pp. 307-346.

Will, H.J. 1974, Auditing in Systems Perspective. The Accounting Review, XLIX (4):pp. 690-706.

Will, H.J. 1975a, Model Management Systems. Proceedings of 1973 International Symposium, Organisational Structure and the Structure of Information Systems, Cologne, (invited paper reprinted in Information Systems and Organisational Structure, Eds. E. Grochla, N. Szyperski, pp. 467-483. De Gruyter: Berlin and New York.

Will, H.J. ACL: 1975b, Audit Command Language. INFOR, 13, 1: pp. 99-11.

Will, H.J. ACL: 1983, A Language Specific for Auditors. Communications of the ACM, 26 (5):pp. 358-361.

Will, H.J. 1990, From Computer Assisted Audit Techniques to Computer-Aided Audit Thought Support. Invited lecture, Proceedings 6th Asia Pacific Information Systems Control Conference, Kuala Lumpur.

Will, H.J. 1992, Why We Cannot Trust Computers - And What This Means for the I.S. Auditor. Keynote Address. Proceedings of the Annual EDP Auditors Conference of Australia. Adelaide, South Australia.

Will, H.J. 1995a, The New CAATS: Shifting the Paradigm. EDPACS, XXII, (11):pp. 1-14.

Will, H.J. 1995b, Accountability, Controllership and Auditability: A Knowledge-Based Framework, Proceedings of the Fifth Biannual Conference of CIGAR (Comparative International Governmental Accounting Research), Paris.

Will, H.J. 2000a, Auditability VS. Security On the Internet. Unpublished Guest Lecture, Bell Labs, New Jersey.

Will. H. J. 2000b, Auditability and Controllership: Extracting Knowledge from Accounting Information. Proceedings SCI'2000, Volume X: Concepts and Applications of Systemics, Cybernetics, and Informatics, pp. 483-488. Orlando: International Institute of Informatics and Systemics.

Will, H.J. 2001, Prűfung nach KonTraG: Rechtliches Gebot als Wissensproblem. Festschrift Professor Dr. Gűnter Minz edited by G.Geib. Kőln: KPMG Deutsche Treuhand-Gesellschaft AG.

Will, H.J. 2002, The Assurance Paradigm. Unpublished Manuscript.

Will, H. and D. Whobrey. 2003, The Assurance Paradigm & Organisational Semiotics: A New Applications Domain. Proceedings IWOS 2003. Reading, UK: Reading University.

Chapter 9

SOCIAL CONSTRUCTS AND BOUNDEDLY RATIONAL ACTORS

A Simulation Framework

Martin Helmhout, Henk W.M.Gazendam and René J.Jorna
University of Groningen, The Netherlands

Abstract: In this paper we sketch a framework for multi-actor simulation of organisations. This framework elaborates the interaction and cooperation of actors based on social constructs. Because of the demands of the task environment, in which tasks often cannot be done alone, actors have to cooperate. Cooperation is only possible based on intertwined habits and mutual commitments that are expressed in sign structures, such as agreements, contracts and plans. At a semiotical level of description, these sign structures are seen as social constructs. Social constructs guide the formation and reinforcement of habits of individual actors that are aimed at cooperation, coordination and socially accepted behaviour. In contrast to many approaches to multi-actor simulation, we design the actors as cognitively plausible actors. We use the cognitive architecture ACT-R for modelling the individual actors. This cognitive architecture implements a part of Simon's bounded rationality. In the recent discussion about bounded rationality, fast and frugal heuristics play an important role. Some of these heuristics will be included in the simulation model as a compensation mechanism for the limits to rationality.

Key words: organisational semiotics, bounded rationality, social constructs, multi-actor systems, act-r, simulation

1. INTRODUCTION

Due to improvements in computer power and software languages, multi-actor simulations nowadays are more applied in research than ever before. This increased power of simulation models makes it possible to investigate armchair thoughts about organisations and the cooperation of (human)

K. Liu (ed.),
Virtual, Distributed and Flexible Organisations: Studies in Organisational Semiotics, 153–179.

actors. Simulation models enable experiments that cannot be done in real life for several reasons, such as the undesirability of interfering with people's ordinary behaviour, the complexity of situations, all kinds of measuring inadequacies and, especially in case of organisations, the long time horizon.

The goal of this paper is to give a framework for multi-actor simulation of an organisation that uses simulated boundedly rational actors (Simon, 1945/1976, p. 80) and social constructs (Liu, 2000, p. 64; Gazendam, 2003, p.205) as the main building blocks. A simulation model based on this framework can be used for investigating the effect of social constructs on the behaviour of actors and organisations. The resulting knowledge could be used for the development of new forms of coordination in organisations, for designing information systems, and for understanding the development of virtual organisations. This paper uses the following theoretical perspectives in the design of a multi-actor simulation framework: cognitive science, organisational semiotics, organisation theory, and multi-agent simulation. It focuses on the design of a simulation framework; however the technical implementation of specific simulation models and the results of the simulation experiments fall outside the scope of this paper.

Multi-actor simulation is based on the idea that a system that shows complex behaviour has to generate this behaviour by performing computations. We see the behaviour of such a system, for instance an organisation or society, as complex because that behaviour cannot be described by traditional mathematical tools; For instance, mathematical equations (Wolfram, 2002, p.3). The shortcut taken by traditional mathematics only works when the behaviour of the system is simple. In the case of complex behaviour, this behaviour can be better simulated by computations that use the interaction of computer agents following simple rules (Holland, 1995, 1998; Wolfram, 2002). The complex behaviour at the system level of description can be seen as *emergent,* relative to the simple rules represented at the agent level of description (Holland, 1995, 1998). This discovery has led to a new form of theory development based on the principle of computational equivalence. *Computational equivalence* means, "that whenever one sees behaviour that is not obviously simple . . . it can be thought of as corresponding to a computation of equivalent sophistication" (Wolfram, 2002, p.5). Because of the idea of computational equivalence, we can study (human) organisations based on simulation models consisting of computer agents.

We see cooperation and coordination as resulting from the use of social constructs, which allows a semiotic orientation. This is in contrast with the common non-social perspective in cognitive science. Cooperation is only possible based on intertwined habits and mutual commitments that are often expressed in sign structures such as agreements, contracts, and plans. At the level of description that organisational semiotics uses, these sign structures are seen as social affordances (Liu, 2000, p.64) or social constructs (Gazendam, 2003, p.205). Social constructs guide the formation and reinforcement of habits of individual actors that are aimed at cooperation, coordination, and socially accepted behaviour. Social constructs can be modelled based on concepts and methods used in organisational semiotics.

In contrast to many approaches to multi-actor simulation, we model actors as boundedly rational actors based on cognitive architectures known from cognitive science. This emphasis on cognitive actors contrasts with the standard empty actor modelling in economy and organisation studies. In order to survive, an actor has to participate in an (social) environment, which provides the actor with enough opportunities for acting, individually as well as collectively. However, a "real life" actor has various constraints that can be formulated in terms of bounded rationality, e.g., an actor is ontologically not able to take all information of the complex world into account. Moreover, even if he can, he is cognitively unable to process all this information. Because of this, actors have to cooperate with other actors in many situations.

The aim of doing simulation experiments based on our multi-actor simulation framework is to gain a deeper insight into what effects the use of fast and frugal heuristics —necessary because of bounded rationality— and social constructs have in terms of the efficiency of individual and collective task fulfilment. Important themes to investigate are (i) how actors learn, select and use social constructs given a certain cognitive architecture and the knowledge of certain heuristics, (ii) which configurations of social constructs emerge in a certain environment, and (iii) how these configurations correspond to known organisational configurations. What we try to do is to make a simulation of a collection of actors that have to do tasks in a task environment, and to see what happens if we drop the knowledge of a certain type of social construct (for instance, the "renaissance company", see section 2.2) into that collection of actors. We are interested in what kinds of organisations are formed and how successful they are.

The structure of this article is as follows. In section 2, the modelling of social constructs is described. Social constructs are units of shared knowledge of a normative character. They are the glue that holds organisations together. Instead of using rather complex social constructs that would give the simulation a large amount of complexity, which makes it more difficult to implement and analyse the outcomes of these social constructs, a selection of rather simple social constructs is discussed. One of the ideas behind the simulation design is that organisations can be seen as glued together by configurations of many small and simple social constructs.

Social constructs are the building blocks for organisational configurations that will be formed. Negotiations about which social construct should be applied will finally result in a relationship or organisation.

The modelling of the individual actor, based on a cognitive architecture and on bounded rationality, is explained in section 3. Psychologically plausible cognitive architectures give simulated actors the ability to interact with the environment in a way that is "somewhat" comparable to real human behaviour. We are talking about humans as information processing systems that interpret, hesitate, think, reason and use their memory. The cognitive processes are based upon mental representations the actors have, construct and use. Bounded rationality means that there are limits to the capabilities of the cognitive system. As a result of cognitive limitations, people use compensation mechanisms, for instance, fast and frugal heuristics. The simulation has to incorporate some of these mechanisms.

In section 4, we start with a discussion of the environment in which actors work together. This environment can be seen as a system maintaining physical laws, a task environment, and a "semiotic environment" - known as "the Semiotic Umwelt" in this discourse.

In section 5, we investigate the systems and levels of description that we have to use in our simulation framework. In this investigation, we use several theoretical perspectives: cognitive science, organisational semiotics, organisation theory, and multi-agent simulation.

Finally, in section 6 we discuss the design of the simulation model.

2. THE ORGANISATION SYSTEM

2.1 Organisation and cooperation

An *organisation* can be seen as group of people that have habits of action aimed at cooperation and coordination of work. An organisation is not a physical, tangible object like an apple or a computer keyboard. Its observation, its demarcation, and its existence are dependent on the existence of human habits and human-produced signs[8]. This point of view is a kind of methodological individualism (Franssen, 1997; Van den Broek, 2001, p.25). Basically, an organisation can be traced back to representations that structure the interaction among people, thereby demarcating the group of people that are members of the organisation (van Heusden & Jorna,

[8] And, possibly, to a smaller extent, based on the representations embedded in information systems, and signs produced by information systems.

2001). Especially the participants in the organisation recognize its existence by their behaviour and their knowledge. According to Simon (1945/1976, p. 16), not only the owners (entrepreneurs) and employees of an organisation - groups that are normally seen as its members - belong to its participants, but also its customers, its suppliers, and possibly other stakeholders in the organisation.

Organisations are only formed if the environment poses such demands on the individual actor that *cooperation* with other actors becomes necessary. Situations in which this can occur are, according to Schmidt (1991) and Gazendam & Homburg (1996) that a single actor has insufficient work capacity, insufficient specialized knowledge, one-sided interests and views, and insufficient power to handle conflicts. *Augmentative* cooperation is based on the fact that single actors are limited by mechanical, physiological and cognitive capacity. Therefore, cooperation is necessary to overcome these limitations. *Integrative* cooperation brings in the specialized knowledge of the participants necessary for performing a common task. *Debative* cooperation brings in a variety of values and interests and aims at acceptable conclusions. Knowledge-based work processes are fragile and contestable. The function of debative cooperation is to alleviate this deficiency. Debative cooperation can be found in scientific communities and, for example, in the organisation of governments in clearly independent executive, legislative and judiciary bodies. Actors can also cooperate in order to handle conflicts efficiently and non-destructively by using authority, negotiation, regulated competition and dialogue between discussants.

2.2 Social constructs

In organisational semiotics, the representations that guide the behaviour of people in organisations are described in terms of social constructs. The social construct concept seems to be an efficient abstraction of shared knowledge in organisations that may be useful for implementing social behaviour in simulated actors.

A *social construct or social affordance* (Liu, 2000, p.64; Gazendam, 2003, p.205) is a relatively persistent socially shared unit of knowledge, reinforced in its existence by its daily use. The semiotical level of description can be seen as a relatively strong system level based on the relative stability of social constructs. Compared to compensation mechanisms, social constructs are not only characteristics of individual actors, but are characteristics of relations between actors or groups of actors. Social constructs are relatively persistent units of knowledge that are shared in groups or social systems and are reinforced in their existence by their daily use. When social constructs are known by a group of actors, the habits that are formed based on this knowledge, help to regulate their behaviour aimed at cooperation and coordination of actions. Cooperation also encompasses nonverbal interaction patterns. They can be studied using the observation of recurrent paths in time and space (Giddens, 1984), or as nonverbal work practices (Clarke, 2001).

In organisations, social constructs take the form of, for instance, shared stories, shared institutions (behaviour rule systems), shared designs, shared plans, and shared artefacts. These social constructs support habits of action aimed at cooperation and coordinated behaviour. Each habit of action consists of a commitment to act in a certain way, and a more or less flexible action program that governs the actual acting. If we look at people in organisations, they do not necessarily require similar representations of the organisation they are participating in. However, people participating in organisations need a certain minimum of shared social constructs, and perhaps other shared knowledge, in order to be able to cooperate and coordinate their actions.

At the semiotical level, social constructs emerge based on individual behaviour and mechanisms of reinforcement and selection. At the organisational level, organisational structures can be analysed as being based on social constructs as building blocks. In this way, organisations can be explained as systems of coordinated behaviour of individual human actors, with complex semiotic processes in a key role.

Commitments to act in a certain way and norms can be seen as being attached to social constructs. For instance, there are norms attached to the general social construct of "property" that are inherited by the specific instance of that social construct in the form of the social construct "ownership of my bicycle". An example of these norms is the rule that no one can use my bicycle without first asking my permission to do so.

We have to explain what we mean when we say that a social construct is a unit of socially shared knowledge. Neither all the knowledge, nor all the norms, attached to a social construct, will be shared by all the people that see themselves as committed to that social construct. What is shared is the knowledge of, and commitment to, the social construct as a "root concept", with some norms or default behaviour patterns connected. For instance, if I fill out my income tax form, I feel committed to the social construct of paying taxes, I recognize the social construct of authority of the tax collection service, but I have a very limited knowledge of all the laws and regulations concerning taxes. What I need to know about filling out certain fields in my tax form, I can look up in a tax compendium, which is only a short abstract of all the relevant tax laws and regulations.

Following Dignum's (1996) stratification of social norms, we distinguish three kinds of social constructs. Firstly, we have plans and models as social constructs to the implementation of which individuals or groups can be committed. These social constructs help to determine the actions to be taken. Secondly, there are social constructs that form a relation between two actors, for instance contracts. The actors create obligations and a certain dependency between them. Thirdly, we distinguish behaviour rule systems or institutions that are shared in an organisation, community, or social system. An important part of these rule systems is the description of punishments and rewards in case of (in)correct behaviour. In these behaviour rule systems, also responsibility, authority and power relations between actors can be described. Sometimes these behaviour rule systems are established and modified by authoritative rituals, or take an authoritative form as formal laws or regulations.

If we try to see an organisation, or a coordination mechanism such as a market, as a network of many small social constructs that people use to regulate their social behaviour, we have to look for some simple, basic social construct types as building blocks for our simulation. For inspiration we have looked at, for instance, Weber's theory of authority (Weber, 1925/1968) and simple forms of cooperation agreements found in medieval times and the early Renaissance (Origo, 1957). Based on these sources, we distinguish five types of social constructs to use in our simulation:

1. Principal-agent contract/labour contract (high inequality): Actor A (principal) *offers* a certain number of hours of work and a certain amount of money, and *gets* profit or loss of the enterprise. Actor B (agent) *offers* a fixed number of hours of work and *gets* a fixed amount of money.
2. Company (Italian com pagno, eat bread together) (low inequality): Actor A *offers* a certain amount of hours of work and a certain amount of money, and *gets* a percentage of the profit or loss of the company. Actor B *offers* a certain amount of hours of work and a certain amount of money, and *gets* a percentage of the profit or loss of the company (sometimes there is a principal/agent or father/son relationship here with respect to who can decide about what).
3. Trade transaction (no inequality): Actor A *offers* goods, or services (e.g., specified hours of work of a certain type), or money, or a mixture of these, and *gets* what B offers. Actor B *offers* goods, or services (e.g., specified hours of work of a certain type), or money, or a mixture of these, and *gets* what A offers (1, 2 and 3 are possible special cases of a more general type of transaction).
4. Action plan (no inequality): Actor A and actor B agree to do certain actions at certain points of time.
5. Authority (high inequality): Actor A and actor B agree that A has the right to decide about certain subjects that are in their common interest. This is mostly based on rational authority, instead of traditional or

charismatic authority (Weber, 1968). Traditional authority means no agreement and charismatic means an agreement, which is more or less tacit (possibly a part of the social constructs 1, 2, and 4, mentioned above, and perhaps a (recursive) part of an agreement of type 5 itself)

In our simulation, we will make the knowledge of these social construct types one by one available to actors and see what organisations are formed as a consequence.

According to the Stamper school of organisational semiotics (Stamper, 2001; Liu, 2000), authority is necessary to start or finish a social construct. So, once authority has been established, it can be used for the specific social construct. The establishment of new authority as part of the establishment of social constructs 1, 2, 4, and 5 has to be distinguished from the existing authority under which the construct is established. Because most social constructs are built up on authority, authority can be used as the main social construct on which norms are attached to regulate authority. However, authority is in the eye of the authoritarian actor as well as in the eye of the perceiving actor. Here the cognitive/actor system comes in. Both have representations and authority only works if both actors share larger parts of the representations.

An architecture of social constructs can be formulated. The Stamper school of organisational semiotics states that there are main social constructs called social affordances, to which norms are attached. Norms can be specified by if-then rules (Liu, 2000). Furthermore, each social construct starts and finishes with an actor having an adequate authority to do this. Each social construct may presuppose other social constructs. For instance, to establish a marriage a law or regulation saying how to establish this and what behaviour rules are attached to marriage have to be present. According to the language action school, there is a more or less standardized process (scenario) for establishing a social construct between two actors. So we arrive at the following architecture of social constructs:

- Main social construct ("social affordance") consisting of:
    - Attached norms;
    - Authority under which it starts;
    - Time of start;
    - Authority under which it finishes;
    - Time of finishing;
    - Prerequisite of other social constructs (from which norms can be inherited, and which defines who has the authority to start and finish);
    - Scenario for establishing the social construct;

- o Authority that is created and allocated as part of the social construct;

This architecture is a good basis for the implementation of social constructs in a simulation model. Social constructs however, must be represented in the (simulated) cognition of actors. This cognitive anchoring of social constructs is different to the social affordance perspective. A social affordance perspective does not explicitly take into account the cognitive actor as a human information processing system with mental representations.

3. THE INDIVIDUAL ACTOR SYSTEM

3.1 Modelling boundedly rational actors

In many economic and organisational studies, organisations, and the human actors within, are considered as behaving in a fully rational manner, searching for optimal solutions. Opposed to that, we describe actors as boundedly rational. Bounded rationality is the concept that Simon (1945/1976, p. 80) coined to conceptualize the limitations of "perfect" representations of the environment by the human actor and also of the mental processing capacity of the actor. They are boundedly rational, because they do not have a complete representation of the world around them (the ontological argument) and even if they have, they are not able to process all the information and opportunities they encounter (the cognitive argument). The ontological argument says that you cannot predict, for example, the weather situation in Reading at September 23, 2009. The system is too complex. The same holds for the behaviour of all humans at September 23, 2003. That is also too complex. The cognitive argument says that even if you could, your mental system is not fit in terms of representations and architecture to accomplish these predictions.

If we go back to how Simon over the years elaborated his "satisficing" organism (including the human information processing system), he never changed the fundamental characteristics. They include the following:

- Limitation of the organism's ability to plan long-term behavioral sequences; a limitation imposed by the bounded cognitive ability of the organism as well as the complexity of the environment in which it operates.
- The tendency to set aspiration levels for each of the multiple goals that the organism faces.
- The tendency to sequentially operate on goals rather than simultaneously, because of the "bottleneck of short-term memory".

– "Satisficing" rather than "optimizing" search behaviour.

However, to model boundedly rational actors for our simulation, we have to give them one or more of the following specific properties:

– Bounded knowledge or information about the environment. Normally, the actor absorbs only a small amount of knowledge or information about the environment by interacting with this dynamic environment.
– Decrease in activation of information and rules, which will further restrict use or application. In this way, bounded rationality will never become fully rational.
– An incomplete and imperfect model or representation of the surrounding environment. The representation of the environment of the human actor in consciousness, presupposing the cognitive architecture, is principally not in accordance with reality.
– Restricted processor capacity. The actors are not capable of computing all the symbolic calculations on the knowledge they possess. When, for example, an actor uses heuristics a boundedly rational actor has a preference for a simple heuristic instead of a difficult one.
– Other resources, such as memory, are restricted, which makes it impossible for an actor to remember everything.

To implement these properties, the actors have to be equipped with a cognitive architecture, which enables them to interact with the environment, to create representations (semiosis), to set goals and to learn. An example of such architecture is ACT-R.

3.2 The actor architecture: ACT-R

A cognitive architecture is an implementation of bounded rationality. Many architectures of cognition have been developed (Posner, 1989). In order to implement the properties mentioned in the previous section, we choose the ACT-R architecture (Anderson & Lebiere, 1998; see figure 1) for this simulation. ACT-R tries to incorporate the functional as well as the physiological level of cognition and it also has a more elaborated account of learning as compared to the cognitive architecture that is described in SOAR (Laird, Newell, & Rosenbloom, 1987).

The architecture consists of three main parts: procedural memory, declarative memory and the goal stack. Procedural memory mostly consists of if-then rules. This makes it possible for the actor to reason. Procedural memory is also responsible for actions of the actor towards the outside world. Declarative memory is more like a database consisting of facts, which are most of the time perceived by the actor by interacting with the outside world. Every part, called a chunk of knowledge, has a parameter, which indicates the importance of that knowledge. The base activation level of a chunk depends on the frequency with which it has been used and on the time lapsed since the last time it was used. Selection of chunks is based on these activation levels. The goal stack makes it possible to divide goals into less complicated sub-goals, which, after solving the sub-goals, makes it possible for the actor to solve the main goal.

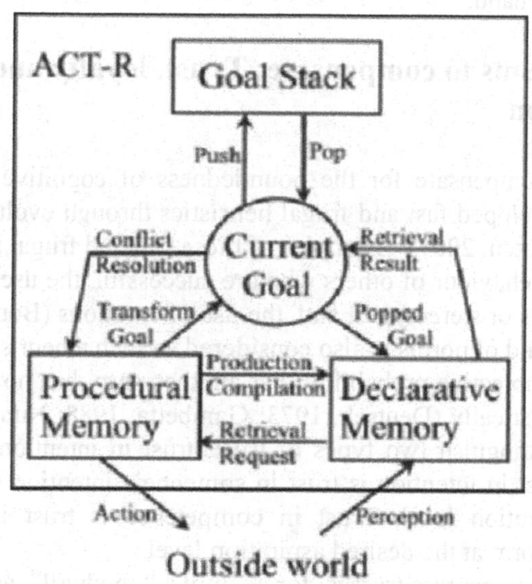

Figure 1. Information flow within ACT-R: a cognitive architecture

The cognitive architecture can also deal with the selection of procedural rules, such as having a preference for simple, instead of for complex rules. One assumption is that different decision strategies need different amounts of processor capacity (Simon, 1955). Another feature is that it is possible to limit the amount of elements (chunks, etc.) of procedural and declarative memory.

The basic assumption within ACT-R (and SOAR and other cognitive architectures) is that at the functional level this architecture mimics the mental processes of humans. This is what Newell and Simon (1972) called the symbol systems hypothesis. Symbols, architectural components and processing are comparable to the knowledge (representations) that we have, for the restrictions that are part of our mental make-up and to the way we think. Architectures of cognition are models of humans, who are conceived to be boundedly rational.

This individual cognitive part is implemented by the actors as a basic element in our simulation. The social part comes in when we look at how we try to overcome our inherent limitations. We argue that bounded rationality, that is to say the restrictions humans and organisations experience, is (partly) compensated for by the use of other mechanisms, such as trust, loyalty and reputation between actors, and the social environment on the one hand, and by coordination mechanisms and governance structures at the organisational level on the other hand.

3.3 Mechanisms to compensate: Trust, loyalty and reputation

In order to compensate for the boundedness of cognitive capabilities, humans have developed fast and frugal heuristics through evolutionary time (Gigerenzer & Selten, 2001). Examples of these fast and frugal heuristics are the imitation of behaviour of others who are successful, the use of culturally transferred models or stereotypes, and, the use of emotions (Bouissac, 2003). The use of trust and of norms is also considered as such a heuristic.

Trust is the subjective probability that another party has no intentions to behave opportunistically (Deutsch, 1973; Gambetta, 1988; Numan, 1998). It is possible to distinguish two types of trust: trust in intention and trust in competence. Trust in intention is trust in someone's intention to perform at the desired aspiration level. Trust in competence is trust in someone's capability to perform at the desired aspiration level.

A mechanism to express trust is, for example, "goodwill", accounting for all actors whom an actor had contact with. "Goodwill" will help an actor to establish a representation of the intentions and competences of other actors. Trust in itself is not an independent characteristic, because it is dependent on behaviour of other actors and on the 'hostility' of the environment. Gulati (1995), for example, states that trust increases with time, when the partner does not show opportunistic behaviour, such as breaking the relationship or not complying with the acquired competence. Trust is subject to changes and can be very unstable in a rapidly changing environment. Loyalty on the other hand is more dependent on the properties and behaviour of the actor itself. Loyalty forms the behaviour of the actor itself and can determine the trustworthiness for this specific actor. For example, when an actor behaves in a stable way in a relationship and is not defecting, even if there is a better opportunity, this actor can be defined as a loyal actor. But what are the benefits of loyalty versus opportunism?

There is probably a clear connection between loyalty and reputation, because when an actor wants to keep a good reputation for not defecting from a relationship, it will behave more loyally towards other actors to preserve this good reputation. Reputation can be seen as a partly shared representation of what all actors think about an actor. To acquire this reputation, an actor has to behave properly; the actor has to have knowledge about how to behave in certain circumstances. McAdams (1997), for instance, argues that every actor has (social) norms, which it has to obey. They are perceived from the environment, from other actors (inheriting of parents) or created/changed by the actor itself. Norms are a result of shared characteristics of proper behaviour and the willingness of individuals to reward correct behaviour and to punish incorrect behaviour. If, for example, you are invited to a dinner that you thought of would be an informal dinner and you are wearing jeans, but everybody else wears formal clothing, you interfere with a social norm and as a result you feel embarrassed. In procedural memory, this norm could look like: if <<personal norm> rebellious == false> and if <formal dinner == true> → then <clothing == formal >. This is just a small example. In reality decisions about what to wear are obviously more complicated. Besides this, norms also provide solutions for coordination problems regarding behaviour, which makes it easier to adjust to one another and causes less time and money expenditure.

Adjusting to one another means that the actor has to have capabilities or social aids to interact with other actors or its environment and to interpret signs of other actors and its environment to coordinate actions and cooperate successfully.

Next to the capability of the actor to use and interpret signs, sign-structures like social constructs will enable actors to interact more efficiently and create more 'stable' interaction patterns.

4. THE ENVIRONMENT SYSTEM

The environment system can be seen from the perspective of multi-agent simulation as a system maintaining physical laws, from the perspective of cognitive science as a task environment, and from the perspective of semiotics as a semiotic Umwelt.

In most multi-agent simulations (Wooldridge, 2002, p. 16), it is assumed that the environment in which agents operate is non-deterministic and dynamic. *Non-determinism* means that agents only have partial control of their environment. They have a limited sphere of influence and a perception horizon. In a non-deterministic environment, the action of an agent when performed twice may have different results. The action may also fail. However, the reaction of the environment on the agent's actions is not totally random. In most simulations it is assumed that the environment has to maintain physical laws.

The environment is also *dynamic*, which means that it changes independently of the agent's actions. This means that the agent has to gather information to determine the state of the environment before deciding about what to do. Furthermore, other processes (like the actions of other agents) may interfere with the actions of an agent. The agents, therefore, have to worry about coordinating and synchronizing their actions; something that is not necessary in static environments.

The environment may also be *discrete or continuous*. In a computer simulation, the environment is per definition discrete. Continuous environments, however, can be simulated to any desired degree of accuracy. An example is the determination of time intervals in discrete event simulation.

If we want to compare the performance of human actors with computer agents, the simulation environment also has to work in *real time*, adapted to the interaction with the human users.

Within cognitive science, Newell and Simon (1972) reformulated the environment system as a task environment. They used the term *task environment* to indicate that a problem space representation does not come out of the blue. Setting goals and determining constraints are necessary for any search activity. The structure of the task environment provides part of the information that is needed to account for intelligent behaviour (Simon, 1969). The cognitive system represents and interacts with the task environment in performing tasks.

A task is defined as a sequence of actions in order to reach (various) goals, taking into account (various) constraints (Waern, 1989). Examples of tasks are giving mortgage advice, diagnosing illnesses, scheduling staff shifts, storing goods in a warehouse and trading. A task always requires an explicit or implicit task model. A task is not a natural entity. From the perspective of organisational semiotics, it is a social construct. This means that task analysis may result in several sub-tasks, sub-sub-tasks, etc. Arbitrary end points may result from this situation. Various dimensions to divide tasks can be discerned. In terms of the dimension of time, keystrokes are at the lowest level (less than one second) and loaning a book from the library is at a realistic level (about 10 to 20 minutes), and writing this article (more than one week) is at the highest level.

From an organisational point of view, the *semiotic Umwelt* is an environment around a human being or animal based on the signs and symbols that it creates and perceives. The types of signs and symbols that can be created and perceived depend on the biological species. The basic structure of the semiotic Umwelt, its space and time, depends on the sign processing capabilities of the living being. Time is dependent on its biological rhythms. Space is structured in such a way that the signs an organism can perceive, are localized in a meaningful way.

"Während wir bisher sagten, ohne Zeit kann es kein lebendes Subjekt geben, werden wir jetzt sagen müssen, ohne lebendes Subjekt kann es keine Zeit geben. . . . das gleiche gilt für den Raum. . . . Ohne ein lebendes Subjekt kann es weder Raum noch Zeit geben." (Von Uexküll and Kriszat, 1936/ 1970: 14; Von Uexküll, 1998: 2189).
Or in EnglishIndicating that in this discourse "the notion of a living subject existing without time, or indeed time existing in a context devoid of a living subject does not arise. This applies to spaces too, without a living subject, neither the concept of space nor time can be meaningfully realised". (Von Uexküll and Kriszat, 1936/ 1970: 14; Von Uexküll, 1998: 2189.

Thus the semiotic Umwelt supports the survival of human and animal actors, and affords certain species-specific behavioural patterns (Gibson, 1969; Von Uexküll, 1998). Based on the development of these species-specific behavioural patterns, an actor has access to a task environment that is structured in terms of space, time, objects, resources, other actors, and signs.

5. SYSTEMS AND LEVELS OF DESCRIPTION

5.1 A meta-theoretical analysis of theoretical viewpoints in terms of levels of description and systems

In the definition of our simulation framework, we have to combine the theoretical perspectives we use, namely, cognitive science, organisational semiotics, organisation theory, and multi-agent simulation theory. Furthermore, we have to combine the systems we have discussed thus far: the organisation, the cognitive actor and the environment. An important point of difference between the theoretical perspectives mentioned is their use of different levels of description. An analysis of theoretical perspectives in terms of the systems they distinguish and the levels of description they use seems to be necessary to be able to integrate them in one framework. This is a meta-theoretical analysis by nature. In order to do this, we will first discuss the concepts of 'level of description' and 'system'. After that, we will examine our theoretical perspectives (cognitive science, organisational semiotics, organisation theory, and multi-agent simulation theory) with respect to the systems they distinguish and the levels of description they use. Then, we present an overview of the results of our analysis before proceeding to the integrated view of the theory behind our multi-actor simulation framework in the next section (5.2.).

Levels of description are defined based on the perspective taken when describing one and the same phenomenon or system (Newell, 1990, p.46, p.118). The perspective taken describes a certain system level at which components can be discerned that interact, thus producing behaviour at that (system) level. *Systems* are distinguished based on their coherence and their functioning as a whole. Systems often have clear boundaries. According to Simon (1996, p.183), a stable system generally will consist of a hierarchy of system levels to which levels of description correspond.

Cognitive science focuses on the human actor system and the task environment system. Human beings, animals, robots, and computer agents are functionally equivalent according to Newell and Simon's physical symbol system hypothesis (1972; Newell, 1990). In setting out a research agenda for cognitive science - the human actor system - in the early seventies, Dennett (1978, 1991, p. 76) introduced the distinction in various levels of description. He discerned a physical, a functional and an intentional level of description (or stance, as Dennett called them). Other authors (Newell, 1982, 1990; Pylyshyn, 1984) have given similar accounts in which, however, the number of levels varies.

The first level of description is the physical stance. It describes behaviour in terms of physical properties of the states and the behaviour of the (individual actor) system. For its proper functioning, the human organism requires a complex interaction of its parts with the external world. The central nervous system and the endocrine system transmit information that reveal the state of one part of the system to other parts. We can also mention the transmission of currents in the synaptive system of neurons. Within cognitive science, the physical level is the endpoint of successful ontological reduction.

The second level of description takes the point of view of the functional design of a system. The behaviour of a system is conceived of as the result of the interaction of a number of functional components or processes. In a functional description, it is important to know what the components of the system are, how they are defined and how the components and sub-components of a system are connected with each other. In other words, if the input and output of every component are known, it is possible, given a certain input at the beginning of the system, to predict the resulting behaviour on the basis of the properties of the states. The physical structure (architecture) of the system is not explicitly taken into account, although it may impose constraints on the behaviour of the system. The capacity limitations of human memory will, for instance, impose constraints on solving very complex problems. From a semiotic point of view, mental symbols and representations are at the functional level of description. Mental representations are said to consist of symbol structures that can be processed within the cognitive architecture (Newell & Simon, 1972). The (mental) symbol structures are the basis of higher system levels, corresponding to the intentional and semiotical levels of description. Although rarely formulated explicitly in most representational theories of mind, the whole of functional, intentional, and semiotic levels are parts of a semiotic system, which means that representational theories of mind are semiotic by nature (Jorna, 1990).

The third level that Dennett distinguishes is the intentional level. Complex behaviour that is adapted to prevailing circumstances, according to some criterion of optimality, is said to be rational or intelligent. A behaving system to which we can successfully attribute rationality or intelligence qualifies as an intentional system. It is not necessary for a behaving system to 'really' possess rationality or intelligence, as long as the assumption allows us to predict correctly the behaviour of the system on the basis of our knowledge of the circumstances in which the system is operating.

The main message Dennett wanted to express with his distinctions in levels is firstly that the functional level is an adequate level of description for cognitive science to study all kind of cognitive phenomena and secondly that the intentional level, although the common level of description within social (and organisational) contexts, can, or better, should be reduced to the functional level. Newell (1990, p.122) follows Dennett's research perspective and distinguishes similar levels (for the same actor system) based on a time and space scale. Adjacent levels are grouped into bands. In this way, the biological band, the cognitive band, the rational band and the social band are distinguished. The physical level of description can be situated at the higher part of the biological band, the functional level resides at the cognitive band, and the intentional level corresponds to the rational band. Newell requires that each level has a relatively stable structure, based on the organisation of elements that are based on lower levels (Newell, 1990, p. 117). Levels with a strong organisation are called strong levels. Newell sees all levels above the rational band as relatively weak.

Organisational semiotics (Stamper, 1973, 2001; Liu, 2000; Gazendam, Jorna & Cijsouw, 2003, pp. 1-12) distinguishes six levels of description in the form of a semiotic framework or semiotic ladder: the physical world, empirics, syntactics, semantics, pragmatics, and the social world. The main focus is on semantics (functional level), pragmatics (intentional level), and the social world. Within the social world, social constructs in the form of social affordances (Liu, 200, p. 64) play an important role. Furthermore, there is the language action perspective within organisational semiotics that distinguishes speech-act based scenarios for establishing social constructs, such as the DEMO scenario (Dietz, 1995, 1998). The systems that organisational semiotics distinguishes are the human actor, and a system of communicating human actors (Liu, 2000, p. 64). Furthermore, an environment can be distinguished in the form of a semiotic Umwelt (Von Uexküll & Kriszat, 1936/ 1970, Gazendam, Jorna & Cijsouw, 2003, p. 8). This is an environment around a human being or animal based on the signs and symbols that it creates and perceives. The types of signs and symbols that can be created and perceived depend on the biological species.

In *organisation theory*, there are three systems or system types that are distinguished: the organisation, the individual actor, and the organisation network. In our simulation framework, we will not use the organisation network. The individual actor is generally a human individual, but can also be, for instance, a computer agent. Organisations can be described at the level of the organisation as a whole, at the level of the individual actor, or at the intermediate level, for instance based on the (inter) actions of actors, the sign structures they use, or as graphs depicting communication and control lines between actors and subsystems (Mintzberg, 1979; Gazendam, 1993, p. 102). This intermediate level, a level that more or less corresponds to the social world of social affordances in organisational semiotics, can be seen as a semiotical level of description.

Multi-agent simulation (Carley & Gasser, 2001; Wooldridge, 2002) distinguishes the agent system, the task environment system, and the organisation as system. There are two levels of description: the agent level and the level of emergent communication and cooperation patterns more or less corresponding to the intermediate or semiotical level mentioned above. The theoretical background of multi-agent simulation has developed rapidly in recent years based on the concepts of computational mathematics (Wolfram, 2002), emergence (Holland, 1995; 1998), coherence (Thagard, 2000), and evolution (Dawkins, 1976; 1986; Dennett, 1995). A basic idea behind these concepts is the abolishment of a static world view in favour of a dynamic world view. Computational simulation models are the backbone of this emerging new kind of science, and replace the equation models and logic models that have been the foundation of science since the days of Newton. For instance, Thagard's computational models explain the intentional level based on more basic computational mechanisms at the functional level.

Our investigation of the theoretical perspectives used leads to the overview in Table 1.

Table 1. Theoretical perspectives and levels of description (1: not distinguished except as Newell's social band)

	Cognitive science	organisational semiotics	Organisation theory	(multi-agent simulation)
Organisational level	1)		•	
Semiotical level	1)	•	•	•
Intentional level	•	•	•	•
Functional level	•	•		•
Physical level	•			

5.2 A combination of theoretical viewpoints as the basis for our multi-actor simulation framework

Combining the perspectives of cognitive science, organisational semiotics, organisation theory, and multi-agent simulation, we can distinguish three systems and five levels of description that are interesting for the development of our simulation model.

The three *systems* are: the individual actor system, the organisation system, and the environment system. A common problem within cognitive science is the neglect of the social environment of the human information processing system (the individual actor). To put it in terms of our simulation, the focus is only on the individual actor system. However, individuals always live in groups, families, firms or/and societies. We can state this more generally in saying that individual actors live in organisations. This means that besides the individual actor system we also have the more aggregate organisation system. An *organisation* is a collection of individual actors, together with the work processes, the sign structures, and the objects they see as belonging to the organisation. The individual actor and the organisation "live" in the environment system. This system defines in particular time and space, and the physical laws actors and objects must comply to.

The five *levels of description* are: the physical level, the functional level, the intentional (or rational) level, the semiotical (or social construct) level, and the organisational level. The first level is the *physical* level of cognitive science, which includes Stamper's physical world and empirical levels of description. The second level corresponds to the *functional* level in cognitive science, which includes Stamper's level of syntactics and semantics, and the agent level in multi-agent simulation. The third level is the *intentional* level of cognitive science, more or less corresponding to Stamper's level of pragmatics, and the human actor level in organisation theory. The fourth level is the *semiotical*[9] (or social construct) level of description that can be seen as a relatively strong level based on the stability of communication patterns, languages, and social constructs. Communication patterns, languages, and social constructs persist through decennia, and even centuries (take, for instance, the social construct of property/ownership). They have a key position in communication, learning, and developing social behaviour by human beings. They can be seen as knowledge units that are shared in groups or even social systems, reinforcing themselves by communication and their daily use. These shared knowledge units can influence individual behaviour by forming habits, thus creating a cycle of selection and reinforcement, where some knowledge units are reinforced and others disappear. The semiotical level of description focuses on sign structures, and processes of sign production and sign use as relatively stable, independent phenomena. In this way, one can focus on communication patterns, texts, knowledge units, knowledge types, habits of action, and social constructs as meaningful kernel concepts. We canabstract from the problem of processing the corresponding sign structures by the human cognitive system and the mental representation of these sign structures in the human mindat the functional (and intentional) level. The semiotical level of description corresponds to the lower part of Newell's social band. The semiotical level of description includes the use of social constructs and language action scenarios in organisational semiotics, the intermediate level of description in organisation theory, and the level of emergent patterns in multi-agent systems. Organisational coordination mechanisms can be analysed as being based on social constructs as building blocks. In this way, organisations can be explained as systems of coordinated behaviour of individual human actors, with complex semiotic processes in a key role.

The *organisational* level of description is the fifth level and abstracts from questions around the emergence and persistence of communication patterns, knowledge units, social constructs, and so on, and focuses on a description of organisations in terms of variables and configurations of these variables. The organisational level corresponds to the higher level of Newell's social band. The organisational level of description includes the description of the characteristics of the organisation as a whole in

[9] It may seem somewhat strange that we use the name 'semiotical level' for a level of description. The problem is that a long name like 'social construct level' may be confusing as well, because not only social constructs play a role at this level, but also speech acts, interaction scenarios, shared knowledge units, and so on. Because organisational semiotics focuses especially on this level of description, 'semiotical' seemed the best choice for a name, giving (organisational) semiotics a place as a discipline that can form a bridge between cognitive science and organisation theory.

organisation theory, like for instance Mintzberg's (1979) description in terms of design parameters, intermediary variables, contingency variables, and structural configurations.

The actor system can be described using the physical, functional, and intentional levels. The organisation system can be described using the semiotical and the organisational levels. The environment system can be described in terms of the physical constraints to the operation of means of communication, production, consumption, transport, and so on, and in this way includes the physical level (see Table 2).

Sign structures play a role in all three systems. They play an important role at the functional level of description of an individual actor. They reside as physical inscriptions in the semiotic Umwelt, that is, the environment. Shared sign structures play a role as social constructs that are part of an organisation.

Table 2. Systems and levels of description in our multi-actor simulation framework

	Actor system	organisation system	environment system
Organisational level		●	
Semiotical level		●	
Intentional level	●		
Functional level	●		
Physical level	●		●

In figure 2, we show the connection between the levels of description and the systems used in our simulation framework. On the left side are the levels of description: the physical, the functional, the intentional, the semiotical, and the organisational level. On the right side we show the three systems: the environment, the individual actor and the organisation. Shared signs in the form of social constructs have to be represented (as 'cognitive' signs) in the minds of individual actors (at the functional level), and are used to define an organisation at the organisational level.

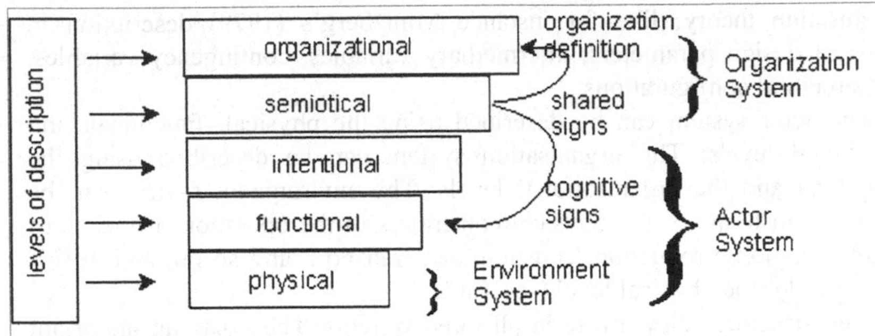

Figure 2. Systems and levels of description

6. THE DESIGN OF THE SIMULATION MODEL

To study multi-actor systems, two approaches can be taken: a) empirical research in real world situations or b) creating and using a (simulation) model that attempts to reflect the reality of organisations. We chose the second approach, because it gives us opportunities to easily change environments, variables and other characteristics of actors without losing time and energy in investigating real world organisations. However, even the best model has to be based on empirical findings, meaning that simulation research can never replace empirical research. It can be complementary to it and, in order to make it stronger, it can be conducted in its own right. Empirical research has to help in (dis)confirming simulation results. Because of this, we haven chosen a layered simulation environment that enables human actors to play roles in the simulated world, much like playing a computer game. This enables the comparison of human behaviour with simulated actor behaviour.

As we already indicated, in this paper we sketch the constitutent conceptual elements of the simulation. Parts of the simulation have already been tried out. Klos (2000) built a first simulation (in Simula) in which he studied the effects of trust, loyalty and profit on the overall performance of two groups of equal buyers and suppliers. In this simulation the organisational level was studied without taking into account cognitively plausible actors. The theoretical background was inspired by the shortcomings of Transaction Cost Economics (TCE). The task environment consisted of a simple trading game. Suppliers can produce goods and sell them to buyers or they can produce goods for themselves. In a number of evolving stages, relations between buyers and suppliers can start, continue or break up. Similarly Van den Broek (2001) developed a simulation of the co-operation between two actors using a SOAR-architecture. A very important result deduced from his simulation was that actors need representations of other actors in order to co-operate. Helmhout (2001) elaborated upon the simulation of Klos by varying the buyers and suppliers in terms of power and by re-programming the simulation in Java. Within the simulation environment of Klos and Helmhout, Kraaykamp (2003) started the implementation of cognitive actors by using the ACT-R cognitive architecture as a psychologically plausible implementation of buyers and sellers. He used Smalltalk as the programming language for this domain.

In our simulation set-up, we see organisational configurations (at the organisational level of description) as derived from the social constructs level (at the semiotical level of description). Actors use social constructs to form relationships and cooperations. When actor A interacts with actor B to complete a certain task, both actors have to come to a certain agreement as to under which conditions a relation starts, under which conditions a relation ends and under whose authority this is taking place. Agreements are often reached by conflicts and compromises. In, for example, the employer-employee relationship, the employer wants wages to be as low as possible, while an employee wants the opposite. If both actors come to an agreement, the relation starts. The agreement is a social construct and is often documented in standard labour contracts. However, both the employer and the employee have their own social construct in memory, which can be copied from former experiences with labour contracts. In the simulation we will give the actors the possibility to choose between different kinds of social constructs that can be learned or discovered in the environment. The simulation probably results in emergent behaviour in terms of knowledge build-up by the actors, the heuristics used most frequently, and the configurations of social constructs learned and used. These patterns of emergent behaviour, especially the social construct configurations, can be interpreted at the organisational level of description as co-ordination mechanisms and organisation structures that emerge.

The simulation experiments will use cognitive characteristics, compensation mechanisms (fast and frugal heuristics), available types of social constructs, and types of environment constraints as independent variables. Dependent variables are the configurations of social constructs formed, their interpretation in terms of co-ordination mechanisms, and the efficiency of task fulfillment in the individual and group/organisation system. Some of the questions the simulation experiments will have to answer are:

I. How, given a certain cognitive architecture, do actors learn, select and use social constructs in order to cooperate effectively?

II. *Which configurations of social constructs emerge in a certain environment?*

III. *Do the emergent configurations of social constructs correspond to known organisational configurations?*

7. DISCUSSION

This article contains a conceptual framework for multi-actor simulation. The idea of building simulation models consisting of actors with a cognitive architecture that cooperate and interact with the help of social constructs is a challenging one. However, the question to what extent the implementation and outcomes of the simulation model are consistent with empirical data still remains open. Empirical evidence, for instance based on the recording of the behaviour of humans participating as an actor in the simulation, can support, or give counterarguments against, the theory implemented in the simulation model. Another point to look at is the complexity of the simulation model. A model with three systems and several levels of description has a lot of parameters that must be tuned. Where possible these tuning factors will be taken from empirical research findings.

Future work focuses on the relationship between the semiotical level of description and the organisational level of description, and will possibly use game theory and sociological network analysis. However, for the shorter and more realistic term, the implementation of, and experimentation with, the model have our attention. The simulation software is now being programmed, and the first experiments will be run shortly.

REFERENCES

Anderson, J.R. 1990. The Adaptive Character of Thought. Redwood City CA: Benjamin Cummings.

Anderson, J. R. 1993. Rules of the Mind. Hillsdale, NJ: Lawrence Erlbaum Associates.

Anderson, J. R. & Lebiere, C. 1998, The Atomic Components of Thought. Mahwah, NJ: Lawrence Erlbaum Associates.

Bouissac, P. 2003. Bounded Semiotics: From Utopian to Evolutionary Models of Communication. In H. W. M. Gazendam, R. J. Jorna & R. S. Cijsouw (Eds.) Dynamics and Change in Organisations: Studies in Organisational Semiotics 3 (pp. 17-39). Boston: Kluwer.

Broek, J. H. Van den 2001. On Agent Cooperation: The Relevance of Cognitive Plausibility for Multiagent Simulation Models of Organisations. Labyrinth Publications: Capelle a/d IJssel.

Carley, K. M., & Gasser, L. 2001. Computational Organisation Theory. In G. Weiss (Ed.), Multiagent Systems (pp. 299-330). Cambridge, MA: The MIT Press.

Clarke, R. J. 2001. Towards A Systemic Semiotic Approach to Multimedia Interface Design. In K. Liu, R. J. Clarke, P. Bøgh Andersen, & R. K. Stamper (Eds.), Information, Organisation and Technology: Studies in Organisational Semiotics (pp. 247-270). Boston, MA: Kluwer Academic Publishers.

Dawkins, R. 1976. The Selfish Gene. Oxford: Oxford University Press.

Dawkins, R. 1986. The Blind Watchmaker. London: Penguin.

Dennett, D. C. 1978. Brainstorms: Philosophical Essays On Mind and Psychology. Hassocks, Sussex: Harvester Press.

Dennett, D. C. 1991. Consciousness Explained. London: Allen Lane / The Penguin Press.

Dennett, D. C. 1995. Darwin's Dangerous Idea: Evolution and the meanings of life. New York: Simon & Schuster.

Deutsch, M. 1973. The Resolution of Conflict. New Haven: Yale University Press.

Dietz, J. L. G. 1992. Leerboek Informatiekundige Analyse. Deventer: Kluwer Bedrijfswetenschappen.

Dietz, J. L. G. 1996. Introductie to DEMO: Van Informatietechnologie Naar Organisatietechnologie. Alphen a/d Rijn: Samsom.

Dignum, 1996. Autonomous Agents and Social norms. ICMAS '96 Workshop paper.

Franssen, M. 1997. Some Contributions to Methodological Individualism in the Social Sciences. Unpublished doctoral dissertation, University of Amsterdam.

Gazendam, H. W. M. 1993. Variety Controls Variety: On the Use of Organisation Theories in Information Management. Groningen: Wolters-Noordhoff.

Gazendam, H.W.M. 2003. Models as Coherent Sign Structures. In H. W. M. Gazendam, R. J. Jorna & R. S. Cijsouw (Eds.), Dynamics and Change in Organisations: Studies in Organisational Semiotics 3 (pp. 183-213). Boston: Kluwer.

Gazendam, H. W. M., & Homburg, V. M. F. 1996. Emergence of Multi-Actor Systems: Aspects of Coordination, Legitimacy and Iinformation Management. In Proceedings of the COST A3 Conference 'Management and New Technologies', Madrid, June 12-14, (pp. 323-327). Luxembourg: Office for Official Publications of the European Communities.

Gazendam, H. W. M., Jorna, R. J., & Cijsouw, R. S. 2003. Introduction. In H. W. M. Gazendam, R. J. Jorna & R. S. Cijsouw (Eds.), Dynamics and Change in Organisations: Studies in Organisational Semiotics 3 (pp. 1-12). Boston: Kluwer.

Gambetta, D., (Ed.) 1988. Trust: The Making and Breaking of Cooperative Relations. Oxford: Basil Blackwell.

Gibson, J. J. 1979. The Ecological Approach to Visual Perception. Boston, MA: Houghton Mifflin.

Giddens, A. 1984. The Constitution of Society. Berkeley, CA: University of California Press.

Gigerenzer, G., & Selten, R. (Eds.). (2001). Bounded Rationality: The Adaptive Toolbox. Cambridge, MA: The MIT Press.

Gulati, R. 1995. Does Familiarity Breed Trust? The Implications of Repeated Ties for Contractual Choice in Alliances. Academy of Management Journal 38(1), 85-112.

Helmhout, M. 2001. Make or Buy? Een Beslissing Gebaseerd Op de Transactiekostentheorie [Make or Buy? A Decision Based on Transaction Cost Theory]. Unpublished Master Thesis, Faculty of Management and Organisation, Groningen University, Groningen, The Netherlands.

Heusden, B. van & Jorna, R.J. 2001. Toward A Semiotic Theory of Cognitive Dynamics in Organisations. In: K. Liu, R.J. Clarke, P.B. Andersen & R.K. Stamper (Eds.), Information, Organisation and Technology: Studies in Organisational Semiotics. Boston: Kluwer. pp.83-113.

Holland, J. H. 1995. Hidden Order: How Adaptation Builds Complexity. Reading, MA: Addison-Wesley.
Holland, J. H. 1998. Emergence: From Chaos to Order. Oxford: Oxford University Press.
Jorna, R.J. 1990. Knowledge Representation and Symbols in the Mind. Tübingen: Stauffenburg Verlag.
Klos, T. B. 2000. Agent-Based Computational Transaction Cost Econmics. Capelle a/d IJssel, The Netherlands: Labyrinth.
Kraaykamp, D. 2003. Cooperation Between Actors: An ACT-R Implementation. Unpublished Master Thesis, Faculty of Management and Organisation and Institute for Artifical Intelligence, Groningen University, Groningen, The Netherlands.
Laird, J.E., Newell, A. & Rosenblum, P. (1987). SOAR: An Architecture for General Intelligence, Artificial Intelligence, 33, 1-64.
Liu, K. 2000. Semiotics in Information Systems Engineering. Cambridge, England: Cambridge University Press.
McAdams, R. 1997. The Origin, Development, and Regulation of Norms. Michigan Law Review, 96 (2), 338-443.
Mintzberg, H. 1979. The Structuring of Organisations. Englewood Cliffs: Prentice-Hall.
Newell, A. 1990. Unified Theories of Cognition: The William James Lectures, 1987. Cambridge, MA: Harvard University Press.
Newell, A., & Simon, H. A. 1972. Human Problem Solving. Englewood Cliffs, NJ: Prentice-Hall.
Numan, J. H. 1998. Knowledge Systems as Companions: Trust, Human Computer Interaction and Complex Systems. Labyrinth Publications: Capelle a/d IJssel.
Origo, I. 1957. The Merchant of Prato: Francesco di Marco Datini. London: Cape.
Posner, M. I. (Ed.). 1989. Foundations of Cognitive Science. Boston (Mass): MIT Press.
Pylyshyn, Z. W. 1984. Computation and Cognition: Toward a Foundation for Cognitive Science. Cambridge, MA: The MIT Press.
Schmidt, K. 1991. Cooperative Work: A Conceptual Framework. In J. Rasmussen, B. Brehmer & J. Leplat (Eds.), Distributed Decision Making: Cognitive Models for Cooperative Work (pp. 75-110). Chichester: John Wiley and Sons.
Simon, H.A. 1955. A Behavioral Model of Rational Choice. Quarterly Journal of Economic, 69, (pp. 99-118).
Simon, H.A. 1976. Administrative behavior: A Study of Decision-Making Processes in Administrative Organisation (3rd ed.). New York: The Free Press. (Original work published 1945).
Simon, H. A. 1969. The Sciences of the Artificial. Cambridge, MA: MIT Press.
Simon, H. A. 1996. The Sciences of the Artificial (3rd ed.). Cambridge, MA: The MIT Press.
Stamper, R. 1973. Information in Business and Administrative Systems. New York: Wiley.
Stamper, R. K. 2001. Organisational Semiotics: Informatics Without the Computer? In K. Liu, R. J. Clarke, P. Bøgh Andersen, & R. K. Stamper (Eds.), Information, Organisation and Technology: Studies in Organisational Semiotics (pp. 115-171). Boston, MA: Kluwer Academic Publishers.
Thagard, P. 2000. Coherence in Thought and Action. Cambridge, MA: The MIT Press.
Uexküll, T. von 1998. Jakob von Uexkülls Umweltlehre. In R. Posner, K. Robering, & T. A. Sebeok (Eds.), Semiotics: A Handbook on the Sign-Theoretic Foundations of Nature and Culture: Vol. 2 (pp. 2183-2191). Berlin, Germany: Walter de Gruyter.
Uexküll, J. von, & Kriszat, G. (1970). Streifzüge durch die Umwelten von Tieren und Menschen. Frankfurt: Fischer. (Original work published 1936).
Waern, Y. 1989. Cognitive Aspects of Computer Supported Tasks. Wiley & Sons: Chichester.

Weber, M. 1968. Economy and Society: An Outline of Interpretive Sociology [G. Roth & C. Wittich, Eds.]. New York: Bedminster Press. (Original work: Wirtschaft und Gesellschaft: Grundriss der verstehende Sociologie. Tübingen: J.C.B.Mohr, published 1925).

Wolfram, S. 2002. A New Kind of Science. Champaign, IL: Wolfram Media.

Wooldridge, M. 2002. An Introduction to Multiagent Systems. Chichester, England: John Wiley.

Chapter 10

E-BUSINESS MODEL IN PC MANUFACTURE:

Learning From Successful BTO Model

Rusdy Hartungi, Oscar Mangisengi, Abraham K. Lomi
Atma Jaya University-Indonesia, Software Competence Center Hagenberg (SCCH)- Austria, Institute of Technology National (ITN) -Indonesia

Abstract: This study analyses an E-Business model of BTO and its applicability to PCs manufacturers in a developing country. A single case of Legend Computers System in China, one of the biggest computer manufacturers is taken as a test case. The Current business model of Legend Computer System is compared and analysed with a BTO PC manufacturer such as Dell.

Key words: BTO, E-Business, ERP

1. INTRODUCTION

A build-to-order (BTO) model is defined as a system that is built based on an actual customer order, with usually standard components. The customer may either be an end user or a member of the distribution channel (Trommer, 1998).

2. ANALYSIS

Our study shows that without the implementation of BTO, most personal computer (PC) manufacturers experience the following problems: a cumbersome system with a complicated process, long cycle time and slow market response, limited choice of configurations, lack of efficient ways in customizing order, high level of inventory, low customer satisfaction because of long time for placing orders and manufacturing. Implementing a BTO model enables PC manufacturers to overcome these problems.

K. Liu (ed.),
Virtual, Distributed and Flexible Organisations: Studies in Organisational Semiotics, 181–182.

3. DISCUSSION

One major factor for a PC manufacturer in shifting to a BTO model is that of reducing the costs of excess inventory (Poirier, 1999). With this new model, a PC manufacturer does not need to carry large inventories because PCs are built as they as they are ordered. This will help to drive down the cost of PCs as well as helping alleviate shortages of PC equipment due to poor forecasting. The companies with BTO will benefit from substantial cost reduction due to eliminating inventory, forecasting, expediting, etc. It drives costs down as BTO utilises less people, machinery, and floor space. Cost reductions are passed to customers in price reductions or in feature enhancements. With BTO a PC manufacturer can increase sales and profits by expanding sales of standard products in addition to customized, derivative, and niche market products, while avoiding the commodity trap. BTO companies are the first to market with new technologies since distribution "pipelines" do not have to be emptied first. The mass customization capabilities of BTO can quickly and efficiently customize products for niche markets, countries, regions, industries, and individual customers. Shipping costs are also reduced. More importantly, customers have the ability to choose from varieties of models and configurations.

4. CONCLUSION

Our study has shown that the BTO model of Dell is applicable and adaptable for PC manufacturers in Asian developing countries. There is, however no guarantee that PC manufacturers in Asian developing countries will be successful as there are several antecedents that have been identified in this study to successfully adopt this new business model. Implementation of BTO model will provide Asian developing countries with more competitive advantage in rapidly growing PC market.

REFERENCES

Poirier, C., 1999, Advanced Supply Chain Management-How to build a sustained Competitive Advantage, San Francisco, Berrett-Koehler Publishers

Trommer, Diane, 1998, BTO: New Order of Business, ebnews, available online on http://www.ebnews.com/extra/1135extra6.html

Chapter 11

CONSIDERING NORMS AND SIGNS WITHIN AN INFORMATION SOURCE-BEARER-RECEIVER (S-B-R) FRAMEWORK

Wei Hu and Junkang Feng
School of ICT, University of Paisley, United Kingdom

Abstract: It seems that Semiotics and semantic information theories are closely related and complementary to each other, and therefore to study the link between them should be beneficial. Here, we briefly introduce our work in this direction.

Key words: Organisational Semiotics, Semantic Information Theories

1. AN S-B-R FRAMEWORK

Information is still an 'explicandum term' (Floridi, 2003) in academic communities today. To facilitate further studies of information within the context of information systems, an overarching framework seems desirable. Through linking, reconciling and synthesising a variety of relevant theories into a coherent whole, we have been developing such a framework, which we call an 'S-B-R' (information *S*ource - information *B*earer - information *R*eceiver) framework. This framework is a highly abstract model for looking at information flow and information systems from a semantic information theoretical (Dretske, 1981) and organisational semiotic perspective.

2. NORM ANALYSIS AND CLASSIFICATION OF INFORMATION BEARER

Considering the roles that norms play in the S-B-R framework is necessary for analysing the existence of links between states of affairs. We

K. Liu (ed.),
Virtual, Distributed and Flexible Organisations: Studies in Organisational Semiotics, 183–184.

observe that norms affect the scope of an information source and give rise to Information Content Inclusion Relationships (IIRs) between states of affairs. Furthermore, we find that norms' existence also affects R (the Receiver) who will receive information from the 'representamen' of a sign. This is a case particularly in an organisation with norms defined as regularities. According to Stamper et al (2000), the condition part in a general structure of norm determines what information the norm-subject (an individual person or a group) requires to be able to obey it, while this leads to the generation of information for others via some means. Therefore, the change of norms existing in an organisation or the capability of knowing those norms will influence the capability of agents (i.e., the Receiver) in the organisation to acquire information.

An Information Bearer can be a traffic light, a physical sign or signal in general, or an IT system. Following Stamper (1997), anything, say x, can function as a sign if it can stand for something else, say y, for the people in some community. Here, x is an information bearer for y. Considering the structure of a sign given by Peirce (Falkenberg *et al.,* 1998), we agree that the 'representamen', which is a thing serving as the 'carrier' of the sign, is independent of its meaning. Furthermore, we classify information bearers by analysing the properties' of a sign with respect to an information source. For an organisation seeking a good information system or attempting to integrate diverse information sources into one IT system, it is in fact a process to design a good cost-effective information bearer.

REFERENCES

Dretske, F. I. 1981, Knowledge and the Flow of Information. Basil Blackwell, Oxford.

Falkenberg, D. E., Hesse, W., Stamper, R., et al. 1998, A Framework of Information Systems Concepts – The FRISCO Report (web edition), IFIP.

Floridi, L. 2003, Information, In The Blackwell Guide to the Philosophy of Computing and Information, Luciano Floridi, ed. Oxford, New York: Blackwell.

Stamper, R. 1997, Organisational Semiotics, In Information Systems: An Emerging Discipline?, Mingers, J and Stowell, F. ed. The McGraw-Hill Companies, London.

Stamper, R., Liu, K., Hafkamp, M. and Ades, Y. 2000, Understanding the Roles of Signs and Norms in Organisations – a Semiotic Approach to Information Systems Design. Behaviour and Information Technology, 19(1): pp. 15-27.

Chapter 12

FACILITATING USEFUL OBJECT-ORIENTATION FOR VIRTUAL EBUSINESS ORGANISATIONS THROUGH SEMIOTICS

Simon Polovina, and Duncan Strang
Sheffield Hallam University, United Kingdom

Abstract: E-business systems are increasingly being developed as nTier architectures. This approach best separates the human-computer interaction (HCI) concerns from those of the system's information content, thus allowing software developers to focus on one without being muddled by the other. Contemporary practice accordingly uses an Object Oriented language with a relational database providing the persistent storage mechanism. It is however well known that object-orientation and relational databases do not sit easily together. Secondly the rewriting of an object's class can cause all the other object classes that it interacts with having to be rewritten in turn, with its consequential knock on effects throughout the application. Through its unifying framework, semiotic offers the optimal way to record an objects' evolution and reconcile the data vs. object divide, and suggests how this might be achieved. (NB: At http://www.polovina.me.uk/publications/os6-full-paper.pdf is the complete version of this paper, including further reference sources.)

Key words: E-business, HCI, software engineering, object-orientation, semiotics, database

1. DATA VERSUS OBJECTS

When considering objects, a key aspect of their success is that data and information is hidden to support effective software engineering (and, hence, usability). As persistent data is in practice handled by a database, typically Relational Databases, then the object to which it is related is forced to have its data divorced from its operations thus undermining the goals of software engineering: encapsulation is lost, cohesion is lost and coupling has to

K. Liu (ed.),
Virtual, Distributed and Flexible Organisations: Studies in Organisational Semiotics, 185–186.

increase. Through this 'object-data divide' we risk, once again, too easily returning to IS (Information Systems) failure due to inadequate software.

2. REFACTORING

As the operations or data belonging to an object can be hidden (encapsulated), internal improvements can be made to the design of that object's class to enhance the application without causing a knock on effect by other objects having to be rewritten. This is known as refactoring. If on the other hand we modify the public interface to an Object then all clients of that object will need to be modified if they wish to use the new functionality. The traditional approach to dealing with this issue has ended up creating 'object litter' by having to spawn numerous new (sub)classes that allow the original (imperfect) object to be used, but add to the information overload as the application's class library size goes out of all humanly manageable recognition.

3. SEMIOTIC APPROACHES

Polovina has illustrated how the semiotically inspired conceptual graphs can bring two divergent disciplines into one unifying, non-compromising framework (Polovina, 1993). This approach could be applied to the object-data divide. Organisational semiotics could usefully be applied to the issues raised in this paper (Liu *et al.* 2002). The Shared Meanings Design Framework (SMDF, http://www.smdf.org/), which focuses on semiotic in requirements engineering, namely from a conflicting user/stakeholder perspective offers a particularly attractive route. How any of these may be appropriated is to be determined, but demonstrates that there is a substantial base of semiotics to tackle the worthwhile problems that this paper raises.

REFERENCES

Polovina, S., 1993, Bridging Accounting and Business Strategic Planning Using Conceptual Graphs, in Conceptual Structures: Theory and Implementation, Lecture Notes in Artificial Intelligence, H.D. Pfeiffer and T.E. Nagle (eds), Berlin: Springer-Verlag, pp. 312-321

Liu, K., Clarke, R. Anderson, P. Stamper, R. with Abou-Zeid, E. 2002, Organisational Semiotics: Evolving A Science of Information Systems, Proceedings of IFIP WG8.1 Working Conference, Boston: Kluwer Academic Publishers.

II

SYSTEMS INTERFACE

Chapter 13

A SEMIOTIC MODEL OF USER-INTERFACE METAPHOR

Pippin Barr, Robert Biddle, and James Noble
Department of Mathematical and Computing Sciences, Victoria University of Wellington, New Zealand

Abstract: User-interface metaphor is an extremely popular technique for creating usable user-interfaces. Although there has been considerable research into its application in practical settings, there has been little investigation into the concept itself. This paper applies Peircean semiotics to user-interface metaphor in order to provide a structured model of the concept. As an end result, a far more detailed understanding of the technique and a useful vocabulary are made available to user-interface designers and researchers.

Key words: User-interface, computer semiotics, metaphor

1 INTRODUCTION

Metaphors are a very popular approach to user-interface design. Two of the largest interface design companies in the world, Apple and Microsoft, both strongly recommend the use of metaphor:

> You can take advantage of people's knowledge of the world around them by using metaphors to convey concepts and features of your application. Use metaphors involving concrete, familiar ideas and make the metaphors plain, so that users have a set of expectations to apply to computer environments (Apple, 1992).

> Familiar metaphors provide a direct and intuitive interface to user tasks. By allowing users to transfer their knowledge and experience, metaphors make it easier to predict and learn the behaviours of software-based representations (Microsoft, 1995).

K. Liu (ed.),
Virtual, Distributed and Flexible Organisations: Studies in Organisational Semiotics, 189–215.

Although there has been considerable research positing the advantages of metaphor in the user-interface (Carroll *et al.,* 1988; Dertouzos, 2001; Erickson, 1990; Johnson, 1997), its problems (Carroll and Mack, 1995; Carroll *et al.*, 1988; Carroll and Thomas, 1982; Halaz and Moran, 1982; Kay, 1990; Mountford, 1990; Nelson, 1990; Norman, 1998; Smyth *et al.,* 1995; Wozny, 1989), and practical advice on its use (Carroll et al., 1988; Carroll and Thomas, 1982; Cataci *et al.,* 1995; Erickson, 1990; Halasz and Moran, 1982; Lundell and Anderson, 1995; Madsen, 1994; Smyth *et al.*, 1995; Väänänen and Schmidt, 1994), there has been little analysis of the concept itself. This lack of investigation into the underlying idea means that discussion is somewhat ungrounded and relies heavily on intuition and empirical studies. We believe that it is necessary to provide a structured examination of the *concept* of user-interface metaphor in order to fully understand its use.

As noted by Ronald Stamper, there is an important need to "build a science of information systems using the operationally secure, primitive notion of a *sign*" (Liu *et al.,* 2002, p.xiv). Computer user-interfaces are a critical part of the study of information systems because they are the primary means of their representation. This is well reflected in the brief literature review in section 3. Within user-interfaces, the concept of a user-interface metaphor is very common. To this end, it is clear that a semiotic analysis of user-interface metaphor is an important contribution to organisational semiotics. Therefore, in this paper we use Peircean semiotics to explain the structure and function of user-interface metaphors. This involves the creation of a detailed semiotic model of user-interface metaphor, based on the Peircean triad.

In section 2 we will provide a basic introduction to the common perception of user-interface metaphors. Next, in section 3 we discuss the already existing application of semiotics to computers, and specifically to the user-interface. This completed, we begin to establish the background required for the semiotic model by outlining important aspects of Peircean semiotics, along with some research by Umberto Eco, in section 4. Finally, with the background in place, we produce models of both metaphor in general (section 5) and user-interface elements (section 6), before presenting our model of user-interface metaphor in section 7. Some thought is given to necessary future work in section 8 before we conclude in section 9.

2 WHAT IS USER-INTERFACE METAPHOR?

A metaphor is a device for explaining some concept or thing, x, by asserting its similarity to another concept or thing, y, in the form X IS Y[1].

The concept being explained is often referred to as the tenor of the metaphor, while the concept doing the explaining is called the vehicle. Thus, in a metaphor such as JULIET IS THE SUN (Shakespeare, 1933, Act II, Scene II, l.2), the tenor is "Juliet" and the vehicle is "the sun". Juliet is described to the audience via their knowledge of the sun. Thus, we understand that Romeo believes her to be warm, radiant, high above him, and so forth.

User-interface metaphor is intuitively the application of this device to the user-interface. Thus, a user-interface metaphor is a device for explaining some system functionality or structure (the tenor) by asserting its similarity to another concept or thing already familiar to the user (the vehicle). The key here is that the chosen vehicle is something already *familiar* to the user and so the intention is to provide a base level of comfort and knowledge without necessarily understanding the underlying system.

Consider the traditional example of the "trashcan" used in most desktop environments today. In this case the tenor is the concept of "file deletion" while the vehicle is the concept of "using a trashcan." The metaphor can thus be written out as FILE DELETION IS USING A TRASH CAN. It is intended to help the user understand how to interact with the system concept of file deletion which, without the metaphor, is an extremely complex process. Thus, the user interacts using concepts such as putting items into a trashcan and emptying the trashcan, rather than requiring detailed knowledge of directory tables, file flags, and so forth.

Although the intuitive idea of user-interface metaphor is simple and easy to understand, it is also clear that it is not sufficiently structured for detailed discussion of the concept. Particularly, it does not offer a strict way to characterise how the metaphor functions or what the metaphor really *means*. The use of semiotics in this paper will help to resolve these issues.

3 COMPUTER SEMIOTICS

Semiotics has been used extensively in the analysis of computer systems, and particularly concerning the user-interface. The treatment of the user-interface as a sign-system, then, is not out of the ordinary.

One of the most important researchers in computer semiotics is Peter Bøgh Andersen. In his major work, *A Theory of Computer Semiotics*, Andersen shows in detail how semiotics can be applied to the understanding of computers as sign-systems (Andersen, 1997). In other papers Andersen investigates semiotics as regards programming (Andersen, 1993) and human-computer interaction (Andersen, 2000).

A second major researcher in the area is Joseph Goguen, who has performed detailed work on the concept of an "algebraic semiotics"

(Goguen, 1999; Malcolm and Goguen, 1998). The theory behind this approach is that semiotics can be formally captured and thus become similar to mathematics in its application. Algebraic semiotics has been applied to the user-interface in considerable detail.

Other approaches to computer semiotics analyse their use for graphic design (Mullet and Sano, 1995), modelling user-interface elements (Nadin, 1988), informing the design process (Andersen and May, 2001; Connolly and Phillips, 2002; de Souza, 1993; May and Andersen, 2001), and analysing sign types in the interface (Barr et al., 2003).

It is clear from this brief survey that semiotics is an accepted approach to explaining computer systems. With this in mind, we now go on to show how Peircean semiotics can be used to analyse and explain user-interface metaphors and their purpose.

4 PEIRCEAN SEMIOTICS

In this section we will first outline the basics of the Peircean triad. Following this we will provide some discussion of the distinction between interpreting and generating signs, as well as the concept of unlimited semiosis. These three ideas from semiotics will be combined to create our model of user-interface metaphor.

4.1 The Peircean Triad

Charles Peirce proposed a triadic model of the sign (Peirce, 1934-1948). In his view, a sign is divided into these three parts: *object*, *representamen* and *interpretant*. Consider, for example, the triad applied to a stop-sign shown in figure 1.

In this example the *object* is the concept that "cars must stop here", that is, it is the referant of the sign. The *representamen* is the stop-sign itself, the sign's manifestation in the world. Finally, the *interpretant* or response to the sign is the successful one of the interpreter understanding they must stop their car.

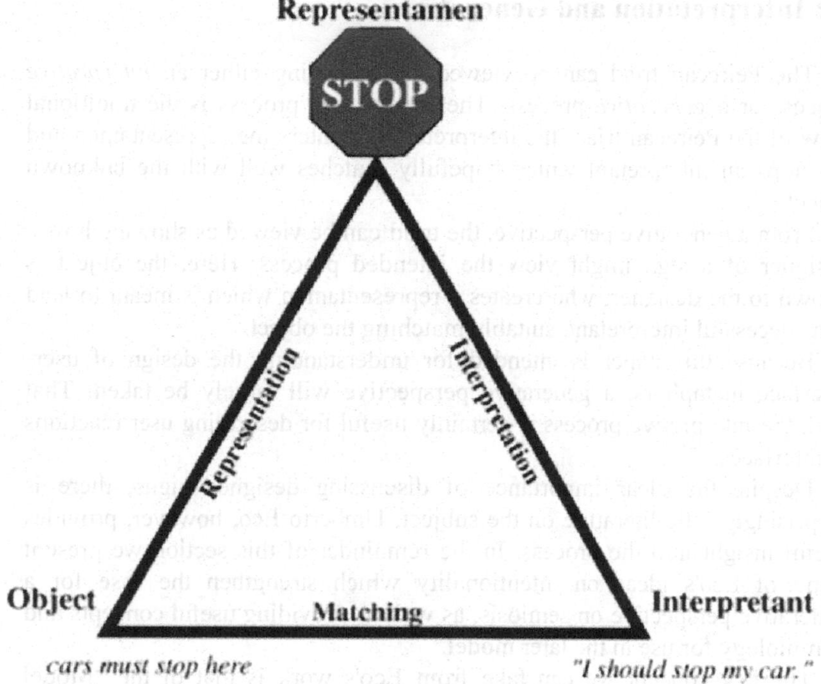

Figure 1. A diagram of the Peircean triad as applied to a stop-sign.

In addition to the three parts of the sign, three relationships between the parts can be identified, as shown in the diagram. We suggest that these relations are revealing, despite Peirce's claim that semiosis is "not ... in any way resolvable into actions between pairs [of sign-components]." (Peirce, 1934-1948, v.5 p.488)

The relation of *representation* concerns the way in which a red sign with white lettering can represent the concept of stopping a car. In this case, it relates to linguistic and colour conventions, among other things. The *interpretation* relation describes the mental process that takes place between the interpreter seeing the representamen, and arriving at an interpretant. Finally, the *matching* relation concerns how successfully the interpretant arrived at matches the actual object of the sign.

Note that here, and for the rest of this paper, it is possible to talk of a "successful" sign because all signs in this paper are intentional ones. An intentional sign has a *specific* object which it is intended to convey. Interpretants which match this object can be considered successful or correct, and those that do not are unsuccessful in their intent.

4.2 Interpretation and Generation

The Peircean triad can be viewed as explaining either an *interpretive* process or a *generative* process. The interpretive process is the traditional view of the Peircean triad: the interpreter encounters the representamen and develops an interpretant which hopefully matches well with the unknown object.

From a generative perspective, the triad can be viewed as showing how a designer of a sign might view the intended process. Here, the object is known to the designer, who creates a representamen which is meant to lead to a successful interpretant, suitably matching the object.

Because this paper is intended for understanding the design of user-interface metaphors, a generative perspective will largely be taken. That said, the interpretive process is certainly useful for describing user reactions to interfaces.

Despite the clear importance of discussing designed signs, there is surprisingly little literature on the subject. Umberto Eco, however, provides useful insight into the process. In the remainder of this section we present some of Eco's ideas on intentionality which strengthen the case for a generative perspective on semiosis, as well as providing useful concepts and terminology for use in the later model.

The key concept we can take from Eco's work is that of the "Model Reader," originally developed in his book *The Role of the Reader* (Eco, 1979). The Model Reader is the reader envisaged by the author of a text or sign who will understand precisely what it is that the author is trying to convey: the object of the text or sign.

The Model Reader helps us to bridge the divide between the generative and interpretive approaches to a sign:

> To make his text communicative, the author has to assume that the ensemble of codes he relies upon is the same as that shared by his possible reader. The author has thus to foresee a model of the possible reader (hereafter Model Reader) supposedly able to deal *interpretatively* with the expressions in the same way as the author deals *generatively* with them. (Eco, 1979, p.7, our emphasis)

We use Eco's terminology to reinforce our explanation of the generative process. First of all, the author of the sign envisages some Model Reader, an interpreter of the sign who has certain beliefs and a certain context such that they will *correctly* interpret the sign. Next, the author of the sign seeks to *produce* the Model Reader "through the use of given ... strategies." (Eco, 1990, p.128) Thus, it is possible to *create* a Model Reader from an actual reader through various forms of influence. It is also clear that this influence must take place through the representamen, which is the point through which author/designer and reader/user are linked.

Based on this discussion, it is clearly justifiable to present a sign model that is from the point of view of a sign *designer*. In this case, the interpretant of the sign may be seen as the interpretant of the Model Reader, rather than a particular reader. Because of this, the interpretant in such a model will be a representation of the *correct* interpretant of the sign, and will thus match the object of the sign via the matching relation.

Eco's comment on the use of strategies to *produce* a Model Reader ties directly to the concept of "narrative strategies" in semiotics. The study of narrative strategies involves considering how a text or sign can produce desired effects in a reader. Clearly, this concept could be highly relevant to the design of user-interfaces, as there is a similar desire to produce particular reactions. For more on narrative strategies in semiotics see Algirdas Greimas (Greimas, 1983) or Gerald Prince (Prince, 1982), for example.

The view of an intentional sign taken in this paper is as follows. The author desires to convey a particular *object* to an audience of readers or interpreters. In order to do this, a *representamen* is created which is intended to produce a model *interpretant* which matches the object. In this way, a sign model can portray the intended effect of the sign, rather than one of the many possible effects. Note that, in order to actually produce the model interpretant, considerable thought as to who the audience of the sign is needed. This links well with the traditional human-computer interaction principle of "know the user" (Nielsen, 1993, pp.73-78).

4.3 Unlimited Semiosis

Before discussing the process of modelling a user-interface metaphor semiotically, it is important to examine the process of semiosis in a little more detail. In particular, it was suggested by Peirce, and furthered by Umberto Eco, that an encounter with a sign is not quite as neat as a single triad. In fact, in Peircean semiotics it is commonly thought that an encounter with a sign involves many interpretants in a process known as *unlimited semiosis*. The term is due to Umberto Eco (Eco, 1990), but the idea is apparent in Peirce's work. For example, Peirce describes a sign as "anything which determines something else (its interpretant) to refer to an object to which itself refers (its object) in the same way, this interpretant becoming in turn a sign, and so on ad infinitum." (Peirce, 1934-1948, v.2 p.300)

What this means in a basic sense is that the interpretant of a sign can be a sign itself. In particular, the interpretant of a sign can become the representamen of a new sign, with a new object and interpretant of its own. This process can go on forever. Hence Eco's terming it *unlimited* semiosis.

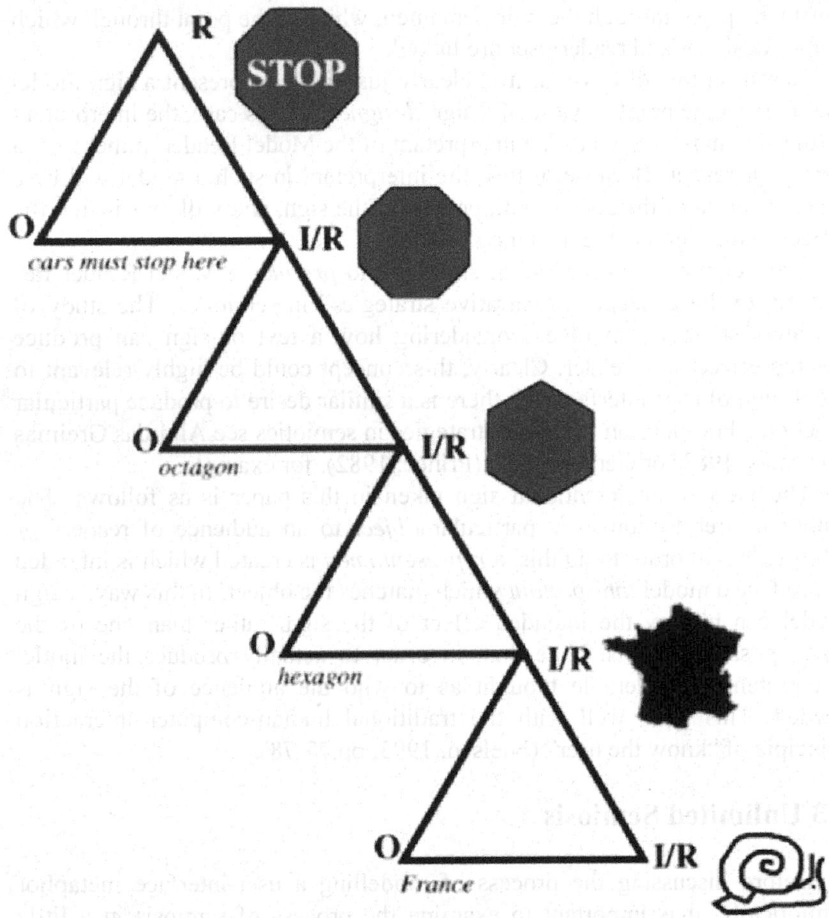

Figure 2. A diagram of the process of unlimited semiosis.

Figure 2 gives a possible example of unlimited semiosis. In this case, the initial sign is the sighting of a standard stop-sign. This makes the interpreter think of an octagon shape, which leads in turn to thinking about another polygon: the hexagon. The shape of a hexagon reminds the interpreter of the shape of France, and, when thinking about France, they think about eating snails. Clearly, this could lead to further representamens and interpretants forever.

Any interpretant can lead to further signs because the interpretant *itself* can represent something else. That is the basis of unlimited semiosis. The chief interest in unlimited semiosis for the purposes of this paper is the concept of joining two signs together. Note also that it is not completely necessary that this *joining* of signs occur strictly *in the mind*. In particular, when seeing a map of France someone might *draw* a hexagon in response. This drawn hexagon can be considered as an interpretant becoming a sign in an important sense. Therefore, we claim that the interpretant of a sign might have a *physical* manifestation as well as a mental one.

5 A SEMIOTIC MODEL OF METAPHOR

Although metaphor is considered important and is discussed in semiotics research, there is no definitive model of the concept readily available. The general view appears to be that a metaphor sign involves the interaction in some way of *two* signs, which are the tenor and the vehicle of the metaphor (Chandler, 2002; Thwaites et al., 1994). The stance we take in this paper is that a metaphor may well be composed of two signs, but can plausibly be treated as a sign in itself as well. Using this perspective, we apply the Peircean triad to metaphor as shown in figure 3, and will now explain the various parts.

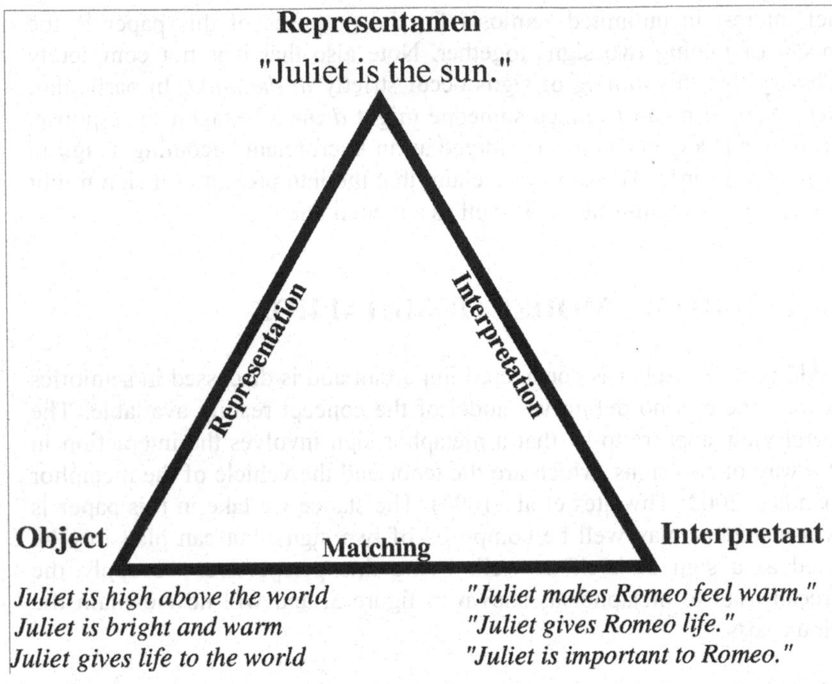

Figure 3. A semiotic model of metaphor.

Essentially, the meaning of the metaphor intended by its author comprises the object, while the expression of the metaphor itself, usually in language, forms the *representamen.* An encounter with the representamen leads a reader to form an *interpretant*, which is what the metaphor is taken to mean by them.

The relations involved are all fairly similar to those already discussed above. The *representation* relation concerns the way the representamen conveys the object. In the case of metaphor this tends to be some linguistic statement which either directly ("Juliet is the sun") or more indirectly ("Arise fair sun and kill the envious moon") specifies the metaphor. The *interpretation* relation concerns the reader's encounter with the metaphor and how they think about it. Finally, the *matching* relation describes how well the final interpretant matches with the intention of the metaphor's author.

An issue, arises, however, when considering the object of a metaphor. Simply suggesting it is the referant of the metaphor is not specific enough for our purposes. To this end, we have turned to the work of George Lakoff and Mark Johnson in *Metaphors We Live By* to provide an answer (Lakoff and Johnson, 1980). In the book, Lakoff and Johnson introduce the concept of *metaphorical entailments*. A metaphorical entailment is the application of some fact about the vehicle to the tenor. Thus, in the example of JULIET IS THE SUN, a metaphorical entailment might be that "Juliet is warm," because the sun is warm and this quality is transferred to Juliet. These metaphorical entailments "characterize the *internal* systematicity of the metaphor ... that is, they make coherent all the examples that fall under that metaphor." (Lakoff and Johnson, 1980, p.91) In other words, a set of metaphorical entailments can be said to be the meaning of a metaphor: the object of a metaphor sign.

The question remains as to *which* possible set of metaphorical entailments we should consider to be the object of a metaphor. The standpoint taken in this paper is that this depends on the position from which the sign is being considered. Because our chief occupation is to examine a generative view of user-interface metaphor, the object of a metaphor is considered to be those metaphorical entailments taken to be the meaning of the metaphor by its designer or author. This will be discussed in more detail when the full model of user-interface metaphor is presented. Note also that the metaphorical entailments provide a more specific means of describing the *matching* relation of a metaphor: the relation is strengthened by aspects of the interpretant which match the metaphorical entailments, and weakened by those that do not.

6 A SEMIOTIC MODEL OF USER-INTERFACE ELEMENTS

It is actually quite straightforward to create a triadic model of a user-interface sign. Much of this section utilises the work on a semiotic view of computer icons covered by the present authors in a previous paper (Barr *et al.*, 2003). Figure 4 provides an example application of the model which will guide the following discussion. The example is of the print button presented by Microsoft Word which is clicked in order to print the currently viewed document.

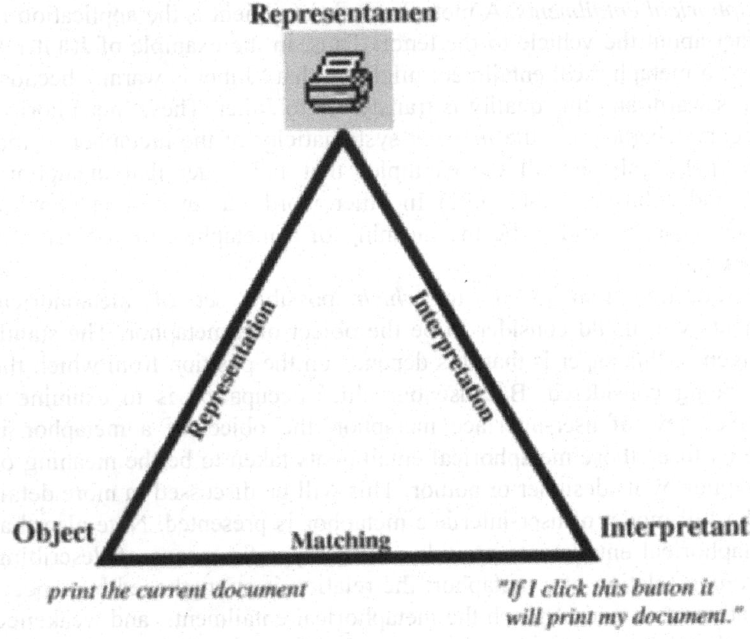

Figure 4. A semiotic model of a user-interface sign.

Essentially, the *object* of a user-interface sign is the functionality underlying it, in this case the ability to print a document. The *representamen* is the perceivable aspect of the interface that is intended to convey the object to a user, who, in turn, develops an interpretant. The interpretant can be thought of as the user's mental response to the sign. Note that it could additionally be thought of as the user's general response to the sign, their reactions to it. It therefore might involve physical reactions, for example.

The relations of the triad are similarly easy to apply. The *representation* relation concerns the way in which the representamen actually depicts the underlying functionality. The *interpretation* relation captures the process gone through by a user on encountering the sign, leading to the interpretant. Finally, the *matching* relation concerns how well the user's interpretation of the sign matches the actual functionality it represents.

7 A SEMIOTIC MODEL OF USER-INTERFACE METAPHOR

In order to create a semiotic view of a user-interface metaphor it is necessary to combine the previously discussed views of a metaphor sign and a user-interface sign. As noted in section 4.3, the concept of unlimited semiosis can be used to join signs together. Traditionally, this transition from one sign to another occurs in the mind of an interpreter as they consider a sign and find that their consideration leads to other signs. As this model is based on the designer's viewpoint, however, the joining of the two signs occurs through the designer instead. What is more, the designer is consciously aware of the joining of the two signs as it is done *intentionally*.

The key point of unlimited semiosis we utilise, then, is the notion that the interpretant of one sign can become the representamen of another. If this is considered as a conscious process, done intentionally, then it is similar to using one concept to fuel another in some useful way. This matches well with the idea of using a metaphor to fuel the design of some part of the user-interface. Therefore, the user-interface metaphor sign will involve a metaphor sign which is linked with a user-interface sign. This reflects the necessity of viewing a user-interface metaphor as a cohesive unit, while also recognising that it is divisible into a base metaphor along with a sign in the user-interface.

Figure 5 displays the model that involves linking the two types of signs already discussed. In particular, the interpretant of the metaphor sign becomes the representamen of the user-interface sign. This presentation of a user-interface metaphor as *two* signs linked together allows discussion of both the perceivable interface elements, and also the underlying metaphor.

The various parts of the sign have been renamed to avoid confusion due to the fact there are now *two* distinct signs involved, the metaphor sign and the user-interface element sign. The following discussion of the model will be guided by the example of the *document* metaphor common to many modern user-interfaces. This example is reflected in figure 5, although note that the figure itself is not intended to convey a *complete* model of that particular sign.

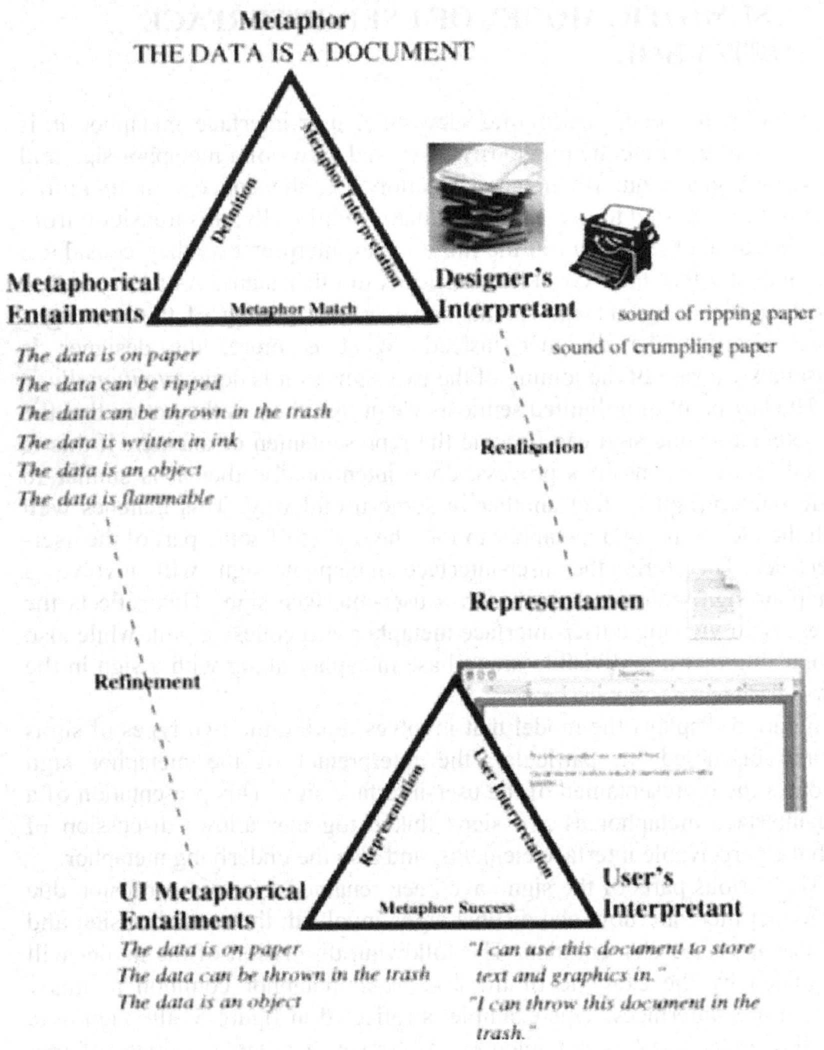

Figure 5. A semiotic model of user-interface metaphor.

7.1 The Parts of a User-Interface Metaphor

7.1.1 Metaphor

The representamen of the metaphor part of the sign is now simply called the *metaphor*. This is in keeping with Peirce's suggestion that the representamen is the sign in some sense. This part reflects the representation of the metaphor that the designer considers while creating the user-interface metaphor sign. It might be a sign in the designer's mind, or more likely should be written down in the project documentation. Note also that by having the representamen be the metaphor, this raises the possibility of having a more detailed model of the metaphor itself, possibly involving two separate signs, as mentioned in section 5 on semiotic models of metaphor. This low-level representation could then be linked through its interpretant to the metaphor which is the representamen of the metaphor sign.

In the context of the document example, the metaphor is that the data is a document. The idea behind this metaphor is that, instead of viewing information input into the computer as amorphous, raw data, it can be cast as a document instead. The metaphor is especially relevant when the data entered into a computer serves a similar purpose as a written document. Although the data is clearly not really a document, the similarity of function allows the metaphor to function.

7.1.2 Metaphorical Entailments

The object of the metaphor part of the sign is now referred to as the *metaphorical entailments* because those are literally what the metaphor is considered to mean. These are the entailments of the metaphor that the overall user-interface metaphor is based on. In particular, these are the entailments the *designer* believes the metaphor to have. They are also *independent* of the user-interface at this point, and are simply entailments of the metaphor in general.

In the context of the document metaphor, the metaphorical entailments are any considerations of documents that might be useful in describing data. Thus a possible (and incomplete) list might be something like:

- The data is an object.
- The data can be written on.
- The data can be read.

- The data contains text, and possibly images and graphs, etc.
- The data can be ripped.
- The data can be typed up.
- The data is usually on white paper.
- The data can be photocopied.
- The data can be written in pencil or pen or ink.
- The data can (sometimes) be edited using twink or an eraser.
- The data contains information.
- The data can be set on fire.
- The data can be picked up and moved from place to place.
- The data can be thrown into a trashcan.
- The data can give you a paper-cut.

It is worth noting here that it is obvious not all of these entailments will be appropriate for use in the final user-interface. Naturally, there are facts about "documents" which are will not be used because they are not applicable in the context of a user-interface. An argument could be made that the metaphorical entailments are those entailments that the designer assumes will be shared by the user. This is similar to Eco's claim that "the author has to assume that the ensemble of codes he relies upon is the same as that shared by his possible reader" (Eco, 1979, p.7).

7.1.3 Designer's Interpretant

The final part of the metaphor half of the overall sign is the *designer's interpretant*. This reflects the result of the designer's consideration of the metaphor. It consists of the various thoughts the designer has about the metaphor overall, while thinking about how to design an aspect of the user-interface. These will be very much related to the metaphorical entailments which are the object of this sign. Note that this interpretant can include mental images, as well as concepts about motion, words, sounds and so forth. In fact, it can be considered as the overall mental reaction to the metaphor. What is more, the designer's interpretant could include any actual work done by the designer prior to actual implementation; it is the thought process which leads to the final implementation and encompasses all that design work.

In the example of the document metaphor, the designer's interpretant is any of the work done by the designer while attempting to figure out the representamen of the user-interface metaphor. Possible aspects of the designer's interpretant might be:

- The designer's mental images of documents, perhaps set down on paper or on the computer for documentation purposes. Specifically, this might involve images of typed documents, documents with images set in them, stacks of paper, and so forth.
- Thoughts and recordings of the sounds involved with documents, such as the sound of a typewriter working, paper tearing, or pieces of paper moving against each other.
- Actions involved with documents, such as typing one up, or throwing one into the wastepaper basket, for instance.
- Thoughts on the tactile sensations involved with documents, such as the feel of paper, or the feeling of hitting typewriter keys.

Note how all of these aspects of the designer's interpretant can be physically documented as a part of the design process. This would make the retroactive identification of the different parts of the user-interface metaphor sign considerably simpler. Note also that all of the aspects of the designer's interpretant can be linked back to the metaphorical entailments that were established. In fact, the designer's interpretant is, in some ways, the realisation of those metaphorical entailments. By comparing the two an idea can be gained of the particular perspective the designer took regarding the entailments of the metaphor.

7.1.4 Representamen

Because of the process of unlimited semiosis, the designer's interpretant now becomes the representamen of a new sign. This makes a considerable amount of sense in the context of interface design: the designer's interpretant is effectively the design process which leads up to the actual implementation of the user-interface metaphor. This implementation is the *representamen* of the user-interface sign as shown in figure 5. The representamen is arrived at when the designer turns their interpretations of the metaphor into an actual user-interface element, and therefore can be considered as the realisation of that design. Here, the designer's interpretant, which is an interpretant of the metaphor sign, becomes the representamen in the user-interface via implementation. The representamen consists of all perceivable aspects of a user-interface pertaining to the particular metaphor.

This can be made clear by considering the example of the document metaphor. The designer's interpretant for this metaphor involves the designer's ideas about the sorts of ways a document behaves, based on the metaphor. The representamen of the document metaphor consists of all aspects in the system that are used to represent these ideas. A few examples of the representamen are as follows:

- The document icon, as shown in figure 6. This visually represents the way that a document might look from afar, in a fairly abstract manner.
- The "Page Outline" view in Microsoft Word, which presents the current document being worked on as a sheet of A4 paper which can be typed on as in figure 7.
- The ability to pick up and move document icons on the desktop, reflecting the concept that documents are physical objects.
- The ability to "throw" a document into the trashcan.
- Explicit referral to collections of data as documents using language, as shown in figure 8.
- The ability to store a document in a folder.

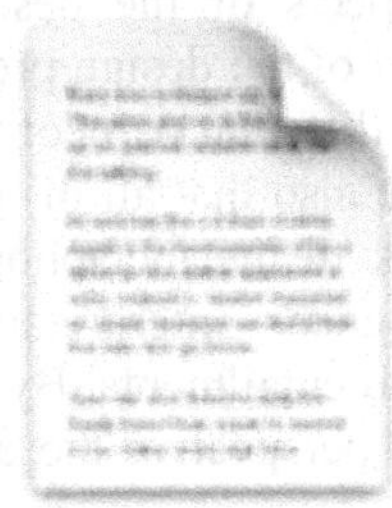

Figure 6. The standard document icon in MacOS X.

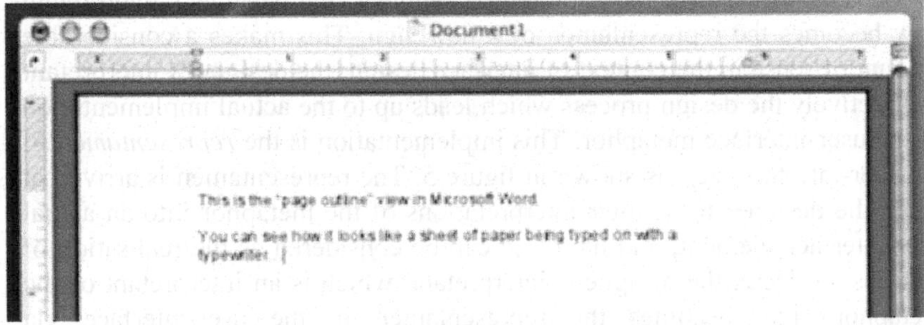

Figure 7. The standard view of the "paper" in Microsoft Word.

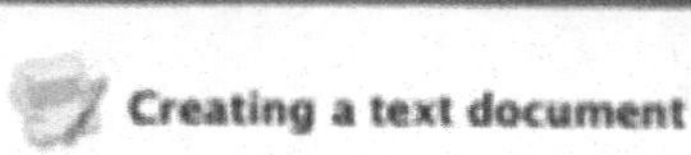

Creating a text document
You can use TextEdit to create text documents. You can change the font, font style and size, and format of your document. You can even add pictures to your documents. As you create your document, you can find and replace text and check the spelling.

Figure 8. Example of explicit referral to a collection of data as a "document" in the MacOS X help system.

Note how, in representing this metaphor, other possible metaphors are invoked, such as a trashcan and a folder. By combining metaphors, the overall illusion of metaphorical interaction is strengthened.

7.1.5 UI Metaphorical Entailments

Given that a new sign is now being discussed, there is therefore a new object of the sign. It is quite interesting to note that the lower (user-interface) sign mirrors the upper (metaphor) sign quite closely. In fact, the user-interface sign can be considered as the realisation of the metaphor sign in a different format: a user-interface implementation. To that end, the object of the user-interface sign is also a set of metaphorical entailments. This new set of metaphorical entailments will be called the *UI metaphorical entailments*, to distinguish it from the earlier set. The UI metaphorical entailments differ from the metaphorical entailments in that they are a set specifically tailored to the user-interface. In particular, they contain only those entailments that are relevant to the implementation of the interface. Basically, the point is that not all of the entailments of a metaphor will be appropriate for actual implementation. Therefore, the set of metaphorical entailments must be refined to the set of UI metaphorical entailments.

In the document example, not every one of the metaphorical entailments is useful for implementation. The designer realises this over the course of establishing the designer's interpretant. Therefore, a new set of metaphorical entailments is established when the representamen is being created. These UI metaphorical entailments reflect the actually applicable entailments about documents which will work in the user-interface. A sample listing could be as follows:

- The data is an object.
- The data can be written on.
- The data can be read.

- The data contains text, and possibly images and graphs, etc.
- The data can be typed up.
- The data is usually on white paper.
- The data contains information.
- The data can be picked up and moved from place to place.
- The data can be thrown into a trashcan.

Note that various metaphorical entailments have been omitted in this listing. For example, entailments such as "the data can be ripped in two," and "the data can be set on fire" are no longer present because such details are not implemented. The complete set of UI metaphorical entailments defines the functionality made available by the implemented document metaphor. Note, however, that they may not define all the functionality associated with the element in the user-interface. For example, it is possible to change the colour of the text in a document at will. This is *not* a metaphorical entailment because you cannot easily do such a thing to a real world document. The ability to combine metaphorical and non-metaphorical functionality is one of the powerful aspects of user-interface metaphors.

7.1.6 User's Interpretant

The final part of the user-interface metaphor model is the *user's interpretant*. As already discussed, this interpretant might be the Model User's interpretant, or a real user's interpretant, depending on what the model is being applied to. If it is the Model User's interpretant, then the model represents the ideal process through which the sign goes, culminating in its successful interpretation. If a real user's interpretant is used, then the model represents a kind of user testing, where the final interpretant can be compared with the UI metaphorical entailments to establish how successful the sign was in conveying the correct way of interacting with it. Note also that the process of unlimited semiosis can be continued upward from the user's interpretant. In this case it can be used to model possible or actual thought processes undergone when interpreting the user-interface. In particular, it might be used as a means to show how the user must "reverse engineer" the perceivable representamen in order to establish the underpinnings of the sign, including the underlying metaphor.

For the document example, the Model User's interpretant will simply be a collection of thoughts which are similar to the UI metaphorical entailments. That is, the Model User will understand, through the representamen, the kinds of things they can expect to do with the user-interface via the document metaphor. This means they will think things such as "I can throw a document into the trashcan" or "I can type into this document." In a user testing context, the user's interpretant will be established by the examination of real users. In this case, the interpretant must be somehow elicited by observation, or by direct questioning, for example. In this case, the designers must have users interact with an implementation of the document metaphor, and then find out what it is they think. If the users think similarly to the Model User, then the metaphor is successful. If the users think things such as "I hope I don't accidentally knock this document off the desktop," then there are issues in the representamen to be resolved.

7.2 The Relations of the User-Interface Metaphor

The relations of this model of a user-interface metaphor are somewhat more complex than those already discussed in sections 5 and 6. This is because of the linking provided by the concept of unlimited semiosis. Not only must the interpretant of the metaphor sign be linked with the representamen of the user-interface sign in a kind of relation, but the objects of the two signs, both sets of metaphorical entailments, have a special relationship too. This section will outline each of the relations in turn and explain what they represent in terms of the design process.

7.2.1 Definition

Between the metaphorical entailments and the metaphor is the relation of *definition*. That is, the set of metaphorical entailments can be considered as the definition or meaning of the metaphor itself. This is reinforced by the position of Lakoff and Johnson, as discussed in section 5. In fact, they even go so far as to list a large number of metaphorical entailments for a metaphor and then write that these entailments "form a coherent whole as instances of the metaphor." (Lakoff and Johnson, 1980, p.140) It can be taken from Lakoff and Johnson that the metaphorical entailments, along with their overall structure and coherence, define the content or meaning of a metaphor.

Thus, in the context of the example, the metaphorical entailments listed (along with the rest which would complete the set) are the definition of the metaphor THE DATA IS A DOCUMENT.

7.2.2 Metaphor Interpretation

The relation of *metaphor interpretation* holds between the metaphor and the designer's interpretant. This relation represents the designer's thought process as they consider the metaphor and ponder what it means. The process leads to the designer's overall thoughts as embodied in their interpretant. This relation, therefore, concerns the designer's brainstorm as to what the metaphor might mean *in general* and independently of any strict design and implementation considerations.

In the example, this relation concerns the process of the designer thinking about the document metaphor, and then coming up with possible ideas for its use in the user-interface. This ultimately yields the designer's interpretant.

7.2.3 Metaphor Match

The *metaphor match* relation embodies how the designer's thoughts on the metaphor tie in to the metaphor's entailments. Because the designer effectively defines these entailments, the match ought to be quite close. It is important to note, however, that this relation can be actively examined. This can be done by having the designer's interpretant assessed for specific matches between it and the metaphorical entailments. This means that it can be discovered whether all of the entailments have been taken into account.

In the example, it can be seen that the ideas in the designer's interpretant do realise various aspects of the metaphorical entailments. Thus, the aspect of the designer's interpretant which concerns the visual aspects of a document realises metaphorical entailments such as "the data is on paper," "the data can have a fold in it," "the data can have text typed on it," and so forth.

7.2.4 Realisation and Refinement

Now that we have discussed the relations relating strictly to the metaphor sign, we must address the important issue of the relations *linking* the two signs involved in the model. There are two links here, one between designer's interpretant and representamen, and one between the two sets of metaphorical entailments. The *realisation* relation concerns the process of the designer's interpretant becoming a real implementation in a user-interface: the representamen. This is the process of actual implementation of the ideas about the metaphor. Thus, in the example, the realisation concerns the transformation of the designers concepts about how documents look and behave into actual interface elements and functionality.

The process of realisation is intricately linked with the parallel relation of *refinement*. The refinement relation concerns the process of narrowing down the set of metaphorical entailments to just those that will be true of the actual user-interface implementation: the UI metaphorical entailments. Because it is so tied to the implementation, this refinement will take place simultaneously with the realisation of the designer's interpretant as representamen in the user-interface. In the example, the refinement relation reflects the designer's consideration of the exact metaphorical entailments that will be used to define the functionality of the document metaphor in the user-interface. This is a culling process, where useful entailments, such as "the data contains text," are retained while inappropriate entailments such as "the data can give you a paper-cut" are jettisoned.

7.2.5 Representation

The *representation* relation concerns how the representamen links with the UI metaphorical entailments. Once again, this can be formalised by specifically indicating what these links are. In this way, it becomes possible to check on the coverage of the interface metaphor. That is, it can be established whether all the UI metaphorical entailments are indicated in some specific way by the representamen, and whether the representamen indicates any non-existent entailments.

In the document example, the representation relation concerns how the implementation of the document metaphor conveys the UI metaphorical entailments already discussed. An example linking the two is that visual representation of the document icon looks like a piece of paper. This ties in with the UI metaphorical entailments which suggest a document can be moved, and even thrown into the trashcan.

7.2.6 User Interpretation

The *user interpretation* relation is the process of the user interpreting the representamen, as is traditional in Peircean semiotics. If the interpretant is that of the Model User then this interpretive process will be the ideal one, making all the correct inferences. If the interpretant is that of a real user, the user interpretation relation will have to be elicited from the user via interviews, thinking-aloud and other techniques.

In the document example, the user interpretation relation occurs while the user is interacting with the implementation of the document metaphor in the user-interface. The relation ends with the user's interpretation of how that aspect of the interface functions.

7.2.7 Metaphor Success

The final relation is that of *metaphor success*. This relation concerns how well the user's interpretant is matched with the UI metaphorical entailments. In other words, this relation is a measure of how well understood the underlying meaning of the user-interface metaphor is by the user. The more the user has made correct inferences about how to interact with the system, the stronger this relation will be.

In the document metaphor example, this relation will concern how well the user has established the entailments about the DATA IS A DOCUMENT metaphor by interacting with the representamen. Instances where the user's interpretant matches with the UI metaphorical entailments indicate a degree of success of the metaphor. Instances where the user imagines functionality not present, or fails to see functionality which *is* present indicate a degree of failure.

8 FURTHER WORK

Although the semiotic model of user-interface metaphor just presented has been shown practically applicable to some degree via the document example, there is clearly more work to be done in that area.

One possibility is to use the semiotic model during user testing. By presenting user responses within the model it may prove possible to trace problems with an interface design back to their origin. Clearly, problems can arise anywhere between the representamen and the metaphorical entailments of a metaphor. For example, a representamen may indicate a UI metaphorical entailment that is not present. Alternatively, this problem might be traced back to the process of refinement, where a metaphorical entailment was removed from the set of entailments, but this was not reflected in the final representamen. Being able to pin-point the cause of a problem for users would be a valuable asset. The work concerning the use of metaphorical entailments to analyse metaphor content in Barr *et al.* (2002) partly concerns this sort of analysis.

A further important avenue of future research is the application of the semiotic model to the design process. Specifically, it would be desirable to teach the model to designers about to begin an interface design, and to see how this knowledge influenced their activities. It could be predicted that the more structured vocabulary would generally aid the designers in discussion, for example.

The analysis of icons using a semiotic model presented in Barr *et al.* (2003) goes some way to suggesting that, once a semiotic model is in place, other semiotic techniques can be applied. In the paper, Peircean sign-types are used to classify computer icons. This kind of transference of traditional semiotic analysis techniques to user-interface metaphors should be made possible by our model.

One more possible step is to perform a detailed case study of actual user-interface metaphors in some software. This has been done to some extent with three major metaphors from Microsoft Office's Project Gallery (Barr, 2003). It will be a major undertaking to analyse an entire interface's metaphors semiotically, but it may well prove very valuable to understanding the metaphors' individual properties, as well as their interactions with each other.

9 CONCLUSIONS

In this paper we have identified a particular issue with the current approach to user-interface metaphors: the concept itself is not well understood. In response to this we have shown in considerable detail how Peircean semiotics can be used to produce a highly structured model of user-interface metaphor. We claim that this model provides interface designers with a consistent vocabulary for discussion, as well as a strong analytical approach to the concept.

Additionally, the application of semiotics to user-interface metaphor clearly allows the possibility of applying further semiotic analysis. In other words, the semiotic model provides a foot in the door of analysis normally applied to other disciplines. Because we now have a semiotics of user-interface metaphors, these analyses can be directed at that concept also.

NOTES

1. This paper will follow the convention of George Lakoff and Mark Johnson's book *Metaphors We Live By* (Lakoff and Johnson, 1980) in presenting metaphors in a small-caps font.

REFERENCES

Andersen, P. B. and May, M. 2001, Tearing Up Interfaces. In Liu, K., Clarke, R. J., Andersen, P. B., and Stamper, R. K. editors, Information, Organisation and Technology: Studies in Organisational Semiotics, pages 299-337. Kluwer Academic Publishers.

Andersen, P. B. 1993, A Semiotic Approach to Programming. In The Computer as Medium, pages 16-67. Cambridge University Press.

Andersen, P. B. 1997, A Theory of Computer Semiotics. Cambridge Series on Human-Computer Interaction. Cambridge University Press.

Andersen, P. B. 2000, What Semiotics Can and Cannot Do for HCI. In CHI'2000 Workshop on Semiotic Approaches to User Interface Design.

Apple Computer, Inc. Staff. 1992, Macintosh Human Interface Guidelines. Addison-Wesley.

Barr, P., Biddle, R., and Noble, J. 2002, A Taxonomy of User-Interface Metaphor. In Steve Jones and Masood Masodian, editors, Proceedings SIGCHI-NZ Symposium on Computer-Human Interaction. The New Zealand Chapter of ACM SIGCHI.

Barr, P. 2003, User-Interface Metaphor in Theory and Practice. MSc. Thesis, Victoria University of Wellington, Department of Mathematical and Computing Sciences.

Barr, P., Biddle, R., and Noble. J. 2003, Icons R Icons. In Robert Biddle and Bruce Thomas, editors, User Interfaces: Fourth Australian User Interface Conference, pp 25-32.

Carroll, J. M. and Mack, R. L. 1995, Learning to Use a Word Processor: By Doing, by Thinking, and by Knowing. In Ronald M. Baecker, Jonathan Grudin, William A. S. Buxtin, and Saul Greenberg, editors, Readings in Human-Computer Interaction: Toward the Year 2000, pages 698-717. Morgan Kaufmann Publishers, Inc.

Carroll, J. M., Mack, R. L., and Kellogg. W. A. 1988. Interface Metaphors and User Interface Design. In M. Helander, editor, Handbook of Human-Computer Interaction, pp. 67-85. Elsevier Science Publishers.

Carroll, J. M. and Thomas, J. C. 1982, Metaphor and the Cognitive Representation of Computing systems. IEEE Transactions on Systems, Man. and Cybernetics, 12(2):pp. 107-116, March/April.

Cataci, T., Costabile, M. F., and Matera, M. 1995, Which Metaphor for Which Database? In M. A. R. Kirby, A. J. Dix, and J. E. Finlay, editors, People and Computers X: Proceedings of HCI'95. Cambridge University Press.

Chandler, D. 2002, Semiotics: The Basics. Routledge.

Connolly, J. H. and Phillips, I. W. 2002, User-system Interface Design. In Liu, K. Clarke R J, Andersen, P. B., Stamper, R. K., and Abou-Zeid, E. S. editors, Organisational Semiotics: Evolving a Science of Information Systems, pages 119-132. Kluwer Academic Publishers.

Souza, C. S. D. 1993, The Semiotic Engineering of User Interface Languages. International Journal of Man-Machine Studies, 39(5): pp. 753-773.

Dertouzos, M. 2001, The Unfinished Revolution. HarperCollins Publishers, Inc.

Eco, U. 1979, The Role of the Reader. Indiana University Press.

Eco, U. 1990, The Limits of Interpretation. Indiana University Press.

Erickson, T. D. 1990, Working with Interface Metaphors. In Brenda Laurel, editor, The Art of Human-Computer Interface Design, pp 65-73. Addison-Wesley Publishing Company,.

Goguen, J. 1999, An Introduction to Algebraic Semotics, with Applications to User Interface Design. In Chrystopher Nehaniv, editor, Computation for Metaphor, Analogy and Agents, volume 1562 of LNAI, pp. 242-291. Springer-Verlag.

Greimas, A. J. 1983, Structural Semantics. University of Nebraska Press.

Halasz, F. and Moran, T. P. 1982, Analogy Considered Harmful. In Proceedings of the Conference on Human Factors in Computing Systems, pp 383-386.

Johnson, S. 1997, Interface Culture: How New Technology Transforms the Way We Create and Communicate. Harper San Francisco.

Kay, A. 1990, User interface: A Personal View. In Brenda Laurel, editor, The Art of Human-Computer Interface Design, pp 191-207. Addison-Wesley Publishing Company.

Lakoff, G. and Johnson, M. 1980, Metaphors We Live By. The University of Chicago Press.

Liu, K., Clarke, R. J., Andersen, P. B., Stamper, R. K. and Abou-Zeid, E. S. 2002, editors. Organisational Semiotics: Evolving a Science of Information Systems. Kluwer Academic Publishers.

Lundell, J. and Anderson, S. 1995, Designing a `Front Panel' for Unix: The evolution of a metaphor. In Irvin R. Katz, Robert Mack, and Linn Marks, editors, Proceedings of CHI'95 Conference on Human Factors in Computing Systems, pages 573-580, New York. Addison-Wesley Publishing Co.

Madsen, K. H. 1994, A Guide to Metaphorical Design. Communications of the ACM, 37(12): pp. 57-62.

Malcolm, G. and Goguen, J. A. 1998, Signs and Representations: Semiotics for User Interface Design. In Ray Paton and Irene Nielson, editors, Visual Representations and Interpretations, pp. 163-172. Springer.

May, M. and Andersen, P. B. 2001, Instrument Semiotics. In Liu, K., Clarke, R. J., Andersen, P. B., and Stamper, R. K. editors, Information, Organisation and Technology: Studies in Organisational Semiotics, pp. 271-298. Kluwer Academic Publishers.

Microsoft Corporation. 1995, The Windows Interface Guidelines for Software Design: An Application Design Guide. Microsoft Press.

Mountford, S. J. 1990, Tools and Techniques for Creative Design. In Brenda Laurel, editor, The Art of Human-Computer Interface Design, pp. 17-30. Addison-Wesley Publishing Company.

Mullet, K. and Sano, K. 1995, Designing Visual Interfaces: Communication Oriented Techniques. SunSoft Press.

Nadin, M. 1988, Interface Design: A Semiotic Paradigm. Semiotica, 69(3): pp. 269-302.

Nelson, T. H. 1990, The Right Way to Think About Software Design. In Brenda Laurel, editor, The Art of Human-Computer Interface Design, pages 235-243. Addison-Wesley Publishing Company.

Nielsen, J. 1993, Usability Engineering. Academic Press.

Norman, D. A. 1998, The Invisible Computer. The MIT Press.

Peirce, C. S. 1934-1948, Collected Papers. four volumes. Harvard University Press.

Prince, G. 1982, Narratology: The Form and Functioning of Narrative. Mouton de Gruyter.

Shakespeare, W. 1933, Romeo and Juliet. Morrison and Gibb, Ltd.

Anderson, M. S. B, and Alty, J. L. 1995, Metaphor Reflections and a Tool for Thought. In M. A. R. Kirby, A. J. Dix, and J. E. Finlay, editors, People and Computers X: Proceedings of HCI'95. Cambridge University Press.

Thwaites, T., Davis, L., and Mules, W. 1994. Tools for Cultural Studies: An Introduction. Macmillan Education.

Väänänen, K. and Schmidt, J. 1994, User Interface for Hypermedia: How to Find Good Metaphors? In Catherine Plaisant, editor, Proceedings of the CHI'94 Conference Companion on Human Factors in Computing Systems, pp. 263-264.

Wozny, L. A. 1989, The Application of Metaphor, Analogy, and Conceptual Models in Computer Systems. Interacting with Computers, 1(3): pp. 273-283.

Chapter 14

THE SEMIOTICS OF USER INTERFACES

A Socio-Pragmatic Perspective

Jonas Sjöström & Göran Goldkuhl
Jönköping International Business School and Linköping University, Sweden

Abstract: Within the IS research field, there are many views on how to understand the use of IT systems. Within the community of organisational semiotics, Stamper's semiotic framework has been used as a tool to understand information systems at different abstraction levels. Another theory related to organisational semiotics, Information Systems Actability Theory (ISAT), argues that social action theories and speech act theory are needed for a thorough understanding of the use of IT systems in organisations. The use of IT systems is considered to be performance of action within a social context. The purpose of this paper is to elaborate on user interfaces of information systems as a means to understand socio-pragmatic and communicative aspects of IS use. The theoretical foundation is based on semiotic and socio-pragmatic theories, and findings from a case study are presented and discussed in order to clarify the argumentation.

Key words: Semiotics, user interfaces, HCI, actability, social action

1 INTRODUCTION

Within organisational semiotics, Stamper's (1973) organisational onion illustrates a view on organisations, business processes and IT systems. It consists of three layers: The informal, the formal and the technical. The organisation as a whole is looked upon as an informal IS, where the values, beliefs and behaviour of individuals are important. The informal layer aggregates the formal layer, which is the way individual actions and business processes should be carried out according to rules in the organisation. The third layer, the technical system, is the part of the formal system that is automated (e.g. through and IT system that supports the processes). The

K. Liu (ed.),
Virtual, Distributed and Flexible Organisations: Studies in Organisational Semiotics, 217–236.

degree of formalisation is the lowest in the informal layer, and highest in the technical layer.

Based on the layered view on organisations (as presented above), the semiotic framework (Stamper 1994) is an analytic tool that suggests that signs can be understood at six different abstraction levels. The lower three levels – physics, empirics and syntactics – are considered to belong to the system platform. The upper three levels – semantics, pragmatics and the social world – are seen as human information functions.

Organisational semiotics has been described as "a discipline that explores the use of signs and its social effects within a social setting" (Baranauskas et al 2002 p 5). Several authors have based their research on this perspective, and some recent papers have treated the subject of how organisational semiotics can help develop user interface design concepts. Connolly and Phillips (2000) conclude that a synergy between the two perspectives of Human Factors (HF) and Organisational Semiotics (OS) can potentially bring benefits to designers of user-system interfaces. Their starting point is the usability theories of Shneiderman (1998). Their discussion is focused on the potential advantages that can be reached through a synthesis between Shneiderman's human factors perspective and the semiotic framework. One of their conclusions is that the meaning of signs is different depending on which semiotic level we are observing. They motivate this conclusion through a discussion on a case study, primarily based on the levels of the semiotic framework. According to Connolly and Phillips, the ideal would be to be able to define future user interfaces (UI) on the pragmatic (or social) level, and to automate the design at lower levels in the framework. They find this approach useful, and make two conclusions based on their argumentation: 1) Signs mean different things depending on which level in the semiotic framework we are currently studying and 2) There might be relations between the different levels in the framework. The example below illustrates how Connolly and Phillips apply the semiotic framework to analyse a part of a user interface. Table 1 contains an analysis of a 'Send' button in an e-mail system:

Table 1. Analysis of UI element using the semiotic framework (adapted from Connolly and Phillips 2002)

Semiotic level	Meaning of 'Send' button
Physical	Group of pixels
Empiric	Visible shape
Syntactical	Icon capable of being distinguished from other icons and of being combined with other icons
Semantic	Carrier of meaning
Pragmatic	Instrument of user-system communication
Social	Tool to help the user accomplish an interpersonal action

The result of the analysis illustrates how the meaning of a sign differs depending on which semiotic perspective we apply to analyse it.

Baranauskas et al (2002) follow the example of Connolly and Phillips, claiming that the referential framework of UI analysis needs to be broadened when designing Internet applications. Furthermore, social and organisational aspects are said to be paid insufficient attention in contemporary literature. The semiotic framework is proposed as a tool to conduct user interface analysis of web sites. Their findings indicate that issues related to organisation and business need to be afforded by the UI, and that it should be taken into consideration in analysis, design and evaluation of web sites. In line with Connolly and Phillips, they consider the framework to be an analytic tool that helps analyse a UI at different levels and from different perspectives.

Andersen (2001) discussed the role of semiotics in user interface design, stating "semiotics is also helpful for positioning design of computer systems in a broader theoretical and philosophical context" (Andersen 2001 p 423). We see a point in using the semiotic framework to direct attention toward different aspects of the user interface, but we believe that we need complementary theories in order to understand how to explain phenomena at different levels in the framework. In the work of Baranauskas et al (2002) and Connolly and Phillips (2000), user interfaces are analysed on a social and pragmatic level. However, it is not transparent *why* certain questions are asked at different levels in the semiotic framework[10].

We believe that the semiotic approach to user interfaces need to be problematized further – a definition of the sign concept needs to acknowledge communicative aspects, in order to be suitable for theorizing on socio-pragmatic aspects of user interfaces.

The purpose of this paper is to present a socio-pragmatic and semiotic concept of user interfaces. Based on a communicative perspective, we believe that this concept is 1) useful to understand socio-pragmatic aspects of IT use and 2) a tool to relate the use of IT systems to an understanding of work tasks and business processes.

This paper does not explicitly handle cognitive aspects of user interfaces – the relation between our user interface concept and cognitive psychology is partially discussed in Sjöström & Ågerfalk (2003), and it will be further discussed in coming publications.

[10] One example of this is the analysis of the social level and the pragmatic level in table 1, which seems to provide a rather narrow view on pragmatics and social action and also an unclear relation between the pragmatic level and the social level.

This paper is based on previously performed case studies and a thorough theoretical reasoning. It is continuation of work reported in Sjöström & Goldkuhl (2002). Parts of a case study will be presented, in order to clarify and illustrate the presented concepts.

Chapter two is a theoretical chapter, presenting our (socio-pragmatic) view on the sign concept and on user interfaces. Chapter three contains an empirical discussion. Finally, we sum up our findings in the conclusions section.

2 A SOCIO-PRAGMATIC PERSPECTIVE ON SEMIOTICS AND USER INTERFACES

Our basic view on signs is that we can apply two different perspectives on signs in relation to action: 1) signs as a pre-requisite for action and b) signs as a result of action. This approach makes it apparent that we consider signs in a communicative perspective[11]. We therefore argue that it is meaningful to take several actors into account when studying a sign; The creator of the sign (the communicator) as well as the interpreter of the sign. Chapter 2.1 contains a fundamental discussion on how to define the sign concept. Chapter 2.2 discusses the implications this definition has on the design of user interfaces.

2.1 A socio-pragmatic perspective on semiotics

There are many approaches to semiotics as the study of signs. Innis (1985) contains an overview and a collection of classical articles. Peirce (1985) has made an important and often quoted definition of sign: “A sign, or representamen, is something which stands to somebody for something in some respect or capacity.” (ibid p 5). In this definition there are several important issues, which can be commented upon. There is one actor identified (“stands to *somebody*”), which we conceive as an interpreter of the sign. Moreover Peirce emphasises the representational aspect of the sign. This is done in the definition and also a bit later in his text: “The sign stands for something, its object” (ibid p 5). We do not deny the importance of this representational or referential aspect of the sign, but there are important aspects not mentioned. Just acknowledging one role – an interpreter – dismisses the communicative character and function of signs. It thereby also

[11] If an action results in a shared message, it is an act of communication

disregards the action character of signs[12]. It might be possible to interpret the peircean position concerning the sign interpreter ("which stands to somebody") as a generic concept applicable both for creator and receiver. In both these roles there is a meaning relation between the sign and the actor. This means that the sign stands as a sign to its creator as well as to its receivers. We admit that this is a possible view. However, this view dismisses the fundamental differences between the sign creator and the sign receiver. The sign for its locutor is not in the first place something to be interpreted. It is a result of a purposive act where a communicative intent is shaped and expressed. The act of the receiver is quite something else. It is an act of reconstructing what is already there. This view will be explicated further below.

A non-natural sign is always part of a socio-pragmatic context. A sign is the result of an actor producing that sign with intentions in a communicative act. The sign will be directed towards one or more recipients. These recipients will interpret the sign and obtain some knowledge as an effect of this communication process. This means that the sign must have relations to these two roles of a communication situation: The locutor creating the sign and the addressee creating an understanding through an interpretive act. The relation between the sign and the locutor can be seen as an expressive sign relation. The sign is an expression made by the locutor of what he wants to communicate to the addressee through his communicative act. The relation between the sign and the addressee is an influence sign relation. The sign will influence the addressee through his interpretive act.

Besides these two actor relations, the sign will of course have a signifying relation to its referent; i.e. the objects talked about. These three relations correspond to the three functions of language described by Bühler (1934) who is another classical semiotic scholar[13]. The three functions are: 1) symptom (the expressive relation), 2) signal (the influence relation) and 3) symbol (the referential function). These functions are depicted in a communication model (figure 1).

[12] It disregards the communicative action aspect of signs. Interpretative action aspects can be said to be at least partially included; see discussion below.

[13] Jakobson (1985), still another classical semiotician, has built on Bühler's semiotic functions and added some more functions (phatic, poetic and metalingual). These other functions seem not to be as basic as the three functions from Bühler and we will not need them for our analysis here.

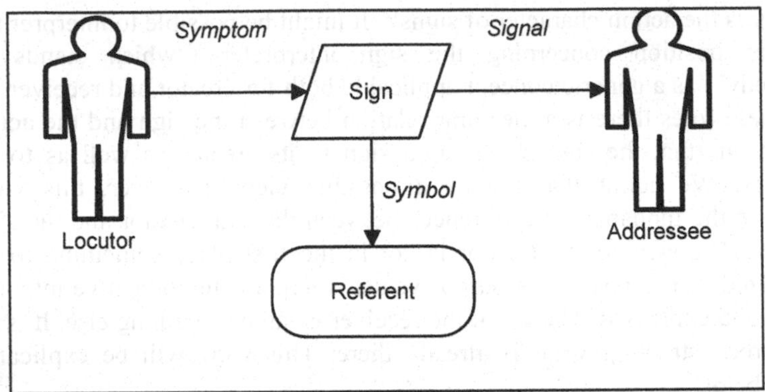

Figure 1. Sign in a communication context describing three basic functions of the sign

Our main message is that a sign should always be seen as a part of such a socio-pragmatic context. It always has a relation to its author as well to its interpreters. And the sign also says something about the world; that it has the capacity to "bring the world" to the communicators. The Russian semiotician Vološinov (1985 p 52-53) describes this socio-pragmatic view of the sign in the following way: "…word is a two-sided act. It is determined equally by whose word it is and for whom it is meant. As word it is precisely the product of the reciprocal relationship between the speaker and listener, addresser and addressee." "A word is a bridge thrown between myself and another. If one end of this bridge depends on me, then the other depends on the addressee."

Even if we like Vološinov's metaphoric and poetic way of describing communication, we must comment upon some issues, which otherwise might obscure our message. The word (which rather should be said to be an utterance) is in itself not an act, but rather a result of an act[14]. Uttered words are not results of one two-sided act, as Vološinov seems to state it. There are instead two distinct but related acts "operating" towards the utterance; the expressive act of the locutor producing the utterance and the interpretive act of the addressee trying to capture its meaning. It is important to not take it for granted that the same meaning will arise between speaker and listener even if this usually is the intention and many times is what is accomplished.

If we should follow the original description of signs by Peirce, we get a limited view on sign pragmatics. Pragmatics, in this view, is restricted to the interpreter's possible actions based on the sign. Morris (1964), following in the traces of Peirce, has elaborated on the pragmatic relation of signs to the

[14] Confer Ricoeur (1991) about his discussion about text as a result of an action and a prerequisite for reading (interpreting).

interpreter. Morris distinguishes between different pragmatic meanings of sign (designative, prescriptive, appraisive), all in relation to the interpreter and what he possibly may do based on the sign. These pragmatic meanings are based on the notion of the act is it described by another American pragmatist, G H Mead (1938). Mead distinguishes between three phases of an act, perceptual, manipulatory and consummatory[15]. Although we find these distinctions useful[16], we claim that this is a limited view on sign pragmatics since there is no reference given to the creator of the sign.

One way to explicate our position further is to relate to the concepts of illocution and perlocution from speech act theory (Austin, 1962; Searle, 1969). Illocution is what is done within the speech act (i.e the communicative intention of the locutor). Perlocution is the possible effect on the interpreter. Pragmatics of signs should include both these action aspects[17]; what the locutor performs in relation to the addressee (the illocutionary aspect) and what the addressee performs based upon the presented sign (the perlocutionary aspect).

Another way to explicate our position is to relate it to the different actions exerted in communication. Clark (1996) describes communication as a joint action consisting of one act of a speaker presenting a sign and one act of an addressee identifying and recognizing the sign. We think that Clark's terminology ("*joint action*") is misleading. Communication is not one joint action performed by a speaker and addressee together; it is rather a *joint activity* consisting of two distinct, but related actions, performed by each actor (speaker and addressee respectively). Although we find his terminology confusing we think that his emphasis on these two interrelated acts is very important. This is also fully in line with Goldkuhl's (2001) differentiation of intervening and receiving actions. To produce a sign is an intervening action and interpret a sign is a receiving action. Through the sign these two kinds of action are interrelated.

A conclusion of the discussions above is that the meaning of the sign (representamen) must be understood not only in relation to the interpreter and the object it refers to (as proposed by Peirce). The peircian position does not include the pragmatic and social aspects that origin from the creator of the sign. When discussing pragmatic and social meanings of the sign, both

15 The designative function relates to the perceptual phase (observable properties); the prescriptive function relates to the manipulatory phase and the appraisive function relates to the consummatory phase.

16 Confer for example Cronholm & Goldkuhl (2002) where these different categories have been used to clarify the different phases of a user interacting with a computer (in the Elementary InterAction Loop).

17 This has been stated earlier by Goldkuhl & Ågerfalk (2002) in a critical analysis of Stamper's (1994) semiotic ladder.

the creator and the interpreter of the sign should be emphasized (c.f. Bühlers view on signs presented in Figure 1). Especially when analysing the socio-pragmatic meaning of a sign, it seems important to acknowledge the creator of the sign.

2.2 A socio-pragmatic perspective on user interfaces

The discussion in section 2.1 considers a sign as either a prerequisite for action or a result of action. This way, all parties involved in creation and interpretation of the sign are acknowledged, which illustrates the pragmatic and social aspects of semiotics and results in a richer picture of communication. This line of reasoning can be transferred to user interfaces (since they can be viewed as groups of signs). The traditional view of user interfaces is that they are parts in a user-system interaction. From a semiotic perspective, de Souza et al (2001) want to expand this view on user interfaces. They distinguish between three different types of communication:

1 User-system interaction
2 User-user interaction
3. Designer-to-user communication

In order to understand and define user interfaces from a semiotic perspective it is necessary to take all these communication situations into account.

In their paper (ibid) they emphasise the communication in a user-interface from its designers to its users. They describe the user interface of an IT-system in this respect in the following way: "They are one-shot messages sent from designers to users about the range of messages users can exchange with the system in order to achieve certain effects" (ibid p 462). This can be compared to the concept of action repertoire (or action potential) within the IS actability theory (e.g. Goldkuhl & Ågerfalk, 2002; Sjöström & Goldkuhl, 2002). The action repertoire of an IS is the possible actions which the system affords to its users. This action potential is a result of the designers'[18] work.

In their discussion, de Souza et al (ibid) focus on the communication between designer and user, while we argue that it is more important to focus the business communication going on: Users of the IT system actually communicate with each other, using the artifact as a medium for communication. This is actually pointed out by de Souza et al (ibid), but it is

[18] It is important to have a broad conception of IT designers in this kind of discussion, including those who are responsible for the design of the IT system.

only discussed in relation to specific types of multi-user applications (e.g. groupware).

We want to stress this kind of communication since we find this to be the core of an information system. A communicative perspective means that *information systems are regarded as systems for technology mediated business communication.* In figure 2 we have described user interfaces contextually, not only in relation to the actual user, but also in relation to other human communicators. We distinguish between three different types of actions: *Business communication*, *UI navigation* and *IT system design,* following the division above from de Souza et al (2001).

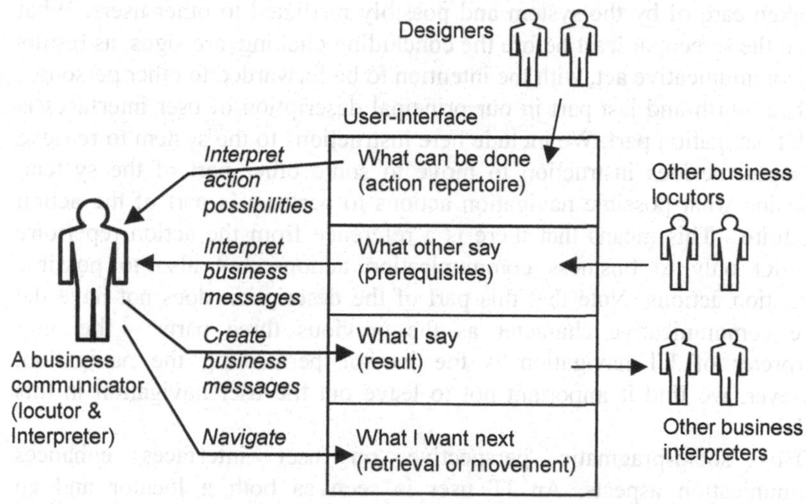

Figure 2. A communicative perspective on user interfaces

We divide a user interface into four parts. One part is the action repertoire. This is to be seen as communication from the designer to the user. By interpreting the user interface the user may hopefully understand what kind of actions it is possible to perform. This part of the user interface is thus made up of signs from designers telling the user what possible actions to perform.

In order to communicate something, through the system, to other persons, it might be necessary to read what others have said/done earlier. Within the IS actability theory, there is one important concept - action memory - which relates to this (e.g. Goldkuhl & Ågerfalk, 2002). An action memory consists of messages about earlier performed actions and other important action circumstances. Before communicating something to other persons, the actual user may read parts of the action memory of the system. These presented messages are thus prerequisites for the user's action. The messages are signs from other persons within the business and mediated by the IT system. To obtain such messages on the screen, the user probably performs some acts of retrieval. We consider this as a part of the UI navigation; which is described below.

After reading such messages, the user may act by expressing something. He may input something through the keyboard and then using the mouse click on a screen button. What is on the screen as a result of his input is a message from him. It is a result of his communicative action. After he has concluded his action (for example through a mouse click), this message will be taken care of by the system and possibly mediated to other users. What are on the screen, at least before the concluding clicking, are signs, as results of a communicative act, with the intention to be forwarded to other persons.

The fourth and last part in our principal description of user interfaces is the UI navigation part. We include here instructions to the system to retrieve messages, besides instruction to move to some other part of the system. Choosing what possible navigation actions to perform is part of the action repertoire. This means that there is a reference from the action repertoire part not only to business communication actions, but also to possible navigation actions. Note that this part of the description does not have the same communicative character as the previous three parts – the only interpreter of UI navigation is the locutor performing the navigation. However, we find it important not to leave out the user navigation in this model.

This socio-pragmatic perspective on user interfaces enhances communication aspects. An IT user is seen as both a locutor and an interpreter. Andersen (2001), in his semiotic analysis of human-computer interaction, describes humans as "compulsive interpreters and compulsive talkers". An IT user is taking part in business communication with other business locutors and interpreters (figure 2).

All these four parts of user interface can be described according to our basic semiotic definition. Each part is 1) an expression of a human acting (symptom) and 2) is directed towards some interpreter (signal) and 3) refers to something (symbol). The user interface is an *interactive action medium*. It contains messages (signs) both directed to the user and from the user. This is of utmost importance to acknowledge. The user interface contains signs to be interpreted and signs, as results of user interventionist action, to be handled by the artefact and possibly forwarded to other humans. In order to explicate this further we have described the different types of communication using the user interface in table 2.

Table 2. Types of communication of different parts of the user interface

Part of user interface	Type of communication and communicators
Action repertoire	A user interprets possible action types afforded by the system (communication from designer to user)
Business communication - for interpretation	A user interprets messages from other users. These messages are mediated through the IT-system. (Communication from user to user)
Business communication - a created formulation to be forwarded	A user creates messages to be mediated by the system to other users (Communication from user to user)
UI navigation	Interaction between user and IT system (No communication between human actors)

Based on the above, we argue that the UI designer needs to treat the matters of business communication and UI navigation separately – one issue is to make sure that business communication is supported in a proper way (in relation to work tasks and business processes), another issue is to make sure that the navigation works properly.

This separation of navigation and business communication points out that we are trying to understand different phenomena. The socio-pragmatic meaning of a sign is clearly related to communication between actors in the organisation. So far we have discussed this issue mainly as one actor (an IT user) being a locutor respectively a recipient. The business communication through an IT system is however usually more complicated since it comprises a many-to-many communication situation. The IT system is a mediator in such communication with the pre-defined ability to transform messages. Sjöström & Goldkuhl (2002) have presented a model describing this complexity of IT-mediated communication (figure 3).

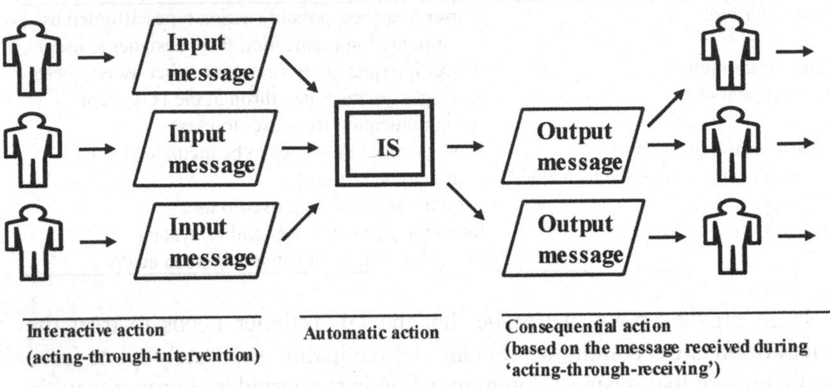

Figure 3. Types of actions related to three IS usage situations (Sjöström & Goldkuhl 2002)

Figure 2 should be seen as a more abstract view of communication through the system, while figure 3 illustrates the complexity of (business) communication using IT systems. The figure is presented in order to relate the previous discussion (based on figure 3) to a discussion on socio-pragmatic aspects of user interfaces. A conclusion from Sjöström & Goldkuhl (ibid) is that an understanding of the communication taking place when utilizing the user interface (the actors involved, temporal and spatial aspects) is vital for an understanding of the socio-pragmatic aspects of the user interface.

In the introduction to this paper we presented a semiotic analysis of a sign (A 'send'-button in a user interface; cf table 1). Within ISAT, there is an important concept called an ae-message (action elementary message); cf Ågerfalk (1999, 2002). An ae-message is the result of an e-action (elementary action), and it consists of propositional content (semantic content describing some part of the world) and an illocution (the intentions of the creator of the message). The ae-message is considered to be the smallest unit of analysis when considering socio-pragmatic aspects of action. The idea is that we need to study a set of related symbols (forming an ae-message) in order to understand their socio-pragmatic meaning. This is also related to our discussion on the sign concept, where we pointed out that utterances (rather than words) are interesting to analyse. We will not deepen the discussion on ae-messages here, but our conclusion is that messages (consisting of signs) are our unit of focus, not single signs.

To sum this chapter up, we conclude two things. First, a communicative view on user interfaces is a step towards an understanding of socio-pragmatic aspects of the interface. Figure 2 presents a communication model on user interfaces, which can be used to guide a designer or evaluator to make the communicative aspects transparent when designing user interfaces for business communication. Second, we need to focus on a larger unit of analysis than a single sign when analyzing socio-pragmatic aspects of user interfaces. The ISAT-concept of ae-messages constitutes a unit of analysis that makes it possible to understand socio-pragmatic aspects of communication.

3 A SOCIO-PRAGMATIC VIEW OF A SCHEDULING SYSTEM

This section contains discussions on an empirical example, in order to illustrate the theoretical concepts presented in section 3.2. The IT system we analyse is a scheduling system for rooms and equipment (projectors and computers). Parts of this case study have been presented in other publications (c.f. Ågerfalk et al 2002; Sjöström & Goldkuhl 2002). The system is used at a number of Swedish universities. Note that the examples (the screen documents) have been translated from Swedish to English. One (for us) known difference is that some letters are underlined in the Swedish version, indicating keyboard shortcuts to some functions in the system. These are not part of our translated versions, due to aesthetic reasons.

This chapter consists of three parts: Two parts describing (central) screen documents in the system, the third part presents some important (socio-pragmatically related) finding from the case study.

3.1 The screen document for overview / searching

The 'introduction' screen (figure 4) in this system is an overview of the bookings currently in the system. All the current bookings (future bookings including today) are displayed. Each booking is a result of a previous action from some actor in the organisation. When a teacher is about to schedule, he/she must interpret the current 'state of business' by looking at this screen and by performing an interpretative act. Furthermore, the teacher has to navigate in the system (e.g. by searching in the schedule). These actions are navigational, in the sense that interactions take place, with the purpose of changing the current view of the system.

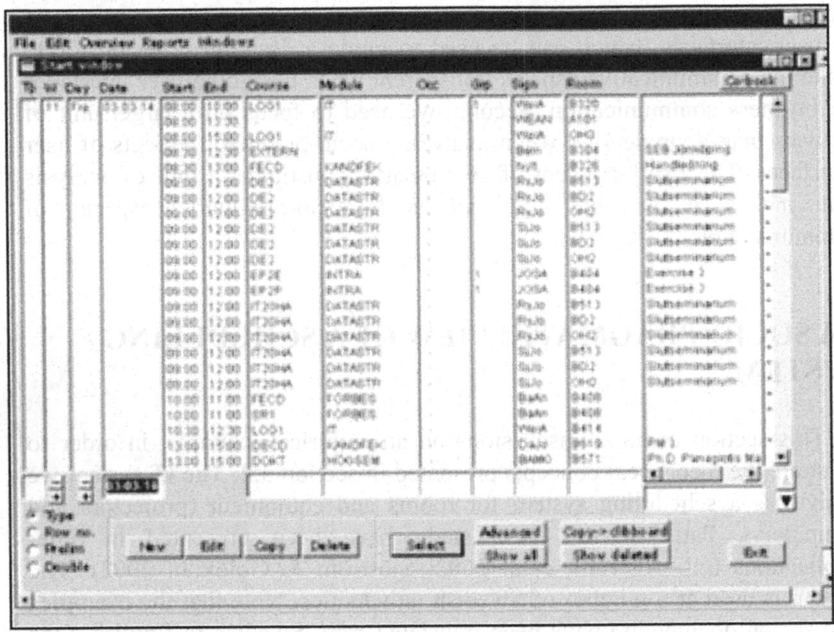

Figure 4. The interactive screen document for overview and searching

Table 3 shows the communication that takes place when this screen document is being used. The table is based on the categories in figure 3. Note that the fourth category (retrieval/movement) is not included. We believe that it is important to understand the UI navigation aspects in order to draw conclusions about the user interface, but in this case we are mainly interested in the communicative aspects; hence we do not focus on navigation at this time.

Table 3. Communication taking place in the screen document for overview / searching

UI part	Description
Action repertoire (designer-to-user)	The designer does not communicate any possibilities to perform communicative business actions. However, different opportunities to navigate in the system are communicated. The user can navigate to various screen documents or filter the current view of business messages using the text fields underneath each column.
Prerequisites (user-to-user)	The locutor has to interpret a set of previously sent business messages, arranged in a table. These are the result of previously performed bookings – an "action memory" that needs to be interpreted by the locutor before scheduling. In this system, it is transparent who is responsible for each business message (the person responsible for the booking is part of the table).
Result	There is no possibility for the locutor to create business messages in this

UI part	Description
(user-to-user)	screen document.

3.2 The screen document for scheduling

When the teacher has got an overview of the current bookings, he/she can create a new booking. Figure *5* shows the interactive screen document used to create new bookings. A set of interactions is needed in order to schedule the booking. This actual scheduling action is directed toward two groups of actors: Students and other teachers. The illocution is different for these two groups. The purpose of communicating the message to the students is that the teacher wants them to show up at the lecture. The purpose of communicating it to other teachers is that the teacher wants to prevent them from booking that same room at the same time.

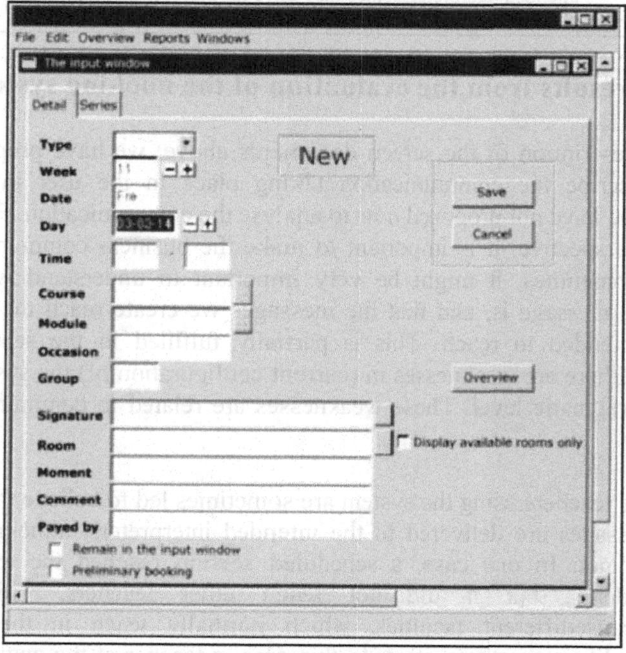

Figure 5. The interactive screen document for scheduling

Table 4 (below) contains an analysis of the communication that takes place when this screen document is being used. Again, the category retrieval/movement has been left out. Note the description of the result, where time aspects and spatial aspects are part of the analysis.

Table 4. Communication taking place in the screen document for scheduling

UI part	Description
Action reportoire (designer-to-user)	The designer communicates the possibility to 1) formulate a booking and 2) to communicate this to other students and teachers. Further, the possibilities to navigate to complementary screen documents (with the purpose of choosing rooms, classes, extra equipment, et cetera) should be communicated to the locutor.
Prerequisites (user-to-user)	No business messages are displayed in this screen document.
Result (user-to-user)	The locutor can use the input fields to formulate and communicate a booking to students and to fellow teachers.
	Spatial aspect: The intended interpreters can receive this message on the school network, the Internet or on video screens in the school. This is not revealed to the locutor in the user interface.
	Time aspect: The locutor cannot be certain when this message reaches the intended interpreters, since they have to 'pull' the message by choosing to view the schedule.

4 Some results from the evaluation of the booking system

In the description of the screen documents above, we have proposed a way to describe the communication taking place in the user interface. However, we have not proposed *how* to analyse the communication. From an actability perspective, it is important to make the business communication visible – sometimes, it might be very important to understand who the creator of a message is, and that the messages we create reach the people they are intended to reach. This is partially fulfilled in the scheduling system, but there are weaknesses in (current configuration of) the system on the socio-pragmatic level. These weaknesses are related to communication aspects:

1) The teachers using the system are sometimes led to believe that their messages are delivered to the intended interpreters, although they are not. In one case, a scheduled session reached the teacher's students, but it did not reach other teachers. This was becausedifferent faculties, which normally teach in their own buildings, use the system. In this case, a teacher at the engineering school scheduled a lecture at the business school. The system indicated that this action was performed correctly. However, the bookings for various schools were stored in different databases, with

the result that the teacher's students could see the booking, but it was invisible for teachers at the business school.

2) Thus last minute changes to the schedule might not reach the students. If a teacher falls ill, and a lecture has to be cancelled, several extra measures have to be taken in order to communicate the cancellation to the students. Of course fone should not argue that an IT system should support every situation in the company, but in this case it was problematic, since it was troublesome to find other ways to reach all the students. Within actability, an analysis of communication includes studying *when* a message reaches the intended interpreters and *how* they receive the message (the place of reception; and whether the message is pushed to the interpreter or pulled by the interpreter). In this case an automatic mail to the affected students would have reduced the size of the problem, since students tend to check mail more often than they check the schedule for changes.

3) Another reflection from our side is that several screen documents are designed to support only one type of user-user communication. The 'overview' window is a one-way communication from other users to a user. In this document, interpretations of previously communicated business messages take place. The 'scheduling' window only supports intervening actions: A locutor creating messages to be interpreted by others. In such a system, a lot of navigation between different parts of the user interface has to take place in order to create new business messages. This could also be related to cognitive theories about not overloading the user's short-term memory (e.g. Nielsen 1993). A way of explaining this phenomenon with our interface concept is that previous business messages that support some user action should be easy accessible, preferably on the screen document that affords the intervening action. The user interface should involve both action prerequisites (messages from others) and possibilities express messages intended for others; confer figure 2 above.

The three examples presented above are examples of an analysis of communication; where actions have been studied. This analysis, where the creators as well as the interpreters of symbols are part of the context, makes it possible to understand socio-pragmatic issues better. If only separate signs – specific parts of figure 4 and 5 – were to be analysed, it would have been harder to draw conclusions about socio-pragmatic aspects of the user interface.

5 CONCLUSIONS

When socio-pragmatic aspects of user interfaces are to be analysed, we need to acknowledge the communicative aspects of signs. In organisational semiotics, Peirce's triadic definition of a sign has a great influence – this definition does however not explicitly acknowledge the creator of the sign, only the interpreter. Other semioticians, such as Bühler, Vološinov and Jakobson, define a sign in a communicative perspective, which leads to a better foundation for an understanding of socio-pragmatic aspects of the sign. Based on our definition of the sign concept, we have presented a communicative view on the user interface concept. We acknowledge interactions on three levels: user-system, designer-user and user-user. The user-user level is made explicit in our view, making it a tool to understand socio-pragmatic aspects of IT-system use. We have also proposed that a suitable unit of analysis for socio-pragmatic aspects of user interfaces is the so called ae-message, as defined in ISAT. Our argument is that in order to understand the socio-pragmatic aspects, we need to focus on something larger than a single sign. Our socio-pragmatic view on signs and user interfaces can be regarded as a complement to the ideas of Connolly and Phillips (2000) and Baranauskas et al (2002), who proposed that the semiotic framework can be used as a tool to understand different aspects of user interfaces. In this paper, we argue that our communicative view on interfaces facilitates an analysis at the socio-pragmatic level of the semiotic framework.

The socio-pragmatic semiotic analysis performed in this paper has also led us to a concept of *pragmatic duality* in human-computer interaction. The prevailing perspective in HCI is that that this kind of interaction is to be seen as a user interacting with an IT artefact. The socio-pragmatic perspective is critical towards this narrow view on HCI and suggests that the user should be conceived as taking part in business communication with other human actors and that the role of the IT artefact (and its user interface) is only a mediator in this human-to-human communication. However, the socio-pragmatic perspective should not be interpreted as a rejection of the view that a human is interacting with an artefact. That would be naïve. Instead we suggest a view on the human-computer interaction as mainly a dual interaction. If we look at the business communication (which can be both interpretation and message creation), described earlier in the paper, we mean that the user is interacting with the artefact and other humans at the same time. The IT system is an artefact with the ability to interact in pre-defined ways with a user. The user must be able to understand how to manage the artefact, for example how to enter information into certain fields and click buttons on the screen etc. When performing such actions, the user is not only manoeuvring the artefact, at the same time, he is actually communicating with other business actors. One can say that (through acts of reading and writing) at the same time he is instrumentally managing the artefact and communicating with other humans[19]. In the same act he is doing several things simultaneously. An interpretative act (when reading information presented on the user interface) means both recognition of what other humans may have said and also finding out how to utilise the artefact. An act of intervention (when entering information onto the user interface) means both an informed act of managing the interface and a communicative act directed towards other humans. Our view on the pragmatic duality of user interfaces can also be a foundation to understand the relation between IT system use and business processes. Important future work will be to relate our work to other contextual approaches to UI design.

To summarize the discussions above, we refer to the purpose of this paper: *To present a socio-pragmatic and semiotic concept of user interfaces.* This conceptualization is useful to understand IT use as social action and how IT artefacts can be seen as communicative instruments in such social action. In future research, we also believe that it can be helpful to relate the use of IT systems to work tasks and business processes.

REFERENCES

Andersen PB. What semiotics can and cannot do for HCI, Knowledge-Based Systems 2001; 14: 419-424

Austin, JL, How to do things with words. Oxford University Press, 1962.

Baranauskas, MCC, Liu, K, Chong, S. Website Interfaces as Representamen of Organisational Behaviour. Proceedings of the 5th International Workshop on Organisational Semiotics; 2002; Delft.

Bühler K. Sprachtheorie, Fischer, Jena, 1934.

Clark HH. Using language, Cambridge: Cambridge University Press, 1996.

Connolly, JH., Phillips, IW. "User-System Interface Design – An Organisational Semiotic Perspective." In Organisational Semiotics – Evolving a Science of Information Systems, Liu K, Clarke RJ, Andersen PB, Stamper RK, eds. The Netherlands: Kluwer Academic Publishers, 2002.

[19] Ågerfalk & Eriksson (2003) have described instrumental and communicative rationality in relation to usability. This is however done in a slightly different way than ours. We emphasize the pragmatic duality in human-computer-interaction.

Cronholm S, Goldkuhl G. Actable Information Systems - Quality Ideals Put Into Practice. Proceedings of the 11th International Conference on Information Systems Development; 2003; Riga.

de Souza CS, Barbosa SDJ, Prates RO. A semiotic engineering approach to user interface design. Knowledge-Based Systems 2001; 14: 461-465

Goldkuhl G. Communicative vs material actions: Instrumentality, sociality and comprehensibility. Proceedings of the 6th Int Workshop on the Language Action Perspective (LAP2001); 2001; Aachen

Goldkuhl G, Ågerfalk PJ. "Actability: A way to understand information systems pragmatics." In Coordination and Communication Using Signs: Studies in Organisational Semiotics – 2, Liu, K. et al, eds. Boston: Kluwer Academic Publishers, 2002.

Innis RE, ed. Semiotics. An introductory anthology. Bloomington: Indiana University Press, 1985.

Jakobson R. "Closing statement: Linguistics and poetics." In Semiotics. An introductory anthology, Innis, RE, ed. Bloomington: Indiana University Press, 1985

Mead GH. Philosophy of the act. The university of Chicago Press, 1938.

Morris C. Signification and significance. Cambridge: MIT Press, 1964.

Nielsen J. Usability Engineering, San Diego, CA: Academic Press, 1993.

Peirce CS. "Logic as semiotic: The theory of signs." In Semiotics. An introductory anthology, Innis RE, ed. Bloomington: Indiana University Press, 1985

Ricoeur P. From text to action. Essays in hermeneutics. London: The Athlone Press, 1991.

Shneiderman B. Designing the User Interface: Strategies for effective Human-Computer Interaction, 3rd edition. Reading, MA: Addison-Wesley, 1998.

Searle JR. Speech acts. An essay in the philosophy of language. London: Cambridge University Press, 1969.

Sjöström J, Goldkuhl G. Information systems as instruments for communication – Refining the actability concept. Proceedings of the 5th International Workshop on Organisational Semiotics; 2002, Delft.

Sjöström J, Ågerfalk PJ. Socio-Instrumental Criteria for Assessing Information Systems. Proceedings of the 8th International Working Conference on the Language Action Perspective on Communication Modelling; 2003 July 1-2; Tilburg.

Stamper RK. "Signs, information, norms and systems". In Signs at work, Holmqvist B, Andersen PB, Klein H, Posner R , eds. Berlin: De Gruyter, 1994.

Vološinov VN. "Verbal interaction". , In Semiotics. An introductory anthology, Innis RE, ed. Bloomington: Indiana University Press, 1985.

Ågerfalk PJ. Pragmatization of information systems - a theoretical and methodological outline [Licentiate thesis]. Linköping: Linköping University, 1999.

Ågerfalk PJ. Messages Are Signs of Action: From Langefors to Speech Acts and Beyond. Proceedings of the 7th International Workshop on the Language-Action Perspective on Communication Modelling; 2002 June 12-13; Delft: Delft University of Technology, 2002.

Ågerfalk PJ, Sjöström J, Eliasson E, Cronholm S, Goldkuhl G. Setting the Scene for Actability Evaluation - Understanding Information Systems in Context. Proceedings of the 9th European Conference on IT Evaluation; 2002; Paris. Reading: MCIL, 2002.

Ågerfalk PJ, Eriksson O. Usability in Social Action: Reinterpreting Effectiveness, Efficiency and Satisfaction, Proceedings of the 11th European Conference on Information Systems; 2003 June 16-21; Naples.

Chapter 15

INTERFACE DESIGN FOR THE CHANGING ORGANISATION

An Organisational Semiotics Approach

Rodrigo Bonacin, M. Cecilia C. Baranauskas, Kecheng Liu
Institute of Computing, State University of Campinas, Caixa Postal 6176 - 13083 970 Campinas, SP - Brazil

Department of Computer Science, University of Reading, Reading, RG6 6AY, UK

{ra000470,cecilia }@ic.unicamp.br, k.liu@reading.ac.uk

Abstract: Within the Organisational Semiotics (OS) perspective, software systems should be designed as part of the whole organisation in which it will be embedded. As organisations are in continuous change, the technical information systems should also be changing in line with their organisation's informal and formal information systems. From the Software Engineering perspective, the difficulties of solving this problem are well known: changes in information systems are usually associated with high costs and its maintenance may cost more than the initial development. While literature in Computer Supported Co-operative Work (CSCW) acknowledges the importance of proposing approaches to deal with this issue, it also acknowledges that we are far from having this problem solved. In this paper we propose a norm driven environment for the system interface configuration, as a way of dealing with the complexity of allowing changes in the system as the organisational norms change.

Key words: Interface Design, Maintenance, Semantic and Norm Analysis

K. Liu (ed.),
Virtual, Distributed and Flexible Organisations: Studies in Organisational Semiotics, 237–255.

1. INTRODUCTION

The real value of a computational system inside an organisation is not the technology itself, but its capacity to improve the performance and effectiveness of the organisation. Therefore software systems should be designed as an integrated part of the whole organisation. As organisations are in constant evolution, we argue that technical information systems should change over time in order to be in line with the organisation's informal and formal systems.

Changes in technical information systems are frequently associated with high costs; maintenance of a software product may cost many times more than its initial development (Boehm, 1975; Manderson and Layzell, 1999). Therefore, if we want the software product to evolve with the organisation we need a mechanism to make it viable. A possible solution would be the use of high-level languages to enable modifications in the software product, without the necessity of changing the code. In this work we propose an approach to construct user interfaces for CSCW systems in order to accommodate changes in organisations.

As stated by Grudin (1994), it is not the organisation that has to adapt to a groupware system; instead, the system must adapt to the organisational practices. A CSCW system should be integrated to the organisational information system, respecting the social norms that are instituted at the workplace. To model and understand the social context, CSCW has been a field open to a wide mix of disciplines encompassing cognitive and social psychology, work oriented sociology and anthropology, and many others (Bannon, 1992).

Literature has shown that the organisational contexts should be understood in order to construct suitable CSCW systems; however the organisations are in continuous development even during system design. Furthermore, the competitive market drives the organisations to constantly improve their work practice. These changes usually have social effects, and the CSCW system should be adapted to the new organisational contexts. In this paper we show an architecture and a methodology based on Organisational Semiotics, more precisely Semantic and Norm Analysis (Stamper et al., 1988) to support organisational changes during system design and use.

The design of systems in which all features are configurable seems not to be viable in practice. In order to deal with the complexity of this problem in the context of organisations we propose a system architecture organised into two parts: a static part that contains elements less probable to be affected by organisational changes and a dynamic part that is more likely to be changed.

According to Sommerville (2000) nomenclature, the static part of the proposed architecture refers to the "enduring requirements" and the dynamic part, the "volatile requirements". Enduring requirements are stable requirements derived from the core activity of the customer organisation; e.g. a hospital will always have doctors, nurses, etc.. Volatile requirements are those which change during development or when the system is in use. In a hospital, for example, requirements are derived from their health-care policy.

The Semantic Analysis, which is presented (Liu, 2000) as a method to produce a stable model of an organisation, is used to construct the first part of the system. The semantic model is translated into an object oriented implementation model. The concepts used to define the system classes results from applying the *theory of affordances* (Gibson, 1968), which is used in the definition of the ontology charts during Semantic Analysis. In this perspective, objects are no longer considered as things that stand by themselves with a set of properties, but they are understood as repertoires of behaviour of agents.

The Norm Analysis is a method for specifying aspects of the pragmatic and social levels of the organisation. With the proposed architecture norms are related to many aspects of the CSCW system interface; as norms change the system can be modified to support changes in the pragmatics and social levels of the organisation during the system usage. Those changes are accomplished by an Interface Engineer through of an Interface Configuration Environment (ICE) without the necessity of direct code maintenance.

The paper is organised in the following way: Section 2 presents some related issues in CSCW research; Section 3 presents the proposed architecture; Section 4 contains a discussion and the analysis of the approach in a case considering a real organisation; and Section 5 concludes the paper.

2. CSCW RESEARCH AND THE CHANGING SYSTEMS

One of the main motivations to search for alternatives for modifying CSCW systems during their use is the dynamic nature of the social groups. In those groups the behaviour patterns usually change over time and new members are continuously being introduced. In OS terms, we are deal with groups of agents that are constantly interacting in social contexts, affecting and being affected by the context.

The CSCW research community has been exploring alternatives so as to maintain the system in line with users' requirements even after the system development completion. They include solutions such as: the design of flexible CSCW systems (Dourish, 1996), "design for unanticipated use" (Robinson, 1993), and, the design of a tailorable CSCW system (Kahler *et al.*, 2000).

"Tailoring" can be understood as "the activity of modifying a computer application within the context of its use" (Kahler *et al.*, 2000, p. 1). The tailoring of a groupware system raises several questions (Teege, 1999, p. 2) such as:

- Which group processes and work culture allow and encourage tailoring by the participants? A successful tailoring by all participants is only possible if it is an integral part of the work process.
- How can tailoring be done collaboratively? In collaborative work settings it is necessary that tailoring steps which affect several participants are performed or agreed upon by all the affected people.
- Do we need different kinds of tailoring mechanism in different areas of groupware?
- How can we transfer developments from HCI domain to implement tailoring support?
- What are the commonalities and what are the differences among user interfaces in general and user interfaces for tailoring groupware?
- How can we include rights and restrictions into tailoring support? When tailoring may affect a whole work group, it is necessary to define constraints for tailoring actions. Who defines and tailors these constraints?
- What system architectures are needed to allow tailoring during system use? How can tailoring mechanisms be integrated in the system?
- How do we take into account diverse and dynamic requirements in the initial development process, i.e. how do we determine the points and the degree of tailorability of a future application?

Research in a tailorable system usually presupposes that the user should be in charge of the tailoring task (Teege, 1999; Morch and Mehandjiev, 2000). Morch (1995) identifies three levels for end-user tailoring: (1) "customisation" in which an end-user can set parameters for various configuration options, (2) "integration" in which end-users can add new functionality to an application through predefined components and (3) "extension" in which the end-users improve the implementation by adding new code.

Although there are some successful applications of end-user tailoring, modification of the system by end-users to adapt to complex social changes, as promoted by changes in norms, are still too far from being a solved problem. Therefore for immediate practical results, in this paper we propose an architecture for easier and economical modification of the system by an interface engineer.

In agreement with almost all CSCW researchers, we argue that as end-users are close to their work domain, their expertise should be considered in the definition of the system modifications. We also argue that the knowledge about the technology and the modelling expertise of an interface engineer is important in complex system modifications. In the approach presented in this paper we propose that the Interface Engineer and the end-user should work together to make changes in the interface. Using Participatory Design (PD) techniques we can include the user in the process of modifying the system, respecting his/her power over decisions.

3. THE PROPOSED ARCHITECTURE

Figure 1 shows the main elements of the proposed architecture, which is organized in two parts: the End-User Interface and the Interface Configuration Environment (ICE). The "End-Users" are people who interact directly with the system in their workplace through the End-User Interface; the "Interface Engineer" are people who configure the End-User Interface (supposedly with the End-User participation) through the ICE. The "Interface Engineer" makes changes in the norms at the ICE, which set-up the End-User Interface.

Figure 1 is a simplified version of the proposed approach, which will be detailed in the sections 3.1 and 3.2. A scenario of the execution will be used in those sections to illustrate the dynamic part of the architecture. A description of the scenario, described in the natural language is as follows:

1. A user named "John" is involved in a problem resolution task, he is at the fourth step of the resolution procedures and he is responsible for this step. The end-user interface passes this data to the Interface Configuration Environment (ICE), as illustrates the arrow with the label "context information" in Figure 1.
2. The ICE, by interpreting norms using an inference machine, concludes that "John" is obliged to specify the actions to be taken at the fourth step in the problem resolution. This is represented in the box with the label "Jess Inference Machine" in Figure 1.
3. The ICE translates this "obligation" in terms of the interface to be showed to the user, by rules that connect the norms to the interface elements. This is also represented in the box with the label "Jess Inference Machine" in Figure 1.

4. The end-user interface is presented to John in accordance to the parameters specified by the ICE, as illustrates the arrow with the label "interface settings" in Figure 1.

The norms and roles evaluated during the steps 2 and 3 of the scenario above are managed by an interface engineer using two application tools: the "norm manager" and the "action manager". This is represented in the boxes with the labels "Norm Specification" and "Action Specification" respectively in Figure 1.

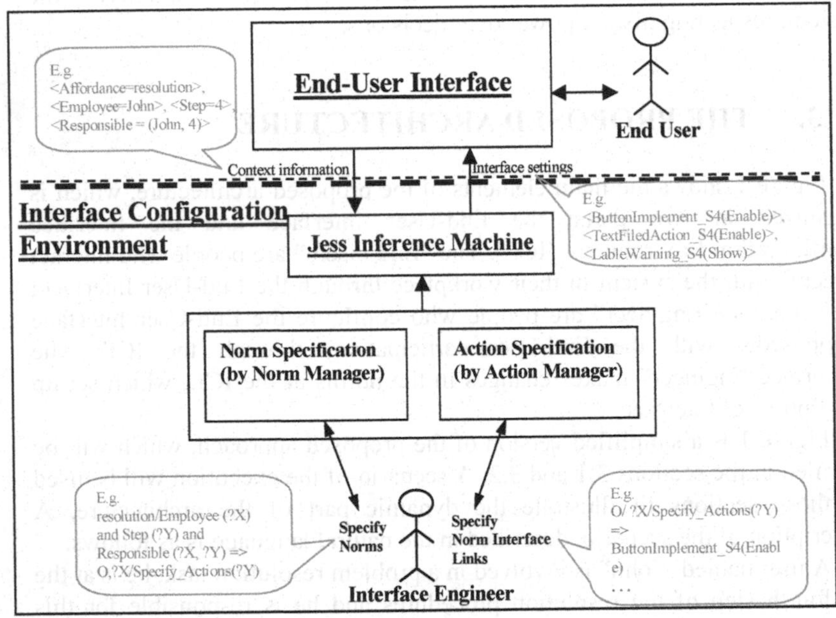

Figure 1. Architecture Overview

3.1 End-User Interface

As Figure 2 shows, the "End-User Interface" is divided into two parts: a static one, which is informed by the Semantic Analysis and a dynamic one, which constructs or configures the interface at run-time, and is informed by the norms specification. To design the End-User Interface we assume that CSCW systems are not constructed to substitute the workers but to help them in improving their work practices. In our perspective Designers and Users should be engaged in the participatory modelling to improve the work practices, constructing new (or modified) social context models (Bonacin and Baranauskas, 2003b, Bonacin *et al.*, 2003).

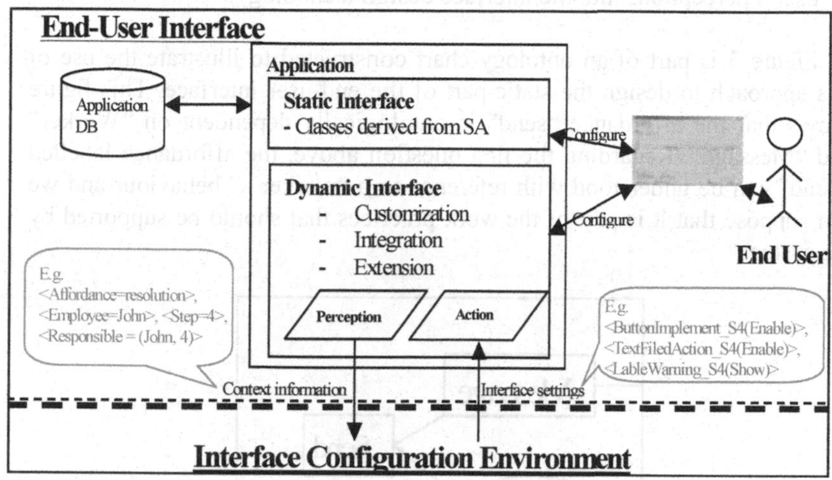

Figure 2. End-user Interface Architecture

Expressed in a semiotic basis, the designers and users should construct a *here-and-now* model of their future work practices and the system should support their human behaviours. "The past and the future, and indeed things over the horizon, do not exist here-and-now. *We have to create them using signs to represent them in the here-and-now*" (Stamper, 2000, p. 27). Therefore we do not have the future workers affordances but the information about what they intend *here-and-now* to have in the future through the opportunities brought about by the CSCW technology.

To construct the first part of the system we focus on the human agents affordances to generate the static part of the interface with the objects that are modified in the dynamic part. For each affordance of the workers in the ontology chart representing the intended work practices we basically try to answer the following questions:

1. *Should the system support this affordance?* It is not all affordances that are directly associated to parts of the work practices that we intend to support with the system. Other affordances may not refer to the workers behaviours.
2. *How to support this agent behaviour?* The interfaces are the part of the system perceived by the end-users, so instead of thinking of the interface as something that stays by itself with a set of properties, we should think about how it would be perceived by the agents in the system.

Participatory Design techniques (Muller *et al.*, 1997) can be used at this stage. After that the designer should translate his/her understanding of the user's perceptions into the interface design technology.

Figure 3 is part of an ontology chart constructed to illustrate the use of this approach to design the static part of the end-user interface. This figure shows that the affordance "send" is ontologically dependent on "Worker" and "Message". Regarding the first question above, the affordance labelled "Send" can be understood with reference to a "worker's" behaviour and we can suppose that it is part of the work practices that should be supported by the system.

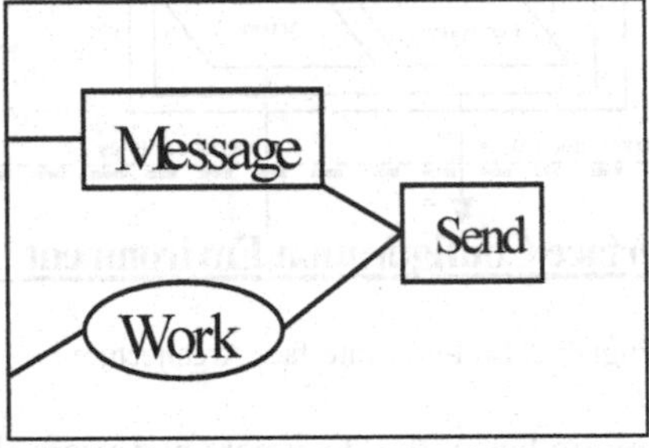

Figure 3. Ontology Chart Example

To answer the second question we should first think about "the meaning of sending a message" in the worker's social context. In this way we can avoid mistakes such as: the use of a "button" as a unique way of sending messages in a social context in which the "button" is not associated to the "Send" affordance. We will use an analogy of a door knob to clarify this point. A knob can be associated with the affordance "open" (the door), and not only with the affordance "turn". Howeverthe fact of a knob being associated with the affordance "open", does not mean that we have to put knobs on all doors; in some contexts automatic doors (without a knob) are more efficient. Usually, in big supermarkets people do not look for a knob in the entrance because the context (e.g. place, shape of the door, and the behaviour of the others) suggests that the door opens by movement detection. Similarly it is not only a button that can be associated with "send", but also the "enter" key would be another option for this. Ontological dependencies mean that certain affordances are only available when others are also available. Therefore some could be used as a condition of displaying interface elements. For example, when an affordance "A" is ontologically dependent on the affordance "B", an interface element associated with the affordance "A" should be displayed only during the existence of the software elements that represent the existence of "B". In Figure 3 the affordance "send" is dependent on the affordance "message"; therefore the interface elements that correspond to the affordance "send" should be displayed only when the software elements (classes, data, or interface) confirm the existence of "message".

The second part of the end-user interface is dynamically generated through the interpretation of norms. The changes that can occur in this part of the interface are constrained by the computational technology: we can configure parameters only if we have configuration options analysed during run-time, we can integrate parts of the interface only if we have used a mechanism that allows the integration of predefined software components at run-time, and we can extend the interface only if we have used a mechanism that allows the inclusion of new code at run-time.

In the same way, the modifications enabled by norm changes is limited by the technology used to implement the end-user interface. One example of how changes in the norms require different types of interface technology mechanisms could be:

– if we change a norm that restricts access to some type of information, we need configurable parameters of the system at run-time,
– if we change a norm to obligate or permit the worker to fill a new form, we have to include this at the worker interface through the integration of components at run-time,
– if we include norms that specify a new procedure to solve a problem, we may need the automatic generation of new code.

Therefore we cannot specify a totally new norm system; the interface engineer should know the limits of the technology. A norm change is viable only if it is associated with an action mechanism of the interface (in the proposed approach it is specified through the Action Manager, see 3.2). Therefore the norms whose changes cannot be reflected at the interface are directly programmed in the system code (if … than …).

As shown in Figure 2 the dynamic part of the interface contains two mechanisms we name as "perception" and "action". Before displaying an interface to the end-user, the application should obtain the interface settings of the "Interface Configuration Environment" ICE. First the ICE should have sufficient information about the context of use. It is necessary to know the agent who is using the system, the task that the agent is doing, and other data of the context of using the application. The perception mechanism is the part of the system that transmits data to the ICE, through messages in a specific protocol. Using this data the ICE can identify the group of the norms to be analysed.

An example of information from context, considering the first part of the scenario showed at the beginning of the section 3 (see Figure 2):

- "<affordance = resolution>" means that the interface element that will be displayed to the user refers to the "resolution" affordance (It is the more abstract affordance);
- "<Employee = John>" John is the worker who is using the system;
- "<Step=4>" the stage in the problem resolution;
- "<Responsible = (John,4)>" John is the responsible for the step 4.

After receiving data about the context, the ICE returns a list of parameters containing interface elements and their actions. The "action" mechanism receives data and translates them in terms of the modifications in the end-user interface, that could be the configuration of the interface (e.g.: an enable/disable button), the integration of new interface elements (e.g.: the addition of a predefined form) or the development of new interface code.

As an example of interface settings, consider the fourth part of the scenario showed at the beginning of the section 3 (see figure 2):

- <ButtonImplement_S4(Enable)> means that the button named "Implement" at the Step four should be enabled;
- <TextFieldAction_S4(Enable)> means that the textField named "Action" at the Step four should be enabled;
- <LabelWarning_S4(Show)> means that the Label named "Warning" at the Step four should be displayed.

In this section we present the proposed architecture for constructing an end-user interface. The static part is based on the semantic analysis, where the designers identify the affordances to be supported by the system and interface solutions. The dynamic part has two mechanisms the "perception" and the "action". The dynamic part of the interface informs the context to ICE using the perception mechanism, and receives back the interface configuration parameters. In the next section the ICE is presented.

3.2 Interface Configuration Environment

Figure 4 is the "Interface Configuration Environment". The first block (from top to bottom) contains a JESS (Java Expert System Shell) Inference Machine and Knowledge Base, and a database with the norms translated to Jess Language.

Jess is an expert system shell with a scripting language written entirely in Sun Microsystem's Java language. Jess supports the development of rule-based expert systems which can be tightly coupled to code written in Java language (Friedman-Hill, 2001). In the proposed architecture this inference machine receives information from the context and by a forward chaining mechanism decides the actions that should be taken.

The information stored in the database in the first block refers to "Norms Specification" carried out during Norm Analysis, translated to the Jess Rules and the "Action Specification", which are rules linking the norms to the interface settings. The Norm and Action specifications are constructed by the Norm Manager (Figure 5) and the Action Manager (Figure 6).

By using the Norm Manager (Figure 5), the Interface Engineer specifies and maintains the norms in a declarative way. Each norm is translated into the Jess language through a Translator module (second block of Figure 4). The Jess Inference machine immediately starts working with the new knowledge base. Therefore changes in norms are directly translated to a new interface configuration without the necessity of code modification.

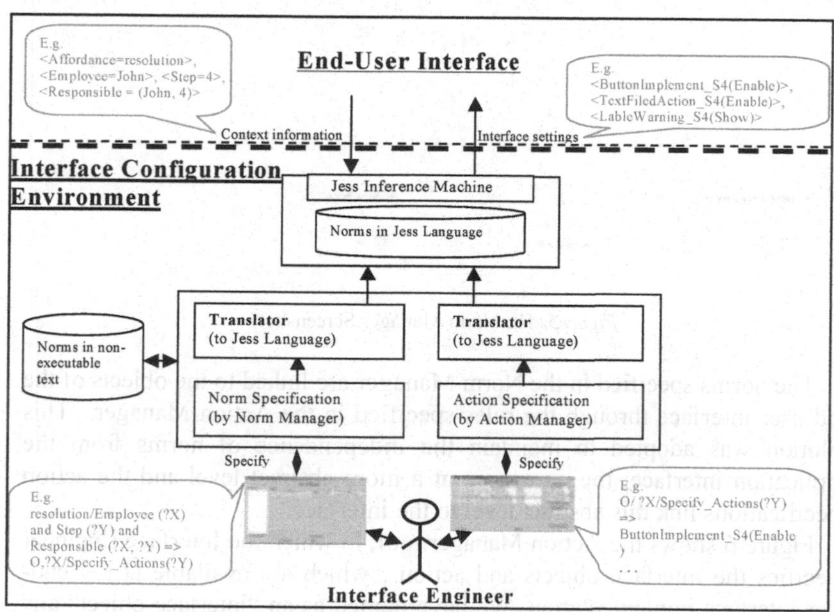

Figure 4. Interface Configuration Environment

As an example of norm in the Norm Manager, consider the second part of the scenario showed at the beginning of the section 3 (see Figure 4):

- <resolution/Employee(?X) and Step (?Y) and Responsible (?X,?Y) ==> Obligated/Specify_Actions(?Y)> means that: *at the resolution affordance, whenever the agent employee is responsible for a step then he/she is obligated to specify the actions of this step.*

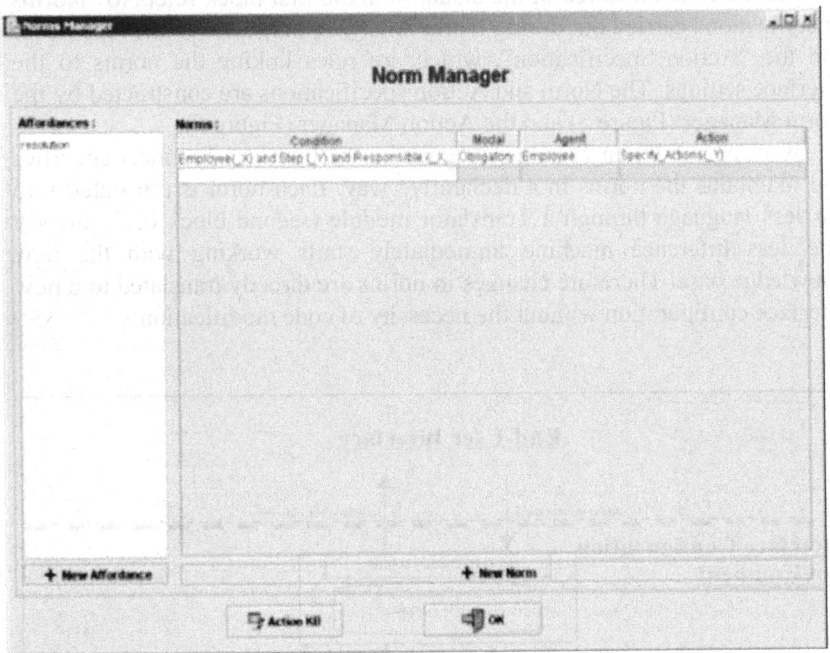

Figure5. The Norm Manager Screenshot

The norms specified in the Norm Manager are linked to the objects of the end-user interface through the rules specified in the Action Manager. This solution was adopted to maintain the independence of norms from the application interface; the norms are at a more abstract level and the action specifications link this abstract level to the interface.

Figure 6 shows the Action Manager tool, in which the Interface Engineer specifies the interface objects and actions, which are available at the end-user interface implementation. We have named as an "interface object" any interface elements and "object's actions" i.e. the possible actions available, such as: a simple button with the actions to show, enable, set the icon, etc, or a complex frame available through the addition of the software components integration with many parameters to configure it. The name object is used because at the implementation level the interface engineer should refer to these interface elements as objects, since they have been implemented using an Object Oriented technology.

After specifying the objects and actions, the Interface Engineer, using the Action Manager tool, should link the "Action Part" of the Norms (specified through the Norm Manager), that reside at a higherabstraction level relative to the objects and their actions atthe interface. The parameters relative to the conditional part of the Actions rules (left side of Figure 5) should be associated to the actions of the norms (right side of Figure 6). When the Jess inference machine concludes that the action of a norm should be triggered, the Actions rules are then fired (through forward chaining), mapping the action of a norm to the list of Interface settings to be applied to the End-User Interface.

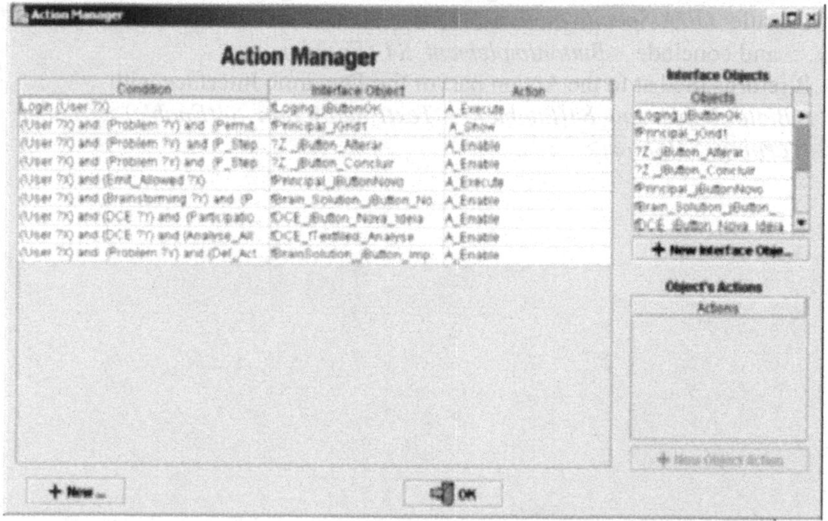

Figure 6. The Action Manager Screenshot

The Interface settings that the Jess Inference Machine returns are a list of elements including the name of the interface objects and the correspondent action to be taken. These interface objects and actions are then interpreted by the "Action Part" of the dynamic interface.

As an example of norm in the Action Manager tool, consider the third part of the scenario showed at the beginning of section 3 (see Figure 4):

- <O/?X/Specify_Actions(?Y) => ButtonImplement_S ?Y (Enable) ...> means that the action "Specify Action (?Y)" is translated to the interface setting "ButtonImplement_S ?Y (Enable) ..." that would be returned to the action part of the dynamic interface.

This example completes the scenario of the execution illustrated at the beginning of the section 3, translated from technical terms (see figure 7 to visualize the example in a detailed view of the architecture):

1. The "Perception part" of the Dynamic End-User Interface informs the Jess Inference machine: *<Affordance=resolution>, <Employee=John>, <Step=4>, <Responsible = (John, 4)>*
2. The inference machine through forward chaining (and unification), fire the rule: *resolution/Employee (?X) and Step (?Y) and Responsible (?X, ?Y) => O,?X/Specify_Actions(?Y)* and concludes *<O/John/Specify_Actions (4)>*
3. The inference machine, through forward chaining (and unification), fire the rule: *O/?X/Specify_Actions(?Y) => ButtonImplement_S ?Y (Enable). . .* and conclude *<ButtonImplement_S4 (Enable). . .>*
4. It returns the list to the Action part of the Dynamic Interface with *<ButtonImplement_S4(Enable)>,<TextFiledAction_S4(Enable)>,<Label Warning_S4(Show)>*

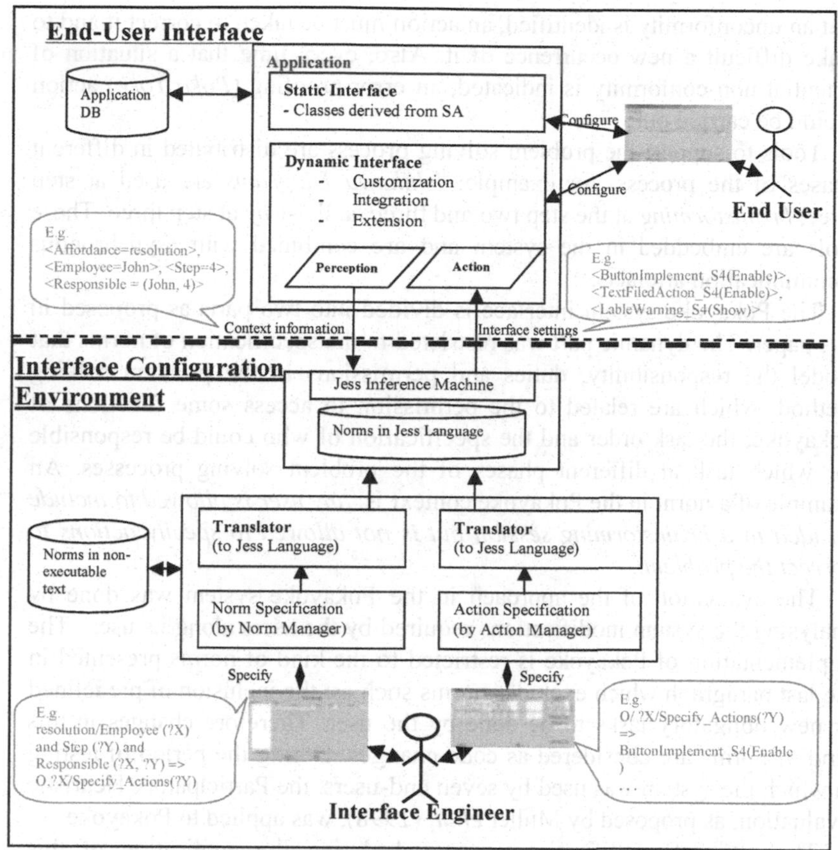

Figure 7. Norm Driven Environment for Interface Configuration

4. DISCUSSION

The proposed architecture has been applied in a case study as illustrated by Pokayoke: a computational system for supporting problem solving and decision making in a manufacturing organisation that adopts the lean production paradigm (Bonacin and Baranauskas, 2003a). Pokayoke is based on a procedure conducted in the factory to analyse and implement corrective, preventative, security, and health maintenance actions, known as the "five steps". The objective of the *five steps* procedure is to define a systematic method for dealing with problems in the routine of production. Every time that an unconformity is identified, an action must be taken to correct it and to make difficult a new occurrence of it. Also, every time that a situation of potential non-conformity is indicated, an error proofing (*Poka Yoke*) action should be carried out.

Tools to support the problem solving process are distributed in different phases of the process, for example: *Ishikawa Diagrams* are used at step three, *brainstorming* at the step two and three, and *5-why* at step three. These tools are embedded in the system and are combined with asynchronous communication artefacts.

The Pokayoke system interface is divided into two parts as proposed in this paper. The dynamic part was restricted to the specification of norms that model the responsibility, duties and permissions in the problem solving method, which are related to the permission to access some functions of Pokayoke, the task order and the specification of who could be responsible for which task at different phases of the problem solving processes. An example of a norm in the Pokayoke context is: *any user is allowed to include an idea in a brainstorming session but is not allowed to specify actions to correct the problem.*

The evaluation of the approach in the Pokayoke system was done by analysing the system modifications required by the users along its use. The implementation of Pokayoke is restricted to the kind of norms presented in the last paragraph which excludes norms such as: the inclusion of predefined or new obligatory tasks to be done by the user. Therefore changes in this kind of norms are considered as code changes. During the period of testing in which the system was used by seven end-users, the Participatory Heuristic Evaluation, as proposed by Muller *et al.* (1998), was applied to Pokayoke.

The total of modifications proposed during the application of this Participatory Design technique, in a group of 7 users and 5 interface experts, was 25. The end-users proposed 14 modifications, whereby 9 referred to modifications of the norms specified in the dynamic part of the interface, 3 referred to small bugs easy to correct but requiring modification in code and 2 referred to modifications in the structure of a screen layout relative to the static part, with more than one day of implementation work.

The interface experts proposed 11 modifications, 4 referring to the norms specified in the dynamic part of the system, 5 referring to small bugs easy to correct but requiring modification of code, 2 referring to modification in the structure of a screen layout in the static part requiring more than one day of implementation work.

Three modifications were proposed during 3 months of use of Pokayoke on a large scale in the organisation, by 48 users, in substitution for the paper-based form for the *Five Steps* procedure. Two modifications referred to the dynamic part of the system and one referred to small bugs; easily corrected.

Analysing the total of 28 modifications proposed to the Pokayoke system we have 54% referring to the dynamic part, 32% to small code modifications at the static part and 14% to modifications that required more than one day of implementation work. The Pokayoke case study indicates the great potential of the proposed approach by the fact that this approach has avoided 54% of the modification to the application code. We have also to consider that this number could even be more favourable if we had included other kinds of norm changes that are not supported by Pokayoke.

5. CONCLUSION

Literature in several fields has shown that the organisational context should be understood in order to construct software systems suitable for the work practice. Understanding the organisation involves considering its formal and informal systems from which the technical system should emerge. Considered as a live organism, this means that the technical system should be allowed to adapt to changes in the organisation. In the context of this work we deal with the complexity of allowing changes in the system as the organisational norms change by proposing a norm driven environment for the system interface configuration. The proposed approach was used during the design and preliminary use of Pokayoke: a CSCW system designed for the context of problem solving in a manufacturing organisation.

The proposed approach does not intend to deplete the problem, quite the contrary, it represents an initial contribution to discussion on the subject. Further work should be done in other case studies specially addressing tailoring and customisation.

ACKNOWLEDGMENTS

This work was partially supported by grants from Brazilian Research Council (CAPES BEX2214/02-4, CNPq 301656/84-3 and FAPESP 2000/05460-0). The authors also thank Delphi Automotive Systems in Jaguariúna, Brazil, and Nied – Unicamp for collaboration and partnership in the Pokayoke project.

REFERENCES

Bannon, L. J. 1992, Discovering CSCW, in Proceedings 15th Information Systems Research in Scandinavia, 507-520.

Boehm B.W. 1975, The High Cost of Software, in Practical Strategies For Developing Large Software Systems, Horowitz E., ed. , Addison Wesley.

Bonacin, R. and Baranauskas, M. C. C., 2003, Designing Towards Supporting and Improving co-operative Organisational Work Practices. Proceedings of 5th International Conference on Enterprise Information Systems, 2003a, v.3, 233-238.

Bonacin, R. and Baranauskas, M. C. C., 2003, Semiotic Conference: Work Signs and Participatory Design, Proceedings of 10th International Conference on Human - Computer Interaction, 2003b, to appear.

Bonacin, R., Baranauskas, M. C. C. and Cecilia, R. M. 2003, Designing and Learning: Joining The Concepts In Work Practices. In Paola Forcheri and Alfonso Quarati (eds.), Journal of International Forum of Educational Technology & Society and IEEE Learning Technology Task Force, 2003, v. 6, n. 1, 3-8. (Online Version: http://ifets.ieee.org/periodical/)

Dourish, P., 1996, Open implementation and Flexibility in CSCW toolkits. Ph.D. Thesis, University College London, (Online Version: ftp://cs.ucl.ac.uk/darpa/jpd/dourish-thesis.ps.gz)

Friedman-Hill, E. J., Jess, 2001, The Expert System Shell for the Java Platform, SAND98-8206, Sandia National Laboratories, Livermore, CA, (Online Version: http://herzberg.ca.sandia.gov/jess)

Gibson,J. J. 1968, The Ecological Approach to Visual Perception. Houghton Miffin Company, Boston, Massachusetts.

Grudin, J. 1994, Groupware and Social Dynamics: Eight Challenges for Developers. Communications of the ACM, 37, 1, 92-105.

Kahler, H, Morch, A., Stiemerling, O., Wulf, V. 2000, Special Issue on Tailorable Systems and Cooperative Work, Computer Supported Cooperative Work, Kluwer, v. 9, Issue 1.

Liu, Kecheng. 2000, Semiotics in Information Systems Engineering, Cambridge University Press.

Manderson R. and Layzell P., 1999, Software Change Control for Maintenance: Some Experiences Of Moving From Black Art To Black Box, Proceedings of the Fifth Workshop on Empirical Studies of Software Maintenance.

Muller, M. J., Haslwanter, J. H., & Dayton, T. 1997, Participatory Practices in the Software Lifecycle. In Handbook of Human-Computer Interaction, M. Helander, T. K. Landauer and P. Prabhu, eds., Elsevier Science, 2 ed, pp. 255-297.

Muller, J. M., Matheson, L., Page, C. & Gallup, R., 1998, Participatory Heuristic Evaluation. Interactions: September + October 1998. V. 5, Issue 5, ACM Press, 13-18.

Morch A. and Mehandjiev N., 2000, Tailoring as Collaboration: the Mediating Role of Multiple Representations and Application Units. Kahler, H, Morch, A., Stiemerling, O., Wulf, V. (Eds), Special Issue on Tailorable Systems and Cooperative Work, Computer Supported Cooperative Work, Kluwer, vol. 9, no. 1.

Robinson M. 1993, Design for Unanticipated use, In Proceedings of The Third European Conference on Computer-Supported Cooperative Work, edited by G. DeMichelis, C. Simone and K. Schmidt, Kluwer Academic Publishers, pp. 187-202.

Sommerville, Ian, 2000, Software Engineering, Addison-Wesley Pub Co, 6th edition.

Stamper, R. K., Althaus, K., Backhouse, J. 1988, MEASUR: Method for Eliciting, Analysing and Specifying User Requirements. In Computerized Assistance During the Information Systems Life Cycle. Olle, T. W., Verrijn-Stuart, A. A. and Bhabuts, L., eds., Elsevier Science, Amsterdam, pp.67-116.

Stamper, R. K. 2000, Information Systems as a Social Science: An Alternative to the FRISCO Formalism. In Information System Concepts: an Integrated Discipline Emerging, E. D.

Falkenberg, K. Lyytien and A. A. Verrijn-Stuart, eds, Kluwer Academic Publishers, USA, pp.1-51.

Teege, G., Kahler, H. and Stiemerling, O. 1999, Implementing Tailorability in Groupware, In SIGGROUP Bulletin, 20, 2, 57-59.

III

COMMUNICATION AND ACTION

Chapter 16

DESIGNING SPACE SYSTEMS IN MULTI-VIEWPOINTS SEMIOTICS

Daniel Galarreta
Centre National d'Etudes Spatiales, France

Abstract: In this paper we examine how complex objects such as space systems can be apprehended by a semiotic approach. Instead of considering this system from a functional point of view or from an economical one etc., we chose to consider the system just as a signifying object whose meaning is to be a space system whatever the point of view we select. We are therefore led to propose multi-viewpoints semiotics to analyse and specify the conditions which allows virtual views of the systems to correspond to one and the same object. We introduce the concept of identity in order to formulate such conditions. Epistemological justifications are proposed.

Key words: Viewpoints, semiotics, design, negotiation, space system

1. INTRODUCTION

In designing business or IT systems a difficult task for the designers who co-operate is to find a common framework where they can efficiently share their knowledge on the same problem. Instead of considering the system they design from a single point of view (e.g. from a functional point of view or from an economical one) we could prefer to consider the system just as a *signifying object* compatible with all the viewpoints involved in the designing activity (see Galarreta et al., 1998). That means that we should use a semiotic framework in order to describe our system. But this framework should accept different ways to apprehend the IT system. Instead of considering that these different ways can be arranged in *IT system ways*, *Formal IS ways* and *Informal IS ways*, we prefer to postulate that each way integrates IT system features, Formal IS features and Informal IS features.

K. Liu (ed.),
Virtual, Distributed and Flexible Organisations: Studies in Organisational Semiotics, 259–275.

This overall ability to describe (even partly) an Information System is typical of what we define as a viewpoint. In contrast with the standard approach of Organisational Semiotics, we do not use a triadic model of the sign. We prefer to start from semiotic of the discourse which favours the *discourse* rather than the *sign* properly speaking.

In the case of the designing of space systems which can be considered as an IT system, there are additional difficulties to take into account since (a) such systems are ultimately inaccessible for validation because of theirlocation and size, (b) these systems involve large communities which are composed of people with different competencies, located in different places.

From the semiotic point of view we adopt here, the question of the semiotic existence of such a system will be examined. To what extent does a space system exist as far as semiotics is concerned? How virtual existences postulated by the different designers (we can also include the users) can match together in order to correspond to one and a same system?

These questions will naturally lead us to examine epistemological issues in relation to them.

2. MULTI-VIEWPOINT SEMIOTICS

Let us recall the basic assumptions of a Multi-viewpoint semiotics[20]

Experiences of projects of realisations of complex systems such as space systems clearly demonstrate the co-existence of specialised languages which are partly impermeable in relation to each other. These languages correspond to the different crafts that are needed during the space project.

These crafts confront each other over the definition –requirement, design, or realisation – of technical objects that are not *apriori* given, but, on the contrary, progressively built up through the negotiation of the meaning they should have to satisfy their requirements. In other words these objects are – at least before their creation, but also after it – semiotic objects belonging to different signifying sets (e.g. thermal, electrical, mechanical representations) likely to be grasped, informed and articulated by a semiotic theory.

The negotiation of meaning, which takes place during the definition of an object of this type, is the work of individuals involved in the project, and is not a pre-existing product of these languages as virtually contained in them. At the same time, the individuals internalise the natural language that they have not built and whose rules they have to observe. In order to account for

[20] In the following paragraphs we quote ourselves from Galarreta (2002) and we hope, with slight improvements.

this situation, we are forced to use the opposition between *natural language* and *speech* (Saussure) or between *natural language* and *the act of discourse* (Benveniste).

The act of discourse, or enunciation, can be defined as a linguistic instance, which is logically presupposed by the very existence of the utterance (which gets traces or marks from it). But who is responsible for this enunciation? In order to avoid the untimely introduction of the concept of subject the term *instance of discourse* has been proposed to designate the set of operations, operators and parameters which control the discourse (see Fontanille,1998, p.92). It designates the discourse as an act and not as a result.

2.1 Definition of a viewpoint and of a multi-viewpoint semiotics

Because we empirically observe it, we make the basic assumption (BA): that given a semantic universe several instances of discourse are necessary in order to account for all possible enunciations[21] that can be realised within this universe.

2.1.1 Definition of a viewpoint

Under the basic assumption (BA), an instance of discourse is called a viewpoint[22].

This definition makes sense provided we define, accordingly, semiotics framework; thisopens a new field of questions concerning these viewpoints.

2.1.2 Definition of a multi-viewpoint semiotics

Given a viewpoint we could ask ourselves how the presence of one or several viewpoints has an influence on its semiotic activity. Although it is a relevant question, it rather belongs to cognitive or even to a "micro-sociological" issue than to a semiotic one.

We prefer to define a multi-viewpoints semiotics as: (Given a semantic universe in the form of utterances and enunciations), a conceptual building, which aims at clarifying the condition of grasping and of production of the

[21] It is not possible to propose a unique model, even a complicated one, to account for all of them.

[22] We proposed elsewhere a very close definition of viewpoint: A viewpoint is the collective or individual instance which is given the semiotic competence which is presupposed by the enunciations it realised. (see Galarreta, 2001)

meaning of "being in the presence of other viewpoints" expressed through the utterances and the enunciations.

Remark: A.J. Greimas and J. Fontanille introduced in the beginning of the nineties in their book the semiotics of the passions the concept of enunciative praxis (see Greimas and Fontanille, 1991; Fontanille, 1998, p.271). "The enunciative praxis is not the semiotic praxis in general. To signify is an act, to discourse is a set of acts [...] whose enunciation takes charge of only what is concerned by the question of the presence [...]. The enunciative praxis is [...] concerned with the appearing and disappearing of utterances and of semiotic forms in the domain of discourse, or else it is concerned withthe event that constitutes the meeting between the utterance and the instance which takes charge of it". (in Fontanille, 1998, p. 271).

"The enunciative praxis manages among other things the existence modes of entities and utterances which compose the discourse: it grasps them at a virtual level (as entities belonging to a system); it actualises them (as beings of language and of discourse); it realises them (as expressions); it potentiates them (as products of the usage)" (in Fontanille, 1998, p.273).

This can be schematically represented (figure 1.) like this (after Fontanille, 1998, p.276).

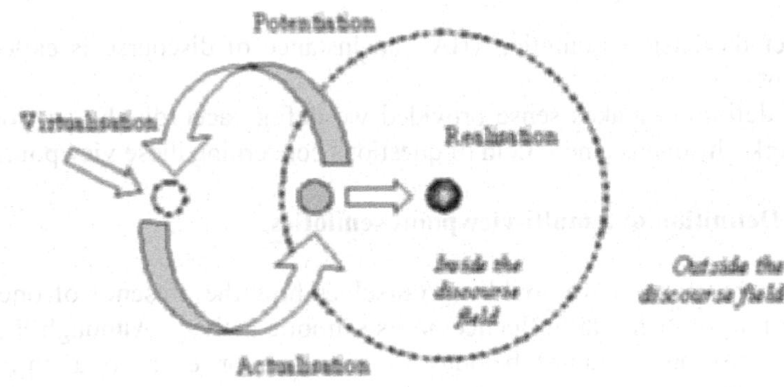

Figure 1. Operations performed by the enunciative praxis with respect to the presence of semiotic forms (after Fontanille, 1998, p.276)

We believe that the enunciative praxis can be better explained if we consider that it results from the interaction of viewpoints. The different levels of presence can be describes in terms of confrontation of viewpoints;

in other words viewpoints are responsible for the enunciative praxis. It also means that all the manifestations of the enunciative praxis cannot be described by just one model.

We describe now the different situations of confrontation of viewpoints. We first recall the definition of a view.

A *view* is an "utterance" which is selected from the representation or signifying set we consider with respect to a given (or reference) viewpoint. An utterance is what is enunciated, but this entity can only be described according to a given instance of the discourse. Therefore in a multi-viewpoints semiotics, an utterance does not have an absolute existence, but should be defined with respect to a reference viewpoint.

A view is usually "transitive", that is, it is usually a view of "something" (see figure 2.). In order to agree with the usual semantic of the term view, we could make the hypothesis that it is sensible to use the phrase "a view of an object from a given viewpoint", but it must be stressed that at this point of our theory, the relevance of such a phrase is only hypothetical. The development of our theory precisely aims at constructing the justification of such a phrase.

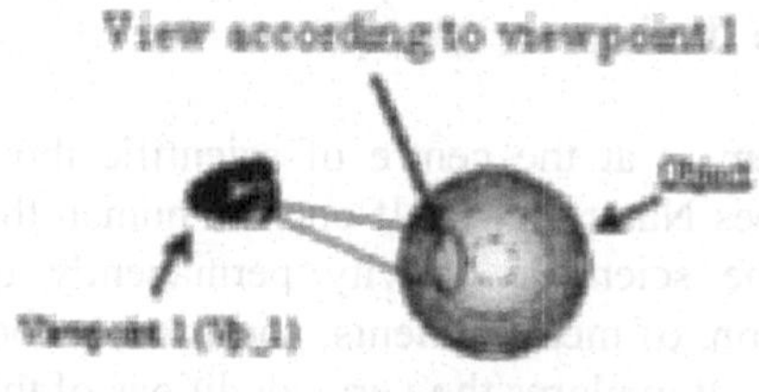

Figure 2. A view produced from a viewpoint

2.1.3 The different levels of presence among viewpoints

Three levels of presence among viewpoints deserve to be distinguished:

– We can consider an enunciation activity of a viewpoint that puts into parenthesis the activities of other viewpoints. Provided the above hypothesis of transitivity of a view is accepted, a view from this viewpoint is a view of a *virtual object*

- If views produced according to these viewpoints are logically or semantically incompatible[23], we say that there exists a *confrontation* of the viewpoints. A view produced in this case is a view of an *actualised object*
- Eventually, after a negotiation process, compatible views[24] can be produced. In such a case we say that the viewpoints are *correlated.* A view produced in such circumstances is a view of a *realised object.*

In order to progress with respect to the constructing of our theory regarding the object issue, we will make an epistemological detour.

3. EPISTEMOLOGICAL ISSUE OF THE OBJECT

"If the myth of physical objects is superior to most of the others from an epistemological point of view, it is because it turned out to be a more efficient instrument than the other myths to insert a tractable structure in the flow of experience" (W.V.O. Quine quoted in Vogel, 1988, p.49)

3.1 From physics to design

"The adequacy problem is at the centre of scientific thought. How is science possible? Why does Nature let itself open to human thought?" (See Ullmo, 1969, p.251). The scientific activity permanently questions the rationality of our perception, of measurements, and models about the world that it grasps and produces. It explores the very conditions of this rationality. The "tremendous effort of the contemporary theory, (which is undertaken by many research workers in many directions) is motivated by rational requirements [...] we can say that the physics of today is rational thought in action" (see Ullmo, 1969, p.293). This underlying epistemological questioning can be put in parenthesis when the objects under study belong to our everyday environment. However when the objects are those which microphysics try to apprehend or are elements of cosmological descriptions epistemological issues emerge.

Epistemological difficulties are also present when one tries to describe the "laws" of design activities since these activities not only involve physical

[23] It means that the signifying elements, which are produced by the activities of enunciation of the different viewpoints, are incompatible when they are considered from a unique viewpoint. The incompatibility may be logical and/or semantic. That does not mean that the "intentions" of the different viewpoints are really incompatible; we just do not know.

[24] In this case compatibility is evaluated in regard to each viewpoint involved.

(and therefore objective) entities but also human subjects their social environment and the representations produced during these activities. "Even promoted to the dignity of observables, the human and social facts remain the produce of interpretative constructs" (see Rastier and Bouquet, 2002, p.4). Therefore it is difficult to use any epistemology which differentiates between the object and the subject.

In the case of the designing of space systems there is an addition of those epistemological difficulties since (a) the objects it produces are ultimately inaccessible to validation because of their location and size[25], (b) space systems involve large communities which are composed of people with different competencies, located on different places[26] and which make an extensive usage of representations. However the necessity to assess the adequacy of the designed system to the expected space system is crucial for the success of the space missions. It is therefore justified to propose an epistemological framework within which conditions of existence of space systems can be asserted. Since in practice this assessment is usually performed through validation procedures taking place within a quality process, the possibility of designing such an epistemological framework remains plausible. In addition if such a framework and assessment conditions existed, they should be integrated into the existing quality processes.

Because of our starting assumption the framework that we have in mind is of course a (multi-viewpoint) semiotics one.

3.2 The practical epistemological answer from the designing activity

Let us examine how in practice the designing activity solves (although incompletely) those epistemological questions. In order to understand it let us mind us the principles of designing large system such as space systems. It is usual to consider a tree-like decomposition of the system

[25] A geostationary satellite is 36000 km away from the Earth. An anomaly detected on a sensor may remain unexplained despite the available data. The size of an entire space system including the satellite and the «ground segment» makes the validation of all its requirements very difficult before launch.

[26] In addition these people may have a different nativelanguage and culture. Using English as a common language does not totally suppress cultural differences.

3.2.1 Designing principles

It is not possible to go into the details of the space system design process although here we can sketch its main principles as deemed relevant for our purposes.

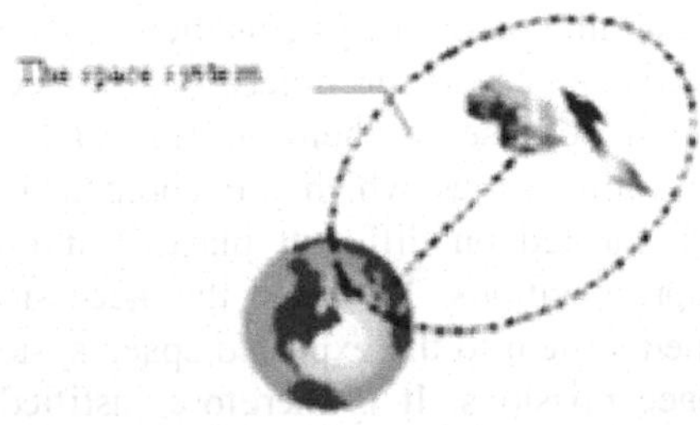

Figure 3. The space system: It includes the ground and onboard components

A first principle is to decompose the space system (see figure 3.) into functional chains which encompass both ground and onboard means in order to satisfy a type of needs which can be apprehended under the banner of a craft; usually this craft is defined by a strong core of scientific knowledge (Mechanics, Science of heat, Electricity, Dynamics, Radiocommunication and Signal processing theory, Optics and so on). It is usual to use six functional chains in order to describe a space system (after Potteck, 1999):

- The mechanical and equipping chain: this is responsible for the mechanical architecture of the satellite and the mechanical environment. It must guarantee compatibility with the launcher: mechanical interfaces, volumes, mechanical environment
- The thermal chain: this maintains thermal conditions acceptable for the equipment by taking into account the various thermal conditions which are created by the different modes of functioning of the satellite and by the outside environment
- The chain of generation and distribution of the onboard electrical power: this guarantees the generation, the storage and the distribution of electrical power to all the equipments of the satellite. It is also responsible for insuring the electrical compatibility between the equipment and the environment.
- The chain of control of the altitude and of the orbit: it guarantees the control of the altitude of the satellite and the performing of the orbital manoeuvring by activating the various thrusters.

- The command and control chain: it manages the data flow onboard from the acquisition of commands to the emission of telemetry. It also guarantees the management of the modes, onboard processing, storing of the data, detecting of the failures, the diagnosing and the repairing.
- The paying service chain: it is dedicated to the delivering of the service, which motivated the designing of the satellite, and of the whole space system. It is usually centred on a principal discipline. For instance, in the case of the SPOT satellite, the payload is centred on Optics and Image processing[27].

Although these different functional chains are not completely independent[28], they are usually used to describe the whole space system and to decompose it in material components, which can be designed and developed by different teams.

It must be stressed again that this functional decomposition follows an existing splitting of scientific knowledge into different domains (Mechanics, Science of heat, Electricity, Dynamics ...). Each domain is characterised by theoretical models which are implemented through material components.

This leads to a second and complementary principle in the designing of space system.

The existence of the system as a space system is reached by merging a functional decomposition of the space system with a parallel decomposition of it into material components. That approach of designing the system avoids the risk of a too radical virtualisation of the system which could make the assessment of the adequacy of the designed system to the expected space system too difficult. Let us describe some aspects of that approach.

The space system is decomposed into the ground segment and the satellite. Let us consider the satellite. It is decomposed into sub-systems which are the set of material components which fulfil the onboard requirements of a functional chain. Equipment assures the implementation of a set of functions in the form of material components located on a particular place onto the satellite. The decomposition of the satellite in the form of subsystems results in a tree-like structure usually called the product breakdown structure. It can be consider as the merging of two tree-like structures: a components tree and a functions tree. This products tree is the reference representation of the system. (see figure 4.)

[27] It can be argued that Image processing is a branch of Signal Processing theory where geometry plays an important role. The position of a particular discipline within a general classification of sciences does not matter here. The key fact is the existence in any of these functional chains of one or several scientific languages.

[28] For instance onboard elements used to implement the mechanical chain may be designed and used in order to satisfy thermal requirements: e.g. their size and shape can be dimensioned in order to dissipate heat.

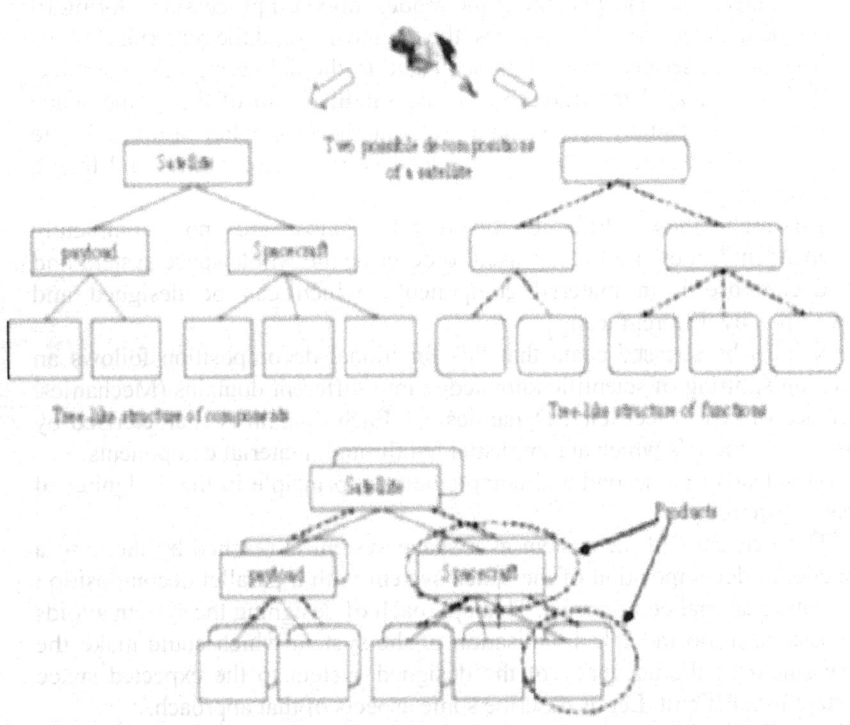

Figure 4. Product breakdown structure. A product has two aspects: a material aspect and a functional one. It results from the merging of the component tree and of the functional tree (after Potteck, 1999).

A product of the product breakdown structure evolves successively as the different states of knowledge which follow the evolution in the designing of a system. These different states are represented by data and documents; they can be considered as different snapshots of these products at different stages of their design[29] (after Chevallier, 1993). The product tree evolves accordingly.

[29] The first state is the origin state which is expressed in the functional specifications documents which describes what the product should perform. The state of the product evolves until it is accepted by the customer (realised state of the product) then operated by him (see Chevallier, 1993).

Whatever its state is, a product differs from a function or a set of functions by the fact that a product is a complex entity which embodies several knowledge dimensions (as a potential solution does) whereas a function is a virtual entity which is neither necessarily feasible nor implemented as such. The indispensable product decomposition is done thanks to the expected system as it is imagined by the designer or the system engineer. The experience shows that this decomposition is consciously or unconsciously directed by a preconceived image of the system taking the existing, the conceivable and the possible options into account. This decomposition is also constrained by the industrial organisation and often by the necessity to reuse physical existing or off the shelf components. The use of the functional tree in order to design the system is obviously limited although it allows a more creative approach (after Chevallier, 1993).

The functions are literally grafted onto products.

3.2.2 The limit of this practical epistemological solution

The products, whatever their states of development, play the role of test elements with regard to the feasibility of the functional requirements considered separately or as a whole. But this role reaches its limits when the (relative) functional independence of products decomposition is no longer satisfying. Let us examine how this independence is managed.

In order to potentially exist, a product belonging to the product breakdown structure should support several descriptions related to the corresponding domains of knowledge that can be identified during the life of the project. However it is usual that only dimension of knowledge is put forward although other dimensions still exist.

For instance a solar panel (see figure 5.) which is composed of solar cells laid on a panel, constitutes a solar array. It is a key element of the chain of generation and distribution of the onboard electrical power. However it has a mass, moments of inertia, a thermal capacity; these other dimensions cannot be ignored but even if they are negotiated during the designing activity, they should not alter the main function of this product. If such alteration occurred, the product would lose its identity: it would no longer be a real solar panel.

Therefore when the whole system is decomposed into products of different ranks in the product breakdown structure, it is necessary to suppose this decomposition allows a relative functional independence of the products. This independence cannot be absolute because of the interaction between functions via the products.

When the complexity of the system increases because of the increase of the number of components or because of the increase in the number of functions which are integrated within one component, it is increasingly difficult to maintain the relative functional independence of the products and the product breakdown structure could locally reach its limits in the engineering of the system.

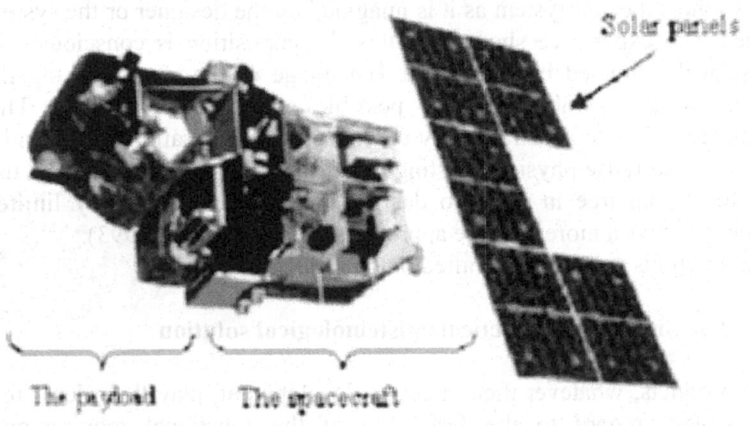

Figure 5. Cutaway view of SPOT4 satellite. The solar panels at the right of the picture are fixed onto the spacecraft, the payload is held onto the spacecraft on the left. It corresponds to the optical functions of the satellite.

Let us summarise what we have observed from the traditional designing activity of space systems. A space system obeys a functional decomposition which follows an existing splitting of scientific knowledge into different domains. Thanks to a decomposition of the whole system into a hierarchical structure based on potential components of the aimed solution, namely products, the issue of the consistency and of the compatibility of the functional requirements can be satisfied to a relatively good extent. However there exist cases where the complexity of the system limits the application of such an approach.

4. SEMIOTIC EXISTENCE OF AN OBJECT

We can now examine the conditions which would permitthe consideration of views as the views of an "object".

Let us consider the collection of viewpoints, which either run "counter to" i.e. confront each other, or, are actually correlated (at a given moment).

As we have already noted in the case of designing of space systems, this collection of viewpoints is structured by the existence of entities that the designers could assimilate from products, but that we prefer to define as *themes* and *common places*:

- A *theme* is a potential site of the correlation of viewpoints, which is established or verified through use; it is therefore an empirical concept. In other words it is a set of viewpoints which usually correlate together. Let us give examples of classical themes frequently encountered in the designing of space systems. They usually correspond to functional combinations. They are lexicalised in various ways; one of the most frequently used terms is "system" or "sub-system" in phrases such as "space system", "ground system", "onboard system", "thermal sub-system", " electrical power sub-system", "control of the attitude sub-system" and so on.
- A *common place* is a realisation of such potential correlations. It can involve several themes. For instance in a discussion involving three designers discussing the design of a space mission of a nano-satellite (i.e. whose mass is less than 50 kg) references were made respectively to the themes of *propulsion*, *information storage* and *propulsion*. They used the "object" *image* as a reference pivot in their discussion. (see figure 6.)

A *value system* is the collection of viewpoints structured by the existence of themes and common places.

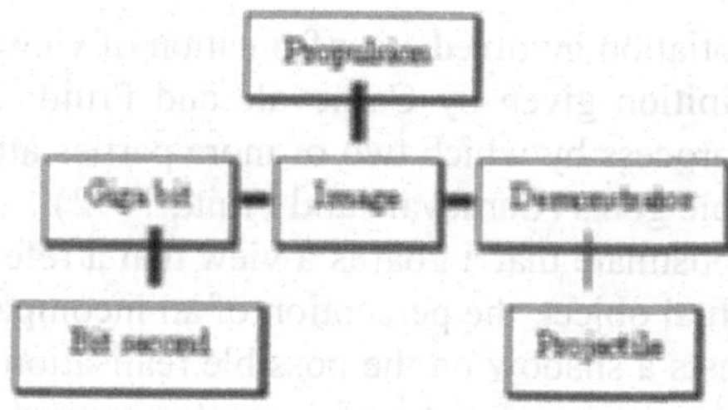

Figure 6. Illustration of a common place by means of a cluster of terms co-occurring among a discussion between designers which refer to the themes of propulsion, information storage and of propulsion.

If we consider the situation where all the viewpoints of a value system are (at a given moment) correlated then a view produced from these viewpoints could be considered as a view of an object; however such a statement needs to be justified.

It follows from our above definitions that viewpoints are not correlated just because the different views they produce are compatible but because a of a negotiation process taking place[30].

But what do we mean by negotiation? Although this concept seems a rather everyday occurrence (negotiation processes take place everywhere in our everyday life[31]), its description is much more difficult to give. In other words it means that negotiation is a convenient concept to encapsulate a correlation of viewpoints in as far as no further details are needed. Otherwise this concept must be carefully examined and closely related to the viewpoints issue… In what follows we just use the heuristic power of the concept.

Let us start by recalling definitions of negotiation

"Negotiation is the process involving dealings among persons, which are intended to result in an agreement and to commitment to a course of action". (Clarke, 1993)

"Negotiation is the process by which a group of agents communicate with one another to try and come to a mutually acceptable agreement on some matter" (Lomuscio et al., 2001).

Artificial Intelligence has striven to determine the structure of the agents and their individual and collective behaviour in order to perform the negotiation process[32].

Since this process of making a decision occurs when there are no rules about how decisions are made, the AI approaches to negotiation face difficulties.

The fact that negotiation involved a confrontation of viewpoints is clearly apparent in this definition given by Carnevale and Pruitt: Negotiation has been defined as the process by which two or more parties attempt to resolve perceived incompatible goals (Carnevale and Pruitt, 1992).

If we accept the postulate that a goal is a view that a reference viewpoint produces about a virtual object, the perception of an incompatible view from another viewpoint casts a shadow on the possible realisation of the object in the real world. But because negotiation is oriented toward the search of a solution which could conciliate[33] all the viewpoints involved in the negotiation, the reference viewpoint will try to "repair" the virtual object that the initial goal described. What is aimed at through this goal needs not to be forsaken but just be adapted to the new circumstances. Repairing supposes

[30] Cf.: "Eventually, after a negotiation process, compatible views can be produced. In such a case we say that the viewpoints are correlated".

[31] See Jeudy, 1996, Tout négocier. Masques et vertiges des compromis. Editions Autrement – Collection Mutations N° 163

[32] For a survey of that question see ZV Zlatev, 2002)

[33] Cf. Getting to the Yes (Fisher, Ury and Patton, 1991)

that despite possible confrontations of viewpoints of the value system, *something* remains which is independent of possible transient incompatibilities. The *object* embodies this permanence which can be considered as its *identity*.

The identity of an object is *what* makes it the object under consideration, and not another, and moreover if time goes by or evolutions occur it will still be the same object: the object whose designing was decided at time T_0, which was designed at time T_1, built at time T_2, launched at time T_3, and so on.

a) In most simple cases this identity can be established if we can describe the context of the object (viewpoints which participate to the semiotic existence of the object) and identify the themes and common places which express the mutual presence of the viewpoints defining the object.
b) But if the context evolves because new viewpoints appear or because themes or common places disappear, it is then possible that incompatible views emerge. The maintaining of the identity of the object is then conditioned by the "repairing" of the object. It consists either in recovering previous theme or common places which were forgotten or finding new views, which are compatible with respect to the new context of the object and can replace incompatible ones.
c) Sometime the preceding case can be anticipated. It consists in allowing for new views which could be necessary in order to "repair" the identity of the object in case of evolution as a preventive measure to enrich the identity of the object before it becomes necessary.

Given a value system, *identity* of an object will then be defined as the "repairing" operation (the negotiation process) which is required in order to establish the correlation of the viewpoints of this value system. Within this perspective, views of "something" are utterances which can be transformed through these operations, that is: *in order to be a view of "something", an utterance should be negotiable within the value system under examination.* We will not further elaborate on this point here.

Let us end by the following remark: our conception of the semiotic of an object is independently consistent with the epistemological conception that modern physics has of an object.

"In order to reach objectivity, it is necessary to take into account altogether every possible point of view of a given observer and of all possible observers –therefore of the most possible diversity of subjects: the paradox of the objectivity is that object is only found through the indefinite diversification of the subjects. It is the [mathematical] group, which solves this paradox, by giving the invariant by the very means of the indefinite diversity of the [group] transformations. The group therefore appears as a necessary condition of the experiment, not because of it would be a frame imposed by the mind to the experiment, but because it constitutes a condition of existence of a knowable objective world; if there is an objective world it will appear to its observers by means of groups" (see Ullmo, 1969, p.280).

"[The] building of the world of ordinary objects (with changes which occur in our conscience) or the building of the objective world (with changes in appearances for different observers) is always and necessarily the introducing and the using of a [mathematical] group, it is properly the constructing of an abstract group and the building of invariants, and then the interpreting of it as the group of changing of references" (see Ullmo, 1969, p.280).

5. CONCLUSION

In this paper we examined how a system such as a space system can be described and understood by a semiotic theory. Instead of considering this system from a single point of view (e.g. from a functional point of view or from an economical one) we considered the system just as a signifying object whose meaning is to be a space system whatever the point of view we select. Obviously these issues are not limited to the domain of space, but can be extended to any designing activity, which involves very distinct crafts and viewpoints. One of the results of this paper is that multi-viewpoint semiotics may be defined which offers a convenient framework to deal with the question of the semiotic existence of objects. Instead of presupposing the existence of an object and then try to define it in itself we suggest to start with the concept of identity as a process. This process assures the compatibility of the different views produced by the viewpoints and takes the form of a negotiation process. During the designing of a complex system such as a space system, in order to be a view of an object, an utterance needs to be negotiable. Future works will further justify such statements.

REFERENCES

Carnevale, P. J., Pruitt, D. G. 1992, Negotiation and Mediation, Annual Review of Psychology, 43: pp. 531-582.

Chevallier, J., 1993, Les Différentes Représentations Système et la Conduite De Projet. Note technique, CT/DA/93-008, CNES.

Clarke, R., Clarke, R., 1993, Fundamentals of Negotiation, [online]. Retrieved June 2003 from: http://www.anu.edu.au/people/Roger.Clarke/SOS/FundasNeg.html

Fontanille, J., 1998, Sémiotique Du Discours. Limoges: Coll. Nouveaux actes sémiotiques. Presses Universitaires de Limoges.

Fisher, R., Ury, W., Patton, B.1991, Getting to YES: Negotiating Agreement Without Giving In. New York, NY: Penguin Books (second edition).

Galarreta D., Charrel P.-J., Orel T., Rothenburger B., Trousse B., Vogel C, 1998, Study of Dynamic Viewpoints in Satellite Design. IFAC-INCOM, 9th Symposium on Information Control in Manufacturing. Nancy-Metz, France. June 24-26.

Galarreta, D. 2001, Mesurer l'évolution Des Connaissances d'un Projet Spatial. Conférence TIA-2001, Nancy, (2001) 3 et 4 mai.

Galarreta, D. 2002, Supporting the Semiotic Quality of Data of A Scientific Community. 5th Workshop on Organisational Semiotics, Delft, The Netherlands, June 14-15.

Greimas, A. J., Fontanille, J. 1991, Sémiotique des Passions. Paris, Editions du Seuil.

Lomuscio, A.R., Wooldridge, M.& Jennings, N.R., 2001, A Classification Scheme for Negotiation in Electronic Commerce' in, Agent-Mediated Electronic Commerce: A European AgentLink Perspective, eds. F. Dighum and C. Sierra, Springer, Verlag, pp. 19-33

Potteck, S. 1999, La Conception Des Systèmes Spatiaux. Editions à Compte d'auteur. www.serge-potteck.com.

Potteck, S. 2001, Elans de Conception. Editions du Schèmectif. France.

Rastier, F. 2002, Bouquet, S. Introduction Aux Sciences De La Culture. Paris: Coll. Formes sémiotiques. Presses Universitaires de France.

Ullmo, J. 1969, La pensée Scientifique Moderne. Coll. Champs. Flammarion.

Vogel, C. 1988, Génie cognitif, Paris, Masson.

Zlatev Z.V. 2002, Examination of the Negotiation Domain. Retrieved June 2003 from: http://www.ub.utwente.nl/webdocs/ctit/1/000000a3.pdf

Chapter 17

ON THE SEMIOTIC ANALYSIS OF INTERNATIONAL COMMUNICATION OVER COMPUTER NETWORKS

John H. Connolly and Iain W. Phillips
Modelling and Reasoning Research Group, Department of Computer Science, Loughborough University, United Kingdom

Abstract: This chapter is concerned with the application of the six-level framework of Organisational Semiotics to the analysis of the problems raised by international communication. Some of these problems involve whole semiotic systems, namely human languages. Other problems, such as speed and bandwidth of data transmission, pertain to the levels of empirics and the physical world. At the other end of the semiotic ladder, which is concerned with the social and cultural aspects of communication, problems include the different notions of politeness that are accepted in different cultures and the different administrative systems that operate in different countries, while institutional differences such as those of currencies and time zones introduce further complications. The semiotic analysis of the problems of international communication via networks thus reveals (i) the fact that all semiotic levels are involved in some way and (ii) which problems affect which levels. How useful is the support offered by IT in coping with these problems? It turns out that while certain problems can be handled straightforwardly, others are far less tractable. The Internet is recognised as offering many opportunities for the conduct of international communication, but it also raises particular problems, which are here considered from a semiotic perspective.

Key words: Internationalisation, Semiotics, Communication, Internet

1. INTRODUCTION

In the present era of the Global Internet and the World-Wide Web, it is easier than ever to establish distributed organisations (whether formal or

K. Liu (ed.),
Virtual, Distributed and Flexible Organisations: Studies in Organisational Semiotics, 277–291.

informal) that transcend national boundaries and involve people from different cultural traditions. The communicative activity in which members of such organisations engage, whether with each other or with people outside, naturally invites semiotic analysis.

The purpose of the present paper is to apply the framework of Organisational Semiotics (OS) to the analysis of international communication over networked computer systems, in the context of distributed and virtual organisations. The thrust of the paper is theoretical, in that it aims to improve our analytical understanding of such communicative activity and the problems thereby entailed. However, it may also be of interest to system designers who are operating within the OS framework and who seek to incorporate the international dimensions of communication into their work.

2. SEMIOTICS AND COMPUTER-SUPPORTED COMMUNICATION

Let us begin with three points of a rather general nature. First of all, when people interact over networks, they have to involve themselves in two types of computer-supported communication (CSC):

- Human-computer communication (HCC) via the user-system interface (USI).
- Computer–mediated communication (CMC) with one or more other human beings.

The issues raised by the need to design international user-system interfaces have been addressed in works such as Nielsen (1990), del Galdo and Nielsen (1996) and Nielsen (2000). More general treatments of the internationalisation and localisation of software can be found in, for instance, Jones et al. (1992), Taylor (1992), Uren, Howard and Perinotti (1993), Martin O'Donnell (1994), Luong et al. (1995), Carey (1998), Hall and Hudson (1997) and Esselink (2000). Studies pertaining to CMC include Kerr and Hiltz (1982), Chesebro (1985), Hiltz and Turoff (1985), Bowers and Churcher (1989), Rapaport (1991), Walters (1995), Herring (1996), Shapiro (1996), Ulijn, Lincke and Karakaya (2001) and several of the chapters in Connolly and Pemberton (1996).

The second point concerns the well-known Peircean classification of signs into symbols, icons and indices. As far as international communication is concerned, all three classes of sign are of relevance. With regard to CMC, a large proportion of this type of communication is textual in nature, a fact which ensures that symbols are present in abundance. However, people can also exchange information by graphical means such as pictures, diagrams or charts, all of which are primarily iconic (though often supplemented with textual material). Moreover, the involvement of indexical signs should not be overlooked. For instance, the language(s) in which an individual can communicate will generally be an index of where they have lived, while the fact that English is so widely used as a means of international communication is an index of its dominance as a result of historical factors.

With regard to HCC, the usual graphical USI makes extensive use of symbols, such as the textually presented options in most menus, and of icons, for example buttons bearing a representation of a disk or a printer, for the purpose of instigating the process of saving a file to disk or printing out its contents. The choice of language in which the textual aspects of the USI are expressed is an index of the locale for which it was designed, while the speed at which, for example, web pages load in response to a click on a hyperlink is an index of factors such as the bandwidth of the network to which the computer is connected.

The third issue concerns the six-level OS framework proposed by Stamper (1991). The topmost level in this framework is termed the 'social world'. However, there are important aspects of CSC, and particularly of HCC, which are not strictly social in nature. For example, launching an email application, although it may facilitate CMC, is not of itself a social act. Nevertheless it is an act of communication (with the computer system), and so it would be unfortunate if this semiotic act could not be described in terms of the full six-level framework. In order to accommodate this, we propose to broaden the scope of the topmost level, so that it explicitly includes the individual as well as the group. Accordingly, the semiotic act of launching an email application from a pull-down menu would be analysable as follows:

- Level of physical world: release of the mouse button, and brief change of values of the relevant pixels.
- Empiric level: pattern of mouse-button movement in the vertical dimension, and brief inversion in the appearance of the relevant pixel pattern.
- Syntactical level: selection, from among the menu options, of the particular option for launching the email application.
- Semantic level: the meaning of the menu option, namely the potential launching of the application.
- Pragmatic level: the practical effect of the action, namely the actual launching of the application.
- Level of (broadened) social world: achievement of a sub-task in the user's interaction with the system.

A further point about the 'social world' is that it needs, of course, to be taken as encompassing cultural phenomena, as well as social phenomena in the narrow sense of the term. Strictly social phenomena pertain to the internal differentiation of society, and include the following (cf. Goodman 1992, pp. 45-46):

– Social groups, such as organisations, communities or families.
– Social categories, such as the computer-literate or the retired.

Under the heading of cultural phenomena would typically be classed the following (cf. Goodman 1992, pp. 31-35):

– Material culture, such as artefacts.
– Non-material culture:
  – Beliefs.
  – Values.
  – Norms of behaviour.
  – Sign systems, such as languages.

Interactions between people from different cultural backgrounds constitute an obvious possibility in international CMC, and must therefore be accommodated within the semiotic framework of analysis.

3. INTERNATIONAL COMMUNICATION: AN ORGANISATIONAL SEMIOTIC PERSPECTIVE

Let us now suppose that an organisation has been formed which is geographically distributed and which relies heavily on networked computer systems to provide its communications infrastructure. Let us further suppose that the organisation includes people situated in different countries, having a variety of cultural backgrounds. What we should now like to do is to consider the communication problems that may arise in this scenario, and how they might be tackled with the help of computer-based support. These problems will be dealt with in terms of the six-level OS framework.

It was suggested in Connolly (2002, p. 6) that the six levels of the OS framework can be grouped as follows:

– The core levels: syntactics and semantics.
– The infra levels: empirics and physical world.
– The supra levels: pragmatics and social world.

This grouping will form a convenient basis for organising our exposition.

3.1 The Core Levels

Probably the most obvious problem that can arise in the context of international communication is the fact that not everyone in the world speaks the same language, and it is therefore possible that people who would like to engage in international communication may be prevented from doing so because they have no language in common. It is true, of course, that English has acquired the status of being the *de facto* international language, but nevertheless there are still many people who do not know English, or whose knowledge of this modern-day *lingua franca* is too limited to allow them to use it conveniently.

Even when people have a language in common, there may still be impediments of a linguistic nature that interfere with their communication. Individual languages can be spoken with different accents and dialects, and even the written standard can vary from country to country. Differences between British and North American English, for instance, are very familiar, though these do not usually cause difficulties of understanding; however the use of slang or of abbreviations can do so. On the other hand, some languages have mutually unintelligible dialects, which will preclude spoken interaction, even if the written medium remains usable.

From the semiotic point of view, the linguistic differences just mentioned extend to the core levels. At the syntactical level they impinge upon vocabulary and upon all the hierarchical layers of sentence structure, while at the semantic level they raise the familiar problem in translation that not only is the same concept generally expressed by a different word or phrase in different languages, but also it is common to find that words do not correspond exactly in meaning from one language to another. For instance, the German word 'Wange' denotes the upper part of the cheek, and has no exact equivalent in English.

Non-verbal communication (NVC) may suggest itself as an alternative when language-based communication breaks down. However, again there are cultural differences that can thwart communication. For example, the thumbs-up gesture used in some countries, such as the UK, to indicate that all is well, would not be understood in this way everywhere in the world. In fact, according to Horton (1994, p. 245), it is a rude sign in Sicily! Such differences in gestural systems are a matter of significance in CMC in circumstances in which the participants can see each other, as for instance in videoconferencing. Moreover, graphical symbols may have meanings which are not universally obvious. For example, an icon depicting a wig and symbolising a document containing legal information might be easily understood in the UK, but less readily in countries where judges and counsel do not wear such a costume.

The connotative aspect of meaning should not be overlooked here, either. For instance, in Western culture the colour black is associated with mourning. However, in Chinese culture, the colour associated with mourning is white.

In addition to those communication problems which involve the relationship between form and meaning, there are some essentially syntactical issues that arise in the context of international CMC; see del Galdo (1990), Taylor (1990), Zobel-Pocock (1990). One important consideration lies in the fact that not all languages employ the same character set. Even the languages of Western Europe that use the Roman alphabet are not identical in this respect. For instance, the character 'å' is found in (for instance) Swedish, but not in English or German. Moreover, languages such as Greek, Russian or Arabic do not use the Roman alphabet at all. Furthermore, not all languages read left-to-right the way that languages like English do. For instance, Arabic reads right-to-left.

Other issues relating to the characters of the written language arise as well. Firstly, punctuation may differ from one language to another. For instance, in Spanish a question not only ends with a question mark but also begins with an inverted question mark. Secondly, there can be differences in the conventions relating to hyphenation. For example, in German, unlike English, if the sequence 'ck' is interrupted by a line break, then not only is a hyphen inserted, but the 'c' is also transformed into a 'k'. Accordingly, the word 'locken' would hyphenate as 'lok-ken'. Thirdly, there can be differences in the collating sequence, which forms the basis for sorting characters and strings (generally reflecting alphabetical order). For instance, in the conventional collating sequence of Swedish, 'x' precedes 'ü', but the reverse is true in German.

In addition, there are several formatting conventions that can vary from one country to another. These can affect:

– The representation of numerals. For instance, in the UK the decimal point is represented by a dot, whereas a comma is used for this purpose in Germany.
– The representation of dates. For instance, in the UK '1/2' means '1st February', while in the USA it means '2nd January'. Of course, some countries, such as China, operate with entirely different calendars.

In some cases the existence of alternative formatting conventions can create ambiguity. For instance, the numeral '10,055' has different meanings, depending on whether the comma represents a decimal point or a separator between thousands and hundreds. It can be interpreted correctly only if one knows which convention is being followed. Similarly, if it is not clear which date formatting convention is in force, then an expression like '1/2' (even if it is known to represent a date rather than a fraction) will be ambiguous.

3.2 The Infra Levels

The variety of character sets in use in the different languages of the world has important consequences at the level of empirics. The latter level is concerned with the patterning of physical signals in such a way as to produce recognisable characters. In CSC, this in reality means the formation of bytes and words, and the mapping of the values in these to actual characters. The traditional mapping system is ASCII, which employs 8-bit sequences to represent the characters of western languages such as English. However, it does not suffice for all the world's languages. This shortcoming led to the development of Unicode, which is an extended scheme, using 16 bits to represent characters, and able to cope with other languages such as Russian, Arabic and so on. See Graham (2000) and http://www.unicode.org.

Another matter of significance in relation to the infra levels is the network infrastructure that supports international CMC. The Internet supports CMC in two manners: realtime and non-realtime. In realtime applications the media are produced as a stream of data by the transmitting software as the application executes and is then transmitted across the network. Such applications include Internet telephony and videoconferencing. In non-realtime applications the transmitted data are prepared and then sent across the network asychronously from the preparation. Non-realtime applications would include applications such as the World-Wide Web, electronic mail and instant messaging applications (such as Internet Relay Chat, MSN and Yahoo Messenger) where two users communicate by typing messages to each other. The network infrastructure needs to be capable of handling all these applications efficiently.

3.3 The Supra Levels

Not surprisingly, international communication raises issues that relate to the social world. As suggested in Connolly (1996, pp. 22-23), we may identify at least three types of difference that may occur at this level when people from different countries engage in computer-supported communication, namely differences in:

- Institutional norms.
- Social norms.
- Environmental norms.

An example of an institutional factor is currency, such as the pound or the dollar. In many situations CMC can involve people in different countries which employ different currencies, necessitating conversion in order to facilitate an accurate appreciation of sums of money, such as the price charged for goods. Within multinational organisations and/or businesses with an international market this can obviously be an everyday occurrence.

Another institutional factor relevant to international CMC is that of time zones. (Although the need for time zones derives from the physical-world phenomenon of the revolution of the earth, the zones that have been instituted are conventions of the social world.) Large distances between time zones can make it difficult to find opportunities to speak to people in other continents during working hours, and can force the use of alternatives such as electronic mail, even if a live conversation would have been more efficient.

Differences in location and time zone between participants in a dialogue can also have implications in terms of the pragmatics of natural language communication. The interpretation of words like 'here' and 'now' will, of course, vary according to the spatio-temporal position of the speaker or writer, while expressions like '1500 hours' or 'three o'clock' have to be interpreted with reference to a particular time zone, and may require conversion for the benefit of people in other zones. Hence, if an organisation is not only geographically distributed but also temporally distributed over time zones, then this can create problems for the coordination of its activities.

A further example of an institutional factor is seen in the fact that different countries have different systems for accomplishing administrative tasks. For instance, financial accounting systems are organised in a manner that is not uniform from one country to another. Again, this can causes complications in the life of internationally distributed organisations.

Social norms are also of importance. It is recognised that differences of this nature from one culture to another can give rise to problems. In this connection Connolly (1994, p. 146) highlights the following aspects:

- Group relationships:
  - Identity.
  - Solidarity.
- Attitude:
  - Politeness.
  - Sufficiency.

People from particular social groups tend to share linguistic characteristics, which are distinctive to those groups. For example, as mentioned above, particular speech communities may have their own language, dialect or accent, while members of an organisation may develop their own jargon, which would not be intelligible to an outsider. Such distinctive characteristics of speech have pragmatic effects, in that they help to confer or reinforce group identity and to give members of a group a feeling of solidarity with their fellow members. However, they can also have an alienating effect upon outsiders. For example, being forced by circumstances to use someone else's language rather than one's own can cause a certain amount of resentment. This would not be a helpful sentiment for a multilingual organisation to provoke among any group of its members.

Another aspect of pragmatics lies in the expression of attitude, both towards other participants in the communicative activity and to what is said and left unsaid. The question of politeness is highly relevant here. Although the norm is to be courteous towards other people, the idea of what is and is not polite varies from culture to culture. For instance, in Japan it is considered very discourteous to say 'no', whereas in British society the word 'no' can be used without necessarily causing offence, even though some tact may be needed if becomes necessary to refuse a request. Another difference concerns the notion of 'sufficiency', which relates to the amount of explicit content it is appropriate to include within a discourse. In Japan it is regarded as proper to talk around a point before reaching the crux of the matter, whereas in British society it is regarded as appropriate to proceed straight to the main point, and doing so does not imply a deficiency in courtesy. See Loveday (1983) for further information on this and related matters.

Another difference between Japanese and British culture relates to the process of decision-making. Ishi (1990) explains that in Japan this is a collective process, based on achieving a consensus. In Britain, however, the process is not always so democratic, and individuals in positions of authority tend to have the right to make a decision on matters falling within their remit. The conduct of business meetings is also different in these and other cultures; see Pan, Scollon and Scollon (2002, pp. 106-136).

As for environmental norms, these manifest themselves via the material culture. Examples are found in the design of buildings, such as office blocks, and of artefacts, such as mailboxes. Although these objects exist in the physical world, their design is a matter of the social world, both because design is a mental and therefore human process and because it is carried out to fulfil functions required by society, such as the accommodation of businesses and the collection of (paper) mail. Furthermore, recognisable styles of design are characteristic of particular cultures at particular periods of history.

The design of mailboxes, in particular, has become an issue in the design of human-computer interfaces; see del Galdo (1990, p. 6) and Sukaviriya and Moran (1990, p. 198). In some instances, an email system has been denoted by means of a mailbox icon, designed in the American manner, which differs considerably from the design of comparable artefacts in, for instance, the UK, to the extent that the meaning of the icon can be obscure to British users. Del Galdo regards an envelope-shaped icon as far preferable, since envelopes are much the same the world over.

4. IT SUPPORT

4.1 Addressing the Problems

As we have seen, numerous kinds of problem arise in the context of international communication. Organisations whose work involves international communication need to address these problems, and they will naturally look to IT for support in solving or at least ameliorating them, where possible. What support, then, can be offered by IT for such purposes?

The provision of computer networks with an adequate Quality of Service (QoS), speed and capacity is a good starting point. Network QoS refers to the network's ability to perform for the distributed application being executed over that network. This performance is related to the specific quality of the network hardware and software, the available bandwidth and the loss performance of the network. The first of these is usually sufficient in modern networks. However, the latter two are affected by the amount of traffic on the network and therefore the effects of congestion caused by too many applications trying to share the same resource. In non-realtime applications, such as web browsing and email, the TCP/IP protocol ensures reliable transfer by reducing the transmit rate of the communication and retransmitting any dropped or corrupt packets. In realtime applications such as telephony and videoconferencing, lost data have other effects. For example video frames will be dropped, causing a jerkiness to the display, or audio streams will be affected by glitches and such like.

In addition, there are various other possibilities for effective IT support, besides adequate quality of service, speed and capacity. For example, the problem of communication between people who speak different languages, or mutually unintelligible varieties of the same language, can be tackled to some extent through the use of machine translation (MT) systems or machine-assisted translation (MAT) systems; see for instance Hutchins and Somers (1992). The major difficulty here, however, is that because human language is so complex and individual languages tend not to admit of straightforward mapping into other languages, high-quality MT is an immensely challenging area of technology, and is far from any kind of general solution. MAT in the form of bilingual dictionaries and so on is less demanding technologically, but has the disadvantage of requiring the involvement of human translation experts, which is more expensive and potentially slower than fully automated translation. Ideally, many organisations would prefer to have the option of spoken as well as written MT, but this increases the technological challenge even further, as it depends on good quality automatic speech recognition and synthesis, both of which present problems of their own.

On the other hand, it is true that certain problems associated with the automatic handling of text by computer are less difficult. The appropriate formatting of numerals and dates is quite straightforward, even though (as pointed out above) it can bring problems of interpretation, while hyphenation and at least some aspects of punctuation are also tractable. The various character sets can be accommodated by means of Unicode, though the input of handwritten text or of non-alphabetic scripts represents a major problem and calls for techniques from the field of AI; cf. Zobel-Pocock (1990).

Inter-cultural disparities in relation to NVC, iconography, the connotations of colours, and so forth, admit of a rather different kind of IT support. Here it would be useful to have available a comprehensive and well-organised on-line encyclopaedia in which the conventions accepted in various cultures were collected. Although of limited use in the live communicative situation, this would at least allow for people to prepare for interaction with people from other cultural backgrounds by consulting the encyclopaedia, and would permit USI designers to obtain information that would be of use when considering internationalisation. The encyclopaedia would probably be web-based and achievable with current technology.

With regard to inter-cultural disparities at the supra levels, some of the problems admit of simple computational solutions, for instance currency conversion or the simultaneous display of times current in different zones. Others could be alleviated by extending the on-line encyclopaedia to include phenomena such as the social and environmental norms prevailing in different places. However, disparities that affect deep-rooted organisational norms such as the way in which decisions are made or accounting systems are organised will not yield to any straightforward technological solution.

4.2 Communication via the Internet

Now that the Internet is so widely used for the purposes of CMC, it is appropriate to consider the particular character of this method of communication. It is clear that the Internet has come to offer various opportunities for CMC that did not previously exist. Newsgroups and chat-rooms are obvious examples, and they have resulted in the building up of virtual communities whose members are linked almost entirely by means of on-line communication. Moreover, the addition of sound and vision that has been enabled through web-based technology can in some cases endow this kind of CMC with an experience approaching that of virtual reality.

From the OS perspective an interesting feature of Internet-based communication has been the emergence and establishment of various norms to help users from around the world to enjoy the benefits of the Internet in a relatively uniform manner. Standards such as MP3 and MPEG-4 have been agreed for the exchange of data regardless of its geographical or cultural origin. Moreover, stylistic conventions have emerged, for instance the fact that the normal format of an email message is header + body + signature, and the use of emoticons (smileys) to indicate humour, sadness and so on, in a manner which is surrogate to face-to-face NVC. Furthermore, a fairly standard Internet-related jargon has developed, for example the use of the word 'summarise' in newsgroup postings, in the sense of simply concatenating a series of other postings on a given topic. In addition, social conventions have become established. Some of these go under the name of 'netiquette', for instance the convention that a private message should not be publicly quoted in a newsgroup posting without the author's prior permission.

An aspect of the pragmatics of CMC that has aroused some concern is the opportunity which in some cases it brings to conceal the true identity of the participants in the interaction. For example, it may be possible to avoid disclosing attributes such as one's gender or age, or indeed to masquerade as a person whose attributes differ from one's own; see Barnes (2001, pp. 135-157) for discussion. Thus one's own name or pseudonym can end up referring to, in effect, someone else. In semiotic terms, Nguyen and Alexander (1996) speak of the sign being split away from its referent. Because of the disquiet that many feel about online deception of this kind, it is the kind of subject that readily becomes a social and political issue.

Matters pertaining to ideology, and to the concomitant phenomena of power and critical dialectic, are, of course, familiar themes in semiotics; and it is not surprising if such issues arise in relation to Internet-based communication. The Internet can be used as a means of reinforcing and/or resisting ideologies; and the ideological conflict between those who advocate free, untrammelled communication on the Internet and those who espouse control, especially in the form of censorship, has been widely documented; see for instance Regan Shade (1996) and Barnes (2001, pp. 207-230). To the extent that the content of the information sources on the Internet is regulated, this may serve as a tool for exerting political and social control; cf. Bromberg (1996). Furthermore, being world-wide in its reach, it has the potential to be exploited for the ends of global hegemony.

Of course, the Internet, as a technology, is morally neutral. Whether or not it is used to benefit humankind is a matter which will be decided at the topmost level of the semiotic hierarchy, namely the social world within which we have our voice.

5. CONCLUSION

Our conclusions from this paper are as follows. International communication is immensely complex. However, by analysing it semiotically in terms of the six-level framework, we can attain a more organised and structured understanding of it. The application of the OS framework clearly demonstrates that the achievement of successful international communication via computer networks is by no means a purely technical problem. On the contrary, all of the semiotic levels of analysis are affected. Furthermore, our treatment of the issues that arise in international communication has shown that different kinds of problem occur at the core levels, the infra levels and the supra levels.

IT can offer some valuable support to people in organisations affected by these problems. Already the Internet is a great boon, even though it raises problems of its own. Moreover, the level of IT support is likely to improve in the future, as research into areas such as MT brings further benefits. However, as is evident from the semiotic perspective that we have adopted, international communication is fundamentally a social process, and it is the requirements that derive from this social purpose which are crucial to the specification and construction of supporting IT that people will find genuinely useful.

REFERENCES

Barnes S.B. 2001, Online Connections: Internet Interpersonal Relationships. Cresskill, NJ: Hampton Press.

Bowers J., Churcher J. 1989, Local and Gobal Structuring of Computer Mediated Communication: Developing Linguistic Perspectives on CSCW in Cosmos. Office Technology and People, 4: pp. 197-227.

Bromberg, H, 1996, Are MUDs Communities? Identity, Belonging and Consciousness in Virtual Worlds. In Cultures of Internet: Virtual Spaces, Real Histories, Living Bodies, R. Shields, ed. London: Sage.

Carey, J.M. 1998, Creating Global Software: A Conspectus and Review. Interacting with Computers 6: pp. 449-465.

Chesebro, J.W. 1985, Computer-mediated interpersonal communication. In Information and Behaviour, 1, B.D. Ruben ed. New Brunswick: Transaction Books.

Connolly, J.H. 1994, Artificial Intelligence and Computer Supported Cooperative Working in International Contexts. In CSCW and Artificial Intelligence, J.H. Connolly, E.A. Edmonds, eds. London: Springer.

Connolly, J.H. 1996, Problems in Designing the User Interface for Systems Supporting International Human-Human Communication. In International User Interfaces, E.M. del Galdo, J. Nielsen, eds. New York: Wiley.

Connolly, J.H. 2002, Accommodating Natural Language Within the Organisational Semiotic Framework. In Coordination and Communication Using Signs: Studies in Organisational Semiotics 2, K. Liu, R.J. Clarke, P.B. Andersen, R.K. Stamper, eds. Boston: Kluwer.

Connolly, J.H, Pemberton, L., eds. 1996. Linguistic Concepts and Methods in CSCW. London: Springer.

Del Galdo, E.M. 1990, Internationalisation and Translation: Some Guidelines for the Design of Human-Computer Interfaces. In Designing User Interfaces for International Use, J. Nielsen, ed. Amsterdam: Elsevier.

Del Galdo, E.M., Nielsen, J., eds. 1996, International User Interfaces. New York: Wiley.

Esselink, B. 2000, A Practical Guide to Localisation. Amsterdam: Benjamins.

Goodman, N. 1992, Introduction to Sociology. New York: Harper Collins.

Graham, T. 2000, Unicode: a Primer. Foster City, CA: MIS.

Hall, P.A.V., Hudson, R., eds. 1997, Software without Frontiers: a Multi-platform, Multi-cultural, Multi-nation Approach. Chichester: Wiley.

Herring, S.C., ed. 1996, Computer-Mediated Communication: Linguistic, Social and Cross-Cultural Perspectives. Amsterdam: Benjamins.

Hiltz, S.R., Turoff, M. 1985, Structuring Computer-Mediated Communication Systems to Avoid Information Overload. Communications of the ACM 28: pp. 680-689.

Horton, W. 1984, The Icon Book: Visual Symbols for Computer Systems and Documentation. New York: Wiley.

Hutchins, W.J., Somers, H.L. 1992, An Introduction to Machine Translation. London: Academic Press.

Ishi, H. 1990, Cross-Cultural Communication and Computer-Supported Cooperative Work. Whole Earth Review: Winter: 48-52.

Jones, S., Mueller, C., Sweezy, M., Thomas, B., Velez, L. 1992, Developing International User Information. Bedford, MA: Digital Press.

Kerr, B., Hiltz, S.R. 1982, Computer-Mediated Communication Systems: Status and Evaluation. New York: Academic Press.

Loveday, L. 1983, Rhetoric Patterns in Conflict: the Sociocultural Relativity of Discourse-Organising Processes. Journal of Pragmatics 7: pp. 169-190.

Luong, T.V., Lok, J.S.H., Taylor, D.J., Driscoll, K. 1995, Internationalisation: Developing Software for Global Markets. New York: Wiley.

Martin O'Donnell, S. 1994, Programming for the World: a Guide to Internationalisation. Englewood Cliffs, NJ: PTR Prentice Hall.

Nielsen, J., ed. 1990, Designing User Interfaces for International Use. Amsterdam: Elsevier.

Nielsen, J. 2000, Designing Web Usability. Indianapolis: New Riders.

Nguyen, D.T., Alexander, R. 1996, The Coming of Cyberspacetime and the End of the Polity. In Cultures of Internet: Virtual Spaces, Real Histories, Living Bodies, R. Shields, ed. London: Sage.

Pan, Y., Scollon, S.W., Scollon, R. 2002, Professional Communication in International Settings. Malden, MA: Blackwell.

Rapaport, M. 1991, Computer Mediated Communication. New York: Wiley.

Regan Shade, L. 1996, Is there Free Speech on the Net? Censorship in the Global Information Infrastructure. In Cultures of Internet: Virtual Spaces, Real Histories, Living Bodies, R. Shields, ed. London: Sage.

Shapiro, J. 1996, Collaborative Computing: Multimedia across the Network. Boston: AP Professional.

Stamper, R. 1991, The Semiotic Framework for Information Systems Research. In Information Systems Research: Contemporary Approaches and Emergent Traditions, H.E. Nissen, H.K. Klein, R.Hirschheim, eds. Amsterdam: North-Holland.

Sukaviriya, P., Moran, L. 1990, User interfaces for Asia. In Designing User Interfaces for International Use, J. Nielsen, ed. Amsterdam: Elsevier.

Taylor, D. 1990, Creating International Applications. In Designing User Interfaces for International Use, J. Nielsen, ed. Amsterdam: Elsevier.

Taylor, D. 1992, Global Software: Developing Applications for the International Market. New York: Springer.

Ulijn, J.M., Lincke, A. and Karakaya, Y. 2001, Non-Face-to-Face International Business Negotiation: How is National Culture Reflected in this Medium? IEEE Transactions on Professional Communication 44 (2): pp. 126-137.

Uren, E., Howard, R., Perinotti, T. 1993, Software Internationalisation and Localisation: an Introduction. New York: van Nostrand Reinhold.

Walters, R. 1995, Computer-Mediated Communications: Multimedia Applications. Boston, MA: Artech House.

Zobel-Pocock, R.A. 1990, International User Interfaces. In Designing User Interfaces for International Use, J. Nielsen, ed. Amsterdam: Elsevier.

Chapter 18

A SEMIOTIC INSIGHT INTO MODEL MAPPING

Hongwei Xu and Junkang Feng
University of Paisley, United Kingdom

Abstract: Model mapping faces many challenging tasks and contemporary work seems to focus on computational issues. As a result it seems to lack an overarching theoretical framework whereby all aspects of model mapping can be investigated systematically. We maintain that the principles of semiotics may well provide theoretical foundations for developing such a framework. In this chapter we report our preliminary work on using semiotics in investigating mapping determination and creation between two independently created models across heterogeneous data sources. By employing semiotic principles, we develop a novel approach to model mapping as sign exchange. We give an analysis of the triadic relationship among data, information and knowledge concerning syntactics, semantics and pragmatics of signs. We present a conceptual view of sign interchange and propose an abstract architecture of information flow between two logic covers that is based upon our model of minimal mapping covers. This minimal mapping cover forms the basis of a set of signs participating in determining and establishing a set of correspondences between two disparate models. Our work considers a set of mappings at three semiotic levels and proposes a notion of the information bearing capability of signs. Our work thus far seems to show that semiotics principles do provide insight in tackling the complexity involved in model mapping, in particular the issue of "meaning".

Key words: model mapping, sign exchange, information flow

1. INTRODUCTION

Model mapping (also known as schema mapping (Miller *et al.* 2000, 2001; Yang *et al.* 2001) or schema matching (Rahm and Bernstein 2001; Madhavan *et al.* 2001; Do and Rahm 2002) plays a central role in data

K. Liu (ed.),
Virtual, Distributed and Flexible Organisations: Studies in Organisational Semiotics, 293–302.

and/or knowledge intensive applications such as enterprise application integration (EAI) and business-to-business (B2B) e-commerce. In this application domain, enterprises and trading partners need to deal with a very large volume of data by accessing exiting systems and the increased new sources of data and Web-based systems (Brodie 2002), thereby involving complex mappings between old and new data, processes and systems. Correctly performing these activities depends on detailed descriptions of data and other aspects of the legacy and new systems, including the relationships between them (Heiler *et al.* 1999). In most studies and applications, the above problem seems to be tackled by looking at the computational issues (namely issues at the data level). There seems a lack of a holistic, effective treatment for understanding and articulating *complexity* and *meaning* involved in the process of mapping determination and creation for information exchange.

In the chapter, we discuss some basic issues for an investigation of model mapping by using semiotic principles. This preliminary investigation treats a task of information exchange as sign exchange.

To achieve this, we develop a model of *minimal mapping cover*, which is concerned with a triadic relationship among data, information and knowledge. This is inspired by the theory of signs being concerned with syntactics, semantics and pragmatics (Morris 1938). The model serves as the basis of a set of signs that needs to be identified for a desired mapping.

We propose the notion of the information bearing capability (IBC) of signs for looking at how data is interpreted by reasoning about pragmatics-to-semantics dependencies. The IBC of signs articulates the relationships between the individual design choice of an input model and the information requested by a given mapping task, which gives a query or a set of queries the *clue* to understanding where the information is located in the data sources.

Our work is based on an assumption that a model (e.g., a relational database schema or an XML schema) can be seen as a set of artificially created signs by different data design processes performed by a human designer or by an automated tool. Thus a mapping between two models can be viewed as the mapping between two sets of signs. That is to say, the model mapping should be done on the basis of the minimal sets of the elements defined in the triangle, and each of which can and should be justified by the ideas of "properties of signs" (Stamper 1997).

This chapter is organized as follows: Section 2 summarizes some related work. Section 3 presents a model of minimal mapping cover with a triadic relationship among data, information and knowledge that is based upon properties of signs. We show a conceptual view of sign interchange between two data sources in Section 4. We investigate the issue of information flow in Section 5, which includes the introduction of the notion of *logical covers* and *pragmatic mapping* in Subsection 5.1. The information flow between logical covers is presented in Subsection 5.2. We summarize our work and give further research directions in the final section.

2. RELATED WORK

Our work is originally motivated by the work on studying information capacity (Miller *et al.* 1993, 1994a) in the context of schema integration. The work of Miller *et al* highlighted the need for a measure of correctness for schema integration tasks and bridging theory and practice. They extended Hull's notion of relative information capacity of database schemas (Hull 1986) and proposed the core notion of information (capacity) preserving mapping and examined it by developing a schema intension graph (SIG) (Miller *et al.* 1994b). This notion today may still be a key to comparing among models (Bernstein et al. 2000).

The work of Fagin et al (2003) addresses the dependencies used in the process of reasoning about semantics and query answering in the context of data exchange where the formalism is relevant to ours when we define dependencies between knowledge (K) and information (I).

Other work on context interchange for intelligent integration of information (Goh *et al.* 1999) is also relevant. They take semantic interoperability into consideration by elaborating the context interchange strategy.

Organisational semiotics (Stamper 1997) forms a basis for using the theory of signs in modern information systems design, which provides us with one of the most stimulating and fruitful ways of approaching the study of organisations (Stamper 1987, Chapter 2). This framework presents many ideas for IT researchers who seek alternative solutions to many aspects of issues relating to the complexity and meaning involved in the design of enterprise applications.

3. A MODEL OF MINIMAL MAPPING COVER

Our model depicted in Figure 1 illustrates a minimal cover of mapping elements with a triadic relationship among data, information and knowledge, denoted by *D*, *I* and *K* respectively. We call them three basic sign-related elements. Each basic element is associated with one semiotic level, namely, *D*, *I* and *K* are associated with the syntactics, semantics and pragmatics of signs respectively. Thus a binary relationship between two of the three would involve two semiotic levels. Each binary relationship represents an activity or behaviour that is featured by a dependency depicted by an arrow shown in the figure. Note that the dotted-line arrow between *I* and *D* indicates that there is no direct dependency from *I* to *D* that involves the activity Representation. The Representation is restricted by the knowledge *K* involved that defines what and how data *D* can be interpreted as information *I* to construct the minimal mapping cover.

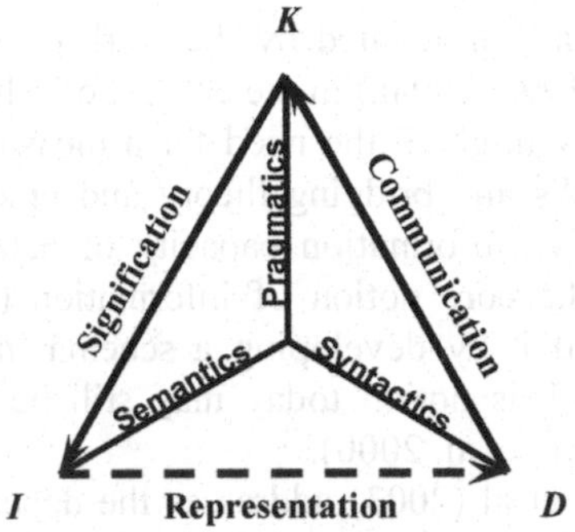

Figure 1. A model of the triadic relationship among data, information and knowledge that based upon properties of signs.

For example, the basic element *I* (i.e., the information content carried by a model to be mapped) is related to the semantics of signs. *I* is involved in two activities or behaviours, namely Representation and Signification, through the dependencies from *I* to *D* and from *K* to *I* respectively. Within this structure, *D* as data sets or schema elements is related to the syntactics of signs, and *K* is the knowledge relating to the pragmatics of signs.

Any two of these elements can be seen as connected by a functional relationship. For example, the binary relationship between *I* and *D* relating to the Representation activity can be viewed as a function that may be embodied by a *rule* or *norm*. It works like this, if $I \in$ dom *K* (this means that following Dretske (1999, page86) *I* causes or sustains an element in the domain of *K*, say k_1), then there must be a minimal *D* such that $(I, D) \rightarrow k_1$, and this *D* is the representation of *I* under a particular rule. This function characterizes aforementioned indirect dependency from *I* to *D*.

This particular relationship (i.e., the activity Representation) presents the information bearing capability (IBC) of signs, denoted by $i \circ d\ (S)$, where *i* is a function from *D* to *K*, *d* is a function from *K* to *I*, and *S* is a sign. Thus the IBC of a sign is actually implied by the activity Communication and activity Signification shown in the figure. Similarly, the model of this minimal mapping cover can be denoted as $k \circ i \circ d\,(S)$ that forms the basis of the set of signs participating in a mapping effort.

The activity Communication is concerned with the *quantity aspect of information* transmission *by means of* signs. That is to say, the Communication embodies the amount of information (e.g., in bits) that is carried by data d_i of D, which causes or sustains some k_j of K. The interested reader may refer to our previous work on the *information quantity* aspect of the information bearing capability of a conceptual data schema (Feng 2002).

The signal transmission could be meaningless for a mapping task since the syntactic representation of D does not completely convey the semantics of different databases (Miller *et al.* 2000). For example, it is hard to know with complete certainty from the D alone whether the **Customer** relation in one data source has the same meaning as the **Customer** in another without identifying the functional relationship between D and K under I. This means that the information content (i.e., I) of D must be identified in order for D to result in K. This is because knowledge is caused or sustained by information, not the syntax of data.

The activity Signification addresses the issue of the *meaning* of signs, which we believe is related to the semantics and pragmatics of signs. A sign may have many meanings, for example Mingers (1995) identified three levels of meaning. In our model, the determination of a particular meaning is achieved by the binary relationship between K and I, which we call the *pragmatics-to-semantics dependency* against the background condition of the syntactics of signs. For example, the syntax of D, such as ordering of entities or a hierarchical structure of a model may be decided as a design choice, which is part of K, in order to represent a certain meaning. This example shows how a particular meaning of D of certain syntax is determined by its pragmatics, namely the use of sign D.

4. SIGN INTERCHANGE

When we are talking about sign, we are actually talking about the meaning it conveys to different users (i.e., model designers in our case) who encode the meaning in a model design process. In order to make a conversation or communicate with others, we must share the meaning (maybe through negotiation) of the signs that we are using. But it could be just part of the semantic information carried by the sign or the pragmatic meaning of the sign (i.e., the particular meaning when a sign, namely a particular model, is defined). In the context of model mapping, the sign might not mean the same to another DBMS, which might be on a different platform (we assume that a model mapping management system is established on top of the DBMS). In order to make the mapping successful, it is crucial to find an appropriate architecture for coupling the DBMSs to accommodate the dynamic development of communication between individual signs.

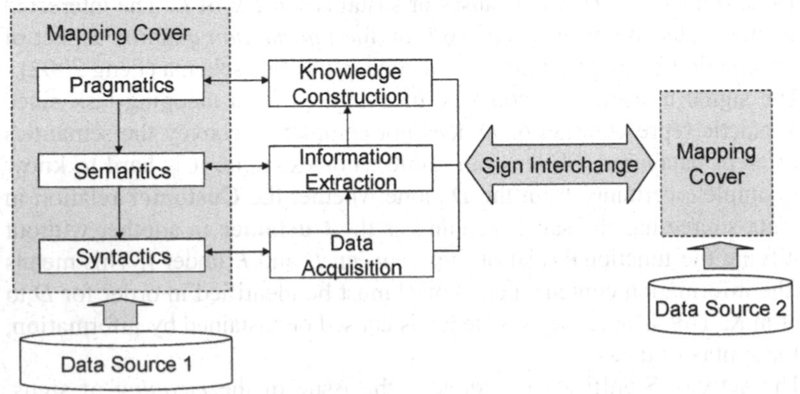

Figure 2. A conceptual view of sign interchange.

Figure 2 illustrates a conceptual view of sign interchange between two data sources. It should be noted that the prerequisite is, for meaning to be shared (or interchangeable) between two systems, each mapping cover must "acquiesce" in something common (e.g., a global schema in schema integration). The challenge is how to identify the complexity of the process of mapping determination and creation.

One possible solution we propose here is to look at the process at each of the semiotic levels. To this end, we must discover what factors should be taken into account in each level of the operation of data acquisition → information extraction → knowledge construction. Most importantly, we must examine the correctness of the mapping generation task by looking at the inter-relations among properties of signs.

As a result, the aforementioned basic elements, data, information and knowledge can be compressed in the mapping cover, which could then be attached in the signs that are interchanged by using, for example, XML messaging between two systems.

5. INFORMATION FLOW

Information flow (Barwise 1993; Barwise and Gabbay 1995; Barwise and Seligman 1997) plays a major role in discovering a set of semantic correspondences between two models. The notion of information flow characterizes information containment (Lalmas 1998) and provides one with a theoretical foundation for reasoning about informational relationship between the sources and receivers in a distributed environment.

5.1 Logical Covers and Pragmatic Mapping

A logical cover (*LC*) is a triple $\langle K, I, \Sigma_{ki}\rangle$, where *K* is the knowledge that defines the pragmatics of *D* carrying *I*, *I* is the information content that defines the semantics of *D* under the condition that the semantics of *D* is the same as the most specific piece of information in the information content of *D*, which is termed "semantic content" (Dretske 1999, page173), and the pragmatics-to-semantics dependencies in Σ_{ki} are a set of assertions relating *K* and *I*, which defines either the *primary meaning* or the *implied meaning* of the *LC*. Note that *D* does not appear in *LC*, which explains why *LC* is said to be logical, namely properties on the *D* level, such as syntactics are not considered in the *LC*.

The *LC* determines the meaning of signs within a certain context. It specifies how data is interpreted to provide information at both the pragmatic level and the semantic level, and the relationship between these two. Understanding and distinguishing pragmatics and semantics can help us find a direct answer to the question: How to determine the meaning derivable from or conveyed by a piece of information carried by a data construct to support a set of meaningful semantic correspondences between two disparate models?

Thus creating mappings between two models becomes a process of determining and establishing a set of correspondences between two logical covers *LC*s, namely $\Sigma_{ki}(\mathfrak{I}1)$ and $\Sigma_{ki}(\mathfrak{I}2)$, where $\mathfrak{I}$ is the minimal mapping cover. We name the result of the set of correspondences between two *LC*s *pragmatic mapping*, denoted by f_p, in our approach.

As model mapping involves the discovery of a query or set of queries that transform the source data into the new presentation (Miller *et al.* 2000), this raises an initial task of creating *LC*s as views to answer those queries. Our on-going work is making use of RDF to represent the *LC*.

In principle, we hope that the pragmatic mapping f_p can help reduce model matching efforts by creating $f_p = \Sigma_{ki}(\mathfrak{I}1, \mathfrak{I}2)$, which is a pragmatic mapping from *LC*1 to *LC*2, and the f_p will help determine the low-level data mapping between two corresponding models.

5.2 Information Flow between Two Logical Covers

The information flow from *LC*1 to *LC*2 can be denoted as $\Sigma_{ki}(\mathfrak{I}1) \rightarrow \Sigma_{ki}(\mathfrak{I}2)$. This formulation underpins a mathematical foundation for our approach to establishing mappings between two minimal mapping covers.

In order to examine the correctness of matching operation on two corresponding *LC*s, we employ the notion of *infomorphisms* by Barwise and Seligman (1997) to test information containment in both directions. Thus we can define that two *LC*s are equivalent if and only if each is contained in the other, denoted by $\Sigma_{ki}(\mathfrak{I}1) \rightleftarrows \Sigma_{ki}(\mathfrak{I}2)$. Based on this idea, we propose an abstract architecture of information flow between two *LC*s illustrated in Figure 3.

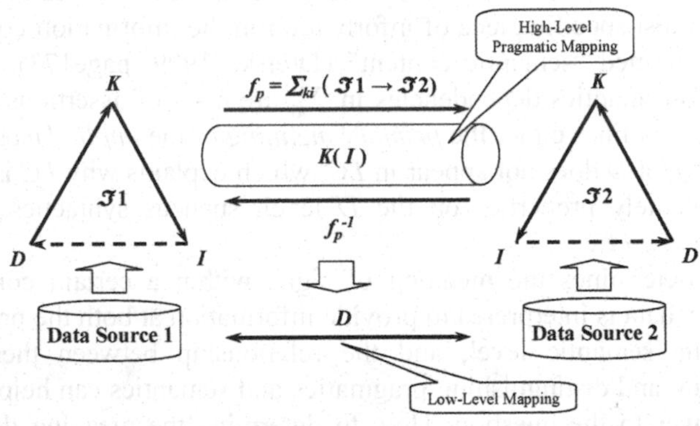

Figure 3. An abstract architecture of information flow between two *LC*s.

The architecture shows that a set of correspondences are determined and established by the high-level pragmatic mapping. The dotted-line arrow between *I* and *D*, as mentioned before, indicates the indirect dependencies between the semantics of signs and the syntactics of it. This feature shows that the semantic information can be independent of the underlying syntactic representation (i.e., the syntactic structure of the data), thereby enabling *semantic interoperability* without interfacing the relevant source data for achieving a mapping task. The feature is also similar to the notion of "data independences" in classic database theory. This will enable an agent component to reason directly about the semantic information and meaning of the data without concerning the structure of it.

The task of information exchange between data source 1 and data source 2 is achieved by the set of mappings at two levels, namely a high-level mapping and a low-level mapping shown in the figure. The high-level mapping task is fulfilled by the pragmatic mapping based on the information flow between *LC*s, which is accomplished by two functions, f_p and f_p^{-1} . The pragmatic mapping, functioning like a compiler, translates the high-level mapping into the low-level mapping by implementing $D = k(I)$ defined within our model, which decides what and how data is transformed from the source to the receiver or is exchanged between two data sources.

6. SUMMARY AND FUTURE WORK

We observe that contemporary approaches to model mapping appear to have focused on computational issues, and therefore seem to lack an overarching framework for understanding and investigating multiple aspects of it. To alleviate this, we propose to make use of semiotics principles in tackling model mapping, which seems to be rather fruitful thus far. In this chapter we have presented our semiotics-based approach to understanding the complexity and meaning involved in model mapping. This is only the starting stage of our work. Our next step will focus on the mechanism for reasoning about IBC preserving transformations based on the framework presented in this chapter.

REFERENCES

Barwise, J. 1993. Constraints, Channels, and the Flow of Information. In Situation Theory and Its Applications, P.Aczel, D.Israel, Y.Katagiri, and S.Peters, Eds. CSLI Lecture Notes, Stanford, California, 3(37):3-27.

Barwise, J. and Gabbay, D. 1995. On the Logic of Information Flow. Bulletin of the IGPL , 3(1):7-49.

Barwise, J. and Seligman, J. 1997. Information Flow: the Logic of Distributed Systems. Cambridge Tracts in Theoretical Computer Science 44, Cambridge University Press, Cambridge.

Bernstein, P. A., Halevy, A. V., and Pottigner, R. A. 2000. A Vision for Management of Complex Models. ACM SIGMOD Record, 29(3):55-63.

Brodie, M. L. 2002. Data Management Challenges in Very Large Enterprises. In Proc. of the 28th VLDB, Hong Kong, China.

Do, H. and Rahm, E. 2002. COMA – A system for flexible combination of schema matching approaches. In Proc. of the 28th VLDB, Hong Kong, China.

Dretske, F. I. 1999. Knowledge and the Flow of Information. CSLI Publications, Stanford, California.

Fagin, R., Kolaitis, P. G., Miller, R. J., and Popa, L. 2003. Data Exchange: Semantics and Query Answering. In ICDT.

Feng, J. 2002. The 'Information Quantity' Aspect of the 'Information Bearing Capability' of a Conceptual Data Schema. In Proceedings of the 7th Annual UKAIS Conference, Leeds, UK. ISBN 1-898883-149. pp.150-157.

Goh, C. H., Bressan, S., Madnick, S., and Siegel, M. 1999. Context Interchange: New Features and Formalisms for the Intelligent Integration of Information. ACM Transactions on Information Systems, 17(3):270-293.

Heiler, S., Lee, W. C., and Mitchell, G. 1999. Repository Support for Metadata-based Legacy Migration. IEEE Data Engineering, 22(1):37-42.

Hull, R. 1986. Relative Information Capacity of Simple Relational Database Schemata. SIAM Journal of Computing, 15(3):856-886.

Madhavan, J., Bernstein, P. A., and Rahm, E. 2001. Generic Schema Matching with Cupid. In Proc. of the 27th VLDB, Roma, Italy.

Miller, R. J., Haas, L. M., and Hernandez, M. 2000. Schema Mapping as Query Discovery. In Proc. of the 26th VLDB, Cairo, Egypt.

Miller, R. J., Ioannidis, Y. E., and Ramakrishnan, R. 1994a. Schema Equivalence in Heterogeneous Systems: Bridging Theory and Practice. Information Systems, 19(1):3-31.

Miller, R. J., Ioannidis, Y. E., and Ramakrishnan, R. 1994b. Schema Intension Graphs: A Formal Model for the Study of Schema Equivalence. Technical Report 1185. Dept. of Computer Sciences, Univ. of Wisconsin-Madison, USA.

Miller, R. J., Ioannidis, Y. E., and Ramakrishnan, R. 1993. The Use of Information Capacity in Schema Integration and Translation. In Proc. of the Int'l Conf. on Very Large Data Bases (VLDB), Dublin, Ireland.

Mingers, J. 1995. Information and Meaning: Foundations for an Intersubjective Account. Information Systems Journal, 5:285-306.

Morris, C. 1938. Foundations of the Theory of Signs. In International Encyclopedia of Unified Science, vol. 1, no 2, University of Chicago Press, Chicago.

Rahm, E. and Bernstein, P. A. 2001. A Survey of Approaches to Automatic Schema Matching. The VLDB Journal, 10:334-350.

Stamper, R. 1997. Organisational Semiotics. In Information Systems: An Emerging Discipline? J. Mingers and F. Stowell, Eds. McGraw-Hill, London.

Stamper, R. 1987. Semantics. In Critical Issues in Information Systems Research, R.A. Boland and R.A. Hirschheim, Eds. Wiley.

Yang, L. L., Miller, R. J., Haas, L. M., and Fagin, R. 2001. Data-Driven Understanding and Refinement of Schema Mappings. In Proc. of ACM SIGMOD, Santa Barbara, CA, USA.

Chapter 19

IDENTIFYING BUSINESS PROCESS PATTERNS USING SEMANTIC ANALYSIS

Boris Shishkov, Zhiwu Xie, Kecheng Liu, Jan L.G. Dietz
Faculty of Information Technology and Systems, Delft University of Technology, Delft, 2600 AJ, The Netherlands E-mail: {b.b.shishkov, j.l.g.dietz}@ewi.tudelft.nl

Department of Computer Science. The University of Reading, Whiteknights, Reading, RG6 6AY, UK E-mail: {z.xie, k.liu}@reading.ac.uk

Abstract: A problem in the business process modelling task is how to grasp correctly and completely the input information about the studied business reality; information which is often unstructured, informal, and vague. We study the usefulness of applying Semantic Analysis for the purpose of "translating" the input information into a structured output. This study is in the context of the development of an approach, namely SDBC, which aligns business process modelling and software specification -in a component-based way.

Key words: Business process; Semantic Analysis; Business modelling

A common challenge for current business process modelling techniques is to cope with the ambiguity of the input information. It is well-known from practice that usually, in the real-life projects related to business process modelling, the information about the business reality under study, provided by the user is completely unstructured, unstandardised, and often vague. The modeller has to perform his/her individual intuitive skills to "translate" the information provided by users into some structured modelling units characterising the particular business process modelling tool applied. The significant problem here is that there is no guarantee of completeness (no missing issues from the user's descriptive information), consistency (no contradictions resulting from wrong interpretation of the user information), and correctness (regarding the integrity/fidelity of the translation process).

K. Liu (ed.),
Virtual, Distributed and Flexible Organisations: Studies in Organisational Semiotics, 303–305.

The DEMO business process modelling environment (www.demo.nl) appears to possess the value of a structured reference to the initial, informal user information. DEMO addresses this issue through the OER-procedure (Organisational Essence Revelation) for identification of transactions (the DEMO elementary business process patterns). The procedure consists of three analysis and three synthesis steps: the PIF-analysis, the CAP-analysis, the PS-analysis, the TP-synthesis, the ATN-synthesis, and the O-synthesis. In the PIF-analysis (Performa-Informa-Forma) one marks the words in a case description as referring to either performative, informative or formative things. In the CAP-analysis one takes all performative things and determines whether they are about coordination (C), about actor roles (A) or about production (P). In the PS-analysis (Product Structure) one determines how the production things are interrelated; this yields tree structures that resembles a bill of material; the root of every tree is the product that is delivered to the environment of the organisation. In the TP-synthesis (Transaction Pattern), all coordination things, production things and actor roles are clustered into transactions, according to the generic transaction pattern. In the ATN-synthesis (Actor Transaction Network) one determines the identities among the actor roles (initiator/executor of every transaction) that are found in the previous step. Lastly, in the O-synthesis (Organisation), one determines the final boundary of the actor-transaction-network, thus separating the kernel of the modelled organisation from its environment.

However, although OER is a well-structured procedure for identification of business process patterns, the first two analysis steps are based on text interpretation; yet, text might be vague. Therefore, facilitating the PIF and CAP analyses, by structuring the information based on which they are realized, would improve the quality of the identification of (DEMO) business process patterns. With respect to this, Semantic Analysis - SA (Liu, 2000) is claimed to be useful for bridging the user information and the business process modelling activities. SA's strengths have been studied from this perspective in the context of the development of the approach SDBC (Shishkov & Dietz, 2004) – Software Derived from Business Components.

Arguments in support of the claimed strengths of SA are:

- Being soundly rooted in the Semiotic theory, SA offers rigorous rules for the reflection of textual information into a semi-formal semiotic model.
- SA possesses the capability of structuring the information concerning requirements in such a way that it is well understandable for both developers and potential users.
- SA allows for a straightforward and precise discovery of both specific and generic issues characterizing the investigated reality, as well as for correct differentiation between these issues.

- Regarding the particular study of identification of DEMO business process patterns, it is useful that DEMO is rooted in the Semiotic theory; this is a good background for relating SA to the further PIF and CAP DEMO analyses.

REFERENCES

Liu, K., 2000, Semiotics in Information Systems Engineering. Cambridge, UK: Cambridge University Press.

Shishkov, B. and J.L.G. Dietz, 2004, Design of Software Using Generic Business Components. Proc: HICSS'04, Hawaii, USA.

Chapter 20

AIDING SEMIOTIC ANALYSIS USING NATURAL LANGUAGE PROCESSING TOOLS

Ken Cosh & Pete Sawyer
Lancaster University, United Kingdom

Abstract: Semiotics treats organisations as sign systems and concerns the study of organisations, human communication and information systems. It is used as an approach to requirements engineering that develops integrated structural and behavioural models. This paper focuses on the MEASUR approach, which has been successfully applied to well-understood, bounded problems. However it is difficult to apply MEASUR systematically to complex, poorly bounded problems. This paper investigates these problems and suggests how the approach could be improved by using Natural Language Processing tools to assist the process.

Key words: Semiotic analysis, MEASUR, requirements engineering, natural language processing, organisational semiotics.

1. APPLYING NLP TO MEASUR

Several authors have pointed out the apparent links between Organisational Semiotics and Natural Language Processing (NLP) (Charrel, 2002; Connolly, 2000). Whenever Semiotic Analysis is used to model any problem or domain, natural language is studied. In the documented case-studies and examples of MEASUR (Liu, 2000), the problem scope is small, and the problem statement is a concise description.

This research has investigated how to apply the method to problems where the sources of information are less clearly bounded, diffuse, scattered and poorly structured. For many real life cases it isn't possible to neatly summarise the problem briefly, so the starting point for analysis could be a long unstructured document. There are several statistical theories, which can

K. Liu (ed.),
Virtual, Distributed and Flexible Organisations: Studies in Organisational Semiotics, 307–308.

be used to analyse natural language, and extract important information from a document. Table 1 shows how some NLP tools can map into the Semantic Analysis Method.

Table 1. The Semantic Analysis Method and corresponding NLP tools.

Semantic Analysis Method	NLP tools
Problem Articulation Method	Long Document e.g. Ethnographic Report
Candidate Affordance Generation	Frequency List Comparison
Candidate Grouping	Collocation Analysis & KWIC
Ontology Charting	Iteration through Collocations.

The first stage in analysing a long document creates a frequency list of each word in the document. By comparing this list to a frequency list of how often words could be expected to occur, created from the British National Corpus, a new frequency list is created with the most significantly overused words prominent (Rayson *et al.*, 1999). These words are the keywords of the problem domain.

The next step investigates the relationships between these keywords in order to develop an ontology chart. Collocation Analysis (Oakes, 1998) is used suggest pairs of words likely to have a relationship with each other, by extracting words that often occur in conjunction with each other from the text. The relationship can then be understood by looking at the Keywords in Context (KWIC), extracting from the text every co-occurrence of the words.

When relationships are discovered, they can be modelled within an Ontology Chart fragment. By iterating this process for each keyword, several fragments can be created and eventually joined to create a complete Ontology Chart for the problem domain described in the report.

REFERENCES

Charrel, P J, 2002, Viewpoints for Knowledge Management in System Design.

Connolly, J H, 2000, Accomodating Natural Language Within The Organisational Semiotic Framework, Third International Workshop in Organisational Semiotics WOS.

Liu, K., 2000, Semiotics in Information Systems Engineering, Cambridge University Press.

Oakes, M, P, Statistics for Corpus Linguistics, Michael P. Oakes. Edinburgh textbooks in empirical linguistics.1998

Rayson, P, Garside, R, & Sawyer, P, 1999, Language Engineering for the Recovery of Requirements from Legacy Documents. REVERE.

Chapter 21

IMPROVING THE FEEDBACK TO CANDIDATES OF MULTIPLE CHOICE TESTS

William Fone
Staffordshire University, United Kingdom

Abstract: **This paper is concerned with improving the feedback to candidates of multiple choice tests by using a speech circuit that introduces autopoietic redundant information to filter noise.**

Key words: Speech circuits, feedback.

Tests using multiple selection questions (MCQs) are easy to automate but there is always concern about detecting guesswork. If a MCQ presents difficulty for the respondent only two paths are available, do the best one can and hope it is correct or give up or not make a selection. Negative marking schemes will deter guessing. However if a student does not attempt a question for fear of losing marks we lose insight into their knowledge or skills. If a candidate avoids a question the responsibility for that rests with the candidate but the test has failed to establish the candidates competence and that is the examiners responsibility. Experiments indicated that students are much more likely to attempt questions that do not carry negative marks and will be prepared to guess when they could not recall the correct answer. More importantly when students admitted guessing, success was sometimes higher than that expected from a random selection (Fone, 2002).

To describe the semiotic mechanisms of a MCQ we can consider Sebock's typology (Sebock 1976 cited by Nöth 1990, p 108.). A sign is associated with an utterance using the convention of the tests' protocol to become a symbol of that utterance. When the respondent makes selections the symbols selected become signals. These signals are triggers for the grader to perform analysis and assign symbols to represent the performance of the respondent. At each of these stages information is filtered and the information content is reduced. Feedback seldom forms part of this process

K. Liu (ed.),
Virtual, Distributed and Flexible Organisations: Studies in Organisational Semiotics, 309–310.

and the respondent takes on the sole role of the transmitter while the grader becomes the receiver. Feedback is important but it is often vague offering an overall performance or a simple checklist of correct and incorrect selections.

In responding to the question the respondent is forming a speech circuit (Saussure 1916 cited in Nöth, 1990, p.176). An associated question can provide additional information that can be analysed to provide an information stream to be used as feedback and complete a speech circuit. By associating questions that ask for responses based upon emotions or 'awareness of feelings or self' we introduce autopoiesis into the conversation. Feedback presented within the speech loop will now take on a consensual role. By asking for information that records the emotional or Confidence State at the time of response, the importance the respondent places upon the selection can be inferred. This information can easily be mapped against each response and used to distinguish guesses from misconceptions and educated guesses from random selection.

In a simple yet effective example employing the above mechanisms the candidate is asked to select an answer. The candidate is also asked to indicate the level of confidence they have in the selection. Choosing one out of:

very confident/ confident/ uncertain/ very uncertain.

If a selection is marked very confident and the selection is correct little need be said. This is also true if a wrong selection is indicated to be a guess. However if an incorrect selection is flagged as confident or very confident then a misconception has been identified. Where low confidence was indicated against correct answers, reassuring feedback can be offered to raise confidence and provide stimulation. This provides a filter for the important issues that need to be raised in the feedback.

REFERENCES

Fone, William, 2002, Improving feedback from Multiple Choice Tests. Proceedings of the 7th annual Conference on Innovation and Technology in Computer Science Education. Page 196.

Nöth, Winfred, 1990, Handbook of Semiotics. Bloomington & Indianapolis: Indiana University Press.

Saussure, Ferdinand de, 1969 (1916), Course in General Linguistics, translation. Baskin, Wade. New York: McGraw Hill.

Sebeok, Thomas A., 1985, Contributions to the Doctrine of Signs. Lanham, Md: University Press of America.

Index